2084
AND BEYOND

UYLESS BLACK

2084

Twenty eighty-four

and Beyond

2084 AND BEYOND
BY
UYLESS BLACK

Available at online booksellers and local bookstores

Communicate with the author at
UBlack7510@aol.com

Go to Blog.UylessBlack.com
and www.UylessBlack.com
for additional
works by Uyless Black

(*IEI* Press)

Information and Entertainment Institute
9323 N. Government Way, #301
Hayden, Idaho 83835

Library of Congress Control Number: 2013906187
ISBN: 978-1-62737-006-6

Publicist: S. G. Mahoney
Cover & Book Design by Arrow Graphics, Inc.
info@arrow1.com
Printed in the United States of America

In DEDICATION

To Bill Bacchus, my friend and critic,
who helped mold this book.

To Ross Black, my brother and father figure,
who helped mold my life.

With gratitude to my publicist, Sylvia Gann (S. G.) Mahoney, who forms a core of past and present times, going back to our third-grade school class in a small country town in New Mexico.

To Carleen Lazzell, who has supported this book and other works as well. And thank you, Carleen, for supporting me in Albuquerque for the book signing.

For Brad Waters, a loyal and supporting friend, who reminds me that still waters run deep. For Paul Kositzka who has offered friendship and wise advice for over thirty years. For Jo Ellen Thompson, an extraordinary friend who has supported my work and our friendship for decades. For Barbara Patterson-Skeen, a loyal friend who helps me maintain ties to my childhood home in New Mexico.

With gratitude to Joel Carson and Frances Dawkins. The Black family thanks the lucky stars that Joel and Frances care.

With thanks to the mysterious cosmos that I somehow have my wife Holly in my corner in all that I do.

CONTENTS

PREFACE

Since early childhood, I have wondered why humans often resort to pointless violent actions. What goes on in the mind of such an aggressive person? In my youth, these people's ability to harm others was limited, because their aggressive arsenals were restricted to their fists, and perhaps knives or guns of modest firepower. Today, this kind of individual can cause great harm to many people. Rapid-fire rifles, bombs, and other weapons of immense force expand the scope of effect of their violent acts. They may be no more numerous than they were when I was in grade school, but the effects of their acts have broadened. Their ability to harm scores, hundreds, even thousands of fellow humans is gradually but surely changing our society.

With good reason, we are becoming more cautious when we take to the streets for our daily activities. We are beginning to have second thoughts about the safety of our workplaces. We are becoming progressively more fearful for our children as they sit in their classrooms. Our reaction is to further arm ourselves and post additional guards at buildings, on streets, and in neighborhoods. If present trends continue, we are in danger of operating like a security state, with associated curtailments to our freedoms.

It is not only our local surroundings that are creating apprehension and concern. It is becoming evident that factions of our species—some identified with a nation, some not—are bent on doing great harm to the human race. They are determined to acquire unconventional weapons to vent their anger, frustration, and perhaps find expression for their sociopathy.

Over the past three decades, I have been exploring ideas and theories about how we humans evolved into a race in which we are creating frightening and frightened societies. In this book, I offer what I believe are plausible explanations about these changes to our cultures.

During this past decade, I have also devoted time to learn about the extraordinary progress being made in human self-change technologies. Genetic research, in consonance with brain imaging, is making astounding inroads in finding the physical and environmental underpinnings of pathological aggression. The advancements are real enough to predict that in the not too distant future, we humans can "re-wire" ourselves to be a less dangerous species.

One theme of this book is a warning: If we do not come to grips with the foundations of our violent behavior, members of our race beyond nation-states will likely find ways to acquire and use weapons of mass destruction on fellow humans. My warning goes further. If we do not address imbalances that exist in the Middle East, we may suffer the same fate from state-sponsored assaults.

The challenges we humans face are both genetically-based and culturally-based. They represent respectively the so-called nature and nurture sides of humans. It is now accepted in most academic and scientific circles that we are products of nature and nurture. We must confront the associated problems that each presents to the well-being of our societies. Thus, this book also deals with the topics of genetics (nature) and environmental factors (nurture).

This book has another theme: that of optimism. We are at the tip of the genetic and cerebral iceberg in understanding the foundations of our behavior. Each day, we humans make new discoveries about our genotypes and phenotypes. Each day, we make advances in improving ourselves.

We need not be locked into an Orwellian world of perpetual hostility, unending aggression, the dodging of snipers' bullets, the fretting about chemical and nuclear weapons, and associated anxieties. If we have the courage, humility, and honesty to examine and confront our nature and the natural causes of our behavior—and be willing to alter age-old "orders of battle," we humans can go a long way toward fixing ourselves.

It is my hope this book helps point the way.

* * *

Because parts of *2084 and Beyond* are views from the future that make reference to the past, most of the passages are written in the past tense. Some of the quoted sources, originally written in the present tense, have been altered to read in the past tense. However, the majority of the reference notes (endnotes) are taken from current sources. With a few exceptions, these notes are written in the present tense. I have made these small changes to ease the reading of the text, the quotes, and the references.

The published date of a source often varies from the original hard copy. As one example, a periodical from that of its online copy. Some of my references are taken from hard copy, some from websites. On numerous occasions, I looked at both hard copy and electronic copy. If I encountered different publishing dates, I noted this fact in the endnote. Also, when doing this duplicate checking, I compared both copies to make sure they were the same. Except for the hard-copy publication date and the online-publication date, I found no differences in the content between the hard copy and its online counterpart.

For much of *2084 and Beyond*, I use the male genders of "he" and "him." I do so because the male has been the dominant player in the themes of this book.

PROLOGUE

Humans, a study in contradictions.

Did they paint the Mona Lisa and sculpt marble images of David?
Did they paint Swastikas and sculpt marble images of Stalin?

Were the Taj Mahal, Museum Bilbao, and St. Peter's Basilica extensions of their intelligence and creativity?
Were the racial internment camps, gas chambers, and death houses extensions of their baseness and evil?

Who else but this race wrote the *Magna Carta* and the *Gettysburg Address*?
Who else but this race wrote *Mien Kampf* and *The Final Solution*?

Did they create the Tango?
Did they initiate death marches?

Did *Water Music* come from nowhere? Did *Moonlight Sonata* spring from nothing?
Did the nuclear bomb come from nowhere? Did Anthrax spring from nothing?

Who invented the wheel, the transistor, and the polio vaccine?
Who invented the flame thrower, mustard gas, and poison vaccine?

Was it the human race who discovered fire, gravity, electricity, and the double helix?
Was it the human race who devised the Inquisition, the Holocaust, Agent Orange, and the double cross?

Did they invent ballet and improvise masterful jazz pieces?
Did they invent art yet improvise banal blank canvases?

Was Lincoln's magnanimity indicative of his fellow humans' compassion?
Was Robiespeirre's depravity indicative of his fellow humans' cruelty?

Did some of these creatures use the cross as a symbol of forgiveness?
Did others burn the cross as a symbol of mercilessness?

Who but these beings, acknowledging their imperfect behavior, possessed the wisdom to nurture ethical laws by which they lived?
Who but these beings, disregarding their imperfect behavior, possessed the arrogance to ignore ethical laws by which they should have lived?

Did they embrace love and kindness, and practice charity and tolerance?
Did they display pride and jealousy, and engage in pedophilia and murder?

Humans, a study in contradictions.

CHAPTER 1

INTRODUCTION

——✐——

Be careful what you wish for. It might come true.

Many years ago, some beings called humans lived on the planet earth. They were odd creatures. Unlike previously departed species, humans did not die out. They modified themselves to become an extended lineage of their ancestors. They transformed themselves to become an altered variety of their own kind.

As time passed, the devolving human evolved into the Cepee. The result was not a new race. But the borrowing from the "old" human line with a lending to the "new" Cepee line led to a greatly enhanced species.

Cepee is an acronym derived from the term: Changed Entity, Programmed for Extended Eons. The word *entity* refers to the human. This lengthy name is written as Cepee and pronounced as the letters *CP*.

Even though the Cepees are different from their predecessors, they share many of the humans' traits. They listen to their music, read their books, and watch their movies. These reminders of human existence are stored in the Human Archives. The Cepees study this vast library to learn more about their curious ancestors.

The Cepees are particularly fond of one song they found in these files. It is titled "Heaven on Earth." They like the tune because its title describes a world the humans desired and a world the Cepees have attained: a never-ending life. To achieve this stupendous goal, the Cepees took to heart the thoughts of one of their human predecessors, Julian Huxley, "The human species can,

1

if it wishes, transcend itself—not just sporadically, an individual here in one way, an individual there in another way, but in its entirety, as humanity."[1]

The Cepees have fulfilled this destiny; one that was initiated in a somewhat happenstance manner by their ancestors; one that was wished-for by Huxley. And one that was predicted by another forebear, E. O. Wilson, "Earth, by the twenty-second century, can be turned, if we so wish, into a permanent paradise for human beings, or at least the strong beginnings of one."[2] As told here, the Cepees' coming to dominate planet Earth was much more than a strong beginning. It was an equally strong ending.

This "permanent paradise for human beings" began to come about in the twenty-first century. The startling progress the humans made each year of that century toward the improvement and prolongation of human life surprised almost everyone. The year 2084 was hailed as a milestone in the human's evolution, one that underscored the visions of Huxley and Wilson.

That year, a century after 1984, was chosen as a date for the humans to congratulate themselves. They were making progress in their battles against perpetual war, totalitarianism, and their ceaseless propensity for engaging in gratuitous violence. The humans themselves had created these Orwellian ills. They were now trying to correct their mistakes. Thus, 2084 provided a fitting benchmark to proclaim *well done*, with an admission that *much remained to be done*.

What did 2084 and beyond hold for the humans? Would the race finally lay to rest its self-imposed nightmares? Or would the humans' ancient legacies, subscribed for them through nature yet assisted by their own hand through nurture, win this battle?

To help answer these questions, we will be accompanied in our journey by a Cepee, who is engaged in studying the Human Archives during the year of 2150. On occasion, we will pause and learn of his thoughts about his human ancestors. For now, let's learn more about this being, and begin our discovery of why and how the Cepees came to exist.

Life Enhanced

The Cepee is able to absorb a vast amount of information from the Human Archives. These retention powers are attributable to an extraordinary brain. Three interplaying factors, initiated by the humans, fostered the improvement of this organ: gene manipulation, the manufacturing of artificial cerebral parts, and the integration of organic-based computers into parts of the brain. These procedures became commonplace in the latter decades of the humans' twenty-first century.

In addition to enhancing their brains, the latter-day humans learned how to grow new skin, bones, organs, glands, and muscles to replace their aging or damaged counterparts. These procedures kept pace with the enhancements they made to their cerebral functions. As time went by, the human body and brain were altered significantly, leading to greatly improved mental and physical capabilities.

Life Prolonged

In contrast to the departed human, death is irrelevant to the Cepee. This being is not ordained to die, one reason it likes the song "Heaven on Earth." This enviable position came about as the latter-day humans discovered the genetic codes pertaining to aging, and the emerging Cepees learned how to manipulate DNA to control the deadly ripening process.

Before long, it became less costly and time consuming to make repairs and improvements to worn-out body components (nicknamed by the scientists as the humans' "peripherals"). With the development of regeneration and restoration mechanisms, the repair or replacement of a part became a routine matter. The operations were simplified as many pieces of the emerging Cepee became biosynthetic, replaceable mechanisms, subject to a long existence.

In addition to the astounding improvements made to the humans' peripherals, neurosurgeons and genetic engineers developed ways to greatly enhance the humans' central nervous system—the mind and spine—which was dubbed by the scientists as the humans' "mainframe."

As a result of the strides made toward human enhancement, during the latter part of the twenty-first century, conventional doctors and surgeons, as well as the monolithic health care industry, began to wither on the organic vine. The human body and mind were changed to become an assemblage of their original compositions, plus manufactured amino acids, altered proteins, hardware, software, and a retailored genome.

In a touch of irony, it turned out the humans never realized their fantasy to achieve heaven on earth. This privilege was bequeathed to the Cepees by virtue of their ability to sustain a never-ending life. As a result of the evolution of the Cepee from an existence encompassing extended eons to that of infinite eons, its name could have been changed to Cepie: Changed Entity Programmed for Infinite Eons. However, the Cepees retain the original moniker because, over many years, they have embedded this name into millions of computers, including those in their bodies and brains. Even in these advanced times, software changes are difficult and sometimes perilous to make.

The Key Questions

Our journey in this story will have us visit the circumstances by which the Cepees have come to exist. We will learn how the last remaining generations of humans somewhat unwittingly modified themselves to become different from their ancestors. We shall see it was a relatively short time before these extraordinary beings—increasingly biosynthetic and genetically tailored—modified, amended, and altered themselves to grow an astonishing branch in the *Homo sapiens'* family tree.

But questions remain. Why did the conventional human devolve to 0s and 1s in computer archives? Why did the Cepee evolve to supplant the human? As this narrative unfolds, we will learn these changes came about for four reasons, identified with the acronyms EGO, ILLS, SANE, and ASSES.

EGO. The first reason for the ascension of the Cepee was the humans' unending efforts to exploit their advances in science and medicine, to improve how they looked to themselves, and especially how they appeared to others. Their goal was to better themselves, including the repair or replacement of damaged or worn-out body parts. As examples, skin, hair, arms, and legs were refurbished or supplanted. Alcoholism, drug addiction, and other maladies were removed from the humans' inventory of miseries. Plastic surgery became as common as paying a visit to the dentist. Unattractive noses, drooping breasts, sagging buttocks, slumping chins, ugly wrinkles, and unsightly warts were altered or removed to improve a person's appearance.

Starting modestly in the twentieth century, the alterations to the human assumed a life of their own. Before long, internal parts in the body, such as organs, were being repaired or replaced. The frequency of changes accelerated as success led to more success. When late twenty-first century came about, the human had taken on a different character than he or she had in the past. By mid-twenty-second century, the Cepee's mental and physical compositions had become quite different from that of the conventional human.

Notwithstanding the transition, some of the earthlings, residing in a transmutation purgatory during this interregnum, were both amused and bemused with their situation. A noted commentator of that time named this period the EGO epoch: **E**nhancements to **G**lorify **O**urselves.

ILLS. As mid-twenty-first century rolled around, the human race had come to understand it was losing the battle against a large number and variety of diseases. Germs were adapting themselves to more accommodating residences in the human body.[3] These organisms were mutating and adapting to drugs and medicines faster than supposed cures could be developed. The battle was hindered by the delay of first, inventing medicinal cures; second, having the medicines approved by government agencies; and third, creating drugs whose side effects were not harmful.

Unlike the EGO programs, which were important but not essential to the preservation of the species, the operations associated with ILLS were fundamental to the species' long-term survival.

Consequently, many ILLS programs were initiated to counter the attacks of micro-organisms such as bacteria, protozoa, and viruses.

As mentioned, genetic engineering slowed and eventually eliminated the aging process. Uncooperative organic residue was removed from the human's flesh container, soon to be replaced with biosynthetic material. In many instances, replacements came from natural human parts; some borrowed from other humans; others grown and often modified in petri dishes. Eventually, faltering or failed functions were taken over by human, and soon, Cepee-designed components.

A medical expert coined the term **I**ncurable **L**atent **L**abile **S**icknesses (ILLS) to describe these problems and the programs to solve them: **I**ncurable, because some of the human's diseases had proven to be intractable. **L**atent, because several of the diseases lay dormant for years, suddenly appearing to do damage to the victim. **L**abile, because many of the viruses changed often and rapidly, resulting in high rates of mutation that offset previous treatments. **S**icknesses, because being sick and miserable were the end results of the process.

In a nutshell, the frequent rate of change enabled a germ to adapt to new medical milieus in order to escape the human's natural immune system and medicines' antidotes. Therefore, the ILLS initiatives took a new approach: Modify the human to make it more resistant to germs *and* modify specific germs to make them, as one scientist quipped, more "user friendly."

SANE. The humans took the ILLS programs to another level as they learned more about the regions of the brain and parts of DNA that had an effect on insanity and psychopathy. But these initiatives went further than combating mental illness. The scientists and researchers came to understand the cerebral and genetic underpinnings of mental well-being—even optimism. These programs entailed the manipulation of genes as well as making changes to both ancient and recently evolved parts of the brain. They resulted in the creation of powerful counter measures to combat mental miseries.

The humans dubbed these initiatives as SANE, for **S**upplying **A** **N**ew **E**go. The acronym and its derivation implied the humans had artificially manipulated their genome and central nervous system to give themselves new and enhanced mental functions. In spite of the acronym, SANE not only fixed the brains of the insane, it also repaired the mental functions of many who were sane. Maybe a bit off kilter, but sane.

ASSES. If the humans had not changed themselves because of EGO, ILLS, and SANE, by mid-twenty-first century, many of the changes would have occurred anyway because of reason number four, dubbed by pundits as ASSES, an acronym for **A**lterations to **S**ave **S**ociety from our **E**gregious **S**elves.

By this time, many humans recognized they had no choice but to alter their mental makeup—their cerebral underpinnings. No choice, because the race was annihilating large segments of its societies. Humans had begun using nuclear weapons, as well as gasses and poisons, on large populations of civilians.

Conclusions

By 2084, the human was a dramatically altered individual in comparison to the early twenty-first-century human. By this time, the early twenty-first century human's physical and mental compositions were little more than historical fodder—stored on disk files, computer memory, and holograms in the Human Archives. To coin a phrase of those old times, the human had assumed a virtual existence.

The Cepee is a member of the same evolutionary tree as the *Homo sapiens*, that of the *Hominidae* (hominid). At the risk of offending genealogists, paleontologists, biologists—likely, every profession that deals with nature's family trees—this altered human might even be identified as *Homo cepees* to honor the ancestry from which the Cepee came. But that name would not be valid because their gene pools were quite similar and during their shared residence on earth, they could jointly procreate.

Because of the many ongoing changes that took place during these times, there were many hybrid human/Cepees walking about. Different models, so to speak. One being might have had gone through a gene splicing procedure to extend his life. Another might have had her trachea replaced with 3-D printing (procedures described in Chapter 11). However, by 2084, the Cepees had become quite different from their forebears, the humans.

But the two lineages were similar in one way: The latter-day humans and the emerging Cepees knew better than to alter their genomes in a happenstance manner. Thus, the human-to-Cepee transformation was—in relation to the hominids' cerebral and genetic makeup—rather modest. But as the song goes, what a difference a day makes was also true using slightly different lyrics: What a difference a gene (splice) makes…here and there.

Regardless of intramural bouts about a proper parentage moniker, scientists report *Homo sapiens* evolved from the *Homo erectus* and the *Homo habilis* over a period of 1.5 million years. Ordinarily, the development of a new species (speciation) took millions of years and required the isolation or splitting of a population into separate groups. Not so for the Cepees. They and their immediate human forerunners took the matter into their own hands.

A scientist, living in the early years of the twenty-first century, and wondering what might be in store for the human race, posed these questions:[4]

> Will we become larger or smaller, smarter or dumber? How will the emergence of new diseases and the rise in global temperature shape us? Will a new human species arise one day? Or does the future evolution of humanity lie not within our genes but within our technology, as we augment our brains and bodies with silicon and steel? Are we but the builders of the next dominant intelligence on the earth—the machines?

That future generation lay in both genes *and* technology. And the next dominant intelligence on earth was *not* a species of machines. It *is* a lineage of the humans consisting of improved peripherals (body) and a significantly enhanced mainframe (mind). All of which have been greatly augmented by genetic engineering.

It took slightly less than a century for the Cepees to begin to emerge from the humans and a century and a half for the Cepee to supplant the human. Thus, the Cepee progression was more of a revolution than an evolution.

You might be curious about some of the details of the Cepee. In simplest terms, and expanded later, by 2084 the now-absent human and the present Cepee physically resembled each other in relation to their exteriors. But their interiors, including their brain, were dramatically different.

Perhaps the best way to gain an immediate and general appreciation of this being is to understand that the latter-day humans and the early-day Cepees engaged in highly skillful filtering of the early twenty-first century human's mental and physical compositions. These remarkable sieves—genetic, cerebral, and physical—separated positive from negative traits. They perpetuated the "good" and terminated the "bad" features of the human.

One critical issue recounted in this story was their effort to, if not eliminate, then decrease their penchant for aggression and revenge. On a lighter level, this writer can assure the reader that the Cepees—like their human relatives—love and make love, sometimes resulting in little Cepees. They engage in these pleasant activities in perpetuity. Another reason they like the song, "Heaven on Earth."

Notwithstanding these positive aspects, how can a society be managed whose members can reproduce and also live indefinitely? What about population control? These questions will be addressed later.

We now have an introductory explanation of the Cepee and general information about its place on earth. In subsequent chapters, we will learn more about this extraordinary being. We will come to understand how its *external* appearance resembles its ancestors, but how its *internal* composition is significantly different. Of equal importance, we will learn in more detail *why* the Cepee replaced the human.

---

[1] Julian Huxley, Transhumanism, "*New Bottles for New Wine*," 1957, in Leonard Roy Frank, *Quotationary* (New York: Random House, 2001), 253.

[2] E. O. Wilson, *The Social Conquest of Earth* (New York: Liveright, 2012), 297, Kindle edition, loc. 4777.

[3] Unless otherwise noted, the term *germ* is used in a general context in this book to describe assorted micro-organisms. More specific definitions are provided in Chapter 7.

[4] Peter Ward, "What Will Become of the *Homo sapiens*?" *Scientific American*, January 2009, 70.

CHAPTER 2

SETTING THE STAGE

Civilization is a race to discover remedies for the ills it produces.[1]

As the Cepees study the Human Archives, they learn much about their predecessors. In so doing, they learn much about themselves. This chapter, derived from these archives, conveys to each Cepee the setting and backdrop for the humans' emergence on earth. This chapter and Chapter 3 also tell the story of how the humans became a dominant species on the planet.

Long before the *Homo sapiens* walked the earth, the biosphere's changes paved the way for the eventual proliferation of plant and animal life.[2] Gradually, over millions of years, plants began to grow in most parts of the earth and flourish in regions of the world that had accommodating climates. Eventually, the profusion of plant life and emissions of oxygen affected the characteristics of the earth's atmosphere. Still later, as animals began to populate the planet, plants and animals entered into mutually beneficial relationships.

Enter the *Homo sapiens*

The humans changed this association as they evolved from a common ancestor or a set of common ancestors about five to seven million years ago.[3, 4] Their family tree began around that time with the appearance of a direct ancestor to the twenty-first-century human. It took a very long time for nature to bring about this remarkable creature.

About four millions years ago, perhaps even earlier, the humans began to assume an upright posture. Around this time the prevalent theory is that they began to increase their brain sizes, and learn to use tools.[5, 6, 7] The first human-like being to live beyond Africa occurred around 1.8 million BC. From that time, the human race continued to evolve and to populate other parts of the planet.

Around 50,000 BC, the *Homo sapiens* began an ascent which resulted in their becoming the dominant large-bodied species on the planet.[8] The race's history points to fossils, tools, jewelry, and other artifacts that reveal this ancient human was quite similar in its behavior and biological composition to the modern human. Still later, other aspects of the human race were revealed: Musical instruments, cave paintings, fishhooks, awls, and statues attested to the fact the race was improving its mental faculties.

From Hunter-Gatherers to Farmers

The ancient humans were hunters and gatherers. Hunters, because they hunted game and fish. Gatherers, because they gathered nuts and berries.[9] During their hunting and gathering forays, they spread from Africa to most parts on earth.

Beginning around 10,000 BC, a monumental shift occurred in how humans fed themselves. Ultimately, it determined how they survived, because this shift influenced not just their food intake but eventually their social habits, such as sex, child rearing, and bonding with other humans. The shift also allowed the humans to increase their populations.

These beings set in motion actions that resulted in a rapid change from hunting and gathering to farming and animal husbandry. They began planting and cultivating food and domesticating animals, at a time called the Neolithic revolution.[10] It was the time when agriculture was invented.

During the early part of this transition, the hunter-gatherers had been increasing in number, leading to the increased consumption of plants and animals. As a consequence of this intake, some of the large mammals in parts of the world became scarce. Some historians claim a number of animals were killed off, hunted to extinction.[11] This situation encouraged some of these humans to find another way to eat. Eventually, they took up the hoe and shovel to become tillers of the soil.

Thus, the early humans changed their existence from the dangerous job of wild game hunters and the tedious job of gatherers to the relatively safe occupations of food production and animal domestication. The increased population of humans, with dense concentrations in smaller places, coupled with their occupation of food producers, fostered further change to a more sedentary life and a less physically dangerous existence.

In a touch of irony, the Neolithic revolution did indeed witness the farmers' ascension. But while they were growing in number, they were experiencing a lower standard of living than their predecessors. Hunter-gatherers spent fewer than twenty hours a week securing their food. The farmers worked all day, each day.[12] Because of weather and pests, they suffered from crop losses. They were not as healthy as the hunter-gatherers. Records show the farmers had "more anemia and vitamin deficiencies, died younger, had worse teeth, were more prone to spinal deformity, and caught more infectious diseases as a result of living close to other humans and to livestock."[13]

Granted, the farmer had a less dangerous physical life than a hunter-gatherer because he no longer had to kill wild animals. (And of course, some were inclined to kill him.) But his overall existence was miserable and subject to a capricious Mother Nature. The old saying, "To plant is to pray," may have had its origins in these early times, perhaps even before prayer came along.

Because populations continued to grow and families increased in size, people had to engage in even more farming just to stay alive. While they succumbed to this cycle, they also gained an advantage from their sedentary life. They could have more children. Gaining strength from their large numbers, they succeeded in killing off most of the hunter-gatherers, or drove them from the land they occupied.[14]

Farming rapidly increased the food available to humans. Because these people were relatively well fed with comparatively fuller-sized stomachs than their ancestors, they could more easily increase the size of their families. This sudden population growth, coupled with humans' move to farming, resulted in much of the land being transformed from a natural state to one contoured by humans: "The rest of the living world could not [change] fast enough to accommodate the onslaught of a spectacular conqueror that seemed to come from nowhere, and it began to crumble from the pressure."[15]

These farmers, conquerors of rugged, stalwart hunters, developed a pattern of life that led to the further proliferation of diseases, the development of specialized occupations, stratified societies, and strengthening the concept of the *tribe*.

The Tribe

Tribe is a key word in the quest to decipher the behavior of the human race. Consulting the humans' dictionary, *tribe* is defined as, "Any aggregate of people united by ties of descent from a common ancestor, community of customs, and traditions."[16]

This definition seems straight forward enough. It states descent was the key factor for defining a tribe, and the term *descent* usually meant familial descents, although the word *clan* is a more accurate identifier for a family unit.[17] At first glance, the statement about a common ancestor is obvious: A son or daughter descended from parents and through an evolutionary tree, those parents descended from other parents.

The term *tribe* also described a group of humans that was much more diverse than a close and almost always loyal family of relatives, a clan. To see why, consider that the human of pre-Neolithic times (and most likely obtaining aspects of these traits from his ancestors), conducted his life in accordance with his understanding of three stark facts directing his motivation for survival.

First, he had to kill game in order to eat. Second, he often had to kill another human to prevent that human from killing game he himself needed to eat. Third, the forming of an association with other humans beyond his immediate family frequently made the snaring and killing of game an easier task. One can imagine an ancient hunter might have been more at ease when stalking a tiger—who was also stalking him—if he had some assistance from other hunters, including members of a tribe outside his small familial clan.

In addition, the burning of precious energy was greater if a lone hunter had to stalk and snare his prey. Given that the hunter had learned to eat meat, thus contributing to the consumption of more protein (which is claimed by some experts to have resulted in a larger body and brain), a shared kill among members of the hunting party gave each hunter "more bang for the buck."

This need for tribal bonds became part of a human's mental makeup. It also created conflicts. While the tribe was a positive force for survival of its members, and the resulting attachments fostered more social bonding and better cooperation, the tribal members sometimes competed among themselves. The competition could have been for a greater share of the food during a sparse hunting time, maybe leading to killing within the tribe to snare more of the reduced menu.

Notwithstanding this competition, cooperation was also important to help avoid one of the humans' constant threats: "unpredictable food shortages."[18] Joint hunting allowed the kill for the day to be shared. During times of drought, or if animals destroyed crops, humans often had agreements among themselves to share farming yields across a diverse landscape. If one tribe's crop failed one year, its neighbor's crop might be shared, with reciprocal sharing assumed if fortunes were reversed.

Diverse Tribal Memberships

The humans were a more complex race than a fixation on basic survival needs. As time moved forward from the ancient Neolithic period to the humans' modern times, each human belonged, or tried to belong to many tribes. Some were based on common ancestors, others based on common customs and traditions. Still others were based on a diverse array of human traits and dispositions.

This narrative will reveal that some humans aspired to become the dominant, most powerful member of a tribe. It will also explain that a position in a tribe was more important to some humans than others. To cite two examples, not all humans were concerned with ascending the ladders of fame and fortune. Some were interested in becoming a powerful leader. Others were not.

But given the curious nature of the human, who could say which tribal preference was more important? The family was important to some people but not others. Some humans placed great stock in their political tribe and their position in it. Others wanted an exalted position in their religious tribe.[19]

Whatever their preferences were, later chapters will describe how many humans took any measure, including subterfuge, deceit, and deadly aggression, to ascend the hierarchies, to get to the top in their respective tribes. Many examples in this story will relate how and why members of one tribe frequently used these measures to subjugate and often kill another tribe.

A Rose by Any Other Name

During the humans' later times, beginning in the seventeenth century, the word *tribe* became a word of disrespect, even contempt. With the exception of "backward" humans who lived in remote parts of the world, less offensive terms were employed to describe a population of like people. Thus, *tribe* became the accepted term to portray a group of primitive humans who slaughtered one another, including humans in other groups, with archaic instruments of aggression, such as knives, spears, and arrows.

Other terms, such as *brotherhood, culture, guild, club, society, unit*, and *nation* became the accepted words to describe an "advanced" group of humans who slaughtered one another including humans in other groups with modern instruments of aggression such as bombs, gas, and chemicals. As the humans liked to say, "A rose by any other name is still a rose."

A Cepee has been studying this part of the Human Archives and will be with us for the remainder of this story. He reflects: *True, but a tribe by any other name is still a tribe.*

The Human Tribal Hierarchy (HTH)
and Maslow's Hierarchy of Needs

Through many centuries, human evolution proceeded to foster a key behavioral concept called the *Human Tribal Hierarchy* (HTH)—in practice, a pecking order. The result was the desire for many humans to be on top of the tribal pack, to be superior to the other humans in the tribe, and ascend the pecking order. Thus, a clan warrior aspired to become the chief of the tribe to which his clan belonged. The parish priest labored to be the Pope of the church. The borough politician connived to be the president of the nation.

This competition, in consonance with nature's mutations and associated natural selections, led to the survival of the most intelligent, the most innovative, and other over-achievers. All in all, the Human Tribal Hierarchy was a brilliant model: Excelling in one's endeavors was a laudable construct for behavior because it led to a more efficient and rugged race. It fostered the preservation and advancement of the species.

The Human Tribal Hierarchy was the foundation for Maslow's Hierarchy of Needs, which was developed by the psychologist Maslow in the humans' later times, and is summarized as a general scheme in Figure 2-1. The bottom of the hierarchy represented the fundamental, basic needs of a human, such as food, water, shelter, and clothing.[20] After these requirements were satisfied, the human needed sex to insure his/her genes were passed to subsequent generations. Sex was placed above some of the other basic needs. After all, copulation was not very high on a person's list of needs if that person was starving or freezing to death.

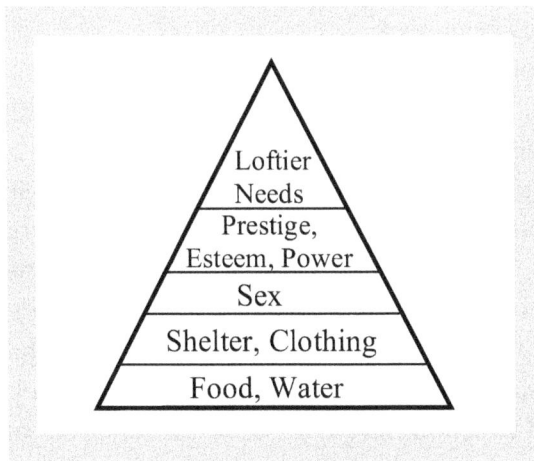

Loftier
Needs
Prestige,
Esteem, Power
Sex
Shelter, Clothing
Food, Water

Figure 2-1. Maslow's Hierarchy of Needs (a general view).

After these essential physiological needs were met, humans sought ways to satisfy their egos and sense of self, such as attaining prestige and esteem, perhaps garnering power. These aspects of behavior did not contribute *directly* to the survival of a human, but they did have an *indirect* (and important) role to play.

For example, a male held in high esteem by his tribal members would likely find more success in spreading his genes than a male who was shunned by the tribe.[21] A powerful tribe member, one who held sway over others, was more likely to survive and procreate than a powerless underling. Even as late as the twentieth century, so-called primitive humans living in remote parts on earth were acutely aware of how much esteem and prestige meant to their ability to find and acquire mates.

In 1961, two warring tribes in New Guinea traded these insults across a river that separated them from each other:[22] "Why do you have so many more women than your low status deserves?" "I have five wives and I'm going to get five more, because I live on my own land. You are landless fugitives. That's why you have no wives." These views came from twentieth-century humans, but reflected values they and their ancestors had possessed for thousands of years. Just as in modern times, in those days possession of land was essential for short range physical survival, as well as the longer range staying-power of one's gene pool.

Nonetheless, a male had to succeed in the lower, basic needs *before* he could aspire to the higher motives of prestige, esteem, and power, with their associated sexual privileges.

The loftier needs shown at the top of Maslow's Hierarchy became important after the basic needs and ego-satisfaction requirements were met. As examples, many humans strived for self-fulfillment by creating works of art or by gaining an understanding of a religion or science. Others wished to engage in politics, perhaps write or play music. And most members of the human race took to the idea that love and affection toward others were important to their lives, that it made them and the recipients of these emotions happier and more fulfilled.

These behavioral attributes were laudable because their existence led to a more harmonious species, one capable of improving not only the human who practiced them, but other humans who interacted with the practitioner.

By drawing parallels of Maslow's Hierarchy to the Human Tribal Hierarchy, it becomes an easier task to examine in more detail how the humans became the Cepees. For this introduction, and a key to understanding these hierarchies: The upper part of Maslow's Triangle (prestige, esteem, power, and the loftier needs) was composed of an almost infinite number of endeavors.

One human desire often coalesced with another. To cite some examples, in the humans' later years the desire to practice politics was coupled with the desire to be a powerful and influential politician. The desire to be wealthy was accentuated by the desire to be proud of one's wealth. The wish to spread the gospel was reinforced by wanting to be a major influence behind a religion. The wish to control more of earth's turf was coupled with a desire to be more powerful.

As can be seen with these examples, the loftier needs were usually accompanied with the desire to attain prestige, esteem, and power in a person's chosen endeavors. This meant that ascending the rungs of the Human Tribal Hierarchy was often achieved by also climbing Maslow's ladder.

Such ascension sometimes had laudable consequences, such as a gifted and benevolent despot taking care of his subjects. The ascension also sometimes resulted in tragic results, such as a despot starving his subjects to death.

For the latter example, excessive pride with a lust for power and influence became major factors in the humans' motives for ascending the Human Tribal Hierarchy, a subject for later discussions.

The Luck of the Geographical Roll of the Dice

The early tribes who, by chance, had the good fortune to live in climates for growing protein-laden food, or who lived in regions abundant with large domestic mammals, gained a head start on other societies, a favorable position with profound consequences for the human race.[23] Eventually, this roll of the dice led to a competitive advantage that affected the tribes' positions in the power and wealth hierarchies. With less time needed to keep their larders full, humans were free to invent new tools. One such tool was steel. Eventually, it became one of the most important factors in a tribe assuming dominance over another. After all, a wooden spear was no match for a blunderbuss made from iron.

This god-given or nature-given advantage (take your pick), set forth in ancient human times, carried through to the humans' stay on earth, even into his modern times of the twenty-first century, often culminating in views of superiority about one's origins. In a touch of irony, many humans thought they were the chosen few. In truth, they were nothing more than serendipitous geographical depositories, so-designated by the place in which they and their ancestors happened to be born.

From around 8000 BC to AD 2000 food producers supplanted almost all the hunter-gatherers, either by killing them off or absorbing them into their own tribes. As farmers stored their surplus food, as they became more specialized and hierarchical, they developed a new occupation: the warrior class, also known as the professional soldier, an important event explained in Chapter 3.

An Introduction to the Rules of Life

The next part of this chapter introduces several concepts related to human behavior, which are excerpts from the humans' *Rules of Life*, rules that this writer suspects will be quite familiar to the reader. They played major roles in the rise of the human race and the later rise of the Cepee. Paradoxically, the humans never gave these rules much thought, even though they influenced, even dictated much of the humans' behavior. Their influence will be in evidence throughout this book and many were an integral part of the *Homo sapiens'* physical and cerebral evolutionary underpinnings. Subsequent chapters introduce more of these rules.

The Immediacy Syndrome

During the humans' relatively brief stay on earth, the Immediacy Syndrome had a great influence on their behavior. This characteristic affected most of the population and manifested itself in the desire for an immediate fulfillment of a wish. In some instances, the wish was a real need, such as a craving for water or warmth. In other situations, the wish was associated with less important matters: a craving for status, an appetite for pride, a hankering for religious succor.

Whatever was desired—pride, sex, food, money, spiritual fulfillment, etc.—its consumption or realization, and (often) satiation required immediate satisfaction. The human had been programmed over many centuries to focus on the present. The future was of no importance.

Until late in the human era, long-range considerations of almost any need or desire were irrelevant to the well-being of the human. Delaying the acts of eating, drinking, or copulation made no sense. Why wait to eat if one was hungry? Why delay an orgasm if copulating couples were trying to expand their gene pool? To the early humans, today was important. Tomorrow would be today soon enough.

This behavioral attribute became part of the humans' genetic makeup, part of their instinctual composition. Seemingly, all well and good, but the Immediacy Syndrome, beneficial to early humans, became a handicap to later generations.

The Autocatalytic Process

The Autocatalytic Process is another concept important to this discussion.[24] It described a positive feedback cycle wherein a process reinforced another process, which in turn, reinforced the first process, which then reinforced the second process, on and on. An example of this cycle is shown in Figure 2-2. Initially, process A had an effect on process B, which in turn affected A. This change to A had another effect on B, which again, affected A. The smaller circles in the figure show the feedback loop of the Autocatalytic Process went faster and faster as it reinforced itself with each successive iteration of the cycle.[25]

The Autocatalytic Process resulted in the human race leading an increasingly faster-paced life. Everything seemed to happen more quickly. While the ancient circadian cycle remained twenty-four hours, the humans continued to compact more events into their hours, weeks, months, and years. The effect of the process was seen in almost all walks of life, and for this story, in the fantastic— and fantastically fast—changes the humans and Cepees made to themselves during the twenty-first and twenty-second centuries.

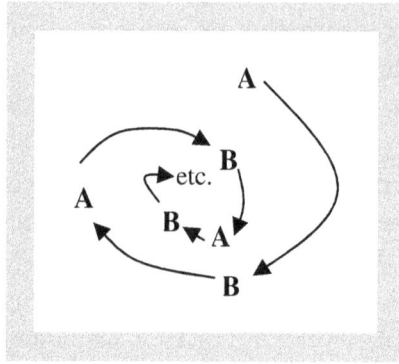

Figure 2-2. The Autocatalytic Process.

But this later century acceleration was nothing new. The Autocatalytic Process in relation to human change had been part of the evolutionary picture for thousands of years. Referring to Figure 2-2, say 50,000 years ago, primitive *Homo sapiens* were positioned at the first A in the process. Then, 10,000 years ago, their smarter and better-off descendants were at the second A. As the Cepees began to emerge, the human/Cepee was at the third A.

Faster and faster: Humans' changes to their mental and physical makeups accelerated. To emphasize: not linearly, but exponentially.[26] And the humans of the twenty-first century sped up the process even more.

The Threshold Lowering Syndrome

Many events in the story about the profound alteration of the human take place in the context of the Threshold Lowering Syndrome. This syndrome described an act by a human, who by committing the act, made it easier for this person or another person to repeat the act.[27] The act could have been beneficial or detrimental to the parties involved. But regardless of its merit, the party who committed the act received positive reinforcement from carrying it out, such as applause, infusions of adrenaline or dopamine, perhaps self-satisfaction, maybe self-preservation.

Examples of this syndrome during the human era were the many Pavlovian stimuli/responses a person experienced during his or her daily activities: a child walking for the first time and receiving kudos from the parents. The first successful sexual exploration. Burning down a building for the first time. Running the first red light. Visiting the first red-light district. Writing the first hot check. Winning the first fist fight. Killing a human for the first time. Executing the first successful heart transplant.

As suggested by these examples, this form of behavior had both positive and negative ramifications for the human race. In some situations, such as the first successful heart transplant, it spurred more attempts to improve heart surgery and humans' lives. In other circumstances, such as killing a fellow human, it could lead to more killing.

Figure 2-3 is used to illustrate the Threshold Lowering Syndrome in relation to its dangerous relationship to the human species. In this figure, the horizontal lines are the thresholds between "Acceptable" and "Not Acceptable" behavior. The Acceptable notation means the behavioral characteristic of a human or tribe was beneficial to the species. The Not Acceptable notation means the behavior was not species enhancing. This figure is read left to right to show: As the threshold barrier lowered, it became easier (more acceptable) for an individual human or tribe to commit species-destructive acts.

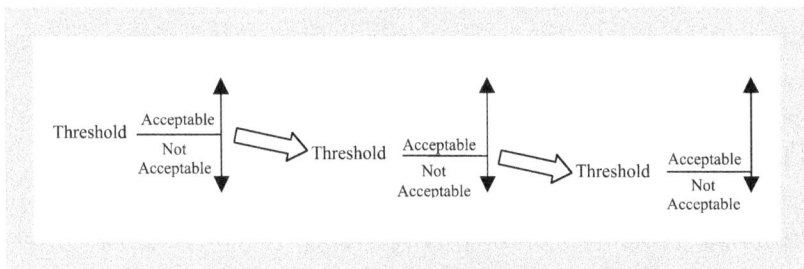

**Figure 2-3. The Threshold Lowering Syndrome
for dangerous behavior.**

Several examples of some (certainly not all) humans lowering their thresholds of acceptable acts were their growing apathy toward violent crime, their increasing acceptance of suicidal terrorist acts, their mounting use of mind-altering drugs, their nonchalance over bombings of civilian populations, their lack of concern about warfare atrocities, their detachment from earth's deteriorating environment, and their indifference to the starvation of populations living in remote parts of the world.[28]

Before leaving this subject, it should be noted that the human race did not begin a slide downward in morals, ethics, and social conscience with the inception of these traits. Indeed, the forebears to modern humans likely started off with a threshold bar set pretty low to begin with. For example, the Kaulong tribe on the island of New Britain routinely strangled to death the widows of their recently deceased mates.[29] The widows took this initiative and selected a member of the family who would kill her. However, the practice was for tribe survival. A lone widow consumed precious food.

As another example, twenty-first century humans could venture vast distances from their homes and encounter complete strangers along their way. With some exceptions, these travelers were safe in those foreign places. In older times, it was unthinkable for a human to venture even a few miles away from his home turf. By doing so, he risked being killed. He was a stranger whose behavior was unknown to those he met, and perhaps a potential killer himself.

Nonetheless, the impact and magnitude of this syndrome achieved greater significance as the human race invented increasingly lethal and powerful weapons to defend themselves and attack others. All of which was happening at an accelerating rate, courtesy of the Autocatalytic Process.

The Disproportionate Ratio Effect

In fairness to this species, it must be emphasized that most of the humans who lived in the twenty-first century were unwaveringly opposed to the destructive acts cited above. It is accurate to state that the vast majority of the humans were neither violent nor aggressive. Furthermore, as the race evolved, it mitigated many of its self-destructive and non-caring acts. Some social scientists in the twenty-first century claimed the race was evolving to become more altruistic and less violent.

Notwithstanding these claims, the Disproportionate Ratio Effect came into play to thwart the well-meaning intentions of this majority. This ratio is defined as n:m, where the value of n is very small and the value of m is very large. As explained in later chapters, as humans developed weapons capable of mass destruction, a limited number of individuals were able to do great harm to many. Thus, as the twenty-first century's clock ticked away, a very few (n) sociopaths, psychopaths, and religious zealots were severely affecting the well-being, even the future of the (m) human race.

During an inter-tribal battle in 8000 BC between two large tribes consisting of a total population of 8,000, it is estimated eleven deaths would have been a likely toll, or about 0.14 percent of the population:[30]

> That's higher than the percentage death toll (0.10 percent) from the bloodiest battle on the Pacific front during World War II.

> To match that percentage, the Hiroshima atomic bomb would have had to kill 4,000,000 rather than 100,000 Japanese and the World Trade Center attack would have had to kill 15,000,000 rather than 2,996 Americans.

Then why was this ratio relevant? Because the older forms of warfare with spears and arrows did not contaminate the land, decimate surrounding wildlife and crops, level all buildings, poison the drinking water, and produce sick people who might survive for years while living in unimaginable pain. The humans' modern "spears" brought forth all these tragedies.

The humans, being an intelligent race, focused on survival. They knew they had to alter the values of n and m dramatically. If not, the race was destined to live a life of chaos, subject to the acts of a relatively few miscreants. The ratio also exemplified positive and courageous characteristics of the *Homo sapiens*.

This ratio will appear in many discussions in this narrative, perhaps to the point where you might think it unnecessarily repetitive. It is not. The frequent references to the Disproportionate Ratio are reflective of the role it played in the history of the human race.

The Disproportionate Impulse Effect

The primitive humans unconsciously relied on a part of the brain called the amygdala to process a sensation of alarm in reaction to a danger. It drove a human to react on impulse, without thinking. The modern human had developed other parts of the brain (the anterior angular cortex and the dorsolateral prefontal cortex) that did not act on impulse, and could subdue the alarm-oriented aspect of the amygdala.

But not always. Often, the ancient part of the brain kicked-in and drove a human to commit an act before the more recently evolved gray matter took control. On many occasions, the damage brought about by a hasty action was already done. It was too late to say, "I lost my head," when that is indeed what had happened.

It was important for the modern human to retain these instinctual impulse alarms and associated precipitate actions. Jumping away from a falling tree branch was as essential to good health to a Neanderthal as it was to a stroller in Central Park.

But some of these instinctual, impulsive actions were not defensive in nature. They were offensive. Often, they were pathologically violent. They stoked the amygdala and suppressed the cortex. The Stone Age humans, like their modern counterparts, frequently acted on impulse. But the modern human's impulse often resulted in considerably more damage being done to others.

As an example: A second thought from an ancient Roman soldier, "I slayed four non-warriors in anger. I should have kept my sword sheathed," had a less disproportionate resonance to it than the lamentation of a more recent killer, "I slayed forty classmates in anger. I should have kept the Glock in my sock drawer."

Taking it to another level, "I should not have ordered that invasion." Too late, the pawns on the chessboard were inching forward into battle. Those on the back row of the chessboard, safe from the effects of their impulsive decisions, had opened yet another Pandora's Box. They were too prideful to put the lid back on.

Better to let the war run its course, later withdrawing with a fatuous declaration of victory.

The Population Concentration-Homogenization Factor (The PCH Factor)

During the twenty-first and twenty-second centuries, the humans' heretofore diverse societies around the world became increasingly homogeneous as people began to eat the same foods, wear the same kinds of clothes, read the same books and magazines, listen to the same music and radio shows, speak similar languages, watch the same movies and TV programs, ride the same subways, drive on the same freeways, and attend the same sports contests.

Sections of humans' cities mirrored one another. Climate aside, travelers often could not discern if they were in London, Las Vegas, or another metropolitan area. The Eiffel Tower in Paris was duplicated for the Las Vegas skyline. The London Bridge was disassembled and re-located to America. New York's Statue of Liberty was copied and put up in several cities that were trying to improve their image.

In addition to the homogenization of their cultures, the humans also increased their population levels in many parts of the world, especially areas of affluence, cities with cultural or religious significance, and places with pleasant climates. Prosperous New York City became a huge human gridlock. The streets of Mecca and Jerusalem began to resemble human canals, stuffed with devout pilgrims. Beautiful places such as Hawaii were eventually engorged with sun-worshipping humans and high-rise condominiums.

As a result of this situation, a new term was coined by the humans, the Population Concentration-Homogenization Factor (The PCH Factor), to describe a highly concentrated population sharing the same consumables and communications facilities. The PCH Factor became important during the ASSES program because the humans' concentrated, homogeneous populations made them more vulnerable to attacks from other humans. It was also a major factor in the ILLS program. Diseased humans and other animals could more easily carry deadly viruses into dense and genetically consistent populations.

The Unlike-Dislike Axiom

Throughout human history, almost anything that was unlike (dissimilar) to a human's expectations was suspect, often disliked. This "anything" could have been a human who dressed differently, was of a different stature, had a different skin color, spoke a different language, consumed different foods, ate with an "incorrect" utensil, shook hands with the wrong hand, crossed one's legs when sitting, practiced an incorrect religion. Almost anything that was unlike was disliked, supporting this axiom: You are unlike me, so I dislike you.

Dissimilar meant this "peculiar" person was likely from another tribe. His presence conveyed a potential danger: *What is this interloper up to?*

Those beings judged to be different were assessed based on an ancient norm, one that had been built into the brains of humans over many centuries. The caution was well placed. In older times, because tribal boundaries were strictly enforced, encountering a stranger or a strange group often spelled danger. A less cautious person, one who was not careful, might be captured or killed by these strangers. After all, this person was likely scouting for a future attack or venturing outside his turf looking for an easy haul.

Even if the human had no acquisitive intent, if he were treading on foreign turf, he had to be especially leery of those he encountered. They may have been the turf's landholders. And within his own property, he was subject to attack from visitors who were shopping—with acquisitive intent—for more attractive hunting and planting land.

The Cepee pauses from his studies. He recalls a reference he came across earlier in the Human Archives: *The writer Jared Diamond coined the term constructive paranoia to capture the idea of exercising caution in the face of potential danger.*[31] *Mr. Diamond stated it was an oxymoronic phrase. Perhaps so, but it's a practical and convincing term.* The Cepee returns to his studies.

These legacies presented serious problems as humans evolved to their more recent state of behavior. Even into the twenty-first century, an "unlike" person was suspect.

In modern times these unlike humans were more often innocent than not. Yet, they frequently paid a price for their distinctiveness. The Human Archives documented a staggering number of deaths and tortures that came about because a person was different from another person, or a tribe was different from another tribe. Once vital to survival, these mind sets became cognitive deficits to modern humans.

The Cepee, when reading this part of the Human Archives about his ancestors, pauses again. He thinks: *Death and torture to a human, just for being something the human could not help being in the first place?* He reads on:

These killers and torturers, frocked in their righteous tribal robes to insure their identification of likeness to others of the same ilk, came to adapt an effective protocol: "Once a group [had] been split off and sufficiently dehumanized, any brutality [could] be justified, at any level, and at any size of the victimized group up to and including race and nation."[32]

In the early twentieth century, a New Guinea man, one not yet accustomed to modern times, spoke about the ease of dealing with strangers, "These people are our enemies. Why shouldn't we kill them?—they're not human."[33]

A few decades later, the situation had not changed much. Can't pronounce "Shibboleth?" Don't have a phoneme of /ʃ/ in your vocabulary? You say "Sibboleth" instead? Off with your head:[34]

Gilead then cut Ephraim off from the fords of the Jordan, and whenever Ephraimite fugitives said, "Let me cross," the men of Gilead would ask, "Are you an Ephraimite?" If he said, "No," they then said, "Very well, say 'Shibboleth' (שבלת)." If anyone said, "Sibboleth" (סבלת), because he could not pronounce it, then they would seize him and kill him by the fords of the Jordan. Forty-two thousand Ephraimites fell on this occasion.

With these Rules of Life now part of our vocabulary, and with others to follow, the pace is changed by examining a major consequence of the Autocatalytic Effect.

Compression of Time

From the cave dweller to the high-rise occupant, the evolution of the *Homo sapiens* took millions of years. It might have been considered fanciful to think a window of less than a century could result in the radical transformation of a modern human into a Cepee. Yet clues to this exponential compression of evolutionary (more accurately, revolutionary) time were in evidence as early as the first decade of the twenty-first century.

A late twentieth-century experiment conducted in Siberia resulted in the transformation of a wild fox into a creature that not only resembled a domestic dog, but exhibited dog-like traits. Thousands of years of domestication (estimated to be about 15,000 years from the time foxes began to be tamed) were compressed into only a few years (nine generations) to bring about these behavioral and morphological changes.[35] The practice was as simple as could be: a screening program. Foxes displaying friendlier behavior toward humans were interbred. Unfriendly foxes were not allowed to propagate.

Of course, a fox was not a human. One could question how an experiment on foxes in Siberia could have consequences on a human in, say, lower Manhattan. The answer was simple: humans wanted to improve and prolong their lives. If manipulation of the human's cerebral and corporal constituents could result in living longer and in being happier, the lowering of thresholds for self-change was foreordained.

From Eugenics to Liberal Eugenics to Preventive Eugenics to Inventive Eugenics

The Siberian experiment used strict breeding controls to produce this change. Such practices, called eugenics, had been banned by most nations because of Nazi Germany's inhumane and murderous implementation of the practice. Nonetheless, forms of eugenics engineering had become a routine part of humans' lives. In order to avoid the stigma of the past, humans usually did not use the term *eugenics*. Some scientists and philosophers called it *liberal eugenics*.

Here are four examples (among many) of humans' practice of liberal eugenics in the early twenty-first century, about the time when the transformation to the Cepee began to gain momentum.

In Israel a program called Dor Yeshorim was implemented to reduce the incidence of several human miseries, such as cystic fibrosis and gland disorders.[36] Used as a screening program, if a fetus was diagnosed with one of several diseases, the pregnancy could be terminated, subject to consent of the parents.

In Russia, the term *liberal eugenics* was used for more assertive actions. As examples, state-sponsored sterilizations were performed on women evaluated to have "psycho-neurological" problems. State-sponsored abortions were performed on disabled women.[37]

In Australia, the country had long practiced the removal of children from their tribes in order to assimilate those of mixed descent into the Australian society.

In China, marriage was prohibited among people who suffered from "impotence, venereal disease, mental disorder, and leprosy." In addition, "Carriers of certain genetic diseases were allowed to marry only if they [were] sterilized, or [agreed] to use some other form of long-term contraception."[38]

Sperm banks opened in China to encourage the proliferation of doctors. One bank, called the Notables' Sperm Bank, only admitted sperm created by registered doctors.[39] The idea assumed doctors carried a medical doctor chromosome in their DNA. This genetic jewel might dictate the career path of the soon-to-be pride of the family.

These limited forms of eugenics were modest endeavors. But with the Autocatalytic Process working in conjunction with the Threshold Lowering Syndrome, it was just a matter of time (and a brief time at that) before a radically modified creature would begin to take shape. Its greatly altered body and mind would come to define, if not a new species, then certainly an extraordinary transformation of an existing species.

More extensive and radical changes to the human followed those cited here. They were dubbed *inventive eugenics* and are explained in more detail in Chapter 11.

Conclusions

Because of the earth's bounty, the sparse human population, and the absence of weapons of any consequence, the early humans led lives in which they did relatively little harm to one another. Certainly, the species members fought among themselves, but their capacity to harm another human and to harm earth's environment was limited in scope.

Within a few thousand years, the *Homo sapiens* became the dominant large species on earth. The evolution to this lofty position resulted in most of the humans becoming sedentary members of stratified tribes, dedicated to food production, the invention of tools, and the creation of more people. The humans became the masters of their surroundings, subjugating almost all of the other species on the planet.

With the use of liberal and preventive eugenics, the human race was gradually improving its physical strength and vigor. With inventive eugenics it was casting aside ancient diseases and other maladies.

Nonetheless, as the humans invented more tools and as their population increased, so did their ability to harm one another and their environment. If these tools had been, say, a better hoe, no harm would have been done. And while the race did invent better hoes, they also invented better spears...in abundance.

The on-going development of an organism sometimes results in a dead-end path during the process of natural selection, an evolutionary blind alley. Sometimes a species develops a behavioral trait that is not in its best interests. The next chapter examines this dangerous course in relation to a human trait: predatory, pathological aggression and the associated use of increasingly deadly tools.

––––––––––––––––––

[1] Jean-Jacques Rousseau, *Discourse Upon the Origin and Foundation of Inequality Among Mankind* (New York: Perennial Library), 1994. Undated comment from William Ebenstein on Rosseau's philosophy.

[2] "Biosphere," http://web.geology.ufl.edu/Biosphere.html. The term *biosphere* is claimed to have been coined by a Russian scientist Vladimir

Vernadsky in 1929, as documented at this website. However, in keeping with humans' disposition toward contention, the Cepee learns from the Human Archives that the term is also claimed to have been coined by geologist Eduard Suess in 1875. In either case, the term refers to the life zone of the earth, including all living organisms, organic matter not yet decomposed, the atmosphere, hydrosphere, and geosphere.

[3] David R. Begun, "Planet of the Apes," *Scientific American*, August 2003, 80.

[4] Katherine Harmon, "Shattered Ancestry," *Scientific American*, February 2013, 49. Recent findings point to fossils that support the theory of humans evolving from multiple lineages, not just a "chimp like ape."

[5] "Early Craftsmanship: Implements in Stone and Bone," http://www. becominghuman.org/. Also, https://www.facebook.com/BecomingHuman. org. According to The Institute of Human Origins, Arizona State University, an upper jaw of a *Homo*, the genus to which modern humans belong, was recovered with primitive stone tools (stone flakes and chopping stones) at Hagar, Ethiopia. The jaw is approximately 2.33 million years old. As of the writing of this book, this site represents the oldest date of the association of stone tools with humans.

[6] Jared Diamond, *Guns, Germs, and Steel* (New York: Norton, 1999), 36. Since Diamond's book was published, paleontologists discovered an almost fully intact human fossil in Ethiopia. It is 3.2 million years old and displays characteristics that most likely gave this being both walking and arboreal capabilities. See Kate Wong, "Lucy's Baby," *Scientific American*, December 2006, 78-85. In addition, discoveries (revealed in 2010) claim a new species, *Australopithecus sidebar* should be placed into the humans' evolutionary tree. See Kate Wong, "First of Our Kind," *Scientific American*, April 2012, 31-39. Nonetheless, these ancestors, while fascinating, and however old they may have been, did not affect the ascension of the Cepee.

[7] Katherine Harmon, "Shattered Ancestry," *Scientific American*, February 2013, 49. In deference to the readers who take offence about the idea of humans descending from the ape, findings supporting more than one set of ancestral lineage for the *Homo sapiens* allow for the possibility that some of our ancestors may not have been tree dwellers. That said, overwhelming evidence points to the chimp as at least one of our very distant and very remote kin. Thus, anti-chimp advocates have a straw of an argument, but a thin straw.

[8] Diamond, *Guns, Germs, and Steel*, 39.

[9] Ibid., 86.

[10] Ibid., 100. See Table 5.1. Researchers are not in complete agreement on the date. Dr. Diamond cites 8500 BC as the first known instances of plant (wheat, pea, olive) and animal (goat, sheep) domestication (in Southwest

Asia). Other literature places these events beginning around 10,000 BC. See T. A. Brown, M. K. Jones, W. Powell, and R. G. Allaby. (2009). "The Complex Origins of Domesticated Crops in the Fertile Crescent." *Trends in Ecology & Evolution 24, no. 2, December 18, 2008, 103-109.*

[11] This hypothesis is not supported by everyone. Some researchers believe climate changes led to some (or all) of the extinction of large animals. Others resent the implication that certain ancient people (Native North Americans, for example) killed-off scores of species. For this narrative, how these large sources of protein became history does not matter. Our ancestors still evolved to be food producers, along with the attendant advantages and disadvantages associated with this occupation. For a view challenging some of Diamond's claims, see Vine Deloria, Jr., *Red Earth, White Lies* (Golden, Colorado: Fulcrum, 1997). Also, http://www.sciencedaily.com/releases/200 1/10/011025072315.htm, which claims the culprit was climate change.

[12] Elif Bautman, "The Sanctuary," *The New Yorker*, December 19 & 26, 2011, 81. Also, http://www.newyorker.com/reporting/2011/12/19/ 111219fa_fact_batuman.

[13] Ibid.

[14] Ibid.

[15] E. O. Wilson, *The Social Conquest of Earth* (New York: Liveright, 2012), 16, Kindle edition, loc. 325.

[16] "Tribe," *The Random House College Dictionary* (New York: Random House, 1984), 1511.

[17] Some historians and other experts on this subject use the word "clan" to describe the smallest number of humans composing a group. Thus, clans formed tribes. This is a useful distinction, and it is used if necessary to distinguish between the two groups. I use the word *clan* in the context of what most of us call our family.

[18] Jared Diamond, *The World Until Yesterday* (New York: Penguin, 2012), 300-303.

[19] Wilson, *The Social Conquest of Earth*, 258, Kindle edition, loc. 4185. The author states, "The evidence that lies before us in great abundance points to organized religion as an expression of tribalism."

[20] Maslow's hierarchy is more detailed than the hierarchy shown in Figure 2-1. This writer has substituted the word *need* for Maslow's word *motive* and separated sex into a separate entry. I've also added the word *power* to the hierarchy. These changes will be explained and justified in Chapter 3. Here is Maslow's complete hierarchy: (1) physiological; (2) security and safety; (3) love and feelings of belonging; (4) competence, prestige, and esteem; (5) self-fulfillment; and (6) curiosity and the need to understand.

I do not go into Maslow's ideas about self-actualization in this book. See Microsoft's Encarta Reference Library.

[21] Even in Cepee times, a female likes to be around successful males. Irrespective of DNA tailoring, a subject for Chapter 11, they offer better genetic material than a lowly follower. The same holds true for the male, but he is often intimidated by an assertive female. Perhaps his reticence is the product of her inherent XX chromosome set in comparison to his paltry XY.

[22] Diamond, *The World Until Yesterday*, 125.

[23] This idea is one of the themes of Diamond's book cited earlier, *Guns, Germs, and Steel*—with which I agree in relation to older societies. For more information on why fertile North America and its inhabitants did not gain a lead at this starting gate, I refer you to Diamond's explanations on pp. 187, 355-370, and his "first set of continental differences," p. 406. Diamond does not discuss why modern societies, those that gained a head start centuries ago, fall behind and fail. In his book *Collapse*, he restricts his examples to Rwanda, Haiti, and the Dominican Republic. For a while, the once great China failed. Modern Russia is headed that way. Mineral-rich nations in Africa are frightening failures. In Chapter 8, I discuss the reasons the once great culture/religion of Islam has fallen behind the west. For now, Jared Diamond is a professor of geology, not a professor of politics, and likely is not inclined to branch out into this subject. Nonetheless, his insights into human behavior would make for an interesting book with international politics as one of the themes.

[24] Ibid., 111.

[25] "Autocatalytic," *Dictionary*, Bing.com. The term *autocatalytic* is used in chemistry to describe the speeding up of a chemical reaction by a catalyst that is a product of the reaction. It also means the speeding up of any process or the production of a faster reaction.

[26] Estimates vary from 10 to 100 times faster than the humans' times of 8000 BC.

[27] B.F. Skinner is credited with this concept, which is known in some circles as the Skinner Effect. This writer coined the term, the *Threshold Lowering Syndrome*, to describe this behavior, but does not claim credit for the idea.

[28] An interesting and controversial variation of the Threshold Lowering Syndrome is an idea called, *Defining Deviancy Down*, a term coined by Daniel Patrick Moynihan in 1993 with a paper published in the *American Scholar*. This paper is available at www2.sunysuffolk.edu/formans/DefiningDeviancy. htm. For another view, Andrew Karmen has written a rebuttal and is available at www.albany.edu/scj/jcjpc/vol2is5/deviancy.html.

[29] Diamond, *The World Until Yesterday*, 21.

[30] Ibid., 128. Before Western civilization had made an impact on the Dani people in New Guinea, such a war was witnessed by westerners who had recently arrived in the area. Diamond devotes Chapter 3 to a description of this battle. I have extrapolated his data with my hindsight view of the past.

[31] Ibid., 243-275.

[32] Wilson, *The Social Conquest of Earth*, 63, Kindle edition, loc. 1065.

[33] Diamond, *The World Until Yesterday*, 125.

[34] Excerpts from Judges 12:5-6 of the Bible. Also,Wahrig Deutsches Wörterbuch, 6th ed, and http://lexikon.meyers.de/meyers/Schibboleth.

[35] Evan Ratliff, "Taming the Wild," *National Geographic*, March 2011, 41.

[36] Shidduchim, Program Dor Yeshorim, http://www.shidduchim.info/medical.html.

[37] *Novaya Gazeta*, December 12, 2005.

[38] M. Bobrow (June 1995), "Redrafted Chinese Law Remains Eugenic," *J. Med. Genet.* 32 (6): 409. doi:10.1136/jmg.32.6.409. PMC 1050477. PMID 7666390. http://jmg.bmj.com/cgi/pmidlookup?view=long&pmid=7666390. Also, Mao X (January 1997), "Chinese Eugenic Legislation," *Lancet* 349 (9045): 139. doi:10.1016/S0140-6736(05)60930-0. PMID 8996454. http://linkinghub.elsevier.com/retrieve/pii/S0140-6736(05)60930-0.

[39] Xinhua News Agency, "China's 1st Notables' Sperm Bank Opens," June 24, 1999.

CHAPTER 3

COMPETITION AND AGGRESSION

———

*Only chimpanzees and humans have enough brainpower to
realize the advantages of removing the opposition.*[1]
(The chimps have their hands and teeth;
the humans have their bombs and gas.)

*Thus was born the human condition, selfish at one time, selfless at
another, and the two impulses often conflicted.*[2]
—E. O. Wilson

*Do not receive overtures of peace or submission...
Kill every male Indian over twelve years of age.*[3]
—Order of General Connor during an
1865 Platte River campaign.

The more things change, the more they remain the same.
—anon

The pace of development of the humans' use of tools for destruction of one another (an exponential, autocatalytic process) outpaced the humans' *possible* hesitations about using them (a linear, non-autocatalytic process). This sudden change created a shortfall between the employment of killing instruments and *reservations* about their use. As discussed in this chapter, the lack of any significant restraining harness on their utilization resulted in calamitous consequences for the human race.

The words *possible* and *reservations* in the previous paragraph are placed in italics to emphasize that anthropologists and other experts on human history are not in agreement on whether the humans of past centuries were hesitant or resolute about using weapons on members outside their clan or tribe.

On one side of the coin, the question was irrelevant, as the Cepees recognize that regardless of the reasons for their use, their predecessors did indeed employ weapons of enormous destructive power on themselves. On the other side of the coin, the question was of utmost importance as its answer might have held the keys for addressing this deadly behavioral deficiency.

Placing the coin on its edge, the fact remained that regardless of either coin side, a biological basis existed for this behavior. It was not ethereal. One way or the other, the humans' behavior had an organic foundation. If an inkling could be gained into the origins of this dangerous malady, perhaps an inkling of a solution could be formed. Perhaps the foundation could be altered. Therefore, the discussions in this chapter will look at both sides of the argument.

During the second and third decades of the twenty-first century, it became evident that several characteristics had to be modified or eliminated from subsequent members of the human species. One trait had to be culled: pathological aggression. The dangers of this violent kind of aggression had been known to the humans for many years. They railed against it when they were the victims and justified it when they were the perpetrators. Yet many members of this race did not realize aggression (that of the non-pathological kind) had been programmed into their makeup thousands of years ago because it was a species-enhancing instinct. Even into humans' modern times, aggression played a vital role in sparking competition within the species, leading to better performances in business, in sports, in practically every walk of life. Thus, it is appropriate to examine the positive traits of aggression the human possessed, with the emphasis on the ancient days.

Since early times, aggression had been a beneficial trait for earth's creatures to possess. It was an instinct contributing to the survival and improvement of each species. For example, aggression within a species (intra-species) and its associated fighting often led to a stronger, healthier, and more intelligent member taking possession of more territory and a more efficacious sexual mate. The control of territory and a gene pool contributed to an enhanced position for the species, because those members who gained dominance in their respective hierarchies often assumed the role of protector against aggressors from other species. For example, the baboon fought for dominance within its species but also fought against other species (hyenas, for example) to protect its family members, including the young.

Furthermore, on some parts of the earth where territory was scarce, intra-species aggression guaranteed a given species would spread out over a limited terrain. Thus ensuring that, say, one pride of lions did not interfere with another pride of lions.

Even with fierce fighting among the species, intra-species killing was the exception and not the rule. After all, unnecessary killing would do little more than reduce the species' vigor. Notwithstanding this fact and the naive beliefs of a number of wildlife enthusiasts, social animals did engage in infanticide and other killings within their species.[4] But the scope and effect of their killing paled in relation to the human species' modern counterparts.[5]

Cooperation within a species also had salubrious effects. For example, flocks of birds, which as individuals were prey to a fox, might attack the fox (inter-species aggression) and drive it away from the birds' breeding grounds. Sometimes the fox was so intimidated that it found another place to steal eggs. As another example, a pride of lions had a better chance of capturing their supper if they attacked a herd of gazelles as a pack, rather than individually.

Likewise, a group of humans had a better chance than a lone hunter of downing an animal for food. If for nothing else, cooperative hunting conserved an individual's protein and energy. But it was more than just preserving strength. In accordance with natural selection, the mutations leading to a more cooperative nature had a profound and positive effect on the species.

Cooperative groups usually triumphed over uncooperative groups. This truth was not at first obvious. Natural selection's focus was on an organism surviving better in certain environments than another organism; that of an individual, such as a human, adapting better to changing conditions. The emphasis had been on individuals more than groups of individuals.

But such was not the entire case. It was concluded, "...selfish individuals beat altruistic individuals, while groups of altruists beat groups of selfish individuals."[6] Common sense really. This trait stayed with the human into his modern era, manifesting itself in many ways: A factious army could not defeat a well-organized army. A sports team with dissenting players was destined to lose most of its games. A discordant company would fall to its less dissonant competitors.

In addition, the altruistic sacrifice of an individual for the benefit of the individual's group had the effect of benefiting this individual—even a soldier who "died for the cause." This seeming contradiction was (again) nothing more than a matter of common sense:[7]

> Altruism actually benefits each group member on average because each altruist shares genes by common descent with most other members of its group. Due to the sharing with relatives, its sacrifice increases the relative abundance of these genes in the next generation.

Nonetheless, as the human changed over thousands of years, manifestations of what was once species-enhancing aggression within and between tribes degenerated into behavior that was severely detrimental to the *Homo sapiens*. In the beginning, mutations that enhanced aggressive tendencies led to both individuals and cooperative tribes ascending a ladder of domination. The results of these changes were better opportunities to procreate and pass their genetic legacy to their progeny. But as time went on, this conduct evolved to a form of *retrograde evolution* because it became an evolutionary dead-end alley.

Creation of the Pecking Order and the Human Tribal Hierarchy

As described in Chapter 2, during their early times on earth, humans developed social systems based on a pecking order that was named the Human Tribal Hierarchy. The pecking order became a common trait of many creatures on earth—not just humans—because it had species-preservation attributes. For example, in a pack of wolves, a dominant male would subjugate other males who were not as strong or as fierce as the lead wolf. In a flock of chickens, a dominant bird (stronger, probably smarter, and perhaps more sexually prolific than the others) would peck its competitors into submission, then go to the head of the copulation queue. Thus, it increased the opportunities of passing its superior genes to the next generation and advancing in the hierarchy of its tribe.

Usually, the strongest and most virile male of a species was given the responsibility of protecting the females. This position gave the male precedence over the other males to spread his sperm and genes into as many females as was physically possible.[8]

Turf: Stimulus for Aggression

Food, shelter, sex, security. Through what means could these needs first be met? How could a human ensure they would continue to be met? These requirements, essential for survival, were satisfied through the acquisition and retention of turf. Possession of turf was the basis for much of the humans' behavior.

Obviously, land was turf. Land had soil for planting. Land had game for hunting. Land had surrounding water to support travel. Land had places for shelter. As well, fisheries and beaches were other forms of turf. Those humans who could live on bounty from the waters were as adept at survival as their land-based relatives.

Land or water, those humans who controlled these "turfs" controlled their destiny. They were the players on the back row of the survival chessboard. All others were pawns occupying the front row.

Wars were fought to gain and hold this turf. Aggression was not a luxury motive for possessing turf. It was the essential drive for survival. All other motives followed the motive to control turf.

So far so good. As long as adequate turf was available from which to hunt, grow crops, drink water, and find shelter, each tribe stayed on its own turf, and humans usually got along with one another. Thus, the species continued to proliferate and expand their presence onto the seemingly boundless turfs on the earth.

But the turf was not boundless. If the population grew to the extent it was taking the resources of the turf and the turf's bounties became scarce, a tribe looked to adjacent turf, often belonging to other tribes. To survive, this turf had to be taken, even at the expense of others.

Nonetheless, so far the performance was being played out with a species-enhancing theme and script: *Take what is needed for survival.*

Aggression Becomes a Negative Factor

As ancient humans evolved to become modern people, as their more recent ancestors began to dominate the earth, aggression took on negative connotations. Humans began to behave in a self-destructive manner in order to ascend the rungs in their Human Tribal Hierarchies. Competition and aggression began to take place without any relationship to species survival and the passing of gene pools. They became ends unto themselves.

"Turf" took on a new meaning. Its geographical boundaries became mental boundaries. The humans were rewiring their brains to redefine their views of turf. But to what end?

Millions of deaths during the humans' last few centuries on earth occurred because of the desire to achieve religious and political domination, to expand humans' mental turf. These actions had nothing to do with physical survival or gene propagation. For example, a murderous despot did not kill his opposition because he needed food, shelter, or a conjugal mate. He killed him because he wanted more power. He did not torture and murder his own subjects because he needed their turf. He already possessed this turf! He tortured and murdered underlings because, to put it civilly, he desired to dominate all around him. *Material needs took a back seat to immaterial desires.*

These humans, small in number but quite significant beyond their quantity, camouflaged their aggression behind guises. But almost any conflict was a contest for domination. In simple terms, toward the later centuries in the humans' evolution: aggression ran amok.

Tools

During the early development of the human, the tools of aggression were muscle power, body speed, and mental agility. Later, external mechanisms such as clubs, knives, and spears became a key part of the aggression toolbox. As the human learned more about the development of these tools, he became skilled at using increasingly sophisticated methods for playing out his aggressive tendencies. Tools evolved from instruments of limited capacity to appliances capable of destroying entire cities.

Thus, the species was making enormous progress in developing aggressive tools for destruction but was not faring so well in changing its gray matter in such a way to display less aggressive behavior, or at least to exercise some control over the tools this species was creating. The seemingly intelligent human did not possess enough intelligence to prevent itself from killing off its own kind, and in many instances, itself.

To be clear about this matter, intra-species killing was not necessarily harmful to the species. It kept weaker members out of the gene pool. It gave a clan or tribe better survival chances by reducing the number of diners around the campfire during times when food was scarce.

The Cepee pauses from his studies of the Human Archives: *I've learned that some of the modern humans looked down on those pre-modern humans who abandoned or killed their sick and elderly. What were they to do? There were no hospitals in ancient New Mexico for an Apache tribe to leave their sick and wounded before they broke camp. Senior citizen residences had not yet sprung up among Bolivia's Siriono Indians for them to drop-off their elderly in the care of others. It's easy to criticize from afar.* The Cepee continues his studies.

Other species adhered to these concepts. For example, certain birds laid two eggs to produce two babies. As the chicks matured, one was going to be weaker. The stronger chick slowly pecked the weaker one to death in order to have more food available for itself. Selective culling, as revolting as it might seem to a bystander, was an efficient strategy on the part of nature.

Nonselective culling was another matter. During the evolution of the humans' DNA and brain, the tools for culling members of their species out of the gene pool became staggering annihilation instruments. In keeping with the Disproportionate Ratio introduced in Chapter 2, they were yielded by a small part of the population, but their weapons were quite effective: bombs incinerating large populations and landscapes, biological and chemical tools causing painful deaths among thousands of humans.

Using these kinds of weapons certainly gave a possessor an advantage over an enemy, at least a tactical advantage. But the long-term consequences did not. The side effects of nuclear explosions were strategically ruinous to both parties.

What went wrong with the human mind? How did the productive aspects of competition and aggression get out of hand? Why did the human not realize that by the use of these staggering destructive forces his race had embarked onto a perilous journey, one that might lead to self-obliteration? To answer these questions, this analysis turns to the subject of how aggression, specifically its after-effects, developed into behavior the humans could not contain.

The following discussion represents a school of thought supported by some, but not all cultural anthropologists and other experts who deal with human history.

Inhibitory Behavior

Before the advent of tools, the human had little need to breed inhibitory behavior into his mental makeup. "In human evolution, no inhibitory mechanisms preventing sudden manslaughter were necessary, because quick killing was impossible anyhow; the potential victim had plenty of opportunity to elicit the pity of the aggressor by submissive gestures and appeasing attitudes."[9] Signals of submission with various kowtowing motions, or retreating from a threatening situation, were usually sufficient to ward off aggression from another member of the species. In addition, without tools, it was usually impossible to kill and difficult to seriously injure another human. Pummeling a fellow to death with one's hands was hard on the killer's anatomy.

Consequently, if possession of turf was not an issue, it is reasonable to assume the prehistory human was likely cautious about attacking another human with the intent to kill. The act was not worth the expenditure of precious energy and especially the risk of death or injury. After all, an injured leg, a damaged shoulder, a broken thumb, would make the attacker vulnerable to his predators, such as tigers or another human. Of course, this risk was lessened if a group of humans attacked an individual. So murder did indeed take place...and often.

But for now, we stay with the plausible idea that *Homo sapiens* intra-species killing without the use of a killing instrument was not a wide-spread practice, that the killing tool had not yet embedded itself into the basic makeup of this species.

> No selection pressure arose in the prehistory of mankind to breed inhibitory mechanisms preventing the killing [within the species] until, all of a sudden, the invention of artificial weapons upset the equilibrium of killing potential and social inhibitions. When it did, man's position was very nearly that of a dove which, by some unnatural trick of nature, has suddenly acquired the beak of a raven.

This seemingly unnatural trick of nature was actually part of nature's natural behavior. The dove's symbolic possession of the raven's beak came about through thousands of years of ongoing mutations and related natural selections.

The Cepee pauses: *I have learned that the person who offered these thoughts, named Konrad Lorenz, was a revered scientist, respected by all, and a winner of the Nobel Prize in Psychology or Medicine. Of course, his research reflected the times of mid-twentieth century. Understandably, some of his ideas were out of touch, but not by very much. Here's one example from the archives:* "If moral responsibility and unwillingness to kill have indubitably increased, the ease and emotional impunity of killing have increased at the same rate." *If Lorenz had changed the idea of killing at the same rate to the reality of killing at a faster and increasingly accelerating rate, he would have captured what his race was becoming. Nonetheless, this man, if the humans had listened, offered alternative paths to their on-going roads toward self-destruction.*

And the raven's beak? Relative to the dove's disposition, it was there. If it was ready for use, why not use it? I've come across a term called the Law of the Instrument. I'll study the archives to learn more, as the Cepee returns to the Human Archives.

The Law of the Instrument

Consider this possibility: If a human could dominate another human (perhaps to the point of murder) to take his food, clothing, shelter, and sexual partner, the result would be to move up the rungs in several Human Tribal Hierarchy pecking orders. The act would also increase the opportunities for the domineering human to pass his genes to subsequent generations.

Even more, if hierarchy ascension could be executed with less risk to his body, the human could become more adventuresome and aggressive. Consequently, the human invented tools as an instrument to abet his aggressive motives. To be fair, most of the tools were used for productive tasks such as tilling the earth, scraping hides, digging holes, and hunting mammals, birds, and fish. But other tools were invented for hunting humans.

Tools eventually became extensions of the hunter's mind and body. The human assumed a tool was part of his makeup. Unto itself, this concept was not harmful to the human. But it became unhealthy when combined with the Law of the Instrument: exemplified by the child who picks up a hammer and looks for something to pound.

Why have a hammer lying around doing nothing? After all, it's meant to nail. Why have thousands of warriors idly sitting around in massive, expensive bivouacs doing nothing but consuming precious food? Why have fleets of warships plying the oceans in never-ending circles, doing nothing but consuming precious fuel? Especially if the use of these hammers could result in the acquisition of more food, more fuel, and in particular: more human turf. A high-level leader of the Israel military (General Rafael Eitan) put it well, "Now that I've built a military machine which costs billions of dollars, I have to use it."[10]

The Aggressive Tools Cycle

According to this school of thought, with less risk, accompanied with the absence of an evolved inhibitor in the brain, it became easier to vent aggression. The invention of a weapon as a tool for destruction upset the humans' otherwise stable behavioral apple cart, leading to a cycle, dubbed as the Aggressive Tools Cycle.

Figure 3-1 is a picture of this cycle. It illustrates how aggression, once a laudatory trait of the human race, became its nemesis, at least in this specific human drama. As the acts unfolded, more powerful theater pieces (destructive tools) were placed onto the stage for its actors to use.

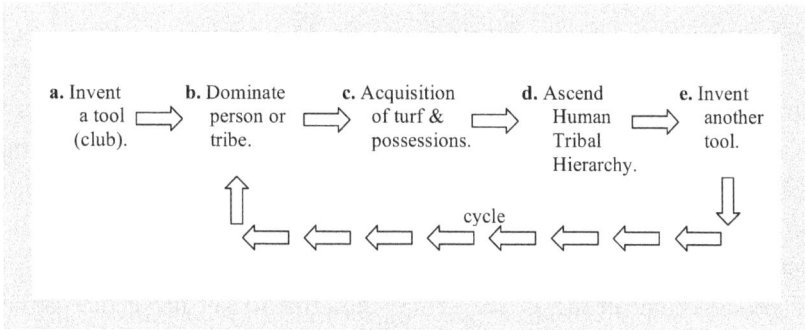

Figure 3-1. The Aggressive Tools Cycle.

Starting at point a in the cycle, thousands of years ago, primitive humans invented the club. (As one example. A hurled rock will do as well.) This tool was used by an individual to attack someone else with less danger to the life and limb of the attacker—especially if the aggressor could carry off the attack to dominate a person or tribe, as suggested in point b.

After this party was conquered, or at least subdued, the now dominant human was able to acquire the vanquished's possessions—food, shelter, clothing, sexual partner, and usually other possessions as well, depicted as point c in Figure 3-1.

One school of thought about this cycle is that through the process of natural selection, a genetic mutation (in simplest terms, an allele) caused one or more humans to be drawn to aggression using tools.[11] The brain of this being (or beings) began to use these tools for assaults. The individual carrying this allele fared better than his counterparts who did not carry this change on their DNA. With each succeeding generation, the individuals carrying this genomic sequence multiplied and spread their gene pool. This group's success begot more success, perhaps subject to other mutations that further aided the process.

The Aggressive Tools Cycle was subject to the Autocatalytic Process, introduced in Chapter 2. Inventing tools reinforced the process of domination, which in turn reinforced the development of better domination tools. On and on, the cycle kept going.

This initial success led to several subsequent effects and transitions through this cycle. One effect was an increased motivation to continue intra-species aggression. As the tools for aggression evolved to distance the human from the object of his mayhem, the human became less inhibited to mitigate his aggressive behavior, an example of the Threshold Lowering Syndrome. After all, blowing a human apart with a remote controlled missile was likely easier on the killer's conscience (and his stomach) than performing the operation with a knife.

A President of the United States had this to say about the use of aerial drones to an enemy located far away, "There's a remoteness to it that makes it tempting to think that somehow we can, without any mess on our hands, solve vexing security problems."[12]

It is logical to assume that the legacy of a human killing at a distance with a tossed stone helped wire the human's brain for killings at longer distances.[13] Otherwise, what was the reason for this reality coming to the front stage of the humans' modern-time drama? Human behavior did not "just happen." Synapses fired and the brain's anatomy changed based on genetic factors and previous experiences.

As the human climbed upward in Maslow's Hierarchy of Needs, he had sufficient food, clothing, and shelter to meet his survival needs. He also had sufficient tools to change his status from a prey to a predator. Because he no longer was in danger of starving, freezing to death, or being eaten by other animals, the human needed something to occupy its increasingly intelligent but potentially idle mind.

As Figure 3-1 suggests (points b, c, d, and e), humans' behavior became cyclical. The pecking order attainments, the resulting successes, the acquisition of more possessions, the availability of more mates, and the expansion of the available gene pool translated into behavior that became increasingly aggressive, acquisitive, and predatory.

Point e in the cycle is labeled, "Invent another tool." After the discovery and/or invention of the club, the spear, and other rather primitive instruments, the tribes continued to refine and improve their tools. As stated earlier, and in fairness to the humans, most of these tools were created for the betterment of the race. Unfortunately, the few exceptions had a huge negative influence on their future.

Why did the early humans not club or axe themselves to oblivion? They needed one another to help in their survival. As stated, they often hunted as a group. As well, aggregate members of a tribe were needed for defense against predators. In addition, a diverse population was needed to maintain a healthy gene pool. The result was the development of mitigations in their minds about using unbridled aggression against individuals within the tribe and especially within the clan.

Thus, one school of thought about this aspect of ancient human behavior was the theory that humans had a reluctance to use weapons on their own kind. But these cognitive disciplines were not balanced against their aggressive propensities, especially as they invented more efficient tools to support their aggressive dispositions.

The other school of thought claimed humans never had these mitigations in their minds in the first place. They thought nothing about doing anything in their power to subjugate their adversary. Regardless of the validity of either school, the facts were not in dispute, as they were there for everyone to see: Humans evolved to the point where they began to employ enormously deadly weapons on themselves.

Evolutionary Arms Race

The aggressive tools cycle shown in Figure 3-1 constituted an evolutionary arms race. To counter the effectiveness of the club, the spear was invented. To counter the spear, the bow and arrow were conceived. Then guns, next cannons, followed by airplanes, bombs, missiles, chemicals, germs, and nuclear devices—to name a few.

On the surface, this arms race could be construed as a race *between* humans. But it was not. It was a race *within* a human. Which part of a human's genetic code, resulting mental machinations, and subsequent physical actions would prevail? The evolution of a propensity to decrease the use of weapons? Or the evolution of an inclination that fostered weapons use?

The Autocatalytic Process:
Stone Clubs to Nuclear Clubs

As seen in Figure 3-2, and as suggested earlier, the humans' tools employed for hunting game and other humans became more sophisticated, more deadly. The inventions of primitive weapons, such as a rock and a carved club occurred at least two million years ago during the Stone Age (using the year 2015 as a reference date).[14] The use of the thrown spear may have occurred during this time, but most studies place the wide-spread use of this weapon beginning about 17,000 years ago. The bow and arrow changed the nature of hunting and warfare. It was the first weapon used that allowed the warrior to be located a faraway distance from game or the enemy. The Human Archives revealed the oldest bow found (in one piece) was estimated to be around 11,000 years old.

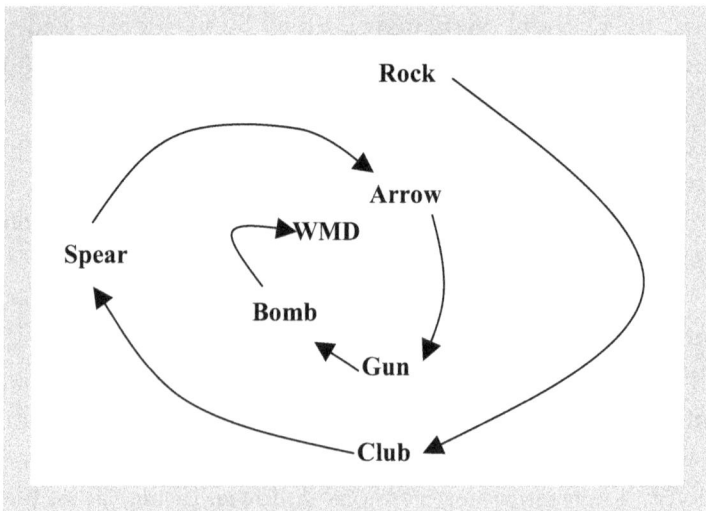

Figure 3-2. Autocatalytic compression of time and use of weapons.

It took over two million years for the humans to evolve from hurling a rock to the shooting of a bow-powered arrow. Afterwards, as depicted by the autocatalytic cycle in Figure 3-2, the evolution of weapons sped up exponentially. In less than 700 years, the humans invented guns (1300s), bombs (1940s), and weapons of mass destruction: poison gas (1915), nuclear weapons (1945).

The Malleable Brain: Rewiring for Aggression

Was the humans' brain development keeping up with the increasing sophistication of their destructive weapons? At the time primitive weapons were coming to the scene, brains of these very early beings were about the same size as that of a chimpanzee. Since that time, the human brain size increased. A modern human in the twenty-first century had a brain three times larger than his predecessor two million years ago.[15]

In the latter part of the twentieth century, technology became available to allow researchers to examine the structure of the brain. Various techniques, grouped under the name of neuroimaging, could display both the surface and innards of the brain.

The humans' brain had been undergoing changes throughout the existence of the species. For this discussion, as they increased their aggressive behavior to perpetuate their gene pool, their brain also underwent transformations. One neuroimaging project showed the composition of different areas of the brain (on the cortex) was significantly different for a person well versed in playing the violin in contrast to a person who played the piano well.[16] One might have thought musical talent—string or keyboard—was confined to one part of the brain, but it was not. Another study showed the creation of new neural connections as a result of participating in an ongoing activity for a prolonged time.[17]

Any human activity had an effect on the brain, and prolonged activity created a change in its structure and operations. The change might have been observable, such as changes that could be seen on the cortexes of piano and violin players who practiced a lot on their respective tools of their trade. Tools of the trade: the hoe, the shovel, the club, the gun, the bomb, the drone. With repeated employment, with practice, their usage modified the brains of their users.

Because the more aggressive humans (with gene mutations likely starting the process) began to dominate their more docile counterparts, the aggressors' predisposition toward violence was reinforced, which fostered a more aggressive culture. This example is the first illustration of the partnership of genes and culture in humans' evolution, a concept called coevolution.

This situation had important consequences: (a) the more aggressive humans increased their share of the gene pool, and (b) their brains underwent further changes. The end result was a segment of the human species who were increasingly disposed toward violence. They were "wired" for more aggression than others. In addition, laboratory experiments proved that, on occasion, parts of humans' brains (the older parts) that veered toward reactionary aggression came to dominate the brain parts (the more recent parts) that mitigated this sort of behavior.

The challenge presented to the human race was how to alter the behavior of these humans before they did further harm to their race. Somehow, these aberrational beings had to be defused. As told later, the Cepee and his later-day human predecessor decided the best way to defuse the human was to "rewire" the human.

Of course, neurologists recognized the complex brain could not be completely re-configured—nothing remotely close. This organ's cortex consisted "of over ten billion neurons, each neuron extending on average of 10,000 branches that connect with other such cells."[18]

Nonetheless, a number of alterations (discussed in Chapter 11) could be and were undertaken. As a result, the humans' brain underwent partial yet significant changes, which in turn changed their behavior. (As did the human genome, discussed in Chapter 11 as well.)

Killing Machines

As stated earlier in this chapter, during the humans' evolution, competition began to come from groups of people—not just from an individual. Of equal importance, intra-species competition was no longer a matter of acquiring food, clothing, shelter, or a mate.

It became a matter of ascending the Human Tribal Hierarchies of power, pride, wealth, and ego domination.

As these events unfolded, intra-species warfare became part of the human mind. Eventually, violent and pointless aggression against one's species was imbued into the human's makeup. Some researchers place this date around the early Stone Age.[19] More recent findings indicate aberrational violence had been part of the human race since it branched off from several lineages about five million years ago.[20]

The exact date is not critical to the point that some time in the past, warfare and intra-species pathological aggression became part of human nature. The constant fighting among humans and between their tribes, spanning over thousands of years, resulted in the genetic selection of those with a better ability and mental propensity to engage in warfare.[21] If a tribe could not protect itself and further its domination, it would fall by the wayside, to be succeeded by a tribe with a stronger disposition toward murderous aggression:[22]

> Our bloody nature, it can now be argued in the context of modern biology, is ingrained because group-versus-group was a principal driving force that made us what we are. In prehistory, group selection lifted the hominids that became territorial carnivores to heights of solidarity, to genius, to enterprise. And to *fear*. Each tribe knew with justification that if it was not armed and ready, its very existence was imperiled.

The human race evolved to become *instinctual killers* of their own species, as well as practically every other species on earth. But instinctual? The idea meant the humans had limited or even no control over their behavior. Countless stories of the humans revealed them to be intelligent, rational, and capable of strategic thought, as well as capable of understanding the destructive path the race was on.

Research in the early twenty-first century revealed that a portion of the human brain dealing with fear and anger, with associated responses, could be activated before other areas of the brain became aware of this mental activity. A person who might be suddenly confronted with a threat often "could not help himself" in evoking his near instantaneous responses.[23]

During the humans' later times on earth they came to understand more about this aspect of their behavior. They named it the *adaptive unconscious*. Much of it originated in the older parts of the brain and was not accessible by the newer parts, such as the frontal cortex. Nor could it be influenced by a slower and more reflective introspective process coming from these "recent" additions to the brain.

The writer Malcolm Gladwell nicknamed this aspect of human behavior "blink." The Cepee learns that Gladwell quoted the psychologist Timothy D. Wilson in his book, titled *Blink*:[24]

> The mind operates most efficiently by relegating a good deal of high-level, sophisticated thinking to the unconscious. …The adaptive unconscious does an excellent job of sizing up the world, warning people of danger.

The adaptive unconscious had been a vital key in a human reacting to a danger to his life, such as an attack from a predator. As a necessity, the brain's processing was faster and more focused on the present. By its very nature, this reaction was much less flexible than an introspective operation. A successful evasion from a stone club assault did not benefit from, "Hmm, should I lower my head or jump backward?" The human under such stress and duress *just did it*, and unconsciously.

Like the musician playing a violin or piano frequently—with the resultant change in the brain's physical composition and functioning—a significant part of the human population experienced the rewiring of their brains to abet violent aggression. These acts often occurred without much forethought. They were part of mental routines that had been wired into the brain for thousands of years. One's frontal cortex was of little use when a human was suddenly attacked by a saber-tooth tiger. Better to let the brain stem and other primitive cerebral parts handle the situation. It was an effective convention, one that became an important part of the rituals of human warfare.

Rituals of Warfare

Large-scale warfare and wide-scale slaughter alternated with small-scale warfare and small-scale slaughter as accepted norms of behavior for the human race. This situation was described in the statements of a twentieth-century statesman, Winston Churchill:[25]

> Instead of a small number of well-trained professionals championing their country's cause with ancient weapons and a beautiful intricacy of archaic manoeuvre, sustained at every moment by the *applause* [my italics] of their nation, we now have entire populations, including women and children, pitted against one another in brutish mutual extermination and only a set of bleary-eyed clerks left to add up the butcher's bill.

This quote was uttered in 1930. In its starkest and simplest terms, it said this man was against war, unless it was conducted with the humans' older weapons. That being the case, war was acceptable. Evidently, Mr. Churchill thought war was just getting out of hand. His race was getting too good at it.

Disproportionate Ratios

The laws of natural selection had not changed during the humans' evolution from their small-sized brains to the large brains of the modern *Homo sapiens*. Without question, the more recent lineage could eliminate considerably more of its kind than its ancestors. Nonetheless, these early cousins were adept killers. Using modern humans as a benchmark, historians were able to deduce the homicide rate of humans who lived centuries ago.[26]

> ...the homicide rate for the [ancient human] works out to 29 homicides per 100,000 person years, which is triple the homicide rate for the United States and 10 to 30 times the rates for Canada, Britain, France, and Germany.

These surprising facts, while useful, must be viewed in the context that primitive humans engaged in combat almost every day of their lives. Modern humans took time off between their wars. Consequently, the ancient ones could tally up dead bodies more frequently than the modern ones. Also, the humans of many generations ago did not take as many prisoners as their successors. They likely had little or no food to dispense to anyone but themselves. These two factors led to what could have been considered a bias in this statistical analysis.

But this bias did not alter a stark reality. What had changed in humans' evolution was a sudden unbalancing of the process. Even if the assumption was made that the modern humans were less "brutish" than their predecessors, that they killed less frequently, an examination of two examples of the Disproportionate Ratio Effect rendered this assumption irrelevant:

> The (n) number of *weapons* that could be used to kill (m) number of persons.
> The (x) number of *persons* needed to kill (y) number of persons.

Let's pause for a moment to consider the significance of these simple statistics. For millions of years—even to the time of the modern humans—the number of weapons (n) that could be used to kill was one. A club, a spear, a bomb: one. The same held true for the number of persons (x) needed to kill: one. Granted, many humans might be involved in designing and creating, say, a bomb, but only one person was needed to explode it.

For millions of years a weapon could kill a very limited number of persons (m and y). But in only seven-hundred years, the humans developed weapons that could kill thousands, even millions of people. In a very short time, the potential values of m and y increased exponentially.

These technical and intellectual achievements attested to the extraordinary versatility and creativity of the modern humans' brain. But the accomplishment led to this anomaly: *The scope of effect of humans' weapons (their inventions) rapidly went beyond their scope of control (their brain's evolution) to manage the very weapons they invented.* The humans' rapid assimilation and proliferation of increasingly more deadly weapons were not counter-balanced by mitigations against their use.

Figure 3-3 shows another way to view this process. For most of the humans' existence, their weapons (such as clubs, stones, spears and arrows) did limited harm. Suddenly, in relation to their time on earth, the race invented guns, bombs, and weapons of mass destruction. In so doing, the humans created the means for themselves to bring about their own destruction.

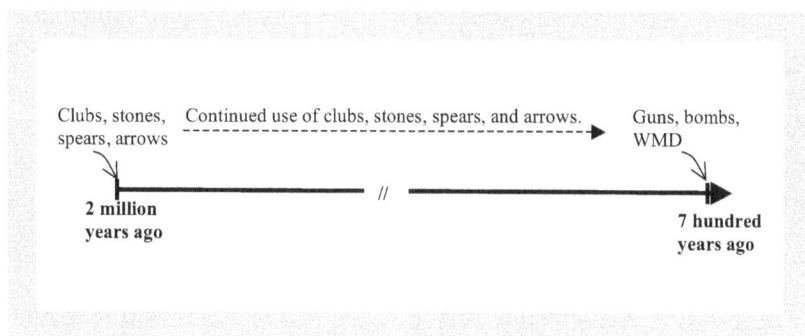

Figure 3-3. Compressing time, expanding weapons, with the year 2000 as a benchmark.

Mitigations in the Mind?

After contemplating the somber fact of the humans' increasing inventory of weapons outpacing their abilities to control their machinery, the Cepee asks himself: *If the humans were so smart to have dominated earth, why were they not perceptive enough to recognize the danger this unbalance presented to their race?* The Cepee turns back to the Human Archives to find answers to his question.

Several comments have been made about the humans' increasing their use of more effective weapons outpacing their possible hesitations about using them. When viewed from the standpoint of natural selection, critics of these theories question why would "mitigation mutations" make their way through the evolutionary process? They claim it made no sense because changes that fostered a human's propensity to use more sophisticated weapons were beneficial to that human. They led to the carriers of these genes coming to dominate those humans who were still carrying around a genome that did not make them as aggressive.

These mutations fared well in relation to the changing environments that witnessed more intra-tribal and especially inter-tribal aggression. According to this school of thought, these less aggressive DNA carriers could not compete and failed to increase their genes' frequencies in this environment.

Aided by Genetic Drift, Revolutionized by Epigenetics

Regardless of the experts' opinions regarding mitigations or no mitigations about using deadly weapons, two additional genetic factors most likely came into play. The first, genetic drift, represented a neutral genome *reacting* to a changing environment. The second, epigenetics, represented a nonneutral genome *changing* itself in a reaction to a changing environment.

Genetic Drift. Natural selection was key to the evolution of the human race toward a species exhibiting a more willful obedience to the Law of the Instrument. The race becoming what some cultural anthropologists in jest called killer machines was aided by genetic drift. Many mutations occurred that were neutral to the well-being of the *Homo sapiens*, having no effect on survival or reproducing. However, "...if the environment changes, some neutral variants can prove beneficial and even essential for survival. Natural selection will then act to increase their frequency [in the population]."[27]

As conditions changed, as more powerful weapons became part of the humans' culture, some of these heretofore neutral mutations led to an increased population of tool-yielding and weapon-yielding humans. These neutral variants were, so to speak, waiting in the genetic wing of the human opera, silently resting on the offstage to come forth if a change in the scene presented an opportunity for the actors to change their scripts in the plot.

Epigenetics. The increase in innate aggression showed itself in the form of a human whose composition leaned toward being a warrior because his father was a warrior. As an example: A warrior father's successful experiences at warfare could be passed down to his sons, making these boys more prone to manning a club than manning a plow.

Heretical! Darwin claimed such changes occurred through millions of years of mutations and natural selections. One generation? Yes. The humans learned about this startling example of the Autocatalytic Process in action:[28]

> ...powerful environmental conditions [starvation, wars, and weapons use, even overeating] can somehow [later, it was known how] leave an imprint on the genetic material in eggs and sperm. These genetic imprints can short-circuit evolution and pass along new traits in a single generation.

This science became known as epigenetics: Heritable changes in how genes might express themselves because of factors other than the basic underlying DNA sequence. The process did not alter a genetic code, but the changes could be passed down to at least one generation.

These patterns of gene expression could come about because of a human's experiences with his environment. Specific chemical combinations called epigenetic marks sat atop genes and could instruct how the genes expressed themselves. Factors such as recursive stress, smoking, over eating, and combat trauma could create the genetic marks, which could influence the children who had the marks passed to them by their parents.

The Cepee reflects about these entries in the Human Archives: *We often study the humans' holy books to learn more about our ancestors. I recall a passage in the Bible,* as the Cepee accesses the archives. *Yes, it's from Exodus 20:5. Here is part of this scripture:* "I, the Lord your God, am a jealous God, punishing the children for the sin of the fathers to the third and fourth generation of those who hate me."

I wonder if these ancient humans somehow sensed the role that epigenetics played in their development? Perhaps they were ahead of their time, but did not know why and chose to blame a supernatural sage for their sins. I need to study this aspect of the humans in more detail. The Cepee will do it later.

The discovery, mapping, and later manipulation of these epigenetic marks had a staggering influence on the human race, not only for eliminating predatory, violent aggression, but for practically every malady in the humans' closet of genetic imperfections. Along with genetic engineering, epigenetic engineering enabled this race to begin to tailor itself toward becoming the Cepee, a story continued in Chapter 11.

The Warrior Class

The stratification of the human race into specialties and hierarchies led to the invention of the professional soldier, a specialized warrior class whom Mr. Churchill lauded. Not evident in Churchill's quote was his love of his soldiers conquering turf for England's British Empire. In the sixteenth through nineteenth centuries, Churchill's England succeeded in subjugating and conquering people in Europe, Africa, Asia, North America, South America, Australia, New Zealand, the Caribbean, Malaysia, Sarawak, New Guinea, and other turfs. At one time, England claimed ownership of almost 25 percent of Africa and over 50 percent of North America. The original residents of these lands were not consulted about their induction into the British Empire.

For what reason did England conquer these parts of earth? Were Maslow's lower level needs a factor? Were the basic requirements for survival the issue? Was England forced to sail its ships to the Caribbean to gather coconuts to prevent the starving of its English citizens?

No. The tribal hierarchies of power, wealth, pride, religion, and language were the factors. The Cepee smiles: *They were not after coconuts? Perhaps Maslow's Hierarchy of Needs and the Human Tribal Hierarchy should have had "better life-styles" as an entry. I joke to myself, but I do not joke. My ancestors' desires for being not only secure but comfortable was an important component of their behavior.*

What is more, many of the warriors for the British Empire were not English. They were conscripted citizens of the conquered countries, forced into the role of commandeering and controlling members of their national, linguistic, and cultural tribes, even their own families.

Of greater consequence: England's aggressive imperialism accompanied the country's sudden, swift, and ill-conceived carving up of its conquered territories. The formerly culturally homogenous lands were divided into artificial countries in such a way that the partitions disrupted what had been centuries of gradual tribal assimilation and integration. These actions proved to be disastrous, a story for Chapters 6, 8, and 9.

The "Warrior Gene"

One of the factors contributing to humans' impulsive aggressiveness was a malfunctioning enzyme, called Monoamine oxidase A (MAO-A). It was dubbed the "warrior gene" by the news media.[29] This enzyme alone was not the sole culprit contributing to aggression or in transforming a conscientious objector into a warrior. This genetic factor did not assure that its carrier would necessarily be anti-social or aggressive. But it was shown to increase the risk of an aggressive response to certain situations, such as that of high provocation from another religious group, or from a nation vying for more turf.

Nonetheless, research supported the theory that an MAO-A deficiency was responsible for at least some aggressiveness.[30] Traits that were detected from a mutation of part of this enzyme were:

- Territorial aggression: Attacking an interloper that was occupying the aggressor's turf.
- Predatory aggression: Hunting and killing a prey.
- Isolation-induced aggression: A sustained lack of normal interactions with fellow members of a species (the lack of normal stimuli).

Impulsive aggression in humans sometimes resulted in disastrous outcomes. World leaders could find themselves boxed in by their previous spontaneous declarations. As three examples: "That country will never attain nuclear weapons." Or: "We will defend this ally at all costs." Or: "Bring 'em on!"

This latter precipitous boast was an example of the Disproportionate Impulse Effect the Ceepe had come across earlier in the Human Archives (Chapter 2). It was uttered in a moment of excitement by an American President when the primal parts of his brain overtook the more rational frontal lobes.

However ill conceived, once such an assertion was uttered, pride and the likely loss of face kept this leader's nation committed to wars having little or no strategic value to his or her country.

The Spanish-American War? The Philippine insurrection putdown? The Vietnam Conflict? The Falkland Islands assault? The second American/Iraq war? Thousands of maimed or dead humans were the products of unnecessary wars. And the toll was not just on warriors. Where was a non-combatant to go? This person, usually unarmed and untrained, in the wrong spot at the wrong time, became a casualty of the humans' killing machines.

These miseries often came about because a leader or a group of leaders were perceived to be weak if they changed their minds. The end result was staggering. Millions of humans were killed because their leaders—chosen to protect them from harm—were too proud to back down and utter, "I need to re-consider my stand on this matter." The Cepee studying this part of the Human Archives could only say: *Incredible*.

Pride Well Placed and Pride Misplaced

As stated, a pivotal failing of the human species was its excessive pride, often bordering on arrogance. Returning to the British, one of their respected leaders told his subjects, "Remember that you are an Englishman, and have consequently won first prize in the lottery of life."[31] To these hubristic egoists, unless a person was born to an upper class, high in the pecking orders of the white race, other people were nothing more than an underclass of the species.

Essential to the warrior class was the assertion of pride and claiming pride to be the lifeblood of the warrior's tribe. This characteristic was vital to the success of the warrior, and it was often well-placed and well-earned. As two examples: the SEALs and the Marines. The participants in these organizations had actively contributed to the performances leading to their well-placed pride.

Not so for many humans. Often their pride had nothing to do with their earning it. The Cepees found this egocentric quirk so fascinating they gave it a name, as well as a definition, and added it to the humans' Rules of Life: The Pride Anomaly: A person who is proud of an act or situation to which this person has made no contribution.

Many examples could be found of this incongruity. For instance, many modern-day humans often proclaimed, "I'm proud to be an American!" They should have said, "I'm lucky to be an American," because they had nothing to do with the greatness of that country. A lifelong civilian would brag, "I'm proud of the Marines!"[32]

These proclamations were largely harmless. But as told later, the humans' pride coupled with their aggressive tendencies had devastating consequences.

The Noble Savage

A Frenchman in the eighteenth century was credited for making famous the term, the *noble savage*. Jean-Jacques Rousseau penned in 1755:[33]

> So many authors have hastily concluded that man is naturally cruel, and requires a regular system of police to be reclaimed; whereas nothing can be more gentle than him in his primitive state, when placed by nature at an equal distance from the stupidity of brutes and the pernicious good sense of civilized man....

> The example of the savages...seems to confirm that...this condition is the real youth of the world, and that all ulterior improvements have been so many steps, in appearance towards the perfection of individuals, but in fact towards the decrepitness of the species.

Many humans were led to believe by the entertainment industry that the Native American was the personification of Rousseau's noble savage, and through movies and pulp fiction novels, the "Indian" was romanticized to the point of farce. This subset of the human species exhibited no more and no fewer of Rousseau's noble savage qualities than any other human tribe on earth. For example, like their counterparts in other tribes, these warriors took delight in torturing their captured enemies.

Unlike some of their *ignoble* savage counterparts, the noble savages routinely killed their captured enemy. This enemy could include every single member of a clan or tribe. Women and children were not exempt. As well, massive massacres—not related to an ongoing battle—of non-combatants was an accepted part of their protocol. The more sophisticated warriors would keep their captives alive in order to use them as slaves and other commercial operations.[34]

Noble savage was a meaningless phrase. Humans were capable of both noble and savage acts. They were simply another set of humans who had no more and no fewer of the characteristics of others in their species. Notwithstanding its inaccuracy, the phrase serves as a convenient moniker for those in the human race who had the misfortune to start their lives with handicaps over which they had no control or responsibility.

Snake Eyes on the Dice Roll. If the American Indians and other noble savages had evolved from hunter-gatherers to high protein food producers sooner than the high-proteined Europeans with their associated culture stratifications, mass populations, and steel weapons; if horses had been available to them earlier; if their populations had been able to achieve immunity to European diseases, their history would likely have been different. They would have been in a better position to ascend the Human Tribal Hierarchy pecking orders. Unfortunately for them, they rolled a losing snake-eyes on the geographical dice game. They became the colonized instead of the colonizers.

Thus, the term *noble savage* was an inaccurate, embellished view of certain members of the human race. Using the term *noble savage* to describe humans or tribes within the human race was both appropriate and inappropriate. Humans were often savage. They were also often noble. Yet a large segment of earth's population associated the noble savage with humans who were simply unlucky enough to find themselves hanging on to the lower rungs of the tribal pecking orders.

The Revenge Cycle

To continue the analysis of the humans, the Revenge Cycle is introduced, as depicted in Figure 3-4. The idea behind this cycle is simple: After a tribe (such as a religious sect or a nation) had been attacked by another tribe, the attacked tribe was obligated (even expected) to strike back and avenge the assault. After the revenge had been taken, the tables were again turned: The avenger became the avenged, the avenged became the avenger, and another battle took place.

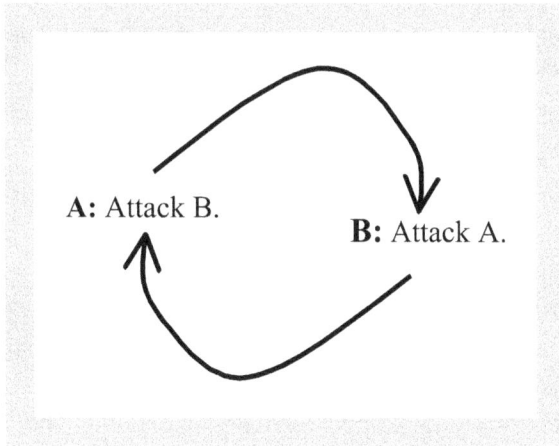

A: Attack B.   **B:** Attack A.

Figure 3-4. The Revenge Cycle.

Then, the tables were turned once again. Humans kept the cycle going until one of the factions admitted defeat, was subjugated, killed off, or became weary from the enervating tedium of invoking revenge. Figure 3-4 represents a startlingly simple diagram of a startlingly simple sickness.

With few exceptions, this cycle never stopped. The humans were so caught up in their day-to-day pursuits of revenge, they failed to understand where it was leading them. They could not break the Revenge Cycle, even though the cycle was surely breaking them.

Misplaced Aggression: Needs Become Motives

The following is a summary of earlier ideas which serves as an introduction to new observations. Through the years, humans realigned their focus on the reasons for their aggression. As seen in Figure 3-5, in earlier times, they killed for food, water, shelter, clothing, and mates. These *material needs* were dependent on their possession of land, of turf. These needs had to be satisfied if they were to survive. In later times, having plenty of these basic requirements on hand, they shifted their priorities to satisfy their egos, their pride, their pursuit of power. These *immaterial inclinations* represented motives, not needs.

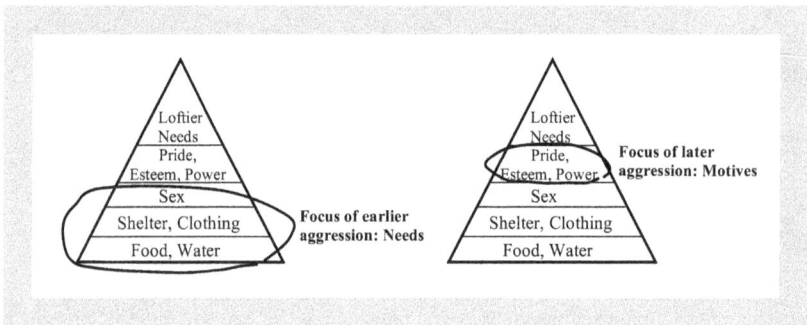

Figure 3-5. Misplaced aggression.

In Chapter 2, the word *need* is used in Maslow's hierarchy instead of his term *motive*. This alteration fits with the idea that the lower levels of Maslow's hierarchy, as well as the Human Tribal Hierarchy, are more accurately described as needs. Certainly, the satisfaction of these needs had to be completed before a human or a tribe could ascend to the next level. But as Figure 3-5 illustrates, the focus of the humans, as they evolved from hunter-gatherers to early food producers, then to the modern humans, shifted from *needs* to *motives*:

– Need: A physiological requirement for survival.
– Motive: A psychological desire for satisfaction.

If the motives were benign to the human race, this cultural and social evolution was for the betterment of the race. But if they were not, problems occurred. The disproportionate ratio raised its head again. A relatively few humans developed motives having nothing to do with anything but brutal carnage, revenge, and pointless aggression. The resident Cepee, who has been studying the Human Archives, comes across thousands of examples, such as:[35]

> At the end of July the Taliban [during a war in Afghanistan] used their new trucks, enhanced with machine guns, to finally capture the northern town of Mazar-e Sharif. This historic center of Shia worship, the "Noble Shrine," had resisted Taliban attacks the previous summer and was now punished with a series of ghastly reprisals [against fellow Muslims]. Ahmed Rashid later estimated six thousand to eight thousand Shia men, women, and children were slaughtered in a rampage of murder and rape that included slitting people's throats, and bleeding them to death, halal-style,[36] and packing hundreds of victims into shipping containers without water, to be baked alive in the desert sun.

Case Study: 1860s New Mexico Territory

Deadly inter-tribal aggression, created and amplified through many centuries, came down to this issue: If the physical needs for survival of a tribe led to the eradication of another tribe, the slaughter, however repugnant to a bystander, was an efficient culling mechanism. Bench-warmer members of a species were removed from the bench to be replaced with better players.

However, if a tribe's eradication of another tribe was an immaterial issue to the survival needs of the tribe doing the eradication, what was the point? If a second-string bench warmer never came off the bench as a replacement for a first-string starter, why would that first stringer go to the trouble of trying to have him cut from the team?

What was the answer? Perhaps it was because he was a limited contributor to the overall human gene pool (the team). Maybe he was—from the tribal standpoint—different. Both factors possibly came into play.

Whatever the answer might have been, with tribal Darwinism, by the eradication of a "lowly" member of the species, one with a woeful gene pool, a superior set of superseding genes would further propagate a subset of the human species.

The Cepee pauses: *Yes, but as the humans evolved, they began to kill others of their species even though their own well-being was not at stake. Hmm, they killed without regard to their survival? Just for domination?* The Cepee continues to study the archives and comes across an article about several noble savage tribes who had the misfortune of simply living on turf.

In an area almost devoid of minerals and vegetation. On terrain that would be of no use to anyone but a noble savage—a semi-desert with almost no water—the American government erected *seventeen* forts in the southwest part of the emerging United States for the principal purpose of subduing the pagan native population and protecting the incoming populace of Christian white people.[37]

Were these immigrants coming to this wilderness from the safe environs of eastern America and western Europe because they were trying to survive or looking for sexual partners? No. Were their needs physical? No. Their physical and sexual inventories, perhaps sparse but adequate, were not their reasons. They wanted more territory, and not only physical territory, but spiritual territory as well.

They masqueraded their lust for turf and religious proselytizing by wearing a mask of righteousness. They would make the local natives moral and virtuous by converting them to the correct religion. The natives' subjugation and conversion would take place while the new arrivals took over their land. None other than their greatest statesman, George Washington, proclaimed his country should embark on a "policy to encourage the 'civilizing' process" of the Native American.[38]

The civilizing process in New Mexico also entailed the commercialization of bison slaughter, but not for the meat of this animal, for its horns and hide. The bison were already being depleted by Indian and comanchero raids, but the tipping point came with the "arrival of commercial hunters from the east."[39] The result can only be characterized as self-cycling paradox. The natives had to resort to cattle rustling to compensate for the loss of their bison food. These cattle belonged to the white man, many who had come west in order to ship the bison hides and horns east. In order to stem the flow of the Indians' cattle stealing, the white men killed the Indians' horses, which further limited the ability of the noble savages to remain noble.

Injury and death were added to insult as the natives were evicted from their homes and forced to live on "reservations." In what can only be called ethnic cleansing—in effect, genocide—fifty-three forced marches from homes to reservations occurred in the mid-1860s. Thousands of men, women, and children perished along the way.[40]

How many of these people were killed to satisfy Maslow's lower hierarchy of needs, for the humans' fundamental lower hierarchy of needs in the Human Tribal Hierarchy ladder? None of them. How many were killed to satisfy the humans' lust for psychological and religious power, wealth, and pride? All of them.

Motives Morph into Needs

Again, it is important to understand the implication of the humans' evolution toward the use of deadly aggression to advance their self-esteem and pride. And as said, the once laudatory use of aggression to advance the needs for survival and the perpetuation of genes began to be replaced by using aggression to advance human motives having nothing to do with either. The result was to reinforce an increasingly dysfunctional mental and genetic makeup.

Fortunately, most humans were able to concentrate their free time on the loftier pursuits cited in Figure 3-5, and achieved self-fulfillment with species-enhancing activities. Unfortunately, others were *stuck in the middle* of the hierarchy. They were unable to get past their lust for power and esteem, and let pride subjugate their potential to be a more positive element in their lives and their societies.

Unfortunately for the *Homo sapiens*, the Disproportionate Ratio raised its head: A relatively small number of these people increasingly employed deadly aggression to satisfy their motives for status, esteem, and power. But how deadly? A few statistics will shed light on the subject.

The World's Records for Murder and Genocide

For this discussion, genocide is defined as the "deliberate killing of a large group of people, especially those of a particular ethnic group or nation."[41] Genocide does not necessarily mean murder, but death is its close ally.

The Cepee comes to the conclusion that an incredible number of humans were killed by other humans. These numbers, and the percentage of a population killed, are depicted in Figure 3-6 and Table 3-1.[42] The term *democide* referred to state-sponsored killings of a state's own people, or those people whom the state had conquered. What is astounding about these facts is that the numbers in Figure 3-6 excluded deaths from outright wars between nation states.

Human aggression was not confined to conflicts just between countries. In the twentieth century, governments murdered almost 170 million people, which in 2003 would have constituted 2.7 percent of the earth's population. During the same time, 34.4 million people were killed from international and civil wars.[43]

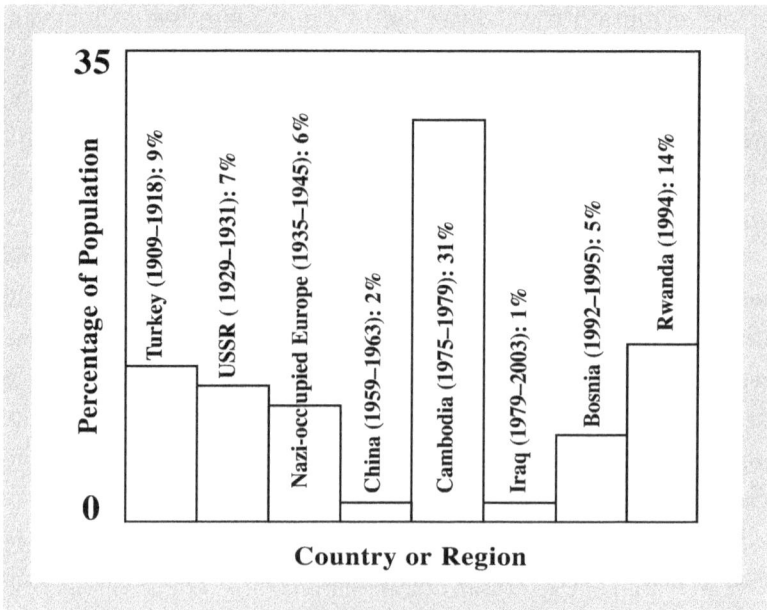

Figure 3-6. The democide chart.
(percentage of population killed in a country, a small sampling)

Table 3-1. The genocide table.

Location	Date(s)	Event(s) or "Reason(s)"*	Toll**
Europe	1930s–1940s	Extermination of Jews	6 to 16 million killed
Europe	Post WWII	Revenge against the Germans	2 million killed
Australia	1900-1970	Children separated from home	25 thousand displaced
Zanzibar	1960s	"Enemies" of the "state"	4,000 killed
Guatemala	1960–1996	Civil war	200,000 killed, ~1 million displaced
Bangladesh	Early 1970s	Minorities (religious & cultural)	1,500,000 killed
Rwanda	1972 & 1993	Cultural: Hutu vs. Tutsi	800,000 to 1 million
North Korea	Early 2000s	Starving the population	Several million died
Equatorial Guinea	1968–1979	Ethnic cleansings	80,000 killed
Laos	1975–1980	Ethnic cleansings	100,000 killed
East Timor	1974-1999	Ethnic cleansings	18,600 killed; 84,200 others died
Lebanon	1982	Ethnic/religious cleansings	700-3,500 killed
Ethiopia	1990s	Any opponent	150,000 killed
Iraq	1980s	Kurds	Thousands
Tibet	1959	Religious cleansings	92,000 killed
Brazil	1988	Indigenous native cleansings	Not available
Congo	1988–2003	Pygmy cleansings	Not available
West New Guinea	1963	Papuan cleansings	100,000 killed
Somalia	1991 onwards	Ethnic cleansings	Hundreds
Bosnia/ Herzegovina	1995	Ethnic/cultural	Thousands
Cambodia	1975–1979	Political/ethnic /religious	1.7 million killed

* Ethnic often also included religious. ** Mid to upper range estimates.

During the last half of the twentieth century alone, millions of people were killed, injured, and displaced from their homes. The New Mexico incident described above was little more than noise in this spectrum of violence. In parts of the world, the human race had created a large number of frightening as well as frightened societies.

The Cepees of the late twenty-second century were cerebrally and genetically wired to avoid harming anyone in their species. Yet even with their advanced intelligence, as they study the Human Archives, they often pause to think about their forebearer: *Was that creature actually our ancestor?*

But the Cepee is not entirely perplexed, because he knows much about the legacy of the human. Still, additional statistics, such as those shown in Table 3-1, would give any caring person pause. The entries in this table reflect a sample of some of the human genocides that took place in the latter part of the twentieth century. The sheer number of killings or displacements and their frequency of occurrence brings forth to the Cepee a quote from one of the Cepees' more astute human ancestors: "Ghost: 'Murder most foul, as in the best it is; But this most foul, strange and unnatural.'"[44]

Containing Collateral Damage

Returning to the human era, as discussed earlier, the tools for aggression became more effective. A prime example of a sophisticated club was the predator drone, an unmanned aircraft flown with remote control, perhaps by a person from thousands of miles away. The remote control operator also gave commands for the drone to fire missiles into a targeted area.

How convenient. While the drone warrior ate his morning Cheerios at his breakfast table, he could direct a drone to launch a missile at a rival. It was a novel way to bid cheerio to his enemy, who might be located on the other side of the planet. By touching his computer screen, the warrior commanded a drone, buzzing over and around the soon-to-be less than cheerful enemy, to fire a rocket at this adversary. Killing with a touch screen took on the patina of toying with an iPad app. Score one for Super PacMan.

Beginning in 2004, it was reported one drone attack (the only publicly substantiated event of that year) killed from five to eight individuals who were fighting in a remote region of Afghanistan. Eight years later, with the Law of the Instrument taking the stage, the United States launched hundreds of drone attacks, not only in Afghanistan, but in countries who were not formally at war with America.[45]

The moralists favored the use of drones over conventional bombs and missiles because they inflicted fewer casualties to people who were not bearing weapons:[46]

> Since drone operators can view a target for hours or days in advance of a strike, they can identify [the enemy] more accurately than ground troops or conventional pilots. They are able to strike when innocents are not nearby and can even divert a missile after firing it if, say, a child wanders into range.

Political scientists' studies revealed conventional military conflicts resulted in civilian deaths in the range of 33 percent to 80 percent of all deaths.[47] One can wonder if some other study might have resulted in a slightly better estimate of the death count. In deference to this huge range, doing body counts in which it was often difficult to discern which body part belonged to a specific body, led this task to be more of a soft art than a hard science. Regardless of these figures, studies claimed that with the use of drones, the proportion of civilian casualties dropped to a range from 4 to 20 percent.

What progress! The only disadvantage to this kinder way of killing was that the enemy quickly figured out their drone-armed enemy had qualms about blowing up smaller humans. Thus, a group of warriors kept a few tiny tots in their company. The children were better protection than armor.

There was another consequence of the precision from "firing from afar." Because drone attacks resulted in fewer casualties to the tribe controlling the drones, the widely accepted concept (in civilized societies) of considering the waging of war as a last resort became passé. Even the so-called political blues (liberal and generally antiwar) became enamored with remote controlled warfare. After all, the use of drones translated to no messy boots on the ground.

The prevalent school of thought was that the human race, by using predator drones, was progressing beyond its past practices of firebombing or nuking entire cities. No more Dresdens. No more Hiroshimas. Only clean kills. All well and good, until the recipients of the drone rockets grew tired of having their breakfasts interrupted, and their Cherrios left untouched. As recounted later in this story, they decided to become human predator drones. Their counter punches were low tech but equally deadly, such as bombs on buses and explosives at the finish line at marathons. Finish, in more ways than one.

The Cepee reflects on this part of the Human Archives: *My ancestors were very smart. Not only did they change their launching technology, they also changed the technology of what they launched.*

The Creeping Momentum Principle

It is at this point in the narrative that the Cepee takes a break from his studies of the Human Archives to reflect on the Rules of Life he has come across so far: *These rules have provided a short-hand notation to help me understand several complex aspects of human behavior. The humans' gradual, but increasingly rapid use of more powerful weapons to kill their enemies is more easily grasped by recalling the Autocatalytic Effect and the Threshold Lowering Syndrome.*

The drones I studied recently are another example of these rules. But these remote devices, and the manner in which they were used, leads me to recall another human Rule of Life: the Creeping Momentum Principle. Here is what the archives say about this principle: A gradual expansion of what begins as a modest endeavor, therefore escaping notice and concern, until the effect of the endeavor renders it too big to be ignored, and sometimes too pervasive for its momentum to be reversed.

The Cepee learns the archives describe two related instances of this principle. (1) Gradually increasing the use of drone attacks. (2) The associated gradual alienation of people who had become potential targets of the drones, many who were innocent bystanders.

The Cepee also learns the modest use of drones, described above, gained momentum because of their success. Creeping along in their growth, under the radar of public scrutiny for a while, they crept into a policy called *signature strikes*. These attacks went after people who were thought to be enemies, who were behaving as if they might be enemies, but might not be enemies after all. If another person (enemy or not) happened to be visiting with one of these suspects, a drone bomb might end the visit on the part of both parties.

The program was quite effective. It killed many enemies of America. It also killed many potential friends. Its remote-controlled cruelty, its disregard for international law, led to a new wave of enemies of America. Those killed by drones were replaced by eager recruits.

The Cepee wonders: *I have yet to come across my forebears asking themselves why they were being attacked? Any person or tribe who was different from another person or tribe was viewed as a potential target for culling. But in humans' modern times, that was an outdated motive. As far as I can tell at this point in my studies, I can find no other motive.* He turns the next page of the archives to find:

Social or Physical Engineering?

Violence and aggression in the human race were not just reactions to external stimuli, such as a threat from a predatory animal, or a threat from another tribe, such as a competing religion or a contending nation. If this were the case, there was hope these so-called "reaction-eliciting factors" could be diminished, perhaps even eliminated.[48] The possibility existed of eventually improving the human species, perhaps to a point where aggressive behavior might be controlled.

While some aggressive tendencies in humans could be repressed or eliminated, many social engineering efforts often came to naught. Help groups, therapy sessions, talk shows, social engineering, emotional nurturing, redistribution of wealth, transfers of power, capital punishment: all were only marginally successful in their attempt to cure this affliction. The humans began to learn that other options had to be pursued, such as the manipulation of parts of the brain and the alteration of their DNA.

Nonetheless, the modern humans came to realize that environmental factors were more influential than had been previously thought, such as epigenetics, introduced earlier in this chapter. Consequently, they also went about cleaning up their social fabrics.

The Disproportionate Ratio vs. EGO, ILLS, and SANE

During this time, substantial progress was being made in the EGO, ILLS, and SANE programs. And to review a key point: Most members of the human race were decent people and managed to sublimate any killing genes that might have been stranded on their DNA. But their world had evolved to a point in which a very small number of people could terrorize a huge population. Once again, an example of the Disproportionate Ratio Effect.

To cite examples of this effect: These organizations and individuals created disorder and mayhem well beyond what their numbers might have suggested they were capable of doing: the Baader-Meinhof Gang in West Germany (20-30 members); the Red Brigades in Italy (50-75 members); the IRA in Northern Ireland (200-400 members);[49] the religious militants in New York, Washington, London, and Madrid; *two* alienated boys killing spectators and runners in an athletic contest.

Before the humans had weapons of mass destruction, a few rebellious people or a few sociopaths did little harm. But armed with readily available nuclear bombs and chemical weapons, they altered the course of human history. All because the humans could not find a solution to their Deadly Trinity.

The Deadly Trinity + Tools for Mass Destruction = Chaos

The availability of weapons of mass destruction to parties other than nation-states upset the humans' aggression apple cart. Because of the diffusion of these weapons into the hands of small but deadly special interest groups, previous methods of obtaining security became ineffective. Confrontation of a nation often did little good. Invasion of the state usually provoked hostility among the citizens of the invaded country. Even worse, many nations eventually found themselves populated by the killers, who were bent on destroying the internal fabric of the very nations to which they claimed citizenship.

Consequently, unlike other times, the twenty-first century humans found themselves in jeopardy, in danger of falling prey to the Deadly Trinity, illustrated in Figure 3-7, and summarized here with three ideas introduced earlier.

- **The Law of the Instrument**: A child with a hammer looks for something to pound. Tools of mass destruction became easier hammers to create, obtain, and use. So, the humans, naturally enough, used them. Succumbing to the Threshold Lowering Syndrome, they committed increasingly violent acts with these weapons.

- **The Revenge Cycle:** The desire of a person or tribe to attack anyone who had previously attacked that person or a tribe.

- **The Aggression Cycle:** The successful execution of an aggressive, violent act leading to more aggressive and violent acts.

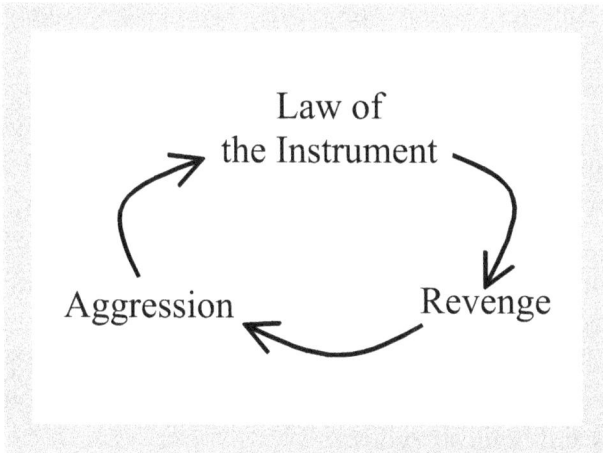

Figure 3-7. The Deadly Trinity.

As seen in Figure 3-7, the Deadly Trinity itself was a cycle. The three members of this trinity influenced and reinforced one another. Revenge led to aggression (or aggression led to revenge, the arrows can be reversed and the cycle is still valid). Of course, the aggression required the aggressor to use the most effective instruments to carry out the aggressive acts. In turn, it led the aggressed to take on the role of the aggressor and restart the process with yet more lethal hammers. Over and over again.

Initially, the availability of weapons of mass destruction was limited. But as the early twenty-first century rolled on into the late 2030s, they became available to almost anyone with the requisite cash to purchase them on the black market. Alternately, a nation-state undertook programs to build them from scratch. Consequently, spats between tribes (such as nation-states), heretofore played out with conventional bombs and guns, were settled with nuclear and biochemical solutions.

The number of participants in these conflicts was as numerous as there were cultures, countries, bloodlines, races, and religions. That is to say: tribes. The list of participants seemed almost endless. To name a few: Chechnyans vs. Russians, Palestinians vs. Israelites, Sunnis vs. Shias, Ossetians vs. Ingush,[50] Indians vs. Pakistanis, Croats vs. Serbs, Mongolians vs. Chinese, North Koreans vs. Japanese, Chinese vs. Japanese, America vs. non-Americans. The result was mayhem and chaos that ultimately affected most people in the world.

Eventually, the rising death tolls and the disintegrating societies of the human race forced humans to come to grips with the perils of their situation. They began to realize the only way out of this dead-end alley was the mental/genetic alteration of their species, a process already underway with EGO, ILLS, and SANE.

By mid-twenty-first century, they began to understand they had to eradicate the Deadly Trinity before the Deadly Trinity eradicated them. And in the end, the utopians' social engineering programs were greatly enhanced by the physical engineering feats of the geneticists and brain surgeons.

Conclusions

The story about the ASSES aspect of the human race is not finished. Pathological aggression was not the only reason for the human to begin to repair itself and later, for the Cepee to take over the process. The humans also made a mess of the earth's habitat. In the next chapter, this situation is examined, another factor contributing to the demise of the human and the rise of the Cepee.

[1] Richard Wrangham and Dale Peterson, *Demonic Males* (New York: Houghton Mifflin, 1996), 25. An interesting quote, but open to question. See the next note.

[2] E. O. Wilson, "What's Your Tribe?" *Newsweek*, April 9, 2012, 44.

[3] Leonard Roy Frank, *Quotationary* (New York: Random House, 2001), 424. General Patrick E. Connor's order to his troops for the Platte River campaign, 1865.

[4] Olivia Judson, "The Selfless Gene," *The Atlantic Monthly*, October 2007, 94. In a study of ground squirrels, researchers discovered at least 8 percent of the young were murdered before they were weaned. Some cliff-dwelling birds produce two offspring to somewhat even the odds of keeping their gene profile alive. The stronger baby bird pecks its weaker sibling to death, thereby gaining more of the food coming from the parents' huntings.

[5] As mentioned, other animals were not above murdering members of their species, but they never learned to use tools. Consequently, their killing capabilities paled in comparison to humans.

[6] E. O. Wilson, *The Social Conquest of Earth* (New York, Liveright, 2012), 243, Kindle edition, loc. 3915. Also, H. Allen Orr, "Testing Natural Selection," *Scientific American*, Dec. 18, 2008.

[7] E. O. Wilson, *The Social Conquest of Earth* (New York: Liveright, 2012), 51. Kindle edition, loc. 863.

[8] For purposes of efficiency and brevity, most of the explanations in this book use the male gender. I chose this gender because males have played a bigger role in human aggression and perpetual war than their female counterparts. In addition, contrary to what some of us would like to believe about the wildlife around us, a mother often has to protect her young from being killed by the father or other males in the group.

[9] Konrad Lorenz, *On Aggression* (San Diego, CA: Harcourt Brace, 1963), 241-247. The direct quotes that are in this section and that follow the section heading of "The Law of the Instrument" are also sourced from pages 241-247 of *On Aggression*.

[10] Patrick Tyler, *Fortress Israel* (New York: Farrar, Straus, and Giroux, 2012), 301.

[11] This example is elementary, but carries the point across about mutation and natural selection. E. O. Wilson has some entertaining and informative examples of alleles in his *The Social Conquest of Earth* using birds and their changing environment.

[12] Lev Grossman, "Drone Home," *Time*, February 11, 2013, 33.

[13] Wilson, *The Social Conquest of Earth*, 28, Kindle edition, 1oc. 513. Wilson writes that the throwing of objects meant "prehumans could kill at a distance. The advantage this ability gave them during conflict with other, less well-equipped groups must have been enormous."

[14] Estimates for the invention and use of the older weapons vary. I have used the most commonly cited dates from several websites. All these dates fall within generally accepted windows of time.

[15] **(a)** C. B. Stringer (1994), "Evolution of Early Humans," in Steve Jones, Robert Martin, and David Pilbeam, *The Cambridge Encyclopedia of Human Evolution* (Cambridge, MA: Cambridge University Press, 1994), 242. **(b)** H. M. McHenry (2009), "Human Evolution," in Michael Ruse and Joseph Travis, *Evolution: The First Four Billion Years* (Cambridge: Belknap Press of Harvard University Press, 2009), 265.

[16] From a series of NOVA programs aired on PBS during the fall of 2012.

[17] Google "Paul Broca" and/or "Paul Bach-y-Rita" for more information.

[18] Wilson, *The Social Conquest of Earth*, 216, Kindle edition, loc. 3490.

[19] Lorenz, *On Aggression*, 42. I am using Lorenz's dates for this reference. Humans were killing each other thousands of years before 40,000 BC, and some scientists believe *mass* intra-species warfare existed in very early times. Notwithstanding these counter claims, most archeologists and anthropologists state that with the appearance of the Cro-Magnon culture (40,000 years ago), tools became more sophisticated. For example, bone and antler became part of the humans' toolbox and were adapted to use for weapons. (www.pbs.org/wgbh/evolution/humans/kind/o.html). For this discussion, these dates (sooner or later) do not matter. What matters is the evolution to the humans' use of weapons of mass destruction on mass populations.

[20] Wrangham and Peterson, *Demonic Males*, 49.

[21] I support this idea, in contrast to the counter view that aggression is solely a learned trait from a person's culture and family. I hold that aggression is both an innate as well as learned mode of behavior. It appears some people espouse the *nurture and no nature route* more from "advocacy than evidence." The phrase in the quotes is from W. Brennan, "Aggression and Violence: Examining the Theories," *Nursing Standard* 12, 25 (1988): 26-37.

[22] Wilson, *The Social Conquest of Earth*, 62, Kindle edition, loc.1045.

[23] Wilson, "What's Your Tribe?" 45.

[24] Malcolm Gladwell, *Blink* (New York: Little, Brown, 2005), 12.

[25] Jon Meacham, *Franklin and Winston* (New York: Random House, 2003), 7.

[26] Jared Diamond, *The World Until Yesterday* (New York: Penguin, 2012), 288.

[27] H. Allen Orr, "Testing Natural Selection," *Scientific American*, January 2009, 47.

[28] John Cloud, "Why Genes Aren't Destiny," *Time*, January 18, 2010, 50.

[29] Information in this section is sourced from: **(a)** A. L. Scott et al. (May 2008), "Novel Monoamine Oxidase A Knock Out Mice with Human-like Spontaneous Mutation," *NeuroReport* 19 (7): 739–43. doi:10.1097/WNR.0b013e3282fd6e88. PMID 18418249; **(b)** G. B. Vishnivetskaya, J.A. Skrinskaya, I. Seif, and N. K. Popova (2007), "Effect of MAO A Deficiency on Different Kinds of Aggression and Social Investigation in Mice," *Aggress Behav* 33 (1): 1–6. doi:10.1002/ab.20161. PMID 17441000; **(c)** H. G. Brunner, M. Nelen, X. O. Breakefield, H. H. Ropers, and B. A.van Oost (October 1993), "Abnormal Behavior Associated with a Point Mutation in the Structural Gene for Monoamine Oxidase A," *Science* 262 (5133): 578–80. doi:10.1126/science.8211186. PMID 8211186; **(d)** Galina B.Vishnivetskaya, Julia A. Skrinskaya, Isabelle Seif, and Nina K. Popova (1 January 2007), "Effect of MAO A Deficiency on Different Kinds of Aggression and Social Investigation in Mice," *Aggressive Behavior* 33 (1): 1–6. doi:10.1002/ab.20161. PMID 17441000; **(e)** J. Hebebrand and B. Klug (September 1995), "Specification of the Phenotype Required for Men with Monoamine Oxidase Type A deficiency," *Hum. Genet.* 96 (3): 372–6. doi:10.1007/BF00210430. PMID 7649563.

[30] First in mice, later in humans.

[31] Uttered by Cecil Rhodes to remind his countrymen of the superiority of their ways.

[32] A small alteration of the declaration would have made it accurate: "I'm proud *for*...."

[33] Jean-Jacques Rousseau, *Discourse Upon the Origin and Foundation of Inequality Among Mankind* (New York: Perennial Library,1994), 61-62.

[34] Diamond, *The World Until Yesterday*, 141. Diamond cites examples of what he calls "traditional" (pre-modern) tribes living in remote parts of the world who routinely kill all the people they capture.

[35] Robert Lacey, *Inside the Kingdom* (New York: Penguin Group, 2009), 209-210.

[36] *Halal* is a term "designating any object or an action which is permissible to use or engage in, according to Islamic law."

[37] James Blackshear, "Boots on the Ground," *New Mexico Historical Review*, 87 (Summer 2012): 329-358. The area described in this essay is located in present eastern New Mexico and northwest Texas.

[38] Robert Remini, "The Reform Begins," *Bill Nye the Science Guy*, History Book Club, 201.

[39] Blackshear, "Boots on the Ground," 333.

[40] Thomas J. Csordas (February 1999), "Ritual Healing and the Politics of Identity in Contemporary Navajo Society," *American Ethnologist* (Blackwell Publishing on behalf of the American Anthropological Association) 26 (1): 3–23. http://www.jstor.org/stable/10.2307/647496; John Burnett (14 June 2005), "The Navajo Nation's Own 'Trail Of Tears," *NPR All Things Considered*. http://www.npr.org/2005/06/15/4703136/the-navajo-nation-s-own-trail-of-tears.

[41] "Genocide Statistics," https://www.google.com/#q=definition+of+genocide.

[42] Bruce Falconer, "Murder by the State," *The Atlantic Monthly*, November 2003, 56-57.

[43] Ibid., 56.

[44] William Shakespeare, *Hamlet*, 1.5.27, 1600, in Frank, *Quotationary*, 530.

[45] "The Year of the Drone: An Analysis of U.S. Drone Strikes in Pakistan, 2004–2012," *New America Foundation*. http://counterterrorism.newamerica.net/drones.

[46] Scott Shane, "The Moral Case for Drones," *The New York Times, The Sunday Review*, July 15, 2012, 4. (With Sunday falling on July 14, but online references point to Monday.)

[47] Ibid.

[48] Lorenz, *On Aggression*, 50.

[49] Brad Knickerbocker, "Classic Guerilla War Takes Shape in Iraq," *The Christian Science Monitor*. Also, excerpted from *The New Mexican*, September 20, 2004, A-5.

[50] The Ossetians claimed the Ingush were responsible for the slaughter of the school children in Beslan, Russia.

CHAPTER 4

WATER, AIR, LAND, AND POPULATION

Earth, earth,
riding your merry-go-round toward extinction[1]

While the humans were busy killing off one another, they were also killing off the earth's biosphere. Signs pointing to the deterioration of the planet were in evidence for many years. The earth had begun to react to the humans' onslaught of its vital organs. Its contaminated water, air, and land served as warnings about the planet's increasingly perilous state.

Generally, the warnings were ignored although some protested their fellow humans' attacks and helped in stemming the trend toward earth's injurious condition.[2] But as slaves to the Immediacy Syndrome, most humans were concerned with winning turf wars at their offices or surviving spouse wars in their homes. The long-range view of evaluating the consequences of behavior detrimental to the earth was subsumed by the need to just get along, to meet the immediate needs of their lives.

One should not be contemptuous or dismissive of this attitude. After all, a short-range view had been programmed into the humans for thousands of years. The early humans had no need, nor did they possess the knowledge to evaluate the consequences of their building systems that emitted to the air, onto the ground, and into the water: methane, carbon dioxide, nitrous oxide, hydrofluorocarbons (HFCs), perfluorocarbons (PFCs), and sulfur hexafluoride (SF_6). Moreover, for most of their existence on earth, humans were too ignorant to assess the impact of their exhausting animal, plant, soil, air, and water resources.

Gradual Accommodations

For millions of years, the earth's flora and fauna developed patterns of behavior that successfully fostered their coevolution. This process took place partially through genetic mutations between, say, a predator and a prey. As one example among many, the prey (a rough-skinned newt) developed a neurotoxin to thwart attacks from a predator (the garter snake). In turn, the garter snake developed a resistance to the toxin. As another example, the hummingbird and bird-pollinated flowers coevolved to help feed the hummingbird with the flowers' nectar and at the same time, spread the flowers' pollen through the hummingbirds' visits to other flowers.

The conflict between the newt (prey) and the snake (predator) was another example of an evolutionary arms race. Both creatures evolved because their survival depended on their changing their makeup.

Coevolution took place gradually. Usually, many generations lived, propagated, and died before a mutation could spread itself sufficiently into a species of flora or fauna to make any significant difference in earth's environment. This slow and steady impact, interacting in complex ways with other coevolutionary processes, gave the earth and its inhabitants time to adjust to one another. Coevolution was a mutual process between competitors involving natural selection.

Exponential Assaults

However, the earth was not prepared for the rapid changes brought about by the human, especially during the seventeenth through twenty-first centuries, when this species assumed dominance over almost all other living creatures:[3]

Overall, the pace of evolution of [nonhuman life, animals, insects, birds, etc.] was slow enough [a linear, non-autocatalytic process] to be balanced by counter revolution in the rest of life. As a result, these [creatures] were not able to tear down the rest of terrestrial biosphere by force of numbers, but became vital elements of it. The ecosystems they dominate today are not only sustainable but dependent on them.

In sharp contrast, human beings of the single species *Homo sapiens* emerged in the last several hundred thousand years and spread around the world only during the last sixty thousand years [an exponential, autocatalytic process]. There has not been time for [humans] to evolve with the rest of the biosphere. Other species were not prepared for the onslaught. This shortfall soon had dire consequences for the rest of life.

Many cultures evolved with the assumption they had access to earth's supposedly unlimited riches. After soil was exhausted, farmers moved on to the next virgin field to repeat their denuding process. When their catches became too low, fishermen sailed to another part of a sea for a more bountiful location. Upon killing off the game, hunters migrated to happier hunting grounds. After chopping down the worthwhile trees, foresters moved to other forests, perhaps replacing the old forest, perhaps not.

The noble savages, those living in sparse landscapes or urban ghettos, were the chosen people to bear most of the burdens associated with the earth's damage. The creation of foul air and water led to the degradation of their health. Many of these humans, those without access to modern health systems, died from drinking foul water, eating contaminated meat, or breathing toxic air.

In addition, while the affluent citizens of the world worried about eating too much, the less fortunate worried about eating nothing at all. Some nations' leaders thought it more important to keep their military larders full at the expense of the cupboards belonging to the starving citizens whom these leaders were supposed to care for.[4] Many of these eminently powerful men built mansions for themselves, while their subjects—dependent on these men for their very lives—died from over-exposure to the elements.

The Cepee learns how humans, once again exhibiting the Immediacy Syndrome, attempted to drive a biospheric nail into their coffin. While they were not completely successful, they created deadly ecosystems that persisted for many years.

A Cepee Diversion. Before the Cepee turns to the next Human Archives pages, he says to himself: *To this point, the study of my ancestors has not been a bed of roses. One of my Japanese Cepee friends tells me she has reached the same conclusion. She says her assessment of the humans' behavior is summed up by an old Japanese saying, "The heaviest rains fall on the leaky house."*[5]

Thus far in my studies, my ancestors have continued to build leaky houses that were far too close to known monsoon areas day after day, year after year. Surely they must have had the sense to come out of the rain, to move away from flood plains. As well as others: To build houses away from known forest fire areas; to move their houses with weak foundations at least a few miles away from earthquake fault lines But they did not.

Again perplexed by the obtuse behavior of the humans—at least a number of them—the Cepee returns to his studies to learn more about *how* or *if* the humans took care of their increasingly leaky-roofed earth.

Controversy about Biosphere Deterioration: Global Warming

For many years, especially in the late twentieth and early twenty-first centuries, the humans could not reach consensus about one key variable in the biosphere deterioration equation: global warming. Some people believed warming of the earth's surface was occurring because of humans' toxic emissions into the atmosphere. Other people believed these emissions had little or no effect on the land, water, or atmosphere.

The opposing parties stalemated each other as the biosphere continued to deteriorate. For example, one side claimed the earth's surface temperature was rising because of human-based emissions of carbon dioxide, methane, and nitrous oxide, which also contributed to lung-related diseases. The other side issued studies to demonstrate no appreciable warming was due to human activity. They claimed warming was occurring because of the ending of the ice age.

As another example, one side predicted vehicles and factories would double, perhaps triple the amount of carbon dioxide in the atmosphere over the next 30 years. The other side claimed these levels would not increase because humans would increase their dependence on nuclear reactors and stop burning coal. They also countered that, even if CO_2 did increase, its effects would be to counter yet another ice age.

In the meantime, as the factions teed off against one another, Iceland lost much of its ice, Greenland finally earned its name, as did the Miami Dolphins. But Glacier Park and the world's coral reefs had to be renamed. These events and many others were attributable to melting glaciers and icebergs, the acidification and oxygen depletion of ocean water, the rise in the levels and temperature of seas and oceans, as well as massive storms, created from increased warm air currents that devastated vast areas of land.

And as it turned out, the humans did not stop using coal. It was too easy to extract from the earth and too abundant.[6] Nuclear plants were judged as too risky, so many were shut down because terrorists and insurgents targeted the sites with the (largely unsuccessful) aim of stealing nuclear material for bombs. In addition, destitute nations sold their material to the highest bidder or the plants blew up on their own accord, sometimes rendering vast landscapes and nearby seas and lakes uninhabitable.

The scientists in this debate got nowhere. They concocted their facts to prove their views. After all, many studies were funded by groups who had their own agenda and turf to protect. Time and again, companies that derived their income from carbon-based products took advantage of the meager incomes of academics and put them on their payroll to write favorable findings about the companies' operations.[7]

Climate Changes and Changes of Policy

An example of this turf protection was demonstrated by another Rule of Life: "Where one stands, depends on where one sits." One of the last technically knowledgeable large organizations to accept the reality of global warming was the American Association of Petroleum Geologists (AAPG). Its 31,000 members steadfastly refused to acknowledge "the effects of human-induced effects on global warming."[8] However, in the first part of the twenty-first century, AAPG changed its policy, at least partially:[9]

> The new [AAPG] statement formally accepts human activity as at least one contributor to carbon dioxide increase, but does not confirm its link to climate change, saying its members are "divided on the degree of influence that anthropogenic CO_2 has" on climate.

What happened to make the world's foremost geologists change their tune? It was likely because of a change in posture from a company who was said to employ more geologists than any other nongovernmental organization on earth: ExxonMobil.

Heretofore, with actions to support the company's stock value, ExxonMobile had taken a stance against almost any effort to diminish its profits from selling fossil fuel-based products, such as gasoline. The company took this stance even if it meant compromising the security of the very nation in which the executives were citizens. They were citizens first to their corporation and its shareholders, second to their country. Lee Raymond, the former chairman of ExxonMobil, was asked by an oil industry executive if the company might build more oil refineries inside the United States to protect the nation against possible gasoline shortages:[10]

— "Why would I want to do that?" Raymond asked, as the executive recalled it.

— "Because the United States needs it…for security," the executive replied.

— "I'm not a U.S. company and I don't make decisions based on what's good for the U.S.," Raymond said.

His stand was in keeping with his job, that of an executive of an international company. But in his zeal to protect his stockholders and his own stock, he overlooked the fact that his passport was not issued by his stockholders, nor the international community. It was issued by the United States. The Cepee thinks: *As my ancestors said,* "Where one stands, depends on where one sits."

In spite of these large companies' policies (organizations that had immense power and influence over lawmakers), the tide began to turn against them. The huge increase in gasoline prices in the early part of the twenty-first century, coupled with their enormous profits and the draining pocketbooks of consumers, placed the petroleum industry in untenable political and public relations positions.

Thus, from the time Raymond gave a speech in Beijing in 1997 claiming that the evidence suggested there was no global warming occurring whatsoever, the company began to shift its stand on the issue.[11]

It was an extraordinary change of policy, with an interesting offshoot: Formerly recalcitrant geologists and pro-oil professors joined this behemoth's bandwagon. The old adage of "All's well that ends well" might have come into play. But the ending was not all's well, as told in the remainder of this chapter.

The Graveyard Shift Law

After a large part of earth's population had come to accept the disastrous consequences of global warming, they also began to understand, "It's too late to reverse the negative consequences of global warming. The best we can do…is get used to it."[12]

Better late than never and another example of a human Rule of Life: the Graveyard Shift Law. This law is not to be confused with a work schedule. Rather, it describes the shifting of priorities to implement a long-known solution to a problem, but only after the problem has created problems. This delay results in unnecessary loss of health, property, and life.

One example was making sure the patients in emergency rooms were periodically checked for their vital signs *after* patients had died while waiting for their vital signs to be checked. Another example was forming committees to address the problems that led to calamitous oil leaks in seas *after* the leakages had already wrought their devastation. And for this situation, governments started taking measures to fix global warming *after* the effects of global warming had already decimated vast swaths of land, deltas, coral reefs, beaches and shores, rivers, homes, buildings, forests, wildlife, and humans.

Glacier Melts

One of the most notable consequences of global warming was the melting of glaciers and icebergs, a point made earlier. Glacial ice was the largest freshwater reservoir on earth, storing water during one season and releasing it later as melt water. It was estimated that one-fourth to one-third of the human population depended on melt water.

This statistic might seem far-fetched. It was not. Many of the thousands of glaciers were huge. The Siachin glacier in the area of Pakistan and India, contained more than two trillion cubic feet of ice, and within fifteen miles, had 45 peaks, which rose to a height of 18,000 feet. The ice mass of the Lambert Mellor and Fisher glaciers in Australia measured 320 miles long and 40 miles wide.[13]

The huge impact of global warming on glaciers was captured on film in the early twenty-first century.[14] Observers happened to have cameras set up when a glacier calving (breaking up) took place. It was the largest calving ever recorded. Its size was comparable to the entire tip of lower Manhattan breaking off and floating out into the ocean, as seen in Figure 4-1.

After witnessing this and similar events, the U.S. Army Corps of Engineers devised a plan for increasing the height and strength of the levees protecting New Orleans. Articles, TV programs, and research papers informed the public about the impact and costs of protecting coastal and river areas of the United States that might be affected, including lower Manhattan, Martha's Vineyard, San Diego, the state of Florida, Houston, etc. In effect, full protection would have had many of America's coasts, deltas, and river inlets surrounded by giant levees. Clearly, such an undertaking was an impossible task.

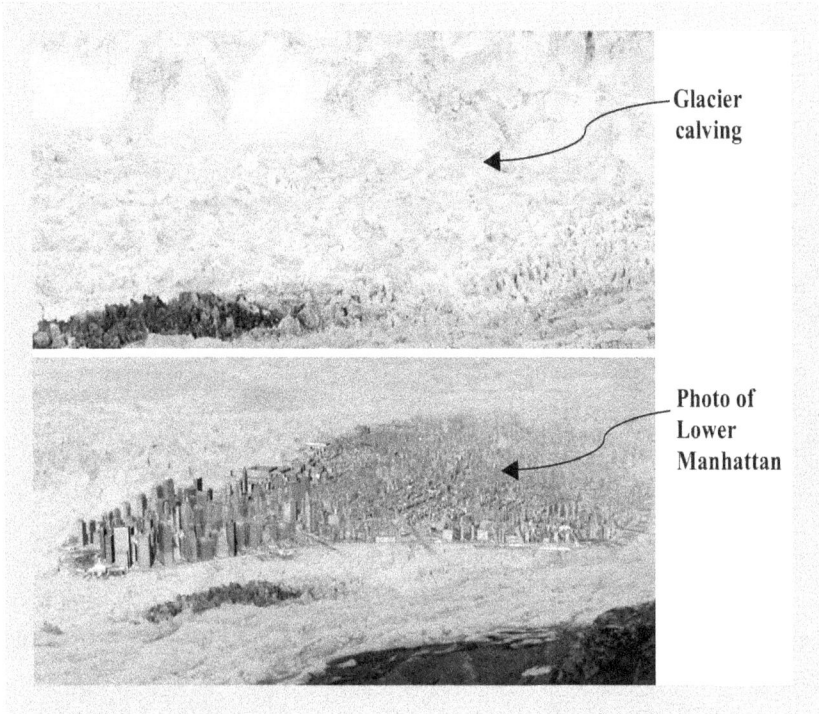

Figure 4-1. Glacier calving.

Other Issues

These debates also revolved around three other issues: (a) humans' population, (b) the Lag Effect, and (c) pollution.

The number of people living on the planet was similar to the global warming debate: widespread disagreement on the subject. Was the number of people on earth too great, too little, or just right? The problem was not overpopulation in general, but overpopulation in specific parts of the planet. Many of the densely populated areas or places of cultural/religious importance became arenas of contest among various tribes (such as ethnic groups), and nation-states. Other parts of the planet were of lesser interest to anyone. For example, unless oil or other vital resources were present, those areas without surface water or a water table rarely became arenas for turf battles.

For this discussion, the Lag Effect is introduced, an important tool for the analysis of the biosphere issue and of the human race in general. This effect represented the time lapse between the occurrence of an action (event A) and when the consequences of the action revealed themselves (event B). The time between events A and B was called the lag window, shown in Figure 4-2.

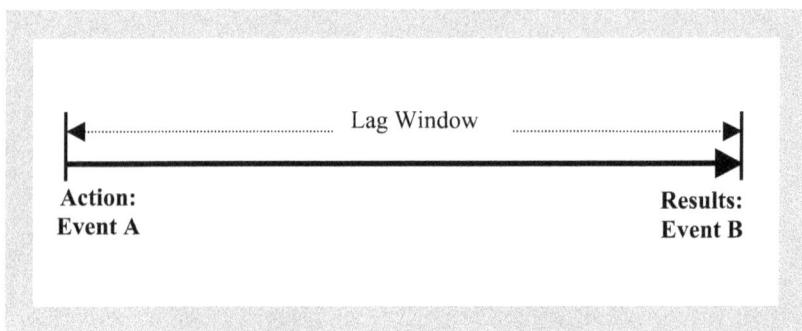

Lag Window

Action:
Event A

Results:
Event B

Figure 4-2. The Lag Effect.

Some human actions and results had predictable lags. For example, pregnancy. The action of event A (when conception took place) had a predictable lag window for the consequences (event B) to emerge. Certainly the lag window could vary, but it usually varied within a known window of time. Some actions and their consequences could not be reversed. That is, after the lag window was opened, it stayed open to its inevitable end. For example, upon a human's birth (event A), the lag window to his or her eventual death (event B) was preordained.

Other actions and their results took place in a gradual manner, and sometimes the results were observable throughout the lag window. For example, a person who continuously ate too much food did not suddenly become fat, but slowly showed signs of obesity almost from the beginning of the lag window.

Another aspect of the lag window was called the Exponential Consequences Curve. Depicted in Figure 4-3, it shows an arrow beginning at the start of the lag window and proceeding to the end. Toward the end of the window, the arrow takes a sharp curve upward, a non-linear, exponential increase. The slope of the arrow illustrates the magnitude of the consequences of the action taken at event A.

Significant ↗

Consequences

Little or None

Lag Window

◄···►
Action: **Results:**
Event A   **Event B**

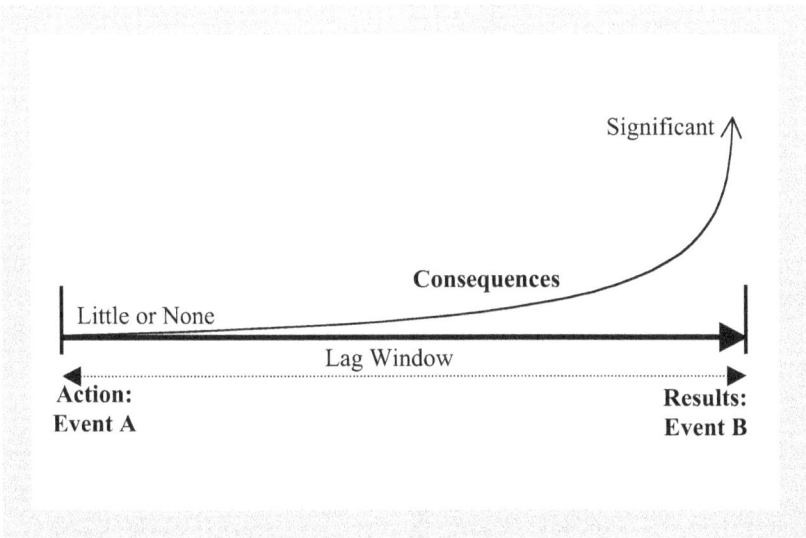

Figure 4-3. The Exponential Consequences Curve.

The curve in Figure 4-3 often manifested itself as the *Unintended* Exponential Consequences Curve, a Rule of Law unto itself. The accumulating results of an action were not evident for a while. Thus, the humans often remained blissfully unaware of the consequences of their behavior and their despoilments.

The global warming and population debates were contentious issues, subject to the vagaries of conflicting evidence, and supported or refuted by which side of the argument a person took. Issues were also clouded because the effects of human-induced global warming encompassed a lag window of many years.

If so, who could fault humans if their primary concern was the lag window of their short time on earth? Why should Joe and Josephine Citizen, residing in the safe environs of their gated community in Kansas, care about the greening of remote Greenland?

Even more, Joe and Josephine lived inland, away from oceans. Why should they care about the tail end of the Exponential Consequences Curve showing the oceans were becoming polluted? That rising waters were flooding New York's subway tunnels during the hurricane season? Likewise, why should Joe and Josephine care if remote China had too many Chinese?

The answers to these questions were: With a few exceptions, they did not care. But they should have. In the early part of the twenty-first century, irrefutable evidence proved humans were creating serious biospheric problems, and that these problems would have severe consequences for…yes, Joe and Josephine.

A Wakeup Call after Waking Up. As time went on, many humans began to understand they were contributing to biospheric pollution. In China, the pollution was so dire, tourists stayed away from the cities. In Beijing, the market for face masks skyrocketed as its citizens donned them to guard against inhaling hazardous particles named PM2-5.[15] These small pieces of pollution were absorbed into the lungs and bloodstream. The air in Beijing often contained four times the amount of PM2-5 that the authorities declared safe to inhale.

The Cepee thinks: *Safe! Inhaling some of these poisonous objects was not considered harmful? Their definition of safe could only have come from an Orwellian dictionary. I've learned the Chinese mortality rate for lung cancer increased fivefold, with no increase of smokers in their population.*

Early mornings in large cities in China would reveal a surreal landscape. Hundreds of people had left their beds to engage in the exercise named t'ai chi. Their goal was to improve their health, combat stress, and strengthen their spirits. Almost all these athletes wore a face mask. It was a good thing t'ai chi did not entail a lot of movement. The pollution was so thick it resembled fog. These keep-fit advocates could have easily collided with one another.

Eventually, most humans no longer questioned that the earth's air was becoming unpleasant to breathe; that many bodies of water were too dirty to drink; that certain chemically contaminated land was dangerous to walk on. Government authorities had to abandon the strategy of downplaying a problem that was asphyxiating citizens before the bureaucrats' eyes. They finally accepted that humans had created a serious problem, and the impact of the problem was increasing exponentially, as seen in Figure 4-3. Given the magnitude of the problem and the reality of the exponential consequences curve, the challenge seemed insurmountable.

Pollution and the Pigsty Paradox

The realities of the situation became clear. Regardless of the debates on global warming; regardless of conflicting computer simulations, emulations, models, and lab experiments, these facts were uncontested: Real-life, practical observations revealed many humans were breathing dangerously dirty air, drinking contaminated water, eating filthy food, and walking on urban and country landscapes that appeared to have been dumped on by a junk yard skyhook. It was painfully plain to see: The humans were destroying their habitats, another example of the Threshold Lowering Syndrome.

As mentioned earlier, many people did not care. They seemed oblivious to their surroundings. Consider pigs living in their sties, heedless of their surrounding muck and swill. Consider the back hills of states such as West Virginia, Pennsylvania, and Virginia where acres of land resembled garbage dumps. Consider abandoned oil fields in New Mexico that left poisonous chemical scars in the soil and on the landscape; dwellers living near dried-out lake beds and forced to wear masks to filter deadly particles in the air; fetid canals in Bangkok, too dangerous to swim in.

The Ceepe is stunned to learn: Deserted strip mines in Montana gave off poisonous wastes into local water supplies, resulting in an enormous toxic lake next to the city of Butte—larger in area than some towns (one mile long, one-half mile wide). Factories on the Shenandoah River dumped carcinogens into the water to be enjoyed by the downstream citizens of Georgetown and Washington, D.C. Tons of used needles and discarded hospital waste washed up on New Jersey beaches. The Russians' contamination of Lake Baikal, which contained one-fifth of the world's fresh water. On and on. It became a never-ending litany of humans abusing the very places in which they lived.

The apathy of the human race, aided by the Lag Effect, and reinforced by the Immediacy and Threshold Lowering Syndromes, eventually created a pigsty habitat on many parts of the planet. Yet a substantial number of humans did not care or were oblivious to it all, a human condition called the *Pigsty Paradox*.

Examples of Problems: Animals, Acreage, and Pollution

The humans' need for space was almost inexorable. Going back in time, if a human were asked why it needed this space, the reply would be, "As a large mammal, I require considerable fresh water and arable land to survive. My ecological footprint is over five acres. I need that amount of space for my livelihood."[16]

Five acres is a lot of land. After all, many humans lived in houses and apartments that took up small fractions of an acre. However, the five-acre requirement encompassed more than living space. This acreage took into account each human's use of common land, such as parks, stores, factories, hospitals, churches, police stations, military installations, highways, and of course, arable land that sustained crops and animals for human's consumption.

In a cattle-growing state, such as Colorado, one cow (or bull) required about thirty acres of land for grazing. Prime acreage could be literally eaten up by a cow. But the food chain above the cow drove the thirty-acre requirement. Many Americans consumed about three hamburgers every week and about sixty-eight pounds of beef every year.[17]

In a typical feedlot, housing about two-hundred-thousand head of cattle, the excrement produced by the animals exceeded the waste produced by the combined cities of Denver, Boston, Atlanta, and St. Louis.[18] Aside from the tremendous problems associated with the disposal of this waste, the many years of feeding cows *corn* resulted in beef that was very high in saturated fat. The government intervened into the cattle industry to provide huge subsidies for growing corn. The result was the mixing of corn into thousands of food products that should not have had corn in them. Besides food for human and livestock consumption, corn was used in paint, paper products, cosmetics, tires, fuel, plastics, textiles, explosives, and wallboard.[19]

Over many centuries, cattle acclimated to the pastures around them. Logically enough, their digestion tracts slowly adapted to the eating and ingestion of grass. Thus, the relatively new food of corn was foreign to them, akin to a non-Hawaiian consuming Poi. Except Poi, residing inside a stomach unconditioned to Poi, only produced starch-induced stomach aches. Whereas, corn residing in cattles' digestive tracts, produced *E. coli* and other pathogenic bacteria.[20] *E. coli* became a major health problem to the human race in the twenty-first century, causing bloody diarrhea, and in some cases, kidney failure, leading to death.

Growth and Progress. In spite of the evidence coming forth in the early twenty-first century about the dangers of a polluted planet, many humans considered the care of the biosphere, their husbandry of helpless, trusting animals, and related conservation programs to be too expensive. This was especially true when their short-range desires for enhancing their living standards conflicted with the long-range needs of adapting to a more modest life style. Indeed, humans often lacked the political will to change their self-indulgent ways. Consider this U.S. government statement, "Sustainable economic growth is the key to environmental progress—because it is growth that provides the resources for investment in clean technologies."[21]

Seemingly, a wise, pragmatic declaration. But compared to what? Rivers polluted with cattle waste that produced five-legged frogs?[22] Lakes polluted with chicken waste that spawned carcinogenic fish? Fishermen falling ill by merely touching the fish's skin?[23] Cattle fed with government subsidies to nurture *E. coli*?

Extinction of Some Societies

At times, it appeared the humans were engaged in an environmental blitzkrieg. They cut or burned away thousands of acres of trees and vegetation, some over many years, some in a few days. Parts of the earth began to resemble a barren moon, as deforestation led to miles of eroded, desolate landscape. Other parts of the land took on a junkyard patina as numerous cultures continued to embrace the Pigsty Paradox. The loss of forests and tree underbrush led to catastrophic top soil erosion rates, ranging between "10 and 40 times the rates of soil formation, and between 500 and 10,000 times the soil erosion rates on forested land."[24] Some societies could no longer grow crops on the sterile, loamless land and migrated to other parts of the planet, fought battles with others for control of a resource, or simply died off.

The surface on several bodies of water, some larger than an entire nation, resembled a dark green oil slick. Underground aquifers were depleted faster than they could replenish themselves.[25] Thus, they could not nourish nearby rivers. Some large lakes simply dried up, leaving hundreds of ships and boats resting on an eerie bed of caked dirt.

The once powerful dams, which had held the lakes' massive waters at bay, stood out as impotent Stonehenge-stark monuments to the humans' inability to manage a vital resource.

Many unlucky residents of the denuded areas (Surprise, they were noble savages.) died from the lack of food, from eating morsels of contaminated food, from drinking foul water, or from having no water to drink. Their weak bodies succumbed to disease or they were killed by their neighbors during fights over scarce resources. An example of this kind of Malthusian birth control was an area in Africa called Rwanda. After experiencing a drought on its already overworked land, thousands of Rwandans murdered their neighbors, including relatives, to acquire a few more feet of land to stave off starvation and to settle old scores.

In earlier times, some tribes, such as the Maya in Mexico, ceased to exist as a viable, productive group of people because they did not manage their land resources. The same fate befell the Anasazi culture in New Mexico. They stripped their land of pinyon and juniper trees, leading to the flushing out of nutrients in the soil. Eventually, the unfertile soil rejected the Anasazis' farming efforts. Without a means to feed a growing population, the Anasazis' societies collapsed. Their once vibrant towns, built centuries ago, became modern-day tourist attractions. The contemporary day tripper walked the Anasazis' former terrain, and beheld acres of low level foundations, offering vague outlines and clues about their once impressive buildings.[26]

Water for Oil

In mid-twenty-first century, the Unintended Exponential Consequences Curve came into play in another arena. The subject was water, or the lack of water. The city of Los Angeles constructed giant aqueducts, snaking them into Northern California to tap the water of several lakes.[27] Within a few years, the lakes were drained dry, leaving hundreds of square miles of dust bowls. Winds kicked up sandstorms, spreading tons of micro-sized particles of dry, powdered earth into the air and lungs of Northern California citizens. This residue never left a human's body and became a contributing factor in respiratory failures.

The city of Las Vegas, housing one of the fastest growing populations in the world, sucked up water from hundreds of miles around. Nearby Lake Mead's water level declined by several meters, leaving erosion marks on the sides of the shores, reminiscent of rings around a recently emptied bath tub. The National Park Service informed the public that the bathtub ring had nothing to do with the lack of water flowing into the lake. The Cepee thinks: *If Lake Mead had ample water, why had many downstream recipients of this precious resource been placed on water hours?*

China, with its burgeoning population, growing industries, and decades of polluting rivers and lakes, let its water supply fall to dangerously low levels. In the early part of the twenty-first century, only one of three citizens living in rural areas had access to safe drinking water. More than 100 cities were in danger of facing a water shortage.[28]

By the time China, other nations, and cities realized they had a water problem, the lag effect of the Exponential Consequences Curve made it impossible to stem the tide (so to speak). The humans could not recover fast enough to reverse the damage done to the lake, river, and water table infrastructure. The oil-rich countries of Saudi Arabia and Iraq eventually ran out of water. Consequently, these nations and other water-starved regions had to resort to importing water from other countries in order to survive.

This program was named the Water for Oil Plan. Countries with ample water, such as Norway, Sweden, and New Zealand, became the newly crowned Potentates for Precious Resources and bartered their water for oil. They one-upped the sheiks of the Middle East for control of a liquid that was even more vital to humans than oil. Gigantic channels and ducts were constructed to pipe the water from one part of the world to another.

In addition to the Water for Oil Plan, massive plants were constructed along the coasts of continents to desalinate ocean water. The demand was so great the pumping of this water might have lowered the level of the seas. Fortunately, thanks to global warming, the North and South Poles and the glaciers had begun melting a few decades before, which resupplied the water in the oceans, resulting in the flooding of thousands of miles of coastlines. These events were more examples of the Unintended Exponential Consequences Curve in action.

Conclusions

Even though the situation in the early part of the twenty-first century was bleak, the human race began to alter its mismanagement of the biosphere. Some of the humans' attacks on the earth's biosphere were reversed as they became aware of the consequences of their actions. Working with scientists, many Evangelical Christians united to take a stand against human-induced global warming. One of the leaders of this movement said that it made no difference how old the earth was, the humans were "messing up" God's creation, and humans had a responsibility to keep God's creation as God had created it.

But these hindsight actions took place only after the Graveyard Shift Law played out its hand. Before the humans could correct their mistakes, vast areas on earth became and remained wastelands. Humans continued to kill one another for sparse water and food resources. Global warming from human emissions became an accepted fact, but the accumulated consequences could not be completely reversed. By the time humans began to take remedial action, the Exponential Consequences Curve for temperature change had progressed too far for these effects to be undone. The melted ice of glaciers and the Poles could not be refrozen, nor could the rising of the seas be reversed. The once magnificent polar bears increasingly drowned as they slipped off floating, melting chunks of ice.

Massive hurricanes, a by-product of global warming, became a way of life for humans and later, the Cepees. Joe and Josephine of

Kansas had their house and themselves sucked up into a tornado tunnel. In a touch of irony, these terrible storms had the effect of helping humans, and later, the Cepees, control their populations.

---

[1] "Ann Sexton," *Time*, September 24, 2007, 17, with the complete poem available at http://www.poemhunter.com/best-poems/anne-sexton/as-it-was-written/.

[2] Thank you Al Gore for your "An Inconvenient Truth." You are hereby forgiven for not inventing the Internet.

[3] E. O Wilson, *The Social Conquest of Earth* (New York: Liveright, 2012), 14, Kindle edition, loc. 299.

[4] The Cepees are especially repelled by the behavior of the leaders of a country in Asia, North Korea. For decades, it was ruled by a brutal one-family dictatorship. Thousands of adults went blind because the regime would not invest in health care, but would invest in the fourth largest army on Earth. Thousands of children died of starvation while this regime spent billions of dollars building a nuclear weapons program.

[5] Anonymous saying attributed to many and none.

[6] Brad Foss, "All Fired Up," *The Spokesman Review*, Spokane, WA, January 25, 2004, D1.

[7] Steve Coll, *Private Empire: ExxonMobil and American Power* (New York: Penguin Press, 2012), 312-313.

[8] "Definition of Anthropogenic Forcing," http://www.chemistry-dictionary.com/definition/anthropogenic+forcing.php.

[9] "Issues related to mitigation in the long-term context," http://www.ipcc.ch/publications_and_data/ar4/wg3/en/ch3.html, in IPCC AR4 WG3 2007.

[10] Coll, *Private Empire*, 71.

[11] Chris Mooney, "The New ExxonMobil: Has the Tiger Changed Its Stripes?" http://www.desmogblog.com/new-exxonmobil-has-tiger-changed-its-stripes.

[12] "Keeping Back the Sea," *FORTUNE*, December 3, 2012, 20.

[13] "Glaciers," http://www.greenpacks.org/2009/04/17/worlds-7-largest-glaciers-by-continent/.

[14] "Impact of Global Warming," http://www.youtube.com/embed/hC3VTgIPoGU?rel=0.

[15] "Something in the Air?" *The Economist*, January 19, 2013, 47.

[16] E. O. Wilson, *The Future of Life* (New York: Alfred A. Knopf, 2002), 215. Thanks to Dr. Wilson for the term *ecological footprint*, as discussed in several parts of his book and defined in the glossary (p. 215).

[17] Eric Schlosser, *Fast Food Nation* (New York: HarperCollins, 2002), 6, 142, 215. On this subject, Schlosser cites several closely related statistics throughout his book.

[18] Ibid., 150.

[19] "Corn Products and Byproducts," http://www.csmonitor.com/2002/1031/p17s01-lihc.html.

[20] Corby Kummer, "Back to Grass," *The Atlantic Monthly*, May 2003, 138.

[21] "Human's Self-indulgent Ways," announcement, Bush Administration, February 14, 2002.

[22] Scott Allen, "Widespread Abnormalities Stump Scientists. Pesticides, Parasites among Explanations," *The Boston Globe*, July 28, 1997, B01.

[23] "Pollution," www.usgs.gov/themes/FS-189-97/.

[24] Jared Diamond, *Collapse: How Societies Choose to Fail or Succeed* (New York: Viking Press, 2005), 489.

[25] Ibid., 490.

[26] The guides at the Bandelier National Monument in Northern New Mexico have conflicting views about the fate of the Anasazis. Their opinions seem to vary in accordance with the political correctness climate.

[27] "Los Angeles' Water Sources," *Life & Times*, January 26, 2007, PBS/KCET, 8 p.m.

[28] "Drying Up," *The Economist*, May 21, 2005, 46.

CHAPTER 5

THE UNIVERSE AND UNIVERSAL DISAGREEMENT

...the universe...can be encompassed in its entire majesty only by a cosmic intellect.[1]

...the universe may not only be queerer than we suppose, but queerer than we can suppose.[2]

The humans' views of the universe were almost as diverse as the universe itself, including their theories about its origins. Clouding the discussion was the religious leaders' opposition to many of the scientists' views about the universe and the possible reasons for its existence. In this chapter, the Cepee learns about the humans' theories on how the universe came to be. He learns that his ancestors, being contentious and curious creatures, engaged in unending debates about the universe.

Theories about the Universe

The inability of a human to accept another's beliefs or a society to accept another society's way of life was partially attributable to the customs associated with their Human Tribal Hierarchy. A key component in the hierarchy was their religious incompatibility with one another. Time and again, religion had the lead role on the stage of deadly aggression. These conflicts often stemmed from the basic questions of how and when the universe was created and for what reason. From these questions, the inevitable thorny issue of the intervention or absence of a divine power—a god or gods—in this process led to confrontations and conflicts.

Regardless of these quarrels, humans were never able to answer fundamental questions about the universe. They were baffled by the possibility of a universe of seemingly infinite size with a seemingly infinite existence. The word *seemingly* is fitting because some humans believed a bound existed on the size and life span of the universe, even though this bound was in the framework of billions of light years in size and billions of years of existence. Others believed the size and life span of the universe were infinite. Some theorists stated the universe was never ending, that it wrapped back onto itself.

Still others held the view that the universe was only six thousand years old and nothing existed beyond earth except a cloud-filled heaven guarded by angels at a pearly gate.

The Big Bang

Numerous theories about the universe had been formulated in the past, and they continued to persist into the Cepee era. One prominent hypothesis, the Big Bang theory, championed the idea of a universe that was at one time extremely compact. Then, according to one (and dominant) school of thought, about 13.75 billion years ago, a cosmic explosion occurred, and the universe began expanding very rapidly.[3] Thus, this school considered the universe to be a bit less than 14 billion years old. The original supposition of this theory held that the universe would eventually stop expanding and begin contracting.[4] This contracting theory was later (largely) discounted.

Regardless of the theories, most everyone agreed that the universe was big. A distant galaxy observed by astronomers (its emanated light) revealed that the light had traveled over 13 billion years to reach the earth—at a speed of 186,000 miles per second.[5] Very big indeed. It was determined that one galaxy was 100,000,000, 000,000,000,000,000 miles away from earth.[6]

The expansion from the Big Bang caused the universe to cool, allowing energy to be converted into various subatomic particles, such as protons, neutrons, and electrons. It would take millions of years for these particles to create atoms and compositions called elements:

"The first element produced was hydrogen, along with traces of helium and lithium. Giant clouds of these primordial elements would coalesce through gravity to form stars and galaxies."[7]

The Big Bang theory originally rested on two assumptions: the universality of physical laws across the entire universe and the cosmological principle. This principle stated that, on large scales, the universe was homogeneous and isotropic (the same in all directions).[8] As discussed later in this chapter, both assumptions were called into question by researchers in the early years of the twenty-first century.

This division among learned scientists, the inability to agree on such fundamental concepts, further alienated many religious communities from the scientific society. They looked upon these academic disputes as silly and atheistic. They believed the Big Bang and results from the bang required a divine creator.

The detractors of a god-created universe claimed the cosmology of the Big Bang and its aftermath made the idea of a creator superfluous.[9]

The religious mountebanks countered by asking, "In your view, who or what powered the bang itself?" They had a point. The Big Bang theory and Einstein's equations broke down "when applied to the extreme environment of the universe's earliest moment."[10] To attempt to answer these skeptics, the scientists came up with the theory of *inflationary cosmology*. This theory put forward the idea that a cosmic fuel could have created the Big Bang.[11]

The religious leaders came back with a similar question, "Then who or what created this cosmic fuel?" The scientists had no answer. They retreated to their equations to devise more postulations.

A variation on the Big Bang theory stated the universe was a four-dimensional system. Its conventional three dimensions were extended by a fourth dimension of time. Others came forth with theories about even more dimensions. Regardless of how many the humans thought might have existed, these dimensions were said by some humans to be infinite, supporting a universe with no boundary and an ad infinitum existence.

This theory clashed with the theory that the universe would eventually contract and fall back into itself to its compact state. With the expansion theory, the Big Bang was really big. It was so huge the metaphorical balloon on which all elements were positioned never stopped enlarging. Well, perhaps only in the context of it bending back into itself. As mentioned, a theory some scientists espoused.

Also stated earlier, according to the Big Bang model, the universe expanded from an extremely dense state. A common analogy offered that space itself was expanding, carrying galaxies with it, like spots on an inflating balloon. The scheme in Figure 5-1 shows how space stretches (expands) as time passes.[12] Space increases between the elements as the overall area expands.

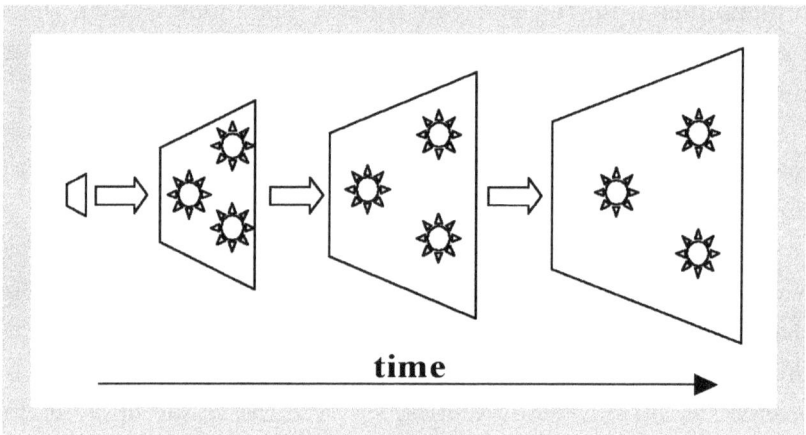

Figure 5-1. Explosion of space.

Consequently, this theory held that the Big Bang was not an explosion of a specific location in space, but an explosion of space itself. That is, it occurred everywhere at once. With this theory, the galaxies were not fragments of a Big Bang moving away from earth. Instead the space between the galaxies and earth was expanding.[13]

Another theory about the universe stated the perception of a three-dimensional universe was an illusion, and reality was more like a two-dimensional hologram. Physicists hoped this idea was a clue to the "ultimate theory of reality."[14] Members of the religious community rolled their eyes.

Dark Matter and Dark Energy

For a while, the humans' scientific community thought it had a handle on gravity. The prevailing theory declared objects attracted one another. As examples, earth's gravity attracted people to its surface, and celestial bodies attracted other celestial bodies. Einstein demonstrated how gravity could bend light rays.

However, according to some scientists, the Hubble telescope's sightings revealed the Big Bang's expanding universe was continuing to expand, and the expansion was increasing in speed—an anti-gravity effect.

Scientists came up with a specific theory about the invisible gravitational effects on particles. The culprit was called *dark matter* because it could not be seen nor was it completely understood. They did not know exactly what dark matter was or if it was dark. The term was coined to convey the idea that it *was believed* to be important to the cosmos, but no one was really sure what it was. It was believed to be related to the gravitational forces in the universe. Dark matter was also called missing mass. Because many religious believers discounted a secular explanation of the universe, they had a field day with this name. A Catholic declared the scientists were not only missing mass but missing the point about the universe.

The scientists also discovered dark energy, although they (again) were not completely certain of what they discovered. This energy—not to be confused with dark matter—seemed to be working against gravity to push the universe outward and had been doing so since the Big Bang.

However, it was also believed that about seven billion years ago, the expansion of space, "went into overdrive and has been speeding up ever since." As a scientist explained, "That's like gently tossing a ball upward, having it slow down initially, but then rocket upward ever more quickly."[15]

In an attempt to explain dark energy to a TV audience who were unfamiliar with the details of astronomy, another scientist took some car keys out of his pocket.[16] He tossed them in the air. As they came back into his hand, he told his audience, "If dark energy exists in the universe, these car keys—representing say a galaxy—might just as well reverse course and take off into space at an accelerating rate."

The TV viewers were both confused and transfixed. They thought about this improbable situation in relation to their everyday lives of dealing with the gravitational reality of drooping breasts and sagging necklines. Dark energy seemed out of this world to these people who dealt in practical earth-centric matters.

The TV evangelists smiled while watching the program: Out of this world? Of course. They believed the ascension of Jesus into a heavenly cosmos was at least as plausible as the scientist's car keys accelerating into a dark cosmos. Besides, the scientists offered no alternative for anything ascending to a "better place." But the evangelists did. They offered solace and hope for anyone who chose to believe in their creed.

As stated, no one knew much about this pushing. They proposed it might be a property of space itself, perhaps similar to an electromagnetic field pulsing in the universe.[17] They also postulated that the dark energy was not visible, something like an "invisible mist [that was] uniformly spread through space—[but] the gravity exerted by the energy mist [was] repulsive."[18] In addition, Einstein's general theory of relativity predicted an "extremely elastic form of energy could actually be repulsive."[19]

Upon making the startling discovery of the existence of dark energy, a noted theoretical physicist said, "It fits the data, but it's not what we really expected."[20] One would think that if it fit the data, it would be what was expected. Otherwise, why do the data in the first place?[21] The answer is that the scientists had to continue to look for answers. By possibly finding their calculations and "data" incorrect, they could move forward to make alternative postulations and seek other solutions.

Mathematically Describing the Unobservable

Many scientists believed that eventually nothing would escape a scientific explanation. Increasingly, they had to use equations instead of observations in their quest for these answers. After all, some parts of the universe could not be observed:[22]

Take black holes. Scientists routinely use general relativity to speak with confidence about what happens inside a black hole, even though nothing, not even light can escape a black hole's interior, rendering such regions unobservable. The justification is that once a theory makes a slew of accurate predictions about things we can observe, as general relativity has, we justifiably gain confidence in the theory's predictions about something we can't observe.[22]

Scientists observed the universe through the analysis of the light emanating from galaxies. A "faint red blob" in the nighttime sky revealed the distance the light had traveled to reach earth. The color was determined by how much the light's wavelength had been stretched as it traveled through space. The light waves became elongated, which had the effect of their taking on red and therefore were dubbed as being red-shifted.

Thus, humans could only see what was observable. They could not see beyond "the distance the light has traveled since the Big Bang."[23] Cosmologists and astrophysicists used sophisticated antennas to detect the shifting. These systems received signals beyond the visible light, even beyond the infrared spectrum. They were designed to receive signals of the microwave spectrum, called cosmic microwave background radiation (CMB).

The analysis of CMB revealed an intriguing fact. The intensity of CMB had slight variations, which scientists believed to reflect a "slight lumpiness in the distribution of matter. The degree of primordial lumpiness was enough to act as seeds for the galaxies and larger structures that would later emerge from the action of gravity."[24]

The observations of the size of the universe and the rate at which it was expanding were derived from:[25]

... formula relating the red-shift of light signals coming from distant galaxies to the distance of these galaxies from [earth] and the time of detecting of these light signals. The red-shift...increases forever as time is running from the past to the future. The...increasing rate of the red-shift coefficient... is...the nowadays value of the acceleration of the expansion of the universe.

This simple explanation was a proxy for thousands of labor-years of research and discovery. These ideas represented feats of startling intellectual achievements. Still, what was out there beyond the observed cosmos? Other than theoretical explanations, no one could say, as it could not be observed. This puzzle pleased some of the religious people. One religious pundit offered, "I told you so. Beyond those light beams is a cloud-filled heaven." Members of the scientific community rolled their eyes.

To complicate matters, some scientists posed the questions of what if the universe were not homogenous and isotropic? What if the laws of physics and the law of relativity were not universally applicable? Shortly, these questions are examined. For now, we examine one of the most remarkable discoveries the humans made about the universe.

As introduced earlier in this chapter, it was concluded that as the universe expanded, its space expanded. This mysterious cosmic fuel replenished itself. Furthermore, it was never used up as the universe continued to expand.

Accordingly, the physicists and astronomers came up with statistics (approximations) about the energy density components that made up the universe:[26]

Dark energy	68.3%
Dark matter	26.8%
Other matter	4.9%

If the scientists were correct, dark energy would continue to take more of the space in the universe as the universe expanded. This meant something was replenishing itself from itself. It was an incredible concept to humans who were conditioned to think that something had to spring from something else.

As the list above shows, about 95 percent of the universe was invisible. As mentioned, it was *dark* in the sense that humans were not sure what it was, and it could not be seen. A number of scientists accepted this ignorance as an admirable lesson in humility. Some quoted Shakespeare's *The Tempest* to remind themselves they had a lot to learn, and that they might never come to know it. In this play, Antonio says, "This thing of darkness I acknowledge mine." But these wise humans were not referring to matters of the universe as "this thing of darkness." They were referring to the fact that "this thing of darkness" was their own ignorance.

If some of the religious radicals, those who routinely informed their subjects their chosen creed provided all the answers, had taken a more humble approach to their practices, the human race would have fared much better.

The God Particle

The physicists and astronomers dealt with other discoveries about particles in the universe. One of their crowning achievements was the discovery of the Higgs particle, also called the Higgs or Higgs boson. This particle was considered to be an explanation of why some particles had mass.[27] It became known, to the chagrin of pastors, priests, and many scientists, as the God Particle. Others called it the god damn particle.

The reason this discovery was so important to the theorists was their claim that without this particle there could be no mass in the universe such as stars, planets, or even atoms, not to mention humans. Of course, everyone knew that stars, planets, atoms, and humans existed, so the Higgs had to be around somewhere.

However, if the Higgs were not discovered, the math that accounted for the relationships of protons, neutrons, and electrons (atomic nuclei)—and yes, humans themselves—"would disintegrate."[28] Naturally, the mathematicians were happy about this discovery. Ordinary humans, had they known about their narrow escape from nothingness, would have been relieved.

These particles were said to obtain their mass by interacting with an almost transitory Higgs field. The field was considered so fleeting that it atrophied so quickly the humans had to construct massive machines to catch it interacting before it decayed and went away.

The Higgs boson experts added that the God Particle had "non-zero strength, even in otherwise empty space." The Sunday morning televangelists took issue with anything associated with God being characterized as a mere "particle," but they silently acquiesced on this specific claim as they—being experts on religion but not on physics—were not sure what "non-zero strength" meant.

As told earlier, according to the dark energy and dark matter researchers, space was not empty. And with the discovery of Higgs, scientists held out hope that further work "might account for some strange stuff called 'dark matter.'"[29] As mentioned, it was hoped the transitory Higgs might lead to an understanding of non-transitory dark matter.

The scientists also proposed that if the Higgs boson was shown not to exist, other "Higgsless" models would be considered. They said there could be multiple Higgs bosons.

Of course. If a theory was shown not to be true, others had to be considered. Meanwhile, even though the discovery of the Higgs boson was quite important, it did not explain creation. But it did help explain the forming of the universe.

After the Higgs discovery was made in 2012, the researchers spent almost a year analyzing the data that had been collected about this event. Finally, in 2013 they announced to the world:[30]

Just in time for Albert Einstein's birthday Thursday, scientists delivered exciting news about how the universe works.

On Thursday, scientists announced that the particle, detected at the Large Hadron Collider, the world's most powerful particle-smasher, looks even more like the Higgs boson.

"The preliminary results with the full 2012 data set are magnificent and to me it is clear that we are dealing with a Higgs boson though we still have a long way to go to know what kind of Higgs boson it is," said a spokesman.

A physicist said, "You can think of it as a kind of molasses-like bath that's invisible, but yet we're all immersed within it,"

But scientists do not know if the particle they've found is truly the one predicted by the Standard Model of particle physics. That model is the best explanation out there for what happens at scales smaller than the atom, but still has a lot of holes in it, and there are other theories out there that go beyond that model.

This newscast was not entirely accurate in that the discovery did not come close to explaining how the universe worked. Aside from this point, even with this important discovery, the scientists were still hedging their bets. They still had "a long way to go." They were not sure what kind of Higgs boson it was.

The Standard Model, a Page from Nature's Notebook

In spite of the scientist's uncertainty, the Higgs became part of the Standard Model. This model was an explanation of how the universe worked (except for gravity, which was considered part of Einstein's general theory of relativity). This model included 17 particles broadly categorized as quarks, leptons, fermions, and bosons.[31] Physicists needed the Higgs boson in their math to give mass to most of these other particles. Otherwise, the Standard Model would have been rendered incorrect.

This endeavor was a work of extraordinary mental creativity, attesting once again to the genius of the *Homo sapiens*. The Standard Model, built over many years, provided a mathematically consistent way of explaining nature's building blocks and how they came together to form the universe.

Barbs Fly. These brilliant minds, displaying a sense of humor, called the particles Quark Soup. An anti-idea televangelist—likely having lost touch with the physical world after flunking long division—in an attempt to make hay with a drowsing Sunday morning audience, used the term "Quack Soup." A fine example of the pot calling the kettle black.

The scientific community usually kept a low confrontational profile with the religious community. With its jargon and equations, the community knew it could not possibly gain the attention of many people. Certainly, leptons and quarks in the model could not compete with easy-to-grasp and compelling parables in the Bible. Behind the scenes, at cosmologists' cocktail parties, a running joke was that this televangelist suffered from the Innumeracy Syndrome: An affliction of the frontal cortex in which the sufferer did not consider 0 to be a number.

Nonetheless, the Standard Model, even with Higgs, was considered to be incomplete. As scientists said at the beginning of the twenty-first century:[32]

> One problem is that, as it stands, the model requires its 20 or so constants to be exactly what they are to an uncomfortable 32 decimal places. Insert different values and the upshot [are] nonsensical predictions, like phenomena occurring with a likelihood of more than 100%.

This statement implied that nature's fixation on precision and fastidiousness was considered an affront to the humans' math. At any rate, associated theories about the Model concluded it did come close to answering other questions about the universe. The humans kept on looking for the final answers, including the concept of spooky actions.

Spooky Actions, Entanglement, and Teleportation

As the humans made progress in learning what they did not know about the universe, they discovered quantum mechanics (QM). It was a discipline that provided a mathematical description of both the particle-like and wave-like behavior of energy and matter. QM attempted to explain an idea that Einstein characterized as *spooky action at a distance*:[33]

> ...an experimenter could entangle a pair of particles, separate them by vast distances, then instantaneously change the state of one by changing the state of the other—even at distances of millions of light years.

...a team at the University of Geneva conducted a particularly dramatic demonstration by entangling packets of light called photons, then sending them in opposite directions down fiber-optic lines to detectors nearly seven miles away. When they measured properties of one photon, it had an instantaneous effect on the other. If the interaction behaved in a classical way, a measurable amount of time would have passed between measurement of one and the effect on the other.

This theory was counter intuitive to common sense, but it was verified through experiments, as discussed above. In addition, another experiment succeeded in transferring photons and verified that the process did not destroy the photons at either end. Prior to this experiment, one of the entangled particles was destroyed.

The implications of particle entanglement were extraordinary, leading to articles and papers about so-called teleportation. If photons could be entangled and show their presence instantaneously miles away, why not atoms? Why not other particles? Why not humans? It was an idea reflected in "Star Trek" episodes.

A professor of physics and mathematics at Columbia University, while stating the idea of teleportation to be complex and hypothetical, did lend it considerable credence by including a lengthy enactment on a TV program of two humans teleporting themselves back and forth between Paris and New York.[34]

Other scientists were not so keen on instantaneously moving bodies around. "Teleportation is a really unfortunate term," claimed one physicist. "It implies moving people from point A to point B," when in fact it refers to "creating a quantum state in one place that used to exist somewhere else" with no intervening connection.[35]

The Cepee pauses from his studies of this part of the Human Archives. He thinks: *It seemed the physicist was upset because he could not account for the speed of light law in his observations. 186,000 miles per second is very fast, but it still entails a delay. There was no delay between the associated actions of A and B. Teleportation? Maybe these scientists were too prideful to be linked to a "Star Trek" fantasy.*

Multiple Universes

In addition to the idea of the Big Bang, the God Particle, and spooky actions, some physicists claimed the cosmic fuel could have powered not just one Big Bang, but countless other Big Bangs, with each bang creating a separate universe. As a result, the humans' universe would have been only one among a huge number of other universes.

The scientists made estimates of the total possible universes that existed. Their tally was 10^{500}. The number was so large no one could comprehend it.[36]

This theory held that multiple earths and their associated galaxies could be scattered throughout this seemingly infinite space. This startling idea also contended multiple copies of everything, including humans, could exist in this space.[37]

> You will probably never see your other selves. The farthest you can observe is the distance that light has been able to travel during the 14 billion years since the Big Bang expansion began. The most distant visible objects are now about 4×10^{26} meters away—a distance that defines our observable universe.

As discussed in Chapter 6, if the concept of multiple universes was startling to the scientific community, it was an abomination to the religious community.

Furthermore, multiple universes (the multiverse) might yield universes that were different from one another. A concept called "string theory" stated that each particle in the universe had a vibrating string-like energy, something akin to the frequency vibrations that occur on a played violin. The manner of the different vibrations could yield different kinds of particles, different basic building blocks, in the different universes. Consequently, the proponents of this idea claimed it was theoretically possible for this multiverse to contain universes that operated with different principles.

As a consequence of this notion, and because the idea of multiverses gained credence, during the twenty-first century a number of scientists advanced theories stating the constants of nature might not be constant.[38] They postulated the velocity of light (c), Newton's constant of gravitation (G), and the mass of electrons (m_e) might not be the same at all places and times in the multiverse. They held:[39]

> First, the equations describing inflation [an expanding universe] strongly suggest that if inflation happened once, it should happen again and again, with an infinite number of inflationary regions created over time. Nothing can travel between these regions, so they have no effect on one another. Second, string theory suggests that these regions have different physical parameters, such as the number of spatial dimensions and the kinds of stable particles.

The implications of these theories were disquieting to many scientists. If they were true, singular natural laws governed different parts of the cosmos. Therefore, what was viewed as an immutable fact on earth might not exist in other parts of the multiverse. DNA in another universe? Not as the humans understood it. Electrons? Not as the humans knew them. Carbon atoms? Not as constructed on earth. Duplicate copies of Joe Citizen? Perhaps, but with changing constants, a human Joe on earth might resemble on a distant planet a growth from the "Little Shop of Horrors."

Counter Views

Some scientists disparaged the theories of isolated universes with their separate laws. Others discounted the notion of dark energy and the accelerating expansion of the universe. One physicist claimed, "The reason dark energy is so mysterious is that it is an illusion."[40] This argument was based on a theory stated in the principal of general relativity that clocks in different parts of the universe could run at different rates, and that time slowed near massive objects. Thus, the flow of time near galaxies would be different from the flow of time in the space away from galaxies.

This view held that the proponents of dark energy and an increasingly expanding universe ignored or misinterpreted the "positions of the distant supernova explosions used to determine how quickly the universe is expanding…creating the illusion that the expansion of the universe is speeding up. Supernova measurements are the key to evidence of dark energy."[41]

This argument also questioned the supposed age of the universe. The debate went as follows:[42]

> In a truly relativistic view, the age of the universe differs from place to place. In empty space over 18 billion years since the Big Bang, but within galaxies only about 15 billion years have passed.

In considering this new way of viewing the universe's time, thus discounting decades of research, TV viewers' eyes clouded over. And the religious believers—once again—rolled theirs.

Debates go Unabated

The humans and later the Cepees continued their quests to try to understand the universe in which they lived. Sometimes, sound reasoning was clouded by debaters who had underlying motives, such as protecting intellectual or monetary turf. Sometimes, it was about protecting spiritual turf. Fortunately, the arguments about the universe often resulted in enlightenment on both sides of the table.

Notwithstanding the humans' holy books, on occasion the arguments between the God-driven universe believers and the godless-driven universe believers gave both parties pause. This pause led the more thoughtful humans in these camps to reflect on the others' views.

Upon this reflection, their thoughts sometimes led to an impression of awe. Awe in the sense that the ideas and theories of both parties, when viewed together, as a whole, left many of these open-minded humans in wonderment and amazement. Once getting past the creationism chimera, there was nothing contradictory about the joint existence of an ephemeral Higgs particle operating in consonance and harmony with a lasting God principle.

The two schools of thought were mutually supportive if a person chose to think so. If the person did not, no amount of blackboard talk from the scientists or proselytizing from the preachers would move either off their respective gluon and God dimes.

When a preacher or scientist read the opening chapter of the Bible, it was easy to see the ancient writers were discussing "how the constituents of the universe—light, stars, life—were created."[43]

Each human and Cepee wondered about how life came into existence. For the human, of how it might end. However silently, both parties knew, "The deity is in the details."

Neither human nor Cepee discovered all the secrets of the universe. Nor did they resolve the religious significance, if any, of its creation and evolution. In the end, it all came down to mathematical verification on one side. On the other side, it all came down to faith.

The Cepee reflects on what he has learned about the humans' views on the universe and their religions, as well as the frequent conflicts brought about by their conflicting suppositions about reality: *Many of my ancestors were able to integrate the new findings of science into their older religions. But many were not. For both factions, they would have had fewer skirmishes by keeping the thoughts of one of their spiritual leaders, the Dalai Lama, in mind.* The Cepee consults two passages from the Human Archives and reads what this man had to say about the subject:

> My confidence in venturing into science lies in my basic belief that as in science so in Buddhism, understanding the nature of reality is pursued by means of critical investigation: if scientific analysis were conclusively to demonstrate certain claims in Buddhism to be false, then we must accept the findings of science and abandon those claims.[44]

> Unless the direction of science is guided by a consciously ethical motivation, especially compassion, its effects may fail to bring benefit. They may indeed cause great harm.[45]

The Cepee concludes: *Sound advice to all, if they had only heeded it. Nonetheless, for both parties, whatever their views may have been, it all came down to opinion.*

[1] Lincoln Barnett, *The Universe and Dr. Einstein* (New York: Bantam, 1980), 72.

[2] J. B. S. Haldane, "Science's Great Leap Forward," *The Economist*, July 7, 2012, 13.

[3] E. Komatsu, et al., (2009), "Five-Year Wilkinson Microwave Anisotropy Probe Observations: Cosmological Interpretation," *Astrophysical Journal Supplement* 180 (2): 330. Bibcode 2009ApJS..180..330K. doi:10.1088/0067-0049/180/2/330.

[4] George Gamow, "Crunch, Bang," *Scientific American*, March 1954. Excerpted from the March 2004 section, "50, 100 & 150 Years Ago," 15.

[5] Alan Lightman, "Our Place in the Universe?" *Harper's*, December 2012, 34.

[6] Ibid.

[7] Komatsu, "Five-Year Wilkinson Microwave Anisotropy Probe Observations."

[8] A. V. Ivanchik, A. Y. Potekhin, and D. A.Varshalovich (1999), "The Fine-Structure Constant: A New Observational Limit on Its Cosmological Variation and Some Theoretical Consequences," *Astronomy and Astrophysics* 343: 459. arXiv:astro-ph/9810166. Bibcode 1999A&A...343..439I.

[9] T. Frame (2009), *Losing My Religion*, UNSW Press, 137-141, http://books.google.nl/books?id=1mb-h1lom9IC&pg=PA137.

[10] Brian Greene, "The Mystery of the Multiverse," *Newsweek*, May 28, 2012, 23. Posted online, May 21, 2012, http://www.thedailybeast.com/newsweek/2012/05/20/brian-greene-welcome-to-the-multiverse.html.

[11] Ibid.

[12] Michael S. Turner, "The Universe," *Scientific American*, September 2009, 38.

[13] Charles H. Lineweaver and Tamara M. Davis, "Misconceptions about the Big Bang," *Scientific American*, March 2005, 38-39. http://space.mit.edu/~kcooksey/teaching/AY5/MisconceptionsabouttheBigBang_ScientificAmerican.pdf.

[14] Jacob D. Bekenstein, "Information in the Holographic Universe," *Scientific American*, August 2003, 59.

[15] Greene, "The Mystery of the Multiverse," 23.

[16] I saw this interview on a television show that I did not record in my notes. The quote is close, but not verbatim.

[17] http://articles.news.aol.com. November 17, 2006.

[18] Greene, "The Mystery of the Multiverse," 23.

[19] Turner, "The Universe," 43.

[20] Ibid.

[21] I do not mean to diminish the power of data and data's associated input to and output from formula to aid these compelling ideas. They are formulated and proved or disapproved with algorithms. Often, math provides a backup to our natural observations. When we cannot make an observation, equations codify our inferences. Einstein conceived many of his ideas first with analogies to life and with thought pictures. Later, he became more efficient in math and substantiated his views with equations.

[22] Greene, "The Mystery of the Multiverse," 25.

[23] Lightman, "Our Place in the Universe," 37.

[24] Turner, "The Universe," 39.

[25] Jian-Miin Liu, "Formula for Red-Shift of Light Signals Coming from Distant Galaxies," Department of Physics, Nanjing University, Nanjing, The People's Republic of China, http://arxiv.org/ftp/physics/papers/0505/0505036.pdf.

[26] P. A. R. Ade, N. Aghanim, and C. Armitage-Caplan, et al., (Planck Collaboration), "Planck 2013 Results 1. Overview of Products and Scientific Results-Table 9." March 22, 2013. "Planck 2013 Results Papers," and "First Planck Results: the Universe Is Still Weird and Interesting," March 31, 2013, "Astronomy and Astrophysics" (submitted). arXiv:1303.5062. Bibcode:2013arXiv1303...5062P. Other sources cite slightly different statistics (dark energy: 68.3%, dark matter: 26.8% intergalactic gas: 3.6%, stars, neutrinos, and heavy elements: 0.4%. Also see Gary R. Hinshaw (April 30, 2008), "WMAP Cosmological Parameters Model: lcdm+sz+lens Data: wmap5." Michael Turner published these numbers in his "The Universe" article cited several times in this chapter: (dark energy: 71.5%, dark matter: 24%, stars and planets: 0.5%, gas: 4.0%).

[27] Unless otherwise cited, sources for this section are extracted from: Peter Higgs (1964), "Broken Symmetries and the Masses of Gauge Bosons," *Physical Review Letters* 13 (16): 508–509. Bibcode 1964PhRvL..13..508H. doi:10.1103/PhysRevLett.13.508. http://prl.aps.org/abstract/PRL/v13/i16/p508_1; Francois Englert and Robert Brout (1964), "Broken Symmetry and the Mass of Gauge Vector Mesons," *Physical Review Letters* 13 (9): 321–23. Bibcode 1964PhRvL..13..321E. DOI:10.1103/PhysRevLett.13.321; Gerald Guralnik, C. R. Hagen, and T. W. B. Kibble (1964). "Global Conservation Laws and Massless Particles," *Physical Review Letters* 13 (20): 585–587. Bibcode 1964PhRvL..13..585G. doi:10.1103/PhysRevLett.13.585.

[28] Haldane, "Science's Great Leap Forward," *The Economist*, July 7, 2012, 13.

[29] Ibid.

[30] Elizabeth Landau, "Scientists More Certain That Particle Is Higgs Boson," CNN, March13, 2013. Posted to http://www.cnn.com/2013/03/14/tech/innovation/higgs-boson-god-particle.

[31] "Science's Great Leap Forward," *The Economist*, 71.

[32] Ibid., 72.

[33] Peter N. Spotts, "Spooky Action at a Distance," *The Christian Science Monitor*, October 4, 2001.

[34] Brian Greene, "Fabric of the Cosmos," PBS, July 25, 2112.

[35] Spotts, "Spooky Action at a Distance."

[36] Yet this is a guess, a supposition.

[37] Max Tegmark, "Parallel Universes," *Scientific American*, May 2003, 41.

[38] John D. Barrow and John K. Webb, "Inconstant Constants," *Scientific American*, June 2005, 57-63.

[39] Turner, "The Universe," 43.

[40] Zeeya Merali, "Gravity off the Grid," *Discover*, 03.2112, 49.

[41] Ibid., 49, 51.

[42] Ibid., 49.

[43] Abraham Loeb, "The Dark Ages of the Universe," *Scientific American*, November 2006. Web; "The Dark Ages of the Universe."

[44] The Dalai Lama, *The Universe in a Single Atom* (New York: Random House, 2005), 2-3.

[45] Ibid., 9.

CHAPTER 6

THE RELIGIONS AND UNIVERSAL AGGRESSION

Why is your religion better than mine? Because you are richer than I am.
—An Australian bushman to his missionary.

In the logic of extremists…both sides can give each other what they want—perpetual conflict between Israelis and Palestinians.[1]

Ideology knows the answer before the question has been asked.[2]

With some exceptions, the humans' religious tenets should have mitigated their dispositions to harm one another. Granted, passages in their holy books countenanced slavery and stoning a person to death. But some believers misread their holy books, often on purpose to meet their own ends, such as placing women in subservient positions, or assaulting unarmed civilians.

Some religious enthusiasts, a relatively small number in the humans' populace, believed they could kill anyone who cast aspersions on their faith or their holy book. Another practice was to stone to death a female adulteress and let the male adulterer go free.

These directives in the holy books reflected pervasive cultural values at the time they were written. In humans' later times, pragmatic worshippers considered many passages in these books to be archaic. This discernment did not diminish the spiritual value of the books to these astute, sensible people.

Nonetheless, the human race could have saved itself a lot of misery if the more doctrinaire believers had taken-on the views of the Dalai Lama, discussed in the previous chapter.

123

These rigid zealots would have been aghast at the Dalai Lama's tolerance. They brooked no arguments or the exchanging of differing views on religious matters. Any possible settlement of disputes would have required the parties to compromise their stands. How does one go about compromising one's beliefs that had become part of a person's prideful dogma? The Cepee is surprised to learn that the "solution" to many religious disputes was simply to murder a noncompliant person and be done with it.

Besides, there could be no resolution to differing views among some humans because a number of religious extremists would never countenance an examination of their beliefs. By eliminating the disobedient heathens, the holy air was cleansed. The killings often included innocent bystanders who were in the wrong place at the wrong time.

For a small but significant number of humans, the mutual acceptance of others' views—to live and let live—entailed forgiveness and acceptance; four letter words to those worshippers who practiced their faith, not through honest soul searching, but rote memory and associated mime-like actions. The concept of tolerance was beyond their horizon.

To further complicate matters, many humans read their holy books, written centuries ago, in a literal way, interpreting each passage as if ancient writers were not capable of allegory or were not subject to error. As mentioned, these ancient writers were ignorant of the discoveries made in the humans' later times that contradicted passages in the holy books. To cite one example: the antiquity of the earth and evidence of a long process in the development of the human race.

In spite of these facts, many religious people (for example, about 40 percent of U.S. adults) believed the earth and universe were created *after* the times in which irrefutable proof revealed humans were very much in existence. Ignoring much of the knowledge gained after the times their holy books were written, they claimed God created the human within the last 10,000 years. It was another example of the Ignorant Therefore Doctrinaire Syndrome.

The basic problem was a cast-in-stone mentality. Once a holy book was written, any change to religious beliefs for which a holy book had dictated was blasphemy. Through the hundreds of years after religion was conceived, the human race underwent changes, notably in scientific knowledge. Yet the holy books that dictated the behavior of members of the human race remained the same, not taking into account a dynamic world of changing technologies, cultures, and values. Not to mention, knowledge.

These humans believed in other aspects of science. They favored science that would prolong their lives, put a man on the moon, create the Internet, and build a smart phone in which the central component was made of sand. But these people were science cherry pickers. They picked the part of science that fit their opinions. Their cell phones could not exist if science did not exist. Such facts were immaterial to their views on a matter in which they believed, but which science could discount.

Notwithstanding these astonishing mental blocks, the majority of the prevalent religions forbade killing, covetousness, acquisitiveness, and other antisocial traits that had been built into the humans' genomes over many centuries. Most of the humans' societies held themselves together by practicing some form of religion. If their social order was indeed social, it was often because of religion.

Some philosophers who lived in the twenty-first and twenty-second centuries claimed the problem stemmed not so much from the practice of a religion, as it did from the malpractice of a religion.

Upon reading this passage in the Human Archives, the Cepee thinks: *I am not so sure about this claim. Yes, my ancestors' religions did offer many benefits to the race. But passages in their holy books...let me see, here it is: Deuteronomy 20:10-18, says:*

When you march up to attack a city, make its people an offer of peace. If they accept and open their gates, all the people in it shall be subject to forced labor and shall work for you. If they refuse to make peace and they engage you in battle, lay siege to that city. When the Lord your God delivers it into your hand, put to the sword all the men in it. As for the women, the children, the livestock and everything else in the city, you may take these as plunder for yourselves. And you may use the plunder the Lord your God gives you from your enemies. This is how you are to treat all the cities that are at a distance from you and do not belong to the nations nearby.

However, in the cities of the nations the Lord your God is giving you as an inheritance, do not leave alive anything that breathes. Completely destroy them—the Hittites, Amorites, Canaanites, Perizzites, Hivites and Jebusites—as the Lord your God has commanded you. Otherwise, they will teach you to follow all the detestable things they do in worshiping their gods, and you will sin against the Lord your God.

The Cepee continues his thoughts: *So many of the humans' religious teachings contradicted one another. Time and again, we Cepees read about the benevolent characteristics of their gods, for the tolerance and forgiveness that these gods proclaimed. Yet here is yet another passage from Exodus 34:6-7 of the Bible that counters these claims about the compassionate nature of their religions:* "Keeping mercy for thousands, forgiving iniquity and transgression and sin, and that will by no means clear the guilty; visiting the iniquity of the fathers upon the children, and upon the children's children, unto the third and to the fourth generation."

Perhaps I should not be surprised. After all, the humans' holy books were written by humans. My ancestors were contradictory in almost everything they did. For their every why, they had a why not? For every opinion they had a counter opinion. Why should their holy books and religions have been free from inconsistencies? That would be counter to the basic makeup of my forebears. The Cepee returns to the archives.

Regardless of the humans' acceptance or rejection of religion or their opinions about the religions' founders, many members of the race recognized religion provided succor to their miseries and fears. Thus, they embraced religion. It was a joyful part of their lives.

It should also be said that the vast majority of humans who practiced a religion used their devotion for the purpose of aiding fellow humans. They had not an ounce of religious-based aggression in their veins. Quite the opposite, they did great things while on earth. Charity and compassion were their watchwords.

No better example could be provided than the ship *Africa Mercy*. It sailed on seas off West Africa, stopping for months in ports of nations that had almost no medical services. Staffed by Christians, it offered hope and cures to thousands of destitute people who had "diseases that could be easily cured if those patients could reach modern medical care."[3] Their motivation? Christian charity.

Another example was the Mormon Church. Because it had differing views about Jesus and the Bible, it was often characterized as a cult by other Christians. (The Christians had come into existence before this church, and therefore had unofficially ordained themselves to declare which factions were cults or true religions.) Regardless of its reputation among assorted religious enclaves, the Mormons' modern system was a model of decorum, non-aggression, and self-supporting independence. Its charitable works were remarkable. Their motivation? Christian offerings. (Granted, with a lot of missionary goals on their agenda.)

Notwithstanding these organizations, which included a large number of gentle and kind people, the facts were evident that religion had catastrophic effects on humans and their societies. This tragedy came about because a small segment of the human population—small in relation to the number of humans—used religion to scale the Human Tribal Hierarchies of power, pride, and wealth.

Believers and Nonbelievers. Before discussing these matters, it is worth noting that many of the humans' genocides and related pillages did not occur because of the belief in a religion. Many of them occurred because of the absence in the belief of a religion. The nonbelievers often wiped out the believers because the believers believed. The USSR's Stalin was a prime example. Like his predecessor Lenin, Stalin said religion was an opiate and had to be removed from society. To meet his goal, he killed over 100,000 believers in two years alone (the 1937-1938 purges).[4] Estimates of his "removal" of believers range from several hundred thousand to millions.

In addition to this toll, and introduced earlier, the earth's soil was fertilized by countless corpses of believers who were killed by other believers. These believers believed those they killed believed in the wrong religion. One example was the Crusades. Spanning three centuries (eleventh, twelfth, and thirteenth), Catholics and Muslims fought for control of religious turf in the Jerusalem area. The word *countless* is appropriate to describe the number of warriors and noncombatants who were killed. During those early days, taking body counts was more of an art than a science. Historians estimate the death toll from the Crusades numbered between one million and three million people.

This count included those who died in the 1212 Children's Crusade. It was so-named because Catholic children from France and Germany believed their cause was more righteous than older crusaders whose extended time on earth made them more prolific sinners than their children. According to the history books (and this crusade is open to question), the campaign was a disaster. Many of the youths who survived were taken as slaves by the Muslims.

The Disproportionate Ratio Effect Raises Its Head Again

In spite of these legacies, most humans simply wished to be left alone to practice their religion, to communicate with their particular deity, and to let others do the same. But the Disproportionate Ratio Effect came into play to wreak havoc on the species. As introduced in Chapter 2, the ratio is defined as n:m, where the value of n is very small and the value of m is very large. In this context, a very few (n) religious charlatans and spiritual sociopaths severely affected the well being, even the future of the (m) human race.

Which Tale Was Stranger?

Chapter 5 describes the debates among scientists about the origin and evolution of the universe. Many of the theories were vehemently debated and defended. Likewise, this chapter describes equally heated (and sometimes deadly) arguments about which religious creed was true and correct.

Before putting the scientific issue aside and focusing on religion itself, here are a few more thoughts on the matter. The average person on the street was not well versed in the details of religious or scientific postulations and proclamations. The claims of the religious and scientific communities created doubt and caused confusion. As examples:

- A scientific idea: An unknown number of universes created instantaneously from near nothingness?
- A religious idea: A son of God created from a human virgin?

- A scientific idea: A never-ending universe?
- A religious idea: A never-ending life?

- A scientific idea: A black hole from which nothing leaves?
- A religious idea: An earth, from which Jesus leaves, but later returns?

The scientist claimed the priest was not attuned to the logical realities of existence. The priest had no ready answer to such a blanket claim. So, the priest countered by asking the scientist to explain the "reality" of the first instant of the Big Bang.[5] The scientist had no ready answer either, as their equations could not factor in what occurred in the first few nanoseconds of the Big Bang.

Multiple Universes? More Than One Jesus?

One of the most intractable issues facing the two communities was the scientific view that multiple universes contained duplicate and identical planets, a subject discussed in Chapter 5. In this multiverse, there were multiple earths as well. Some of these planets had identical cultures and histories to that of earth. This multiplicity included more than one Jesus, multiple Muhammads, and duplicate Buddhas.

This theoretical possibility went to the heart of earth-centric religions. Jesus, Muhammad, Budda, and other religious icons were revered figures to millions of people. The thought of multiple copies of these honored beings was considered blasphemous to their believers.

But some religious souls were not so inflexible about the matter. They were not upset with the idea of more than one Jesus trekking around the multiverse. Their idea was that God created multiple images of Jesus to help spread the word around the expansive cosmos about God's work in this multiverse.

Aping Apes?

An even more intractable issue that disturbed and aroused a substantial number of people in the religious community (make that many communities, but the focus here is religion) revolved around the humans' ancestry. The conventional scientific view claimed humans descended from a common ancestor of the ape (more accurately, the chimpanzee).

This idea, based on impartial investigations of fossils and DNA, did not claim humans came directly from the chimp. The assertion did not presuppose that sometime in the past, two chimps mated, and nine months later, out dropped a baby human. It claimed that humans and chimps, while different species, came from the same branch in the evolutionary tree.[6]

But true to the Ignorant Therefore Doctrinaire Syndrome, a cadre of prideful and prejudiced people brought forth scathing denunciations of this theory. They claimed this sort of evolution was a blasphemy against their holy books. They insisted humans came from a white man, who God created from (white?) dust. They also insisted the first woman came from this man's rib. Consequently, in this first instance of human cloning, the woman was also white.[7]

These people, who were of fair skin, modest noses, and thin lips, said they could not have come from an ape. This lowly beast was ugly and unintelligent. The very idea of any kind of kinship to the ape, however far removed in the branches of a family tree, was revolting to these individuals.

Interestingly, the ape's dark countenance, wide nose, and large lips looked eerily similar to the African noble savages who supposedly benevolent humans had captured and turned into slaves. These "savages," who were obviously members of the human race, were considered by their captors to be subhuman and, quite possibly, a relative of the ape.

But something was amiss. If the ape was indeed a remote cousin of the slave, the slaveholder had placed a relative, however distant, in chains. As the supposedly superior white-skinned slaveholder looked at his supposedly inferior black-skinned captive, he beheld a being—possibly a distant relative—subdued and bound in iron shackles. What were the reactions of the white humans to this situation?

Some thought: *This African man resembles those apes behind bars at a local zoo. They must be cousins. Apes are dangerous, so must be their kin. Chaining the ape and the African, keeping them in their place, will keep us safe.* Others thought: *This African man resembles me. We must be cousins. I've chained and subjugated a member of my own species, all because he and his forebears, subject to Mother Nature, developed dark skin to protect themselves from an equatorial sun.*

This latter human had deep reservations about his position in life relative to the black man. For the black man, it was a position largely governed by being born in an area on earth with a lot of sunshine with an associated need for ample melanin in the skin. For the white man, who had lived on parts of the earth where the sun's rays were not as intense, less melanin in his skin gave him a white-like countenance.

The Cepee pauses: *Am I reading that some of my white-skinned forebears equated their disdain for apes with their disdain for black-skinned humans? That apes and blacks looked too much alike for the fair-skinned human to accept? It's illogical and frightening nonsense, but it appears to be the case.*

The Cepee is on to something that he will discover in a more complete way later: Regardless of a religious credo (ancient humans likely did not have a religion), the early *Homo sapiens* developed a well-founded suspicion of any stranger in their midst who was different. These strangers often meant danger. The difference could have been the manner of clothing worn or an intonation of a spoken word. It could have been facial features or skin color.

These suspicions and intolerances were keys to survival for the pre-modern human. But for the modern human, they were for the most part, irrelevant. Diversification became a more accepted pattern of life, at least for many of the humans' tribes. For others, these heretofore species-enhancing intolerances became prejudices. They no longer had merit, but true to the old saying, "habits die hard," these tribes clung to them throughout their lives.

Prejudice against those who were different showed itself in religions, the subject of this chapter. This kind of discrimination also showed itself in practically every aspect of the humans' behavior. Even though it was a holdover from ancient times, acts of prejudice created enormous problems in modern times.

Religion and the Theories

Some religions claimed the earth was created by God (with no mention of a Big Bang) in six days, not in a few nanoseconds—with God taking a seventh day off to rest from his arduous labors. And while the scientists wrote millions of pages of documentation on the development and evolution of the earth, many of the religious writers covered the same bases with about one page in the Bible—their documentation.

As introduced in Chapter 5, some scientists postulated mankind would never know the complete story of the universe (and therefore God) because of the Observer Effect. The idea was that in order to know God, one had to understand how an atom functioned. This requirement was important because the atom formed the underpinning of the universe. In order to understand God's universe, God's atom had to be understood as well.

However, to understand an atom, one had to observe an atom functioning. This notion seemed straightforward, except for one problem. A collection of atoms could be observed, but an individual atom was shy. The observation of one atom could not reveal the behavior of this atom, because the act of observation would change the behavior of the atom.[8] The humans were never able to resolve this dilemma.

St. Thomas Aquinas did not know about an atom and its introverted personality. Nonetheless, with fewer than 300 words, he offered a way for humans to deal with the inherent contradictions between science and religion. He addressed the conflicts between religious philosophers and scientists by distinguishing between faith and reason:[9]

> St. Thomas Aquinas's approach to the problem of faith and reason denoted as great a concession to rationalism in relation to the Augustinian solution, as the Augustinian solution had been in relation to the antinationalism of Tertullian. St. Thomas conceived of faith and knowledge as divine in origin; therefore, conflict between them could never be real, only apparent. He thought that the previous trouble had been due largely to the fact that theologians introduced theological criteria into philosophy, and philosophers attempted to philosophize in theology.

> Faith is not contrary to reason, but above reason, and the results of faith are no less certain than those of reason; they are, in fact, more certain because faith is based on direct revelation of God, and therefore closer to the source of all truth than is philosophy, which is based on human insight. If articles of faith could be rationally proved, they would become philosophy, and theology as a separate branch of thought would become unnecessary and disappear; the articles of faith, because of their very nature, however, cannot be intellectually proved...What man can therefore believe, he cannot know, and what he can know, he cannot believe.

St. Thomas Aquinas provided a view of faith and philosophy, not faith and science. As one human put it, "Religion, the philosophy of the heart...and philosophy, the religion of the mind."[10] Nonetheless, his ideas opened a way for the secular scientist to deal with religion and the believers to deal with science.

The Cepee pauses a moment from his Human Archives research. He thinks: *It is also reasonable to claim, Religion, the science of the heart...and science, the religion of the mind. Both ideas are in harmony with the wisdom of St. Thomas Aquinas's beliefs.* The Cepee returns to the archives for further study.

Religion and Aggression

It is believed by some historians that the first wide-scale occurrence of religious-based patriotism and aggression occurred around 3,000 BC in a region known as the Fertile Crescent, considered by many to be the cradle of Western civilization. The Crescent was located in Iraq and eastern Syria.[11] In this region, each community (town) built a temple to honor a god, who was believed to be the town's owner. The citizens labored to understand what the town god desired, because if the god became displeased, misfortune fell upon the town.

A few people convinced the town's citizens that they knew the god's wishes. As a result of their public relations campaigns, they were able to claim privileges, such as supervising the rituals they established to gain the god's favor.

The daily goings-on in a town went well with this approach. The god's worshippers welcomed the intermediaries. After all, these mediators helped an ignorant resident understand why his tithe to them would aid in the worshipper's eventual but perpetual residence in a pleasant garden in the afterlife.

This procedure was especially beneficial to the intermediaries. By knowing god's wishes, they became powerful and wealthy. By managing their god's property, such as places of worship, they were able to take control of the most important facet of humans' life: turf.

As these intermediaries became clerics for the god or gods, they built small windows in the walls of the churches. These openings were used by non-clerics to pass food—through the clerics inside the building who were manning the windows—for the gods to eat. The food was passed through the clerics in more ways than one.[12]

Eventually, matters did not go well between towns that worshipped competing gods. Frequent inter-town wars occurred to prove the claim, "My god is better than your god." The assertion, new at that time, became a popular proclamation in later years, often shouted just before one religious group attacked another. From this modest start, religious-based wars became a dominant part of the humans' lives.

As time moved on, this type of behavior manifested itself in other parts of the world. For example, the Aztec gods were different from the Inca gods. Even the various gods' prophets, seers, and disciples were different: Jesus, Muhammad, Buddha, Mary Baker Eddy, and Joseph Smith, to cite a few. And as societies grew from a few members of a tribe to scores, hundreds, and later millions, they developed elaborate customs, rituals, and warfare to advance their beliefs and make certain their neighbors came to the same point of view.

If only humans could have recognized that there was indeed a religion, *but many acceptable versions of that religion*, their self-imposed acts of religious intolerance and brutality might have been mitigated.[13] But this fanciful vision was not to be. In certain areas of the modern humans' world, such as northern Africa and the Middle East, one person's liberating religion was a contrived falsehood to another, a falsehood that had to be eradicated.

The Crusaders and Their Crusading Work

For about 180 years (during the eleventh through thirteenth-centuries), Christians and Muslims launched nine major wars to capture or recapture (and restore access to) Jerusalem, a sacred city to the Jewish, Christian, and Islamic faiths.[14] The stated motive was to reestablish the religion that had been disestablished from the previous reestablishment of the other religion.

Religious turf was not the only motive. The first crusade unleashed by European Catholics—and ordained by the pope—gained support from the fragmenting Roman Empire by promising the Empire leaders some of the spoils (including land) of the crusade.

End results? One million to three million people were killed, representing 0.3 to 2.3 percent of the world's population. No permanent conquests of the Holy Land were made by the Christians or Muslims. The once mutual respect between Christians and Muslims became sentiments of resentment and intolerance, attitudes that persisted into the modern human and early Cepee eras. In addition, the Crusades helped foster a revival of anti-Semitism.

The Cepee asks himself: *Who gained from these wars?* He delves further into the Human Archives to find: The current rulers gained much. In addition, "The removal of a considerable number of unruly barons to the east also helped the growth of monarchical power..."[15]

The Cepee has answered his own question: *Those who gained were already at the top of their hierarchies. They gained more of what they already had. They had much. They ended up with too much. I recall a Jewish proverb from an earlier entry in the archives, "Where there is too much, something is missing."*

As suggested in this narrative about the Crusades, religious-based wars had a long history, even up to the beginning of the Cepee ascendency. As one example of a more recent "crusade" in 2012, an extreme Islamist group in Nigeria began killing off otherwise peaceful Christians. The killers proclaimed they would continue to kill and "threatened that Christians 'will not know peace again' until they accept[ed] Islam.'"[16]

Missionary Fervor

As suggested in the quote above, many of the origins of humans' warfare could be traced to the belief that a religious tribe, say tribe A, was obligated to become missionaries and convert persons of other religions to tribe A's religion. As one example, the Bible contained a section known as the Great Commission.[17] The gospel according to Matthew stated, "Therefore go and make disciples of all nations, baptizing them in the name of the Father and of the Son and of the Holy Spirit, and teaching them to obey everything I have commanded you."[18]

One could certainly question the practicality of this so-called Great Commission. Given humans' turfmanship, coupled with their pride, it was doubtful many of them would have accepted another religion to be their own. To complicate matters, while tribe A missionaries were busy trying to convert tribe B's missionaries, tribe

B's missionaries were busy trying to convert tribe A's missionaries. Conflict was inevitable.

Fortunately, many religions did not include missionary zealots. The members of these religions had no desire to convert anyone. They just wanted to be left alone. Unfortunately, some of these people were not in a position of power to influence the other religious factions. Often, they were so powerless they became the coveted objects of the messianic zealots who were obsessed with converting them to the "true" religion. As stated, if these religious candidates remained unconvinced about taking on the new spiritual credo, they were often enslaved or killed.

The idea (and motive) was to remove the opposition. If needed, the other tribe was eradicated. It was a necessary action in order to preserve a tribal hierarchy.

Why the Missionaries Were Not the Missioned

Why were some humans destined to be missionaries and others the "missioned"? Without question, the missionaries were the preferred religious tribe. After all, they received the benefits of occupying the upper rungs of the religious Human Tribal Hierarchies. The ownership of vast riches of land and property and the possession of wealth and power became part of a missionary's lifestyle.

The answer is simple. Other human tribal hierarchies, other pecking orders, came into play. Some humans were the missionaries and not the missioned because the missionary humans had succeeded earlier in their lives—often through the geographical roll of the dice—in ascending the upper rungs of the power and wealth pecking orders, a topic discussed in Chapter 3.

Indeed, if the missionaries had *not* been sufficiently powerful and wealthy (as well as acquisitive), they would have been the missioned. In turn, the missioned, if they had possessed the proper tools, would have been the missionaries. The scenario of thousands of humans paying respects at St. Peters in Rome instead of smoking a pipe inside a kiva in Taos was not determined by who practiced the "correct" or "best" religion. It was who had the power and wealth to dictate the religion that was to be practiced.

Did the Navajo Indian convert the Catholic? Did the New Guinea native change the Lutheran? The African Pygmy, the Baptist? The Australian Bushman, the Mormon? No. The Navajo Indian, the New Guinea native, the African Pygmy, and the Australian Bushman were noble savages. By the very nature of how they lived and because of the geographical roll of the dice, they were relegated to the bottom rungs of the hierarchical pecking orders. In contrast, the Catholics, Lutherans, Baptists, and Mormons belonged to tribes occupying the upper rungs of the power and wealth pecking orders.[19]

Consequently, the humans' religious laws ordained the non-noble savages to subjugate the noble savages—killing them, if necessary—in order to convert them to their religion. The powerful and wealthy became the missionaries. The powerless and poor became the missioned.

Upon studying this aspect of the human, the Cepee asks: *What happened if the competing religions decided not to take an advantage in regard to power and wealth? What if, say, a Christian tribe was as well armed and economically advantaged as an Islamic tribe? Did they stand off, allowing each other to practice their religion?*

As the Cepee delves further into the Human Archives, he finds the answer. Generally, yes. Often those in power had a live-and-let-live approach. It was not unusual for a believer to accept a nonbeliever's refusal to convert to the believer's religion. This notion is surprising to the Cepee, because tolerance between religious factions was not a preponderant theme in human history. Yet under certain circumstances, the human race was capable of notable religious forbearance. Disparate religious groups often tolerated and even supported one another.

Even in the Middle East, where members of the same religion (but different denominations within the religion) routinely beheaded one another, some societies and nations were remarkably tolerant. For example, the United Arab Emirates (UAE) let its citizens pursue the religion of their choice.

As another example, in the country of Yemen, the Ibadhi religion was practiced by over 70 percent of the population. Yet this majority let the minority religions alone to practice their faith. This tolerance was not insignificant, as one difference dealt with how long a sinner would stay in hell.

The Ibāḍīs believed that anyone who entered hell would burn forever. In contrast, Sunnis believed those who entered hell would live there (granted, quite uncomfortably) for a fixed time. This bath of fire would purify them of their shortcomings. Thereafter, they would be sent to Paradise. A bit of sacrifice for an eternity of pleasure.

If so, then what circumstance or circumstances tilted the seesaw of religious acceptance toward widescale religious mayhem and killing? The answer is that humans' religious altruism was often defeated by a very few individuals who could not control their avarice, pride, lust for power, and inability to forgive past transgressions. These people had abandoned or never espoused the ideas of tolerance and acceptance of a differing view. The small numbers afflicted with this societal illness was another example of the Disproportionate Ratio in action.

Pizarro and His Missionary Work

Religious-based deadly aggression did not happen only recently in the humans' time on earth, such as the twenty-first and twenty-second centuries. As an earlier example, on November 16, 1532, at a South American highland in present-day Peru, the Spanish soldier Francisco Pizarro subjugated an astounding number of people. Acting for the Holy Roman Emperor Charles V, with 164 soldiers Pizarro conquered an army of about 80,000 warriors of the Inca emperor Atahualpa. On this day, religious zeal contributed to the death of about 7,000 Inca citizens. The Spaniards made these comments about their slaughter of these native people:[20]

> The...labors...and battles of the Spaniards...will cause joy to the faithful and terror to the infidels. For this reason and for the glory of God our Lord, and for the service of the Catholic Imperial Majesty...[I] write this narrative...It will be the glory of God, because [the Spanish soldiers] have conquered and brought into our holy Catholic Faith so vast a number of heathens, aided by His holy guidance.

The humans' actions were nothing more than pious poison. How could one rationalize this philosophy? The humans only needed to summon up their self-interested interpretation of God's presence and their desire to vent their aggression, and then proceed to execute, if not anti-religious concepts then certainly anti-humane acts, all in the name of God.

Killing Machines: Across the Species

The story of Pizarro is not intended to cast aspersions on a solitary group of people. In this retrospective examination of the human race, it is merely cited as an example of the disguises the humans employed to play out their lust for wealth and power. In this instance the camouflage was religion.

If it was not Pizarro, it was someone else. In the same part of the world, the Spaniards' pillage and carnage paled in comparison to the Aztecs' slaughtering practices. During the 1300s, the Aztecs developed a large, complex society built on religion and militarism. The religious cadre extracted human sacrifice from neighbors. The military cadre extracted tribute from those neighbors who had survived the religious sacrifice. The empire was not self-sustaining because it did not produce its own wealth. It relied on a steady supply of "payments under duress" from its neighbors by threatening or carrying out military reprisals. The Aztecs relied upon a steady supply of bodies for sacrifice to their god, the sun.[21]

> The Aztecs saw the sun as a warrior who fought a daily battle across the sky against the forces of darkness. As long as the sun remained strong, he would prevail in combat and the universe would survive. The Aztecs believed they could keep the sun strong by nourishing him with a source of vital energy: human blood, preferably the vigorous blood of warriors captured in battle. To the Aztecs, unceasing warfare and human sacrifice were sacred duties upon which the preservation of the universe depended.

Before another Spanish conqueror, Cortes, wiped out the Aztecs with small arms and smallpox, this tribe was killing approximately 50,000 people a year as sacrificial victims to the sun, their version of a god.[22] Cortes stopped the sacrificial tributes, but continued the economic tributes by bankrupting the Aztecs with payments (tributes) to Spain's church and monarchy.

As suggested with the examinations of the Spaniards and the Aztecs, intra-species killing was not confined to, say, the noble savages or the non-noble savages. All participated. Indeed, the early European explorers to North America correctly concluded that carnage and massacre was routinely practiced among "les savages."[23]

Cultural Assimilation

Later, in the seventeenth through nineteenth centuries, the Europeans continued their quest to force many people of the noble savage world to practice the Europeans' religious beliefs. Taking heed of the well-known British boast, "I would annex the planets if I could," they proceeded to take control of entire cultures around the globe.[24]

Once again taking their pride to extremes, if they could not annex the savages, they eliminated them. These genocides, performed in the name of cultural assimilation, sought to convert the savages to the correct religion: Christianity.

This absorption process was dubbed as making religious apples. The Indians, as they were called, would still be seen as red on the outside, but they would be white on the inside. Their pagan skins would be red, but their Christian souls would be white.

Even into the twentieth century, Indian spiritual leaders in America ran the risk of serving jail time for practicing their religion. What had happened to this country's vaunted freedom of religion credo? The Indians were not practicing a religion. They were practicing a spiritual cult. Thus, the freedom of religion idea was not invoked. The Indian medicine man was forced to take spiritually lethal doses of the white man's religious medicine.

Small wonder many of these oppressed people clung to one of their ancient religious traditions: ingesting hallucinogenic drugs. The peyote cactus became an elixir beyond its religious significance. Fortunately for these oppressed souls, the United States passed the Native American Free Exercise of Religion act (in 1993), which allowed the tribe of Peyote Indians to use the peyote cactus in their religious practices. The humans, practicing the Feel Good Law, had a large number of white-skinned apples applying for membership into this red-skinned tribe.

A Few Exceptions to the Rule

Not all humans fought to subjugate their neighbors. As examples, the Toda, Tikopia, Dorobo, and Copper Eskimo were physically isolated from other tribes and could not fight with their distant neighbors, an example of the Geographically Undesirable Law in action.[25] This law stated: A potential attacker would not go to the trouble of assaulting a potential victim if the victim was located in an inconvenient place in relation to the potential attacker.

The ancient tribes' funding and staffing of warriors to support geographically undesirable wars would have placed an unsustainable burden on tribal budgets. However, within these tribes, they fought and killed one another, just to stay attuned to their basic human natures.

In the humans' early days, the Geographically Undesirable Law held sway over most of the earth because humans were unable to interact across dispersed parts of the globe. But with the advent of airplanes, the law became more circumscribed. And with the advent of modern nuclear weapons, missiles, the highly mobile drone, as well as the ambulatory terrorist, this law became obsolete in regard to world-wide warfare. All locations on earth became, if not geographically desirable, then certainly geographically feasible to attack.

More Religious Killings, Courtesy of al Qaeda and Others

The story of Pizarro's murders and the Aztec's human sacrifices took place a few centuries before the humans began their self-change procedures. One could ask, did this race alter its behavior and the practice of its religions during its later times on earth? To answer this question, the remainder of this chapter places us in the early to mid-twenty-first century, the time when humans began the EGO,

ILLS, SANE, and ASSES programs in earnest. The focus is on two religions: Islam and Christianity.

Islamic doctrine contained passages about a concept called jihad. Some Muslims understood the word to mean "holy war." However, the word in Arabic was originally defined as "to struggle" or "to exhaust one's effort" in order to please God. This effort could be individual or collective. It also applied to leading a virtuous life, such as helping other Muslims through charity or education, preaching Islam, and fighting to defend Muslims from aggression.

A number of people took a different view of jihad. For example, a Muslim branch, the Sunnis, believed jihad was fulfilled by the heart, the tongue, the hand, and the sword. In contrast, groups such as the Imami and Bohra-Ismaili Shias were forbidden from participating in a hostile jihad. As a whole, many Muslims believed war was a very small part of jihad and was taken only for self-defense or in defense of justice, such as the protection of homes and home turf. (Thus, the Palestinian issue was viewed by many Muslims as a justifiable cause for a jihad-based war.)

However, to some Islamic militants, their concept of jihad justified acts of murder against innocent people, all in the name of Allah. This issue was confusing. Did this religion sanction killing or did it not? A passage from the Human Archives revealed this information.[26]

> Islamic legal scholars, during the early centuries of Islam, divided the world into dar al-Islam (abode of Islam) and dar al-harb (abode of war—that is, of non-Islamic rule). Islamic law further stated that it was the duty of dar al-Islam to strive to bring as much of dar al-harb as possible under its control, preferably by conversion but by force if necessary. The Qur'an (Koran),[27] the sacred scripture of Islam, states that those who die in this type of jihad, while fighting for the faith, automatically become martyrs and are awarded a special place in heaven. Most modern branches of Islam, however, stress the inner, spiritual jihad.

But not all branches. Tolerance was foreign to a militant sect called al Qaeda and its leader, Osama bin Laden.[28] The following passage was part of the al Qaeda training manual.[29]

In the name of Allah, the merciful and compassionate. To those champions who avowed the truth day and night...And wrote with their blood and sufferings these phrases...The confrontation that we are calling for with the apostate regimes does not know Socratic debates...Platonic ideals...nor Aristotelian diplomacy. But it knows the dialogue of bullets, the ideals of assassination, bombing, and destruction, and the diplomacy of the cannon and machine-gun.

Islamic governments have never and will never be established through peaceful solutions and cooperative councils. They are established as they [always] have been by pen and gun, by word and bullet, by tongue and teeth.

During an interview with a grand imam, a position of authority and influence in the Islamic faith, Mohammed Sayed Tantawi stated jihad was purely defensive and could not be aggressive.[30] Furthermore, he emphasized jihad could be proclaimed only by a head of state or a recognized leader of Arab people when Arab lands were invaded, great numbers of Arab peoples were abused, displaced, or exiled, or when the tenets of Islam were directly attacked or abused. He quoted the Quran (al-Baqarah2:190) which stated:

Fight in Allah's cause against those who wage war against you, but do not commit aggression, for verily, Allah does not love aggressors.

The imam distinguished between jihad and irhab. Whereas jihad was defensive, the word *irhab* was interpreted by some militant Muslims to mean the waging of war. For these militants, it could consist of aggressive violence against civilians. However, the imam stated Islamic law forbade killing innocent people, a retreating enemy, a surrendering enemy, or the destruction of buildings and civic centers.

According to this Islamic scholar, Osama bin Laden's philosophy was flawed. Like so many other killers in the human race, he succumbed to the Deadly Trinity; in this situation, in the guise of religion. Killing armed combatants was one thing, slaying civilians was quite another.

First, Kill. Second, Justify. Osama bin Laden's warriors and later successors had no religious justification for the killing of noncombatants, including women and children. An email on this subject was written by al Qaeda *after* the organization had masterminded and executed attacks on civilian populations.[31] The email was a form letter sent to various Islamic scholars.[32] If the theme of the letter had not been so frightening, one might have thought a script writer had created it for a satiric skit. As before, comments in brackets have been added by this writer:

> Dear highly respected _____
>
> I present this to you as your humble brother...concerning the preparation of the lawful study that I am doing on the killing of civilians. This is a very sensitive case—as you know—especially these days...[And especially for those civilians being killed.]
>
>> It is very important that you provide your opinion on this matter, which has been forced upon us as an essential issue in the course and ideology of the Muslim movement...
>> [Our] questions are:
>
> 1. Since you are the representative of the Islamic Jihad group, what is your lawful stand on the killing of civilians, specifically when women and children are included? And please explain the legitimate law concerning those who are deliberately killed.
> 2. According to your law, how can you justify the killing of innocent victims because of a claim of oppression? [If the victims were innocent, they were not involved in the oppressive acts to begin with.]
> 3. What is your stand concerning a group that supports the killing of civilians, including women and children?
>
> With our prayers, wishing your success and stability.

The Cepee puts the Human Archives on hold. He reflects: *The al Qaeda killed people who had nothing to do with their wars. Yet they were not certain their killings were religiously sanctified. What if the responses to their questions directed them not to kill women and children? How could they go about resurrecting the persons they already murdered? They could not, but their damage was done. I am reminded again of one of humans' Rules of Life, The Graveyard Shift Law.*

Even after the 9/11 attacks, bin Laden had not attained sufficient religious rationalization for justifying the destruction of the World Trade Center buildings. The justification for his cause was provided months later by a Saudi cleric who wrote "A Treatise on the Legal Status of Using Weapons of Mass Destruction against Infidels."[33] This missive explained why using weapons of mass destruction on believers and nonbelievers alike was, under Islamic law, lawful.

Osama bin Laden and his al Qaeda comrades first murdered women, children, and other noncombatants and then looked to their holy men to justify and rationalize their actions. Holy Wars? Jihad? Nonsense. These wanton murderers were doing nothing more than playing out their lust for power, pride, turfmanship, and revenge.

Bin Laden was eventually tracked down by warriors of the United States, a nation his own warriors had attacked. This psychopath's minions assassinated thousands of innocent civilians, all in the name of jihad. Revenge was had by the United States when bin Laden's family hideout was discovered. During the subsequent attack, bin Laden was killed.

Yet, unlike his debased style of combat, the U.S. warriors left unharmed most members of his family, including assorted wives and children. The Cepee thinks: *A fine touch of irony.*

Equal Extermination Opportunity (EEO) Assassins

The Islamic terrorists did not discriminate between civilians or military, between white, black, or yellow races, between young or old. What was good for one was good for the other. What was good for the Christian was good for the Jew, the Hindu, or the Buddhist. Even a parent, if a nonbeliever, could be in their crosshairs, a turn around of the ancient human practice of succoring and protecting one's family:[34]

Allah warns the parents, siblings, offspring, and other relatives of the Muslim that their relation to him will be of no use to them on the day of judgment, if they have not themselves died as true believers. So, don't be complacent, or let the Devil deceive you into thinking that your connections will intercede for you on that terrible day.

Their cardinal EEO rule was: All people associated with their enemies fell under their sword. Children? Women? Noncombatants? No matter. They were equal beneficiaries of the terrorists' EEO program.

From the standpoint of body counts, the EEO program had a decided advantage over a program named Rules of Engagement (ROE), a policy practiced by the United States. These rules required a warrior to take extreme caution when dealing with non-combatants and helpless combatants.[35] In contrast, EEO stated all people could be targets of the terrorists' blood lusts.

As suggested above, exceptions to the EEO rule might be Muslims. Religious largesse came into play here, although, in several Muslim countries, Muslims killed other Muslims as part of their penal code. For example, Saudi Arabia executed Muslim men and women for assorted transgressions against Islam. In addition, Islamic intra-faith vendettas were as common as inter-faith feuds: Sunnis beheading blindfolded Shias and Shias shooting blindfolded Sunnis. This mayhem occurred because one side accused the other side of claiming an incorrect religious lineage from their prophet, Muhammad.

The humans often justified their murderous measures by quoting passages in their holy books. They avowed to practice their religions in accordance with the dictates of those documents. As discussed, these books contained passages directing the followers of the books' credos to carry out some appalling actions on their own race.

The Cepee gives this contradictory and confusing aspect of his ancestors' behavior considerable thought: *In relation to the teachings of one of their revered beings, Jesus, it appears the problem was their neglecting his advice. Their behavior often disavowed his counsel, his warnings. It mattered not if a human was a believer, an agnostic, or an atheist, Jesus had some Cepee-like ideas that could have improved the humans' lot. He was zealous for sure and sometimes one-sided, deficiencies that he himself discouraged.*

But then, Jesus was supposed to be…well, partly human, from his mother's side. So why could he not be partially contradictory, just like the human side of his gene pool?

That stated, the Cepee concludes that the holy books of Islam and Christianity, written during aggressive times, contained their fair share of passages that fostered aggression. But how could they not? After all, they were written by humans.

Animosities within Religions

When first encountering the history of the humans in the Human Archives, one might think the practice of a specific religion would assure peace and tolerance among the people who practiced the religion. But such was not the case. Religion partially cloaked, but did not completely disguise, humans' genetically based distrust of practically any difference shown by another person: skin color, clothing, hairstyle, covering the face with a veil or a beard, speech, even inflections of the same language. These differences raised an observer's suspicions, however subtle, of this different human, a point introduced in previous chapters. Suspicions even carried over to different interpretations of the same religious faith.

As mentioned above, one example of these differences was the animosity existing between two Muslim denominations: the Sunni and the Shia. From the view of a Sunni:[36]

> They were not Shia. Quite the contrary. They were proud to be Sunni. …To them the Shia were a heretical and miserably misguided sect whose loyalties lay with "the Persians"—the Shia of Iran. Unlettered Sunnis (as well as a few who were well educated) spread stories of how the Shia had forked tails hidden beneath their [clothes] and enjoyed unnatural sexual practices. …They would gather in their husayniyahs (meeting rooms) to switch off the lights, strip off their clothes, and engage in

writhing mounds of group sex. The resulting babies, many Sunnis believed, were then venerated by the Shia community and grew up to become their mullahs [religious leaders].

The Other Side of the Coin

The militaristic Islamic fanatics were the most doctrinaire and murderous religious group of the humans' modern times, but by no means were they the only people who held intolerant, extreme views. Another group who advanced their supposedly passive, religious views with aggression was known by several names. The term Christian Soldier Crusaders is used for this discussion.

Their legacy spanned over centuries. Pizzarro was one example, cited earlier. The Crusaders were another. One of the better known groups was the Knights of Malta.[37] The Knights, also referred to as Hospitallers, was the oldest institution among the three military orders of the Roman Church in Palestine. Originally founded to perform charitable works, they increasingly assumed military duties, including defending the Holy Land from Muslims and other non-Christians.

They had an interesting meld of duties in that they were soldiers and thus engaged in killing and injuring people. On the other hand, they were also hospital people and thus tasked with caring for the people they had only injured. Even more, they followed the monastic Rule of Saint Augustine and carried the additional responsibility of trying to convert to Christianity any non-Christians they had not yet killed.

Onward Christian Soldier Crusaders

Toward the latter times of the humans' reign on earth, another player entered the religious warfare stage, the United States. This country, like that of the many Islamic societies, was deeply steeped in the belief that its religion of Christianity was superior to others. These beliefs came from their holy book and thus formed part of the cultural DNA of the country. From its creation in the 1500s and 1600s to its formal founding in the 1700s, the United States was populated with many religious zealots whose calling in life was to bring others into their religious circle.

Yet in spite of America's religious foundations, until the latter part of the twentieth century, the United States usually kept religion separated from dominating its foreign policy. As mentioned, religious zeal played a role in the country's founding and its expansion. The missionaries were so-named for a good reason. But for the most part, militaristic evangelism was atypical of America's mainstream international politics.[38] Even though religion was often invoked to rationalize the takeover of turf, the church people themselves played a secondary role to land grabbers.

For many U.S. citizens, the rule for international behavior was Christian pacifism, not Christian militarism. But after World War II, this emphasis began to shift. Six factors led to this change.

First, the term *neoconservatism* is introduced, whose roots can be traced back to the 1930s and 1940s. At the City College of New York (CCNY), a group of intellectuals had formed a profound distaste for Communism and for the liberals who supported it.[39] Because of the effects of Stalinism, they also opposed social engineering.[40] On the other hand, they believed in the promotion of democracy in other states, a contradiction to their views against social engineering. One can only gather that they did not mind engineering democratic solutions, but other options were off the table.

They believed American power should be used for principled purposes. They proclaimed military aggression was sometimes necessary to bring morality and virtue to the world. This motive was clouded by differing views on what was moral or virtuous. Was regime change moral? Was the imposition of one's religious views on others virtuous? Prudent world leaders cautioned about using power for social engineering purposes, advising that all other avenues be explored before using force. Others were not so restrained.

One could argue that disposing of a deadly despot in a corrupt country was the morally correct thing to do. The problem with placing this noble idea into practice was the messy job of creating a morally-correct democracy from scratch among groups and nations who had no experience with, or fondness of democracy. To compound the problem, armies were organized for fighting, not democratic nation building.

Unfortunately, the ideologues had yet to learn that nation building was more than the application of raw power, that democracy did not happen by default. In reality, the principles of democracy ran counter to many facets of the humans' behavior and their tribal hierarchies. If the institutions of democracy were not in place—such as a body of law, property rights, uncorrupt government agencies, courts, due process, and accepting election results—a regime change sometimes did more harm than good.

Second, after World War II, the Soviet Union became the major power in Europe, filling in the vacuum left by the prostrate countries of Britain, Germany, France, and Italy. After overthrowing the Tsar in 1917, Russia, a newly appointed American enemy, wore the noble crown of a revolutionary country, the same crown worn by the United States. Heretofore, the United States' adversaries had been corrupt despots. The kings and queens of Europe, the dictators in Mexico, the mandarins and princes of the Far East were all venal oppressors without a scintilla of idealism beyond their feigned postulations of religious and racial righteousness. But now, America was facing a foe as idealistic and visionary as Uncle Sam.

Third, the Soviet Union's economic and political mantras were the opposite of those of the United States. They were as different as could have been possible: Communism vs. capitalism; dictatorship vs. democracy. And each side was bent on proselytizing its way, on instilling its philosophy into other cultures and societies around the globe.

Fourth, of equal importance was the diametrical difference between the USSR and the United States regarding the countries' views about religion: Soviet atheism vs. American Christianity. In the United States, this conflict of views led to a substantial number of influential writers and intellectuals setting forth doctrines positing the struggle between the two counties as one of good (the United States) vs. evil (the USSR). Many ministers, priests, apostles—evangelists of the religious establishment—proclaimed America's most important mission in the world was to defeat the USSR because this country did not embrace Christianity. The handle "Godless Communists" became a catch-all phrase for vilifying America's former WWII ally.

Fifth, a post-WWII USSR military of 2,600,000 personnel required the USA, with only 640,000 people in uniform, to build-up and maintain a huge and expensive counterforce.[41] Prior to the Cold War, America had no Department of Defense. In 1947 this organization came into being and eventually evolved into an establishment that was almost another branch of the government. And true to the adage, "Monks do not dissolve monasteries," after the Cold War was over, the defense establishment reflected this age-old incantation with a slight variation of, "Defense departments do not dissolve defense departments."

Sixth, a (seemingly) powerful USSR posed a threat to America's worldwide economic hegemony. Time and again, economists warned U.S. citizens and politicians of the growing power of the Soviet economy. But these experts discarded the fact that Communism bred inefficient marketplaces. Even the sacrosanct U.S. National Intelligence Estimates failed to assess that the Soviet Union was living on borrowed time.[42] This illusion led to further ignite the flames of suspicion and insecurity, with the inculcation into America's psyche of combating an evil and affluent enemy.

The Factors' Effects

The situation became increasingly intractable as more citizens in the United States turned to religious militancy and militant neoconservative ideas to advance their beliefs. A second invasion of Iraq by the United States came about partially because the neocons pushed their views of fostering democracy through war onto a well-meaning but naive American president (who himself thought God wanted him to be president). This debacle opened Pandora's terrorist box, spawning thousands of Islamic militants who came to the assistance of their "oppressed brethren," and to rid their turf of the Christian Soldier Crusaders. It was history replaying itself one more time.

To complicate matters, 44 percent of Americans believed Jesus would return to Earth within 50 years, accompanied with genocidal wars.[43] These people thought the wars would be right and just. As mentioned, a powerful leader of these movements could proclaim that God wanted him to be president and get away with it.

Several countries assumed they were in a perpetual war. As an introduction to this idea, here is a brief look at the Vietnam War and its effects on the humans' later wars.

Paradoxically, America's haphazard management of its 1960s/1970s military forces and the resultant debacles at the close of the Vietnam War led to a strengthening of the U.S. military. It also led to closer ties of the military with evangelical Christianity and helped pave the way for the ascension of the American Christian Soldier Crusader.

In the past, many clerics believed the military was not a desirable occupation for a young man because of its reputation for hard drinking, hard talking, and hard loving. Not to mention a line item in the job description of a soldier: killing. Likewise, the military did not view the religious establishment as one supporting its mission, because "turning the other cheek" was a clause absent in the military field manuals.

Not all Christians were skeptical of the military establishment. Conservative Christians supported the armed forces. After Vietnam, the, "evangelicals gained respect and influence within the armed forces as a result of the support they demonstrated for the military services, the war, and the men who fought it."[44]

The Vietnam defeat was a humiliating experience for the military. It was the first time in the history of the country that American soldiers were withdrawn permanently from a major war. Notwithstanding this debacle, military leaders recognized the flaws in the system and began the process of creating a different type of fighting operation. The all-volunteer force made a huge difference because it led to smarter and more dedicated troops. A significant number of enlistees were evangelicals, which reflected the nation's population at large as well as the type of person who would volunteer for a potentially dangerous job to better the world.

During these times, the decay of traditional American middle-class virtues was perceived by most Christians (and many non-Christians as well) as the loss of the country's moral compass. The 1970s was a wrenching decade for religious groups as they believed the country was drifting toward decadence with the wide use of drugs, abortions, free-wheeling love, and the disregard for authority.

Increasingly, the military saw the Christian evangelicals as people who cherished many of the values of the military. Likewise, the Christian evangelicals viewed the military in the same light. Thus, the two found themselves marching to the beat of the same drummer.[45]

To most Americans, the all-volunteer force was beyond reproach. Soldiers were cheered at public gatherings. They went ahead of the queue in lines at stores. They boarded and debarked commercial aircraft before anyone else. The arch conservative media frequently espoused army generals as crucibles of combat against immoral left wingers. Their zeal was somewhat moderated when one of their heroes, and the newly appointed director of America's premier intelligence establishment, was discovered to be having an adulterous affair with another army officer. Thankfully, the adulterous affair was between a male and a female. The military zealots breathed a righteous sigh of relief. In the meantime:[46]

> ...evangelicals came to see the military as an enclave of virtue, a place of refuge where the sacred remnant of patriotic Americans gathered and preserved American principles from extinction.... For their part, the armed forces, feeling themselves to be prime targets in the ongoing culture war, came to see the evangelicals as allies—sharing the same enemies and sharing at least to some degree in a common mission of restoration.

A telling example of the prevalence and influence of Christian evangelicals in the military was the United States Air Force Academy, a government school that was supposed to keep church and state separated. To cite some examples: An academy chaplain instructed cadets to try to convert classmates by warning them they would "burn in hell" if they did not accept Christ. During basic training, cadets who did not attend after-dinner chapel were marched back to the dormitories in "heathen flights" by upperclassmen. A Jewish student was taunted as a Christ killer. The head football coach posted a banner in the locker room stating, "I am a Christian first and last. ...I am a member of Team Jesus Christ."[47]

Onward Jewish Soldiers

The Christian Soldier culture was interwoven into America's way of life. But these relationships were nothing compared to the influence the military had on Israel's affairs.[48] The military (the Israel Defense Forces, or IDF) held "a virtual monopoly on policymaking."[49]

Because of the military's dominance, the country's foreign policy was viewed through a military lens, and opportunities for diplomacy were often passed up in favor of military actions.

After Israel declared itself a state in 14 May 1948, it was involved in the 1948 war with the current (Arab) residents, many of whom were displaced from their homes. The Israelis were involved in the "1951–1956 Retribution operations, the 1956 Sinai War, 1964–1967 War over Water, 1967 Six-Day War, the 1967–1970 War of Attrition, the 1968 Battle of Karameh, the 1973 Operation Spring of Youth, 1973 Yom Kippur War, 1976 Operation Entebbe, 1978 Operation Litani, 1982 Lebanon War, 1982–2000 South Lebanon conflict, 1987–1993 First Intifada, 2000–2005 Second Intifada, 2002 Operation Defensive Shield, 2006 Lebanon War, 2008–2009 Gaza War, and the 2012 Operation Pillar of Defense."[50]

The nation had mandatory conscription except for the ultra-conservatives and, of course, the Muslim citizens. The latter individual would not have made for an amiable foxhole companion to a Jew who might be busy shooting the Muslim's cousin.

Many career military people, upon retirement, moved into industry and politics. During a crisis, unlike the United States—which had several intelligence agencies working on the problem—Israel's military intelligence was the only institution in that country with the capacity of performing a thorough analysis. It was as if the United States only had the Defense Intelligence Agency, and the CIA, State Department intelligence, and other intelligence organizations did not exist, or were largely discounted.

Using Israeli military/private industry networks, a number of Israeli citizens became some of the most powerful and rich players in the world's economic-military culture. Yet, some had no ties to political or national boundaries. For example, the Israeli citizen Mark Rich sold the oil of Israel's archenemy Iran, even during embargoes against Iranian oil. Yet, he gave Israeli Mossad agents (the premier intelligence service) contacts in Iran to enable them to conduct their anti-Iranian business.[51]

At times, the analysis favored war and not negotiation. The child holding the hammer, and looking for something to pound, was usually not a politician. It was a general. If it was a politician, the person was a retired general who knew the path to political power in Israel was an early career in the military.

In many situations, during the wars cited above, the civilian (supposed) leadership of Israel was not involved in critical decisions dealing with the tactical and strategic welfare of the nation. They were preempted by the military, not unlike a third-world junta in operation.[52]

With this background about the military dispositions of the radical Islamic Muslims, the Christian Soldier Crusaders, and the Jewish Soldier in mind, a flashback is taken into the humans' early twentieth century. A bitter religious turf battle took place in Israel and Palestine; one that led to the use of weapons of mass destruction; one that was instrumental in paving the way for the emergence of the Cepee.

Palestine and Israel

After WWI, parts of the dismantled Ottoman Empire—now under the administration of Great Britain—were to be allocated as homelands for Jews and Arabs, two groups who had aided Britain during the war.[53] Unfortunately, both groups wanted parts of the same land. But this land, Palestine, was largely inhabited by Arabs, most of whom were Muslims. Nonetheless, the British Balfour Declaration, supported by several other European colonialists, proclaimed it favored a national home in Palestine for the Jewish people. And the Holocaust removed any hesitations from Britain and other Western countries about enforcing the Balfour Declaration.

Below are two paragraphs written by Arthur Balfour, the British Foreign Secretary. The first was written in 1917.

> His Majesty's Government views with favor the establishment in Palestine of a national home for the Jewish people and will use their best endeavors to facilitate the achievement of this object, it being clearly understood that nothing shall be done which may prejudice the civil and religious rights of existing non-Jewish communities in Palestine.[54]

Two years later, he declared:

> In Palestine, we do not propose even to go through the form of consulting the wishes of the present inhabitants of the country. ...The Four Great Powers are committed to Zionism. And Zionism, be it right or wrong, good or bad, is rooted in age long tradition, in present needs, in future hopes, of far profounder import than the prejudices of the 700,000 Arabs who now inhabit that ancient land.[55]

The Imperialists' View. Balfour was an imperialist. He occupied the top rungs of this hierarchy. He was a predatory plunderer who proved disastrous to his fellow humans for his stand on Palestine and other former colonies of the United Kingdom. He believed the world belonged to the British, to keep or give away. When Balfour was prime minister (1903), he "offered Uganda to the Zionists."[56] The Ugandans, being noble savages, had no say in the matter.

But Great Britain was not the only country in a long line of European nations whose arrogant and aberrant actions led to the dismemberment of long-established religious and linguistic cultures. The sudden rupture of these societies created dysfunctional populations. Many members of these groups, especially those devoted to their religions, developed a profound hatred for the "heathens" who had dissected their ancient and revered tribal ways. Seed for revenge cycles were planted. The imperialists were the cultivators.

During his reading of the Human Archives, the Cepee is growing accustomed to the hubris of the humans. But their behavior after WWI renews the Cepee's astonishment.

After the defeat of Germany in the WWI conflict, the winning players on the back row of the war's chessboard met to divide their spoils and to rearrange the various pawns that were at their disposal. After minor negotiations, France was given control of the land that became Syria and parts of Iraq. The boundary and the turf the French controlled were altered after the French Prime Minister Georges Clemenceau got together with Lloyd George, the Prime Minister of the United Kingdom. Clemenceau was pleased about the Syrian carving. Part of the dismemberment came about as a result of a conversation:[57]

> In return for Syria [which became a League of Nations mandate], Clemenceau was accommodating:
>
> Clemenceau: Tell me what you want.
> Lloyd George: I want Mosul. [An oil rich region in north Iraq.]
> Clemenceau: You shall have it. Anything else?
> Lloyd George: Yes, I want Jerusalem, too!
> Clemenceau: You shall have it.

Thus, it transpired. The faction that had a strong lobby, campaign money, votes, and personal friendships with Western world politicians got the turf. The others got nothing. The ordinary humans living on this turf became little more than titleless occupants of land they and their ancestors had occupied for centuries. As stated in the conversation above, Britain obtained the Palestine land and arranged for it to be partially bequeathed to the Jews as part of a joint venture among careless and heedless men. Their hubristic ignorance isolated them. They had no appreciation that their sudden, happenstance decisions would disrupt decades, even centuries of inter-tribal accommodations.

A tragic play was being written, largely by these imperialists. Unbeknownst to them, they were writing a scene in this play for the Deadly Trinity to take the center stage.

The Jewish View. In hindsight, one can understand the Jews' determination to find a sanctuary. Even before the time of Christ, and through no fault of their own, they had been relegated to positions of degradation. Lacking any geographical protection and forced into the financial world because of ancient religious dictates against money lending, they evolved into a successful and wealthy culture, one that was also intellectually astute.

In yet another touch of irony, frequently encountered with this tribe, their success (and their alleged complicity in the death of Jesus) led to more resentment and abuse. Still, against huge odds, they persisted and prospered. With the Holocaust, the tide moved additional Jews toward the Zionist movement to forge a home in the Middle East, the birthplace of their religion. They were no longer going to play the pawn on the European chessboard of prejudice and power. They were going to practice their culture and religion of Judaism by playing their own chess game, but on a chessboard of their own choosing.

It so happened that the chessboard on which they wanted to play was also claimed by another tribe who was bent on practicing its cultures and the religion of Islam. Consequently, both Jews and Arabs found themselves on the same chessboard, each determined to take the match to a checkmate at the other's expense. No stalemate, no draw, no compromise, only a checkmate.

The United States View. After World War II, Arabs in the region beseeched the United States not to support the partitioning of this land. The U.S. President (Truman) convened the U.S. Chiefs of Mission of Saudi Arabia and other countries to listen to their concerns about the increasing anger and fear of the Arabs about the situation:[58]

"I'm sorry, gentlemen," said the President, summing up his position with the utmost candor, "but I have to answer to hundreds of thousands who are anxious for the success of Zionism; I do not have hundreds of thousands of Arabs among my constituents."

Truman codified his decision with a short note the Cepee finds in the Human Archives dealing with the Truman Museum (on display in Independence, Missouri):

"The government has been informed that a Jewish state has been proclaimed in Palestine, and recognition has been requested by the provisional government thereof.

The United States recognizes the provisional government as the de facto authority of the State of Israel.

Harry Truman
Approved, May 14, 1948."

Unfortunately for other repressed people around the world, they were unable to migrate to America to form a political coalition. As three examples, the dictator Pol Pot killed 25 percent of the Cambodian population. The North Korean dictators starved to death hundreds of thousands of their helpless citizens. The repressed Palestinians were denied basic human rights by the Israelis.

These people did not have the means to come to the United States. But the Jewish people did. Thereafter, Truman and *practically every* American politician that followed him were subject to the Jewish constituency. Democracy in action.

The short-sightedness of this man was understandable. How could he know the immigration of several thousand Jews into the centuries-old home of several million Arabs would lead to a problem that would haunt his successors and most of the Western world for many years to come?

Besides, the citizens of the United States knew this area was once the home of the Jews, and they believed the Arabs had taken it away. The truth was the land had been alternately occupied by both tribes since Christianity, Judaism, and Islam were first founded. The proclamation of, "I was here first," depended who was speaking.[59]

The Cepee is now watching a television program from the Human Archives. It is a talk show in which an American, and a strong supporter of a Jewish Palestine, proclaims, "The Jews were there first! It belongs to them." His debater replies, "So what? It is known that non-Jew and non-Arab tribes were there in America: 'Indians.' They have first dibs on the land. So, to which Indian tribe do you want to give your home in Ohio?"

The United States was strongly committed to the Jewish state, often at the expense of its relations with the Arabs. This one-sided support became so asymmetrical that much of the world held the view that America was in Israel's pocket. This view, from practically all people who practiced the Islamic faith, became one that America was as much the enemy of the Muslim as Israel.

A few far-sighted Americans saw the danger of not resolving the problems associated with the displacement of the Palestinians. An American Secretary of State (George Shultz) said, "The continued occupation of the West Bank and Gaza Strip, and the frustration of Palestinian rights, is a dead-end street. The belief that this can continue is an illusion."[60]

The Cepee responds to the Shultz statement with this thought: *A dead-end street…an apt metaphor.*

The Arab View. In 1947, this contested area in the Middle East contained a population of Arabs (just under 92 percent of the total) and Jews (just under 8 percent). Other religious factions lived in the area, but they were not a factor in the conflict.

That same year, the United Nations passed Resolution 181, which called for the partitioning of Palestine into Jewish and Arab turfs. Logically enough, the Jews accepted the resolution. The Arabs did not. After all, the disproportionate ratio of 8 percent Jew to 92 percent Arab with a proportionate ratio of 50 percent to 50 percent in governance virtually guaranteed the 92 percent would resist this fiat. (Not counting a small Christian population.)

The Arabs pleaded with Truman not to make the decision he made. They brought forth arguments, even pleadings. Sometimes an abstract remonstrance was offered, such as this entreaty spoken by the king of Saudi Arabia:[61]

"Give them [the Jews] and their descendants," he said, "the choicest lands and homes of the Germans who oppressed them." There was no reason why the Arab inhabitants of Palestine should suffer for something the Germans had done. "Make the enemy and the oppressor pay," he said. "That is how we Arabs wage war."

Prior to 1947, since the Zionists first began a migration into the Holy Lands, the Arabs fought them. The Zionists kept coming. The Arabs kept fighting. No stalemate appeared on the chessboard.

Consequently, the Jewish cultural and religious leaders persuaded their followers to migrate to a part of earth (the Middle East) whose inhabitants were noted for their intolerance of other cultures and religions. In some parts of the Middle East, a person was not allowed to enter a region if the person was of a faith different from those occupying it. Even more, a person who did not practice Islam was considered unworthy of treading on sacred religious turf. Yet there they were: Jews in the middle of some of the Muslims' sacred sites. The Jews considered this small part of earth to be their oasis. The Arabs were deeply offended by the Jews' presence, whom they considered to be debasing a holy place.

But this defilement was going to be temporary. The American and European imperialists, oblivious to the Unintended Consequences Law, did not realize the non-Jews in this part of the world would never turn the other cheek…not when pride and turf were involved. A Pandora's box had been opened, not to be closed again until the Cepees came along and put the lid back on.

Thereafter, one war followed another as the Arabs and Jews fought for "their" land. The 1948-1949 war was followed by the Six-Day War, which was followed by the wars listed earlier. Then to be followed by even more destructive wars, a story told in Chapter 9.

A Pragmatic Zionist's View. Albert Einstein was a Zionist in heart and mind. But his mind detected the danger of an emerging tragedy:[62]

> Despite his association with the Zionist cause, Einstein's sympathies extended to the Arabs who were being displaced by the influx of Jews into what would eventually be Israel. His message was a prophetic one. In 1929 he wrote to a colleague, "Should we be unable to find a way to [an] honest cooperation and honest pact [with the Arabs] then we have learned absolutely nothing in our two thousand years of suffering."
>
> He recommended a privy council be set up consisting of four Jews and four Arabs, who would be independently minded, and would resolve any disputes. He also said that two great Semitic people (Jews and Arabs) had a great common future. But he cautioned that if the Jews did not assure that both sides lived in harmony, the struggle would hurt them in decades to come.
>
> For these insights, Einstein was labeled as naïve. His warnings were prophetic.

The Deadly Trinity View. These conflicts might have ended in battles solely for geographical turf, but this aspect of a human's dominance over another was not so simple. It became a battle for religious and economic turf, which was a more complex variable in the Human Tribal Hierarchy equation. Both Muslim and Jew claimed parts of the region as theirs because of their past religious legacies to that region.

Time and again, the Revenge Cycle was front and center. As one example among thousands, in a television news program about the shelling between Israel and Hezbollah in Lebanon, the Prime Minister of Lebanon was asked if he could act as an intermediary to influence the Hezbollah to stop their missile firings into Israel. He replied, "Blood calls for blood."[63]

Regarding Hezbollah, this militant resistant group and political party was formed in Lebanon as a consequence of Israel's invasion of that country. It retaliated with attacks on Israel from the safe haven of Lebanon. Little did Israel know that its action would lead to the creation of an effective and deadly enemy, one that did not go away when Israel withdrew its forces from Lebanon. The Cepee reflects: *It's another example of the Unintended Consequences Law.*

Neither Jew nor Muslim was going anywhere. They were home but in the same place. They were on the same chessboard playing for their very existence. Both parties refused to compromise on the most fundamental issue: holy turf. Any ally of the Jew was the enemy of the Muslim. Any ally of the Muslim was the enemy of the Jew.

At this juncture, the fusion of religious zeal, religious turf, and military aggression, mixed with the technology of deadly weapons, became a lethal compound for a sizable number of earth's inhabitants.

Averting the Deadly Trinity? Perhaps this tragedy could have been avoided if the Arabs had not openly vowed to destroy the Israel state. What can one do if one's very existence is threatened? Diplomacy's passive words have little effect on deeds that deal death blows to conciliatory gestures. It was akin to a gazelle negotiating its fate with a circling lion.

The original Zionists did not come to the Holy Land with swords. Often under the sponsorship of wealthy American Jews, they came with plows. Plows? Plows dealt with sod, with earth, with land, with security. As recounted in Chapters 2 and 3, plows dealt with turf, the most coveted and sought-after commodity in the human race.

If the Jews had infiltrated into the Holy Land as investment bankers, and as Wall Street traders did in America, silently and opaquely taken over the finances of the region, there may very well have never been a modern Armageddon. But banks and stocks were not sod. Nothing could replace humans' primeval disposition toward the physical possession of turf.

The Arabs were not naïve to this reality. They often responded with guns. If the Jews were to survive, some of their plows would have to be re-forged into guns. The Cepee learns this re-forging process led to an Israel that became one of the most potent military nations in existence.

On the other hand, perhaps this deadly situation could have been defused if Israel had not continued to illegally occupy more and more land outside its mandated borders. Perhaps events would have turned out differently if Israel had not evolved into a state that was increasingly imperialist with disturbing trends of becoming, if not an apartheid state, then one that was exclusionary and increasingly militaristic (at the expense of diplomacy). Perhaps the Deadly Trinity's outcome could have been modified if Israel had possessed the will to take care and embrace the people its own people displaced.

No, true to the immutable laws of the Human Tribal Hierarchy, Israel not only refused to dissolve its turf, it expanded it. It began building communities in areas that were in violation of international law.

As a consequence of Israel's intractable colonialism, the countries bordering Israel, (even those who said otherwise or remained silent on the matter) wished for the annihilation of this interloper.

Besides, it made no difference which faction was correct, be it Jew, Muslim, Zionist, neocon, pacifist, liberal, or conservative. One or more of these groups might have been correct, but that was immaterial. Being correct was no shield against a bomb.

The Cepee pauses for a moment and thinks: *I've learned that the Israeli leadership was fearful of having an Arab political party in its cabinet.*[64] *Yet that idea was integral to the founding of Israel in the first place. But then, how could an Arab party join an Israeli coalition? How could an Arab belong to a government that bombed Arabs? It was a hopeless situation. Surely, someone must have known the path these factions were on was leading to disaster.* As the Cepee turns back to the archives, he ponders: *What happened to the leadership of the United States?*

Religious Turf Mismanagement

A skilled tennis player knows how to move his opponent around the court to prevent his rival from hitting offensive shots. A skilled golfer knows how to play different lies on the course to make his next shot easier. A skilled nation knows how to manipulate both friends and foes around earth's chessboard to protect that nation's turf, its citizens, and its national interests. This exercise is called statesmanship.

In what can only be characterized as catastrophic mismanagement, the United States bowed to special interest groups and allowed Israel to continue its expansion into territory that from the view of the international community, it did not own. This land was internationally recognized as belonging to the Muslim people that the Jewish people supplanted. Even if the expropriation had been legal, in the eyes of the Arabs, it did not matter. Turf was being confiscated.

The Israeli occupation of land mandated to others—and the manner in which the Jews treated the native Muslims—was one of the major reasons the terrorists became terrorists. (Perhaps the major reason, see endnote at the back of this chapter.[65])

America's more astute leaders knew if the Palestinians were not granted their due process of international law, not to mention a dollop of humaneness, the Middle East would wallow in never-ending jihads and counter-jihads. These wise souls were shouted down by a vociferous, ignorant populace.

But what could a country such as Israel do if its neighbors espoused its annihilation? Expand its turf to form protective geographical buffers? Vow that no nation in the region but itself would ever possess nuclear weapons? Disenfranchise potentially dangerous Muslims who were Israeli citizens? Build huge barriers separating the two tribes? Batten down its hatches to become a permanent state-under-siege? To all these questions, the answers are yes, that is what Israel did. The approach worked in the short run, but these actions were not a prescription for long-term success.

It took little imagination to see that the actions cited above would eventually result in bitter revenge battles. What better way to play out revenge than to employ the most lethal instruments available, to hammer with the best tool?

In the interim, a powerful collection of America's religious/ military/industrial establishments insured a politician would be voted out of office if he/she even obliquely suggested a change in U.S. policy. Thus, the Zionist community, greatly aided by America's

Christian Soldier Crusaders, put their signatures onto proclamations codifying long-term lunacy.

This bizarre charade played itself out for many years. Given mighty America's largesse to Israel, the insistence of the Arabs to dismember Israel could be considered little more than stupid.

But the very nature of stupidity is its insistency.[66] As the Cepee learns in his study of the Human Archives, the humiliated and disenfranchised Muslims were not stupid in their insistence on claiming turf. Because they had nowhere else to go or any other turf to occupy, they could not and did not go away.

The Cepee reflects: *The key to preventing my ancestors from using weapons of mass destruction on one another was to give one of their tribes, the Palestinians, their own turf. They made that gesture for one tribe, the Jews, after WWII. Why not grant another tribe their sovereignty as well? Yet they did not. They did not insist on Israel pulling back its imperialistic operations. It's incomprehensible. We Cepees need to undergo some reverse engineering in order to understand the humans' mind set. They misplayed a chess game, one of enormous significance, one that led to a catastrophic stalemate between Muslims and Jews.*

Duplicitous Diplomacy

Israel's protector and sponsor, the United States, was deceived countless times by Israel. America projected its idealistic naiveté onto a hardened Zionist movement that was dedicated to not only creating a home for Jews, but expanding the turf of that home well beyond the UN mandate.

The humanist aspects of the original Jewish movement were subsumed by an ever increasing militaristic and imperialistic Zionism. As examples:

> Ben-Gurion, though he would be the last to admit it, was aligning himself with the nationalistic forces on the right, who called for seizing more land even if that meant war with the Arabs.[67]

A former president and prime minister of Israel, Shimon Peres, stated, "We have to aspire to alter the state of Israel's borders," he told a closed meeting of senior government officials in 1957.[68] [In a touch of irony, Peres won the 1994 Nobel Peace Prize (together with two others) for formulating and participating in peace talks.]

After invading Lebanon, another future prime minister, Ariel Sharon, informed Israel's enemy (Yasser Arafat) his army could move from Lebanon to Jordan (another exodus), "...it would take only a word from Sharon to force [Jordanian] King Hussein to abdicate his throne. 'One speech by me will make King Hussein realize that the time has come to pack his bags,'" Sharon said.[69]

Another Israeli leader had this to say about the matter, "...all of the peace proposals he had floated as prime minister were fraudulent. His 'moderation' as prime minister was merely tactical. The goal had always been, and still was, the seizure of the lands that had been designated for a Palestinian homeland." "It pains me greatly that...I will not be able to expand the settlements in Judea and Samaria [West Bank and part of the UN designated Arab state] to complete the demographic revolution in the land of Israel. ...I would have carried on autonomy talks for ten years, and meanwhile we would have reached half a million people in Judea and Samaria."[70]

Time and again, the doctrinaire military-imperialists of the Jewish tribe clashed with the doctrinaire religionists of the Muslim tribe. Supposedly, the clashes occurred in the names of noble causes: maintaining cultures, reverence for religions, honoring ancient legacies. All were guises in the never-ending quests to ascend their Human Tribal Hierarchies, ultimately realized by controlling religious turf.

In what could only be characterized as an apartheid practice, Israel's Prime Minister, Benjamin Netanyahu stated the goal of dealing with the displaced Palestinians was to create a Palestinian "Bantustan"—referring to South Africa's practice of setting aside territories for black people. Netanyahu and his minions planned to take over well over 50 percent (not counting Jordan) of historic Palestine and force the former inhabitants to seek refuge elsewhere.[71]

The Cepee closes the Human Archives file that chronicles this part of human history: *I read in the archives that one definition of a statesman was,* "The expansion of his own class or nation at the expense of others." *By this definition, these Israeli leaders were supreme statesmen.*

Armageddon?

As written in Revelation 16:16 of the Bible, "And he gathered them together into a place called in the Hebrew tongue Armageddon," where the final struggle between good and evil took place. Those Christians who interpreted the Bible literally (usually designated as fundamentalists but also including many conservative evangelicals) believed a necessary forerunner to Armageddon was the return of the Jews to the "Holy Land."[72]

The Zionist movement and the Jewish takeover in this region were strongly supported by conservative evangelicals and fundamentalists as a prerequisite to the final battle between good and evil. Consequently, Israel could do no wrong in the eyes of a very large part of America's population. Preemptive wars? Annexation of territory? Secretly building and later possessing nuclear arms without being a member of the nuclear arms nonproliferation groups? Yes, they were justified in the context of a much larger cause: Armageddon and the second coming of Jesus Christ.[73]

The radical Muslims had their own vision of an Armageddon. They held the view that "the annihilation of Israel is not only a religious and national duty, but also a universal human duty, from which no Muslim or free human being can be exempt."[74]

The stage for war between two religious factions had been set. For certain, past history revealed similar acts. Religious wars over irresolvable differences did not happen only in the humans' modern times, they existed centuries before. But this situation was different. In the past, the conflicts were resolved with primitive instruments of war: swords, knives, and spears, resulting in the deaths of a few thousand people here and there. In more modern times, the instruments were TNT bombs, and shortly thereafter, nuclear bombs and biochemicals, instruments that could kill hundreds of thousands of humans.

Upon reflecting about these aspects of the humans, the Cepee thinks: *The Christians supported the Jews taking over much of the Christians' holy lands. But their ideas about the second coming of Jesus Christ could not have made the Jews very happy about their long-term future.*

Conclusions

The religious wars were not about religion. Religion was the pretext, a facade. Many humans who killed in the name of religious righteousness were disguising their motives for domination and revenge behind religious symbols and incantations.

Like Pizarro, al Qaeda's soldiers and his minions killed innocent men, women, and children, later searching the religious documentation to justify their actions. And those latter-day Pizarros, the Christian Soldier Crusaders, were not the innocent lambs of Jesus. They also pushed their religious agendas with military actions.

During these so-called religious wars, Maslow's basic survival needs never came into play. Nor did the lower rungs of the Human Tribal Hieararchy. The contenders were climbing over each other to reach the higher rungs in the Human Tribal Hierarchies of pride, esteem, prestige, power...and turf.

---

[1] Richard North Patterson, *Exile* (New York: St. Martin's Press, 2007), 408.

[2] "George Packer Quotes," http://www.goodreads.com/quotes/376986-ideology-knows-the-answer-before-the-question-has-been-asked.

[3] CBS, "60 Minutes," aired February 17, 2013.

[4] Alexander N. Yokovlev, Anthony Austin, and Paul Hollander, *A Century of Violence in Soviet Russia* (New Haven, CT: Yale University Press, 2002), 165.

[5] For example, Einstein's equations cannot account for the first instants of the Big Bang.

[6] In Chapters 2 and 12, I offer (somewhat) ameliorating ideas about our great...great grandparents swinging around in trees.

[7] A reflection not favored by all.

[8] For example, an atomic-level microscope affects the behavior of the atom that is being examined.

[9] My apologies to the unknown author of this passage. In 1965, I copied these thoughts down in my notebook. My practice is to record the source of references, but I failed to do so on this occasion. I searched the web for the content but to no avail.

[10] Louis Kossuth, *Speech*, Lexington, MA, May 1982, in Frank, *Quotationary* (New York: Random House, 2001), 712.

[11] William R. Polk, *Understanding Iraq* (New York: Harper-Collins, 2005), 19-20.

[12] A few years ago, I visited the Hargar Qim site in Malta. Some archeologists believe Hagar Qim is the oldest standing building on earth. This temple was built around 3000 - 2500 BC, but archeologists claim temples were being built on Malta as early as 4100 BC. A guide showed me a window used to pass offerings to the priests inside the building, who let it be known they, in turn, passed the offerings to the gods. He called this window "The Oracle Hole." Also, see John Samut Tagliaferro, *Malta, Its Archaeology and History* (Luqa, Malta: Miller House, n.d.).

[13] Paraphrased from George Bernard Shaw, *Preface to Plays, Pleasant and Unpleasant*, vol. 2, 1898, in Frank, *Quotationary*, 713.

[14] Some historians cite seven; some cite eight.

[15] Williston Walker et.al., *A History of the Christian Church*, 4th ed. (New York: Charles Scribner's Sons, 1985), 290.

[16] "Getting Worse," *The Economist*, July 14, 2012.

[17] David Van Biema, "Undercover: Christianity in Muslim Lands," *Time*, June, 30, 2003, 39. The Web has many sources of information on the Great Commission.

[18] "The Bible Collection Suite" CD. This writer was unable to find the exact match to Mr. Van Biema's quote. Matthew 28:19 and 28:20 are close approximations: Matthew 28:19: "Go ye therefore, and teach all nations, baptizing them in the name of the Father, and of the Son, and of the Holy Ghost." Matthew 28:20: "Teaching them to observe all things whatsoever I have commanded you... ."

[19] The term *wealth* is used in this discussion to describe a tribe possessing appliances such as ships, steel, and horses—not just caches of gold.

[20] Jared Diamond, *Guns, Germs, and Steel* (New York: Norton, 1999), 68-74. See Diamond's book for a more complete description of this incident.

[21] Microsoft's Encarta Reference Library.

[22] Fred Anderson and Andrew Cayton, *The Dominion of War* (New York: Viking, 2005), 4.

[23] Ibid., 9.

[24] Hannah Arendt, Cecil Rhodes' Quote, *The Origins of Totalitarianism*, in Frank, *Quotationary*, 392.

[25] Diamond, *Guns, Germs, and Steel*, 81.

[26] Microsoft's Encarta Reference Library.

[27] The English spelling of the Islamic holy book varies. Koran, Qur'an, and Quran are the most common spellings. This book uses all three.

[28] The name of Osama bin Laden is spelled differently in several publications and manuscripts. *The 9/11 Commission Report* spells it as Usama Bin Ladin. Some news journals spell it Osama bin Laden; others as Osama Bin Laden.

[29] *The al Qaeda Training Manual* found at an al Qaeda member's home by Manchester, England, Metropolitan Police. http://www.usdoj.gov/ag/manualpart1_1.pdf. Quotes found on page 1.

[30] James Reston Jr., "Seeking Meaning from a Grand Imam," *The Washington Post*, March 31, 2002, B4.

[31] The U.S. embassies in Kenya and Tanzania, in which over 220 people were killed and approximately 4,000 were wounded.

[32] Alan Cullison, "Inside Al-Qaeda's Hard Drive," *The Atlantic Monthly*, September 2004, 60. Mr. Cullison had the good fortune to buy two of al Qaeda's computers after al Qaeda retreated from Kabul. One computer was used by Ayman al-Zawahiri, bin Laden's top deputy. I have altered the format of the letter to improve legibility, but I have not altered the contents.

[33] This article should be available from www.al-fhd.com. However, my browsers and search engines could not access it. Thus, my secondary source is [Michael Scheuer], *Imperial Hubris* (Washington, DC: Bassey's, 2004), 154-155.

[34] Raffi Khatchadourian, "Azzam the American," *The New Yorker*, January 22, 2007, 63. Posted online with a date of January 31, 2007.

[35] James Lyons, "Civilian Casualties vs. Rules," *The Washington Times*, September 3, 2006, B1.

[36] Robert Lacey, *Inside the Kingdom* (New York: Penguin, 2009), 40.

[37] Uyless Black, *The Mediterranean* (privately published, 2006), 18.

[38] Jimmy Carter, *Our Endangered Values* (New York: Simon and Schuster, 2005), 19. *Fundamentalism* and *evangelism* are terms open to wide interpretation. For this discussion, I cite Jimmy Carter's *Our Endangered Values*. He cites the Random House Dictionary of the English Language for the definition of evangelical, "belonging to or designating Christian churches that emphasize the teachings and authority of the scriptures, especially of the new Testament, in opposition to the institutional authority of the church itself and that stress as paramount the tenet that salvation is achieved by personal conversion to faith in the atonement of Christ; or (b) designating Christian, especially of the late 1970's, eschewing the designation of fundamentalist but holding to a conservative interpretation of the Bible."

[39] Francis Fukuyama, *America at the Crossroads: Democracy, Power, and the Neoconservative Legacy* (New Haven, CT: Yale University Press, 2006), 15-17.

[40] I use the past tense in this narrative, but current neocons also hold these views.

[41] David McCullough, *Truman* (New York: Simon & Schuster, 1992), 764. Other sources cite different numbers, but all agree the Soviet Union had an overwhelming superiority in military personnel.

[42] During the mid-1960s, this writer was a U.S. Navy Officer. One of my collateral jobs was that of "second officer-in-charge" for a vault in a Defense Intelligence Agency building containing the NIEs. Copies of NIEs were sent from this location to specific military departments. Other agencies were responsible for NIE dissemination to non-military organizations. I often ate my lunch in the vault while I read scores of NIEs, ranging from assessments of the USSR and China, to personal profiles of Stalin and Mao. I had no "need to know," but I had a curiosity to learn. I discovered that a great deal of this super-secret information was public knowledge, published in newspapers, books, and magazines.

[43] Sam Harris, "The Case Against Faith," *Newsweek*, November 12, 2006, 42-43.

[44] Andrew J. Bacevich, *The New American Militarism* (New York: Oxford University Press, 2005), 140.

[45] Ibid., 141.

[46] Ibid.

[47] "Team Jesus Christ," *The Washington Post*, June 4, 2005, A16.

[48] Aluf Benn, "Israel's Warlords," *Foreign Affairs*, March/April 2013, 164-169.

[49] Ibid., 165.

[50] "Israeli Military Decorations by Campaign," http://www.google.com/#psj=1&q=Israeli+Military+Decorations+by+Campaign.

[51] "Marc Rich," *The Economist*, July 6, 2013, 86.

[52] Patrick Tyler, *Fortress Israel* (New York: Farrar, Straus, and Giroux, 2012). Tyler provides scores of examples throughout this book.

[53] I use the word *Arab* in a general sense for this discussion to identify the native populations in this part of the world. The word precedes Islam, so it should not be linked to this religion. However, most of the people in the *western* part of the Middle East are Muslims who practice the religion of Islam. Those in the eastern part of the Middle East prefer the term *Persians*. During the early discussions about the creation of Israel, the term *Arab* was an accepted short-cut description of anyone who was born in this part of the world who practiced any form of Islam.

[54] Malcolm E. Yapp, *The Making of the Modern Near East 1792-1923* (Harlow, England: Longman, 1987), 290. Also, Patterson, *Exile*, 535.

[55] "British Mandate for Palestine," http://www.mideastweb.org/Middle-East-Encyclopedia/british_mandate_palestine.htm. Also, *The New Yorker*, April 25, 2011, 20.

[56] Simon Sebag Montefiore, *Jerusalem, the Biography* (New York: Alfred A. Knopf, 2011), 428.

[57] Ibid., 447. (Author's parody of a somber conversation.)

[58] Robert Lacey, *The Kingdom: Arabia & the House of Sa'ud* (New York: Avon, 1981), 275.

[59] Most historians agree that Muslims arrived as occupiers in 637, five years after the death of Muhammad.

[60] Tyler, *Fortress Israel*, 334-335.

[61] Lacey, *Inside the Kingdom*, 71.

[62] Walter Isaacson, *Einstein*, AUDIOWORKS, Simon & Schuster, 2007, disc 13, track 6.

[63] CBS program, "Face the Nation," aired July 30, 2006.

[64] "What's the Point?" *The Economist*, January 12, 2013, 42.

[65] Some Middle East experts believe the United States' military and diplomatic intrusions into Islamic holy lands were the major source of Arab resentment. Others think it was American movies and Madonna.

[66] John Peers, Gordon Bennett, and George Booth, "Sam's Dispair," *1,001 Logical Laws* (New York: Fawcett Columbine Book - Ballantine Books, 1980), 137, in Frank, *Quotationary*, 831. I altered the quote slightly. The original is, "The worst thing about stupidity is its insistency."

[67] Tyler, *Fortress Israel*, 61. Mr. Tyler is incorrect by stating, "...he would be the last to admit it." Ben- Gurion declared, "My approach to the solution of the question of the Arabs in the Jewish state is their transfer to Arab countries." See Ari Shaivit, *A Promised Land* (New York: Random House, 2013), 74-75.

[68] Ibid., 103.

[69] Ibid., 306.

[70] Ibid., 351.

[71] Ibid., 406.

[72] Carter, *Our Endangered Values*, 17. This word-by-word reading of the Bible was explained by Jimmy Carter, "We received the Holy Scripture in its entirety as the revealed will of God, agreeing that the words and actions of Jesus Christ are the criteria by which the Holy Bible is to be interpreted."

[73] See Matthew 24:29-31; Mark 13:24-27; Luke 21:25-28.

[74] David Remnick, "Danger Levels," *The New Yorker*, July 31, 2006, 22; http://www.newyorker.com/archive/2006/07/31/060731ta_talk_remnick.

CHAPTER 7

EGO, ILLS, AND SANE

Looking into a reflecting pool of water,
Narcissus fell hopelessly in love with his own face.
Thus smitten, he pined his life away.[1]

I am now the most miserable man living.
If what I feel were equally distributed to the whole human family,
there would be not one cheerful face on earth.[2]

I feel better all over, more than anyplace else.
—anon

The EGO procedures and the ILLS therapies performed on the humans in the early twenty-first century were instrumental in lowering the threshold of acceptability for making yet more changes to the species. As time went on, the exceptional became the ordinary. For example, plastic surgery was once performed in secret, and a person undergoing this procedure stayed in hiding until the scars healed. Shortly thereafter, the younger-looking person rejoined his circle of friends and colleagues, ostensibly having returned from a wrinkle-removing vacation in Hawaii. Before long, this hush-hush maneuver became passé, and a prospective makeover patient would proclaim, "It's time for another facelift." No one cared, as long as they had equal access to the cosmetic ("plastic") surgeon's knife.

The Cepee remembers a Rule of Life he came across in the Human Archives. It is titled, the Feel Good Law: The disposition to disregard almost any taboo or proscription in order to attain a sense of pleasure and gratification. Acting in accordance with The Immediacy Syndrome, the goal was to feel good as quickly as possible.

The ILLS programs eased or eliminated the day-to-day miseries of a person, and in many cases, prolonged his or her life. Humans were vulnerable to germ-induced sickness. Eighty percent of their infectious diseases, such as the common cold, the Ebola virus, and AIDS, were transmitted by touch. ILLS eventually kept the germs at bay, while allowing the humans to continue their disposition to touch, hold, and love one another.

The Cepee now learns in more detail why EGO, ILLS, and SANE were implemented. More detailed examples of the programs are discussed in Chapter 11. Figure 7-1 depicts a time line, which is expanded in later chapters to show the major events contributing to the development of the *Homo cepees* (again, a designation chosen, not for its genetic accuracy, but to acknowledge this extended linage of the *Homo sapiens)*. As noted, EGO, ILLS, and SANE became popular in the early decades of the twenty-first century.

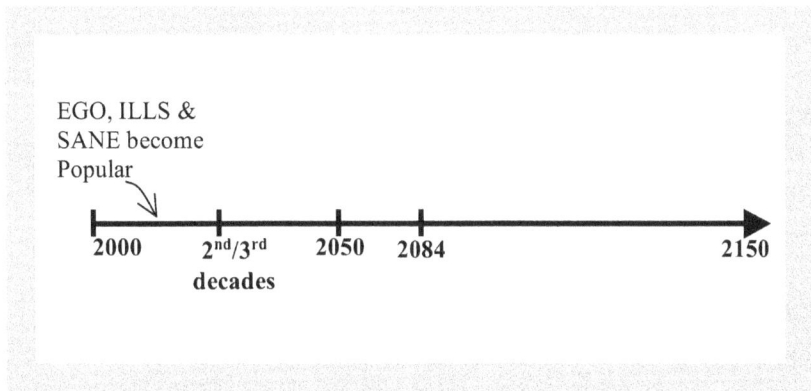

Figure 7-1. Introducing the time line.

Part I: EGO

Enhancements to Glorify Ourselves (EGO) was a fitting phrase and acronym to describe the humans' preoccupation with their physical appearance. Notwithstanding this egocentrism, the caring for and taking care of their body was not pointless ego stroking. A neat, attractive human attracted the sexual attention of another human, easing the way toward producing attractive little humans. Thus, having regard for one's looks was a positive attribute in the human's makeup, because it led to an increased population of above average looking people, decidedly more pleasant to behold than the unaltered gargoyles living next door.

Most members of the human race wanted attention and recognition from other humans. Indeed, the definition of a human's self-worth was largely determined by other humans. A seventeenth-century French scientist and philosopher, René Descartes offered this observation about his contemporaries, "I think, therefore I am."

Humans often took the position of, "They think, therefore I am." The ego of a hardy, healthy human followed Descartes' dictum, but at the same time was mindful of the second pronouncement. The gregarious nature of the humans required they walk a fine line between these two philosophies.

In any case, the humans brought EGO to a fine art. Their hair was center stage. They cut, shaved, and dyed the hair on their head, face, armpits, arms, legs, pubic area, ears, feet, toes, hands, fingers, nose, eyebrows, back, chest, and nipples. Their physiques were a close second to hair in their grooming zeal, and the wise person stuck to healthy diets and exercise programs. Others took shortcuts with steroids.

Fat and Lack Thereof

A large part of the population in the non-noble savage countries, overburdened with discretionary income, consumed enormous amounts of food. A few of these fat humans recognized the dangers of their indulgence and attempted to diet and exercise themselves back to a reasonable facsimile of a person. Others had surgeons remove their fat. Still others had their stomachs stapled in order to reduce the size of their gluttony reservoir.

In contrast, the noble savages, living in less accommodating conditions, were blessed because they did not worry about obesity. There was no anxiety about tummy tucks or stapled stomachs, no concern with clogged arteries. Their lot in life was simpler. They did not worry about eating too much food. Their concern was eating too little.

Toward the end of the reign of the non-biosynthetic humans, the look-good industry in non-noble savage societies was larger than the pet food industry, which was saying a lot because humans cared for their pets as if they were a part of their family. For example, a dog in Beverly Hills consumed more calories per day than a child in Biafra—and the dog's food tasted better. EGO expenditures were larger in America than many countries' gross national product.

Tattoos and Body Piercings

Tattoos were a popular way to adorn a human's skin. They evolved from the process of applying ink to the body. Originally, the procedure was performed with a sharp object (of metal or bone), which held ink on its point. Using a hammer, a tattooer tapped the point repeatedly into the skin, driving in the ink just under the skin's outer layers. The term *tattoo* was derived from the noise made by repeated tappings, heard as "tatu."[3] This process was painful. Therefore, the more humane electric needle replaced the hammer and skin chisel.

Tattoos were controversial, even during their renaissance years. Some people wondered why a person would cover a beautiful body with modified India ink? The answer to this question: Most bodies were not beautiful. Even more, a tattoo made a statement on behalf of the person who wore it. The tattoo expressed the person's individuality and this person's views about life.

Nonetheless, many humans regretted having their skins impregnated with colored ink. Even though the tattoo did not wear off, its novelty often faded, as did the interest of the person wearing the tattoo.[4]

> When she was 16, Miss Li had a tattoo ingrained onto the back of her hand simply on a teen-age whim. Today, five years later, she works in a Taipei office and has tried everything from salt to chemicals—including hydrochloric acid—to remove the cartoon images of Calvin and Hobbes.

"It bothers me the way my co-workers stare at the tattoo," she confessed.

Li said laser treatment could get rid of the multicolored design. "But several 30-minute sessions are required to completely remove a tattoo," she noted, adding that the process costs around US $750. So, until now, she remains stuck with the design on her hand for all to see.

Perhaps this woman became disenchanted with Calvin and Hobbes because of their sudden retirement from the comic strips. Perhaps she found other role models as she grew older and more mature. Maybe portraits of Sun Yat-sen or Chaing Kai-shek would have impressed her co-workers. Many humans liked their tattoos for a while but changed their minds about them. They came to realize their tattoos would be part of their lives as long as they lived.

Body piercing was another EGO practice. It consisted of drilling a hole in a person's body and inserting an ornament, such as a stone, a crucifix, or an image of an animal. The humans showed great ingenuity in positioning the holes and ornaments. Every part of a body was fair game for a piercing to accommodate an associated adornment.

Young and old alike decorated themselves with tattoos and body piercings, making for interesting looking humans, especially older people. A popular advertisement for motorcycles displayed a picture of a senior citizen, mounted on the seat of a motorcycle. Outfitted in black leather, he was decorated with tattoos, earrings, and nose rings.

He didn't look the part of a rebel. The motorcycle's musculature disavowed the softness of his physique. The tattoos on his pale skin were wrinkled hangers-on from his younger days. The earring and nose ring were not of his generation. Nonetheless, the motorcycle advertisement was on the mark. This company's booming sales were not attributed to the Easy Riders of the world, but to aging white collar workers who were trying to latch on to something missing in their lives. Their quest was modest. A morsel of freedom for a short while. A brief journey into independence while cascading down a congested highway populated with SUVs, eighteen wheelers, and Holiday Inns.

Plastic Surgery and Other Cosmetic Makeovers

The humans used plastic surgery for many years to correct birth defects such as a cleft palate or a harelip. It was also used to repair disfigurements resulting from injuries or disease. In some ancient societies, a person's nose could be amputated as a punishment for a crime. This draconian penalty had a significant impact on a person's looks and vanity. What is more, few people looked forward to being in the company of a noseless person. Fortunately for all, the nose-impaired as well as the nose-endowed, the potters' caste developed a method to rebuild the nose by using part of the forehead of the noseless person.[5] The problem was not entirely solved because the person now had a restored nose but an unattractive forehead.

Plastic surgery and other cosmetic makeovers became widely accepted operations among the general populace. During the first part of the twenty-first century, business for plastic surgeons quadrupled each year. In one year alone, 15 million people worldwide underwent various forms of a cosmetic procedure.[6] Approximately 65 percent of the procedures were for the noninvasive techniques: Botox injections (injecting *botulinum* bacteria into facial muscles to reduce wrinkles), chemical peels (removing layers of skin), microdermabrasion (sand blasting the skin), and collagen injections (filling in lines and wrinkles with the skin protein collagen).

The invasive techniques required surgery. Common operations entailed reshaping the nose, lips, ears, breasts, and removing wrinkles from all parts of the face. Another popular surgery was cutting away excess flesh around the chin and neck and a related procedure called liposculpture, which removed excess fat deposits from various areas of the body.

Consequently, most of the EGO operations resulted in a more attractive human: taut buttocks, a flat stomach, uplifted breasts, an erect penis, a wrinkle-free forehead. The human's ego was assuaged with EGO.

Notwithstanding these renovations, some procedures, such as tattooing and body piercing, were considered to be extreme displays of self-worth. But as mentioned, humans continued to lower the threshold for what was considered acceptable in their emerging self-change programs.

Part II: ILLS

The performance of the pre-biosynthetic humans' organic components, such as flesh, organs, and muscles, were constrained by several design problems. First, their shelf life was short, usually less than a century. Second, they were fragile, subject to breaking, tearing, cutting, and bruising. They were also vulnerable to cold and heat, as well as attacks from assorted micro-organisms such as germs. The third problem dealt with aesthetics. When the human was alive, its body often emitted odors, principally from the goings-on of these tiny organisms. When dead, its body always emitted odors, also courtesy of these critters. That is, until its constituent parts entered the food chain cycle and became fodder for other creatures who emitted their own designer scents.

The Incurable Latent Labile Sicknesses (ILLS) programs focused on critical aspects of the humans' health and life. Several programs are discussed that deal with subjects such as pain, hypertension, depression, the over-use of steroids, and the nature of disease. Another ILLS initiative, prolongation of life, is examined in Chapter 11.

Pain

The human was quite susceptible to pain, the unpleasant experience caused by an injury, or the illusion of an injury. The minds of some humans were conditioned to think they were hurting when they were just fine. For this perceived pain, a doctor prescribed perceived pain pills, called placebos. Lo and behold, the pain often went away.

Assuming the pain was real, this feeling was part of the human's makeup for sound reasons. It alerted the person that something was amiss, such as an injury. Pain often invoked a reflexive response to move away from the cause of the injury. It sometimes forced the person to reduce activity, providing time for an injury to heal.

Humans experienced pain because specific nerve endings in their tissues and organs specialized in detecting noxious stimuli—a catchall term for injury-causing events, such as heat, extreme pressure, and cuts. The nerve endings responsible for detecting pain were called *nociceptors*. Several million of these organic receivers were interspersed through the human's tissues and organs.

The typical human ingested almost anything to rid himself/herself of pain. The remedies included (a) simple pills, consumed to relieve mild pain; (b) narcotics, taken for pain, but also to feel good; (c) alcohol, which was not advertised as a pain killer but did indeed kill a lot of pain—until the next morning; and (d) acupuncture, which appeared to cure a lot of ills, but no one knew exactly why.

The modern human and the emerging Cepee made inroads in combating pain signals that had outlived their usefulness. Medicines were invented to diffuse the nociceptors' communications to the brain. By the twenty-second century, pain was becoming an antiquated term. By 2150, pain was found only in passages of the Human Archives.

Hypertension

Hypertension was a medical condition in which constricted blood vessels resisted blood flow, causing the blood to exert excessive pressure against vessel walls. The heart had to work harder to pump blood through the narrowed arteries. Hypertension was a major health problem to the Cepee's ancestors. It affected 25 percent of people living in North America. Many were unaware of their condition until they suffered from a stroke or a heart attack.

To combat this disease, a doctor usually prescribed diet and lifestyle changes to lower blood pressure. Because obese people often suffered from hypertension, many heavy patients lowered their blood pressure by losing weight. Often, a discerning physician's first prescription to an obese patient was an abrupt statement to gain the patient's attention. While not accurate, it proved effective: "If it tastes good, spit it out." The second prescription offered vital and truthful advice: "Get off the couch." Exercise was a cornerstone of fine health for humans (and Cepees).

The physician usually prescribed medications whose actions promoted excess salt and water excretion This procedure reduced the amount of fluid in the bloodstream and relieved pressure on blood vessel walls. Other drugs reduced the heart rate and the amount of blood the heart pumped. Still others prevented the narrowing of blood vessel walls to control blood pressure.

Taking these drugs could cause major side effects, some of which seemed worse than the cure. A hypertension pill might damage the digestive system, liver, pancreas, skin, bones and muscles, nervous system, eyes, and the sense of taste. The pill could lead to the loss of sexual desire and performance. It could cause allergy problems as well as wheezing and shortness of breath. Nonetheless, hypertension was eventually removed from the humans' stock of illnesses.

Steroids

Most of the humans' medicines were beneficial. Occasionally things went awry, resulting in painful or injurious side effects, and (rarely) death. But overall, the medicines were helpful to the human race.

Not so for certain steroids. These medicines were initially created to treat a variety of skin ailments, rheumatoid arthritis, asthma and allergies, eye diseases, and the malfunctioning of the adrenal cortex. All well and good, except they were often misused.[7]

Anabolic steroids, derived from testosterone, increased the weight and muscle mass of those who took the pills. They were developed for medical purposes (for example, fighting cancer), but they were abused by many athletes who hoped to improve their performance on sports fields and arenas. Unfortunately, the pills produced serious psychological and physiological side effects in these athletes, including increased aggressive behavior, cancer of the liver, and other indispositions.

The answer to the steroids epidemic was simple. The latter humans and the emerging Cepees stopped taking them.

Mental Illness

Because of the humans' genetic and mental makeup, as well as their environmental surroundings, approximately 22 percent of adults (based on studies conducted in America) suffered from mental disorders.[8] Brain images revealed the circuits (synapses) between parts of the brain failed to perform correctly in people with depression. The chemicals used by nerve cells to communicate with one another, called neurotransmitters, were out of balance. Consequently, the brain of a depressed person often malfunctioned in its attempt to control moods, thoughts, sleep habits, and appetite—the person's overall behavior. The illness, called clinical depression, could not merely be wished away. No amount of will power could force a person's mind to right itself.

The illness of depression took three forms: depressive disorder, dysthymic disorder, and bipolar depression. A person with (1) depressive disorder experienced a depressed mood or loss of interest in normal activities, which occurred in periodic episodes. On the other hand, (2) dysthymic disorder was characterized by milder symptoms, sometimes lasting for years. The humans suffering from (3) bipolar disorder cycled despairingly between episodes of deep depression and episodes of mental highs known as mania. In the manic phase, a person might act on delusional schemes, ranging from unrealistic romantic aspirations, to robbery, even killing.

Fortunately for the afflicted humans, clinical depression was usually treatable. Unfortunately, the treatments were sometimes accompanied with unhealthy side effects, such as suicide.

Notwithstanding this side effect, up to 70 percent of clinically depressed people responded positively to antidepressant drugs. If the drugs did not help, and psychotherapy was not effective, electroconvulsive therapy (ECT) was applied to the human's brain. Electrodes, placed at precise locations on the head, delivered electrical impulses and caused seizures within the brain. Medical experts thought ECT also improved the chemical balances of the neurotransmitters. ECT was controversial because it could cause disorientation and memory loss, but it was effective in alleviating severe depression.

During the twentieth and twenty-first centuries, the sales boomed for antidepressant medications. In one year alone, 213 million antidepressant prescriptions were filled for a population of about 284 million people.

Side effects accompanied the intake of many of these medicines and drugs. Some pills had no associated problems, but for others, side effects were significant. The antidepressants produced disagreeable behavior in some people. As an example, after ingesting too many antidepressants, a pill taker might exhibit restlessness and direct his or her hostility toward other people. This reaction often had the unfortunate effect of these people reciprocating the aversions, producing even more hostility.

As mentioned, another side effect resulted in the antidepressants evoking suicidal acts in some of the pill takers. This sad peculiarity of proven remedial medicines resulted in significantly reduced depression on the part of the pill taker, but not one that the drug industry advertised during prime time.[9]

Still, one would think an expensive pill, designed to reduce or eliminate depression, could be designed to at least keep the patient alive. In theory perhaps, but a human's brain was very complex.

Killer Brains and Brain Killers

The problems discussed in the previous section could often be treated with medicines. The challenge was to find and then treat those who were mentally ill. Before these people were discovered, they sometimes wreaked havoc on others, leading to frightened societies (discussed in Chapter 8). Other times, they were not discovered or they assumed such positions of power they could not be curtailed or controlled, leading to dangerous societies (also discussed in Chapter 8). These mass killers came in three varieties: psychopaths, psychotics, and severe depressives.[10]

Psychopaths. Some (rare) humans were "born with no capacity for empathy, a complete disregard for the suffering of others." While this illness manifested itself in varying degrees of severity, the sadistic psychopath enjoyed the pain he inflicted on others.

He gained pleasure by killing and maiming anything living, even helpless animals.

This person might not have come across as dangerous because he was usually able to disguise his disease by flattery and persuasion. During the humans' times on earth, no treatment was ever discovered that would help this person. To the grave detriment of those around him, he was destined to live his life without a cure.

Psychotics. A psychotic person did not kill for his self-gratification, but massacred fellow humans to somehow relieve himself of his own anguish. Unlike the psychopath, the psychotic, the victim of an unfortunate generic roll of the dice, was open about his torments.

The psychologists of the early twenty-first century described this person as follows: "Psychotic killers are, most commonly, suffering from schizophrenia, a disease marked by delusions, hallucinations, and loss of emotion, speech, and motivation." Their loss of touch with reality was often accompanied by fears they were being threatened. One such man, who slaughtered students on a university campus, proclaimed:

> You have vandalized my heart, raped my soul, and torched my conscience. You thought it was one pathetic boy's life you were extinguishing. Thanks to you, I die like Jesus Christ, to inspire generations of the weak and defenseless people.

Depressives. Many humans suffered from and dealt with depression. None other than Abraham Lincoln, a legend among some of the humans, had bouts of depression. But most of these people did not suffer from *vengeful* depression. This particular person blamed his sour moods on those around him, even the society in general. What to do to assuage his anguish and distress? As an example of the mass murders of the humans' later times on earth, a tragedy known as Columbine, one of the killers had this to say:

> In 26.5 hours I will be dead, & in happiness. The little zombie fags will know their errors & be forever suffering & mournful. HAHAHA.

These deranged humans usually intended to die during their acts of killing others. They made a mockery of the old saying, "To take life is always to die a little."[11] This simple statement acknowledged the preciousness of life and of the care that should be taken to sustain it. These pathetic and sad beings had no respect for either.

Was it evolution gone amok? Yes. Could the human repair this part of itself? Yes, as described shortly with the SANE programs.

Diseases

As the humans developed an impressive inventory of medicines to combat diseases, as their bodies digested the chemicals and associated antidotes, the complex interactions of the drugs often created unwanted side effects. More seriously, their immune systems became increasingly reliant on the medicines to do their work for them as their natural, at-one-time remarkable biological defenses began to atrophy. Instead of allowing the body to build its own defenses against an invading germ, the ailing human paid a visit to the local pharmacy and bought a pill to do the job.

The Cepees often study the Human Archives records about the Roman Empire, a remarkable dominion that held sway over many parts of earth for almost five centuries.[12] Initially, in the early days of Rome's reign, the Roman citizens took care of their defenses, manning the forts and other strongholds surrounding the city, and later, their large empire. These citizen soldiers fended off invaders who coveted the Romans' wealth and regal living styles. However, the Romans gradually turned these defenses over to foreign soldiers. In turn, the citizens gradually became lethargic and inept in the important task of defending themselves against foreign assailants.

Like the Romans, who made the mistake of buying too many foreign legions for their defense against the Visigoths, the modern humans made the mistake of buying too many pills for their defense against germs.

With a four-billion year-old resume, the germs had devised many tactics, many line items in their job description, for infiltrating and living off the human. Usually, they were "smart" enough not to make the human too sick or to kill their host. The latter act would result in a self-imposed eviction from their residence, an action of no benefit to them or their human innkeeper. With some exceptions, the germs were welcome guests, because they helped the host in its ongoing housekeeping tasks, such as digestion.

Mutants to More Misery

Notwithstanding this fragile landlord/tenant relationship, antibiotic-resistant bacteria came to pose a major threat to the health of many humans. As one example, a mutant superbug named NDM-1 allowed a bacterium to produce an enzyme that could neutralize, "any antibiotic, including last-resort medications known as carbapenems, which had proved impervious to other bacterial enzymes."[13]

Equally alarming to the humans, these resistors to carbapenems, the last line of defense, at least for a while, threatened to render many medications useless in treating common infections.[14]

It became evident that stronger antibiotics were not the answer. Invariably, a number of bacteria developed a mutated resistance to even the most powerful antibiotic. These bacteria would proceed to multiply, requiring the invention of another antibiotic. Efforts to defeat tuberculosis in several thousand sick people in India caused the TB bacterium to mutate into a more deadly strain. Other approaches discussed later had to be placed into the humans' ILLS programs.

Symbiosis

The association between the germ and the human was complex. Their symbiotic relationship took on one of three forms. The first was *mutualism* wherein the germ and the host derived benefits from the germ's presence. For example, the germs in a human's intestinal tract aided in digestion. As another example, anaerobic mouth flora kept an unwanted mate on the other side of the bed in the morning. The second relationship was *commensalism* in which a germ took something from the human, gave nothing in return, but did not harm its host. For example, some humans' tonsils were guests to a food lith. It contained bacteria that did no harm to the human and provided a home for the organism. The third relationship was *parasitism*. This germ-to-human relationship was an example of one-way symbiosis because the germ harmed the human by (a) making a person sick, (b) embarrassing the person, (c) killing the person, or (d) any combination of the three.

The Invader's Thrusts, the Invadee's Parries

The humans' diseases became more sophisticated. So did the germs living in their bodies or residing in nearby residences, such as cats, sheep, and monkeys. As the humans and other mammals evolved, so did the germs.

The humans' body cells possessed a protein marker on their cell membranes. The marker detected the presence of another agent (an antigen) that might harm the cell. Thus detected, protein molecules called antibodies hunted down the culprit antigens. Antibodies prevented antigens from attaching to a cell, and thwarted the potential initiation of a parasitic cycle of growth and reproduction. Furthermore, helper cells aided in the rescue by releasing proteins designed to kill the invaders.

The human's defenses did not stop with this germ repulse. Some of the cells involved in the defense remembered their encounter with the interloper. If the attackers attacked again, the body was conditioned to react faster to the invasion, thus executing a concept called immunity.

But the germs were often able to adjust their behavior as well. In order for a germ to attack a human and initiate an illness or disease, it had to attach itself to the cell. Some germs could change their external makeup by producing different proteins from those antibodies thought to be their marker, and execute a successful attachment. One germ (the gonococcus) could select about three hundred different camouflages to fool the antibodies.

Some germs disguised themselves by coating themselves with a cover, which protected them from attack by the human's immune system. Others attacked the body's T cells, which were the human's forward defense against invasion. The disabling of T cells allowed other germs to attack the human, leading to more diseases. Still others produced enzymes that disabled antibiotics.

The battle loomed on. First the germs took an advantage, next the humans countered, then the germs retaliated, and so forth. The combatants used every weapon in their arsenals. Toward the late twenty-first century, the humans began to gain the upper hand. First, they came to rely less on antibiotic medicine because of the germs' ability to fight off these drugs. Second, they altered the germs to make them less parasitic and more mutualistic. Third, they altered their own defective genes to make them healthier and less susceptible to the germs.

In the end, the humans' immense brain power's thrusts eventually overcame their brainless enemies' parries. But it was a humbling experience for the humans. These "brainless" organisms were disturbingly intelligent. One saving grace for the humans to deal with these surreal microbes was to make them more "user friendly," a topic for Chapter 11.

Part III: Beyond ILLS: SANE

The success of the ILLS efforts brought forth a multitude of related projects. Many of them combined the ILLS initiatives to forge yet more radical changes to the human. Some of ILLS programs were extended to make a person disposed toward better mental health, the subject of the remainder of this chapter.

I place the words "initially" and "unwittingly" into the mix to emphasize once again the happenstance manner in which humans began the transformation to the Cepee.

The humans dubbed these initiatives as SANE, for **S**upplying **a N**ew **E**go. The programs entailed the manipulation of genes, as well as making changes to parts of the humans' brains. These efforts, which were quite successful, masked, improved, and often eliminated humans' mental miseries. Many of these efforts produced marked declines in human aggression and greatly diminished the damage of the actions of psychopaths, psychotics, and severe depressives.

Hello Psychopaths, Psychotics, and Severe Depressives, Meet Pleasure and Trust

The word *pleasure* was used by most humans to connote frivolous pursuits. An old saying, "Pleasure is a thief to business," conveyed the idea that pleasure was secondary to more serious activities. But the philosopher Aristotle put the concept into perspective, "The love of pleasure is one of the great elementary instincts of human nature."[15] The Feel Good Law was not a pointless cliché.

The sensation of pleasure, both to the human and to the Cepee, was central to living a good life: "Pleasure nourishes and sustains animals' interest in the things they need to survive."[16]

In early experiments with rats, researchers discovered animals would often purposely evoke a pleasure stimulus to their brain. Even more, they would opt for this seemingly anti-survival behavior over basic survival needs, such as food. These same animals, if given an opportunity, would induce a pleasure stimulus over 1,000 times per hour to specific regions of their brains.

The humans discovered that certain areas of their gray matter could be stimulated to decrease depression and increase pleasure. These so-called hedonic hot spots, in the sub-region of the brain's *nucleus accumbens*, and another area near the base of the forebrain, were increasingly manipulated by the humans to give themselves more pleasure, with associated decreases in mental illness and aggression.

Some extreme forms of mental illness came about from a dysfunction of the amygdala, which were almond-shaped groups of gray matter located in the midbrain.[17] Brain scans of psychopaths revealed the paralimbic regions of their brains were different from those of normal humans.[18] As well, researchers also found genes that were linked to psychopathic alcoholism.

On the other hand, other studies substantiated the commonsense notion that trust was one of the more important components of a healthy society. The most successful societies set up by humans had trust built into their culture. Research showed an "ancient and simple molecule in the brain play[ed] a major role" in trust.[19] The molecule was named oxytocin. Several research projects proved that higher levels of oxytocin produced more trust in people and led to decreased aggression.

In addition, researchers also discovered that testosterone, the (mostly) male hormone associated with physical and sexual assertion, could interfere with the release of oxytocin. This discovery was in keeping with the humans' evolution. After all, the species had long developed the tendency to be mistrustful of strangers because of the dangers that came along with them. As well, the build-up of a bit of testosterone here and there often led to a bit of aggression here and there.

Thus, as a gesture toward long-held genetic efficiency, it was natural to release testosterone into the body instead of oxytocin. If nothing more, to keep one's battery charged and alert to interlopers. For old times, physical predators. For more recent times, predators of many ilks.

But what if the opposite could be made to happen? What if humans could be re-tooled? As stated by the social engineers:[20]

> So what can we do to shift behavior a bit more toward the expression of oxytocin and thus improve the workings of our entire society?

This aspiration required only the manipulation of a "short protein, or peptide, which [was] composed of just nine amino acids."[21]

How simple! As an added bonus, it was shown that levels of oxytocin spiked in men and women during a sexual climax. This fact led to a huge surge in commercial products that could be taken to further increase the pleasure of copulation.[22] The only problem with this use of oxytocin was the awkwardness of its ingestion. Timing was critical, sometimes leading to anti-climaxes.

The scientists who studied human aggression were not surprised to learn that the malfunctioning of the amygdala led, not only to psychopathy and psychotic illnesses, but to depression as well. They also discovered the rostral anterior cingulated cortex (rACC) played a major role in determining a person's overall outlook on life.

Concerted efforts began in the early part of the humans' twenty-first century to engineer the amygdala, the rACC, as well as other parts of the brain (the brain stem and hypothalamus, discussed shortly) to give their race a much healthier ego. As stated, one that exhibited significantly less aggression.

Tribalism and Racism

The humans came to understand that their elevated prefrontal cortex operations could be disconnected from their physical actions. Parts of the brain, such as the amygdala, commandeered the stage to alert them to potential dangers.

These dangers had come from members of different ethnic groups, of different races, of different religions, even from people who dressed differently. (In Chapter 6 the topic of prejudice is introduced. See section with heading "Aping Apes.")

One study, which focused on racial prejudice, revealed that try as one might (even for the liberal-minded), the ancient viaducts of the brain could not be plugged. Magnetic resonance imaging revealed:[23]

> White subjects respond with greater activation of the amygdala—
> a region that processes alarm—when shown images of black
> faces than when shown images of white faces. "One of the
> amygdala's critical functions is fear-conditioning. ...You attend
> to things that are scary because that's essential for survival."
> Later studies showed similar results when black subjects looked
> at white faces.

Later discussions in this chapter focus on the role that the amygdala played in other acts of pathological aggression. Chapter 11 returns to the subject of modern humans' prejudices, and examines their efforts to alter some of the amydgala's functions.

Epigenetic Rules

In addition to the knowledge gained about the cerebral underpinnings of violent aggression, the humans made extraordinary gains in understanding the relationships of genes and culture during the process of their evolution. Through the co-evolution of genes and the environment, it was determined humans inherited predispositions to commit certain actions. These actions were often determined by epigenetic rules. The word *epigenetic* was coined to connote mechanisms relating to gene behavior, but not the alteration of the genes themselves. Thus, the Greek *epi* (over, above) was used in front of the word genetics.

These rules altered humans' perceptions and behavior. "They [led humans] differentially to acquire fears and phobias concerning [real or perceived] dangers in the environment." They determined the predispositions humans possessed in how they communicated with each other, how they bonded with others, how they loved and made love, how they reacted to chronic depression. In essence, they determined the "inherited regularities of mental development" called "human nature."[24]

Furthermore, scientists learned that epigenetic features played a role in the *Homo sapiens'* ability to make short-term changes in their behavior *without* changing their DNA organization.[25] This feature gave the human (and other organisms as well) remarkable adaptation capabilities.

Armed with this knowledge, the later time humans and the early Cepees were able to make enormous progress in combating societally dangerous epigenetic and genetic disorders, as told in Chapter 11.

Thus, the SANE initiatives led to significant inroads in finding ways to ameliorate the debilitating residues of the humans' primal genetic and cerebral legacies. And there was more. The mental engineers turned their attention to stress and its effects on world-changing decisions the humans' leaders made during times of crisis.

Stress and Behavior

Even with the discoveries just described, the humans remained puzzled about how they could "lose it?" Why they would seemingly bound off into irrational, self-defeating behavior? After extensive introspection and inspection, humans found many of these mysterious actions were attributable to the ancient parts of their brains taking over the otherwise composed operations of their prefrontal cortexes. These precipitous acts, in the past vital to survival and holding on to the lower rungs of the Human Tribal Hierarchy, became severe handicaps to modern humans' interactions with a world that was disposed to attending to the upper rungs of the Hierarchy.

Neuroimaging techniques revealed several activities taking place in the brain during periods of stress and periods of composure. These somewhat technical explanations can be summarized as follows: In times of stress, the humans' older parts of their brains (designed to react to danger) often took over their more recent additions, which were designed for acting in benign and non-threatening situations.

The humans eventually passed these vital discoveries to the Cepees:[26]

- During an unstressed period, signals from the prefrontal cortex made their way into parts of the brain that ordinarily subdued primal actions: striatum (habits), Hypothalamus (hunger, sex, and aggression), and amygdala (fear). The brain also regulated the activity of neurons that enhanced the activity of neurotransmitters (emitting dopamine and norepinephrine) that strengthened the brain's connection to the neocortex.

- The humans' neocortex's functions often assuaged and controlled the humans' quick, spontaneous—often deleterious—acts. Acts that increasingly made little sense in a world that had a bounty of food and ample shelter. And one with more open opportunities for having the pleasures of sex.

- Yet, the humans had to deal with their ancient tribal legacies. During periods of stress—in past times, protecting themselves from assorted predators—their amygdala took over the production of dopamine and norepinephrine. This assertion shut down the operations in the neocortex and "strengthen[ed] activity in the older parts of the brain, thus lessening the brain's ability to control emotions and impulses."

As a consequence of these changes, the ancient, survival-oriented protocols of the hypothalamus, brain stem, and amygdala subdued the neocortex and dictated the human's actions. The result of a stressed mind? Often, it led to precipitous proclamations such as, "Bomb 'em!" or "You are with us or against us!" or "He's a Shia, not a Sunni! Off with his head!" or "The infidels have invaded sacred land. Kill 'em!"

A particularly precipitous statement, "Saddam Hussein…is addicted to weapons of mass destruction," was the driving force for an American president to initiate a war against another man whose country had no nuclear weapons.

After Hussein was dislodged, the president declared, "The tyrant has fallen, and Iraq is free." As a result, Iraq changed from a Sunni theocratic state to a Shia theocratic state, which further upset the balance of power in the Middle East.[27]

These kinds of responses had been built into the human's DNA over many centuries. If an ancient man—acting as a hunter or prey to being hunted—did not act quickly to a situation, he often was subdued or even killed. Thus, the humans' primal wirings, vital to survival in past times, often overcame the more rational operations of other parts of their brains.

Unfortunately for the modern human, once these statements had been uttered, one could not back down. Second thoughts would show weakness. Once said, they became physical realities. A hindsight reflection of, "Maybe I have over reacted," did little to recover the dead bodies strewn about in response to a world leader making proclamations because of an overactive amygdala, hypothalamus, or brain stem.

Moreover, leaders' hindsight reflections and their statements about their actions usually supported their precipitate declarations. How could any prideful human possibly accept the blame for engaging in a worthless war that had led to thousands of deaths or maiming of soldiers and civilians, untold numbers of former combatants who became mentally ill because of the war, destroyed cities, and wrecked economies? Yet, examples were abundant, from ancient to modern times. From Rome to Rhodesia, leaders routinely killed-off their own subjects for spotty reasons, or for no reason at all.

The Cepee pauses from his reading of the Human Archives. He thinks: *I read earlier that one of the human philosophers said,* "Pride is prosperity's common vice."[28] *Yes, but to think one human's prideful actions could have such catastrophic consequences. It's another example of the humans' Disproportionate Ratio in action.* The Cepee clicks the archives' continue button.

Altering Reality?

In spite of these daunting legacies, by manipulating cerebral areas, mental surgeons were able to influence their patients' outlooks on life. The same held true with the genetic engineers. They also succeeded in changing a person's personality. These behavioral alterations inevitably led to moral philosophers debating the question: Can cerebral and genetic changes to humans lead to a change in the overall behavior of the species? Can the human be re-wired by humans themselves?

A large segment of the human population, reading their holy books as if their passages were medicinal prescriptions for spirits in the brain, said no. They said only God permitted such soulful manipulations. The scientists and surgeons said yes. So did the Cepees. As recounted in Chapters 10 and 11, the views of human doctors—and later, Cepee surgeons—prevailed.

SANE for the Sane and Insane

As discussed in this part of the chapter, humans began efforts to give themselves more pleasure and make themselves more optimistic. At the same time, they reduced and sometimes even eliminated mental illness.

The regions of the brain pertaining to trust, stress, and optimism were engineered to produce a happier and less contentious human. In addition, the manipulation of DNA produced remarkable advances in combating psychopathy, psychotic illness, depression, Alzheimer's, social anxiety disorder, schizophrenia, and Huntington's disease.[29]

Finally, the humans accepted the idea that harboring and showing distrust was a big factor in provoking aggression. With the progress made in their ILLS programs, the SANE initiatives led to dramatic changes to the human's mind. These changes formed the foundations for the psyche of the Cepee.

Conclusions

The EGO programs, valuable for their time, provided fixes to the human's unwieldy, unreliable, and often unattractive bodies. The biosynthetic elements that became part of the Cepee solved many of the problems the EGO initiatives had addressed.

The ILLS initiatives complemented EGO's agenda and went to the heart of the issues associated with human's health. These tasks were immensely complicated and frequently resulted in genes being delivered to an incorrect spot in the DNA code, a mistake that could activate genes leading to other problems, such as cancer.[30] Nonetheless, after many centuries, the human race had begun its successful quest to conquer germs.

Both EGO and ILLS, with their phenomenal successes, led to even more ambitious programs to retool the human's psyches. SANE manipulated both ancient and modern brain parts, eventually leading to a decidedly different human being, and later, the Cepee.

These changes, significant as they were, reflected only the tip of humans' self-change iceberg. Chapter 11 continues this discussion with a more detailed examination of how the humans made deeper inroads toward becoming a dramatically altered lineage.

---

[1] Microsoft's Encarta Reference Library.

[2] Doris Kearns Goodwin, *Team of Rivals* (New York: Simon and Schuster, 2005), 99. The quote from Abraham Lincoln should be taken in the context that he had a few things on his mind, such as winning the American Civil War and reuniting a bitter, fragmented nation. Nonetheless, Lincoln was known to be a melancholy man and experienced episodes of depression during his life. These times were not restricted to his presidential years.

[3] "Tattoos—From Taboo to Mainstream," *National Geographic News*, October 11, 2002. Some doctors caution about the potential dangers of using laser surgery for tattoo removals.

[4] http://www.chinapost.com.tw/http://www.chinapost.com.tw/.

[5] Microsoft's Encarta Reference Library.

[6] Claire Bates, "15 Million People Worldwide Had Plastic Surgery in 2011... But Why Are South Koreans so Much More Likely To Go under

the Knife?" http://www.dailymail.co.uk/health/article-2271134/15million-people-plastic-surgery-world-just-year--SOUTH-KOREA-leading-way.html.

[7] Microsoft's Encarta Reference Library.

[8] This section was sourced from several papers (authors Carol Lewis and *Liora Nordenberg)* on the Food and Drug Administration website; FDA. Also, *FDA Consumer* magazine, January-February 2003.

[9] Shankar Vedantam, "FDA Wants Anti-Depressants to List Warnings," *The Spokesman Review*, March 23, 2004, A1.

[10] Dave Cullen, "What a Killer Thinks," *Newsweek*, August 6, 2012, 30-34. These three major categories are taken from this article, and the quotes that follow about these diseases are also sourced from this article.

[11] John Wain, "A Song about Major Eatherly," *Weep Before Gods*, in Leonard Roy Frank, *Quotationary* (New York: Random House, 2001), 425.

[12] Philip M. Tierno, Jr., *The Secret Life of Germs* (New York: Atria Books, 2001), 66-67.

[13] "Lab Report," *Time*, October 4, 2010, n.p.

[14] Maryn McKenna, "The Enemy Within," *Scientific American*, April 2011, 48.

[15] Aristotle, "Nicomachean Ethics," 10.1, trans. J. A. K. Thomson, in Frank, *Quotationary*, 604.

[16] Morten L. Kringelbach and Kent C. Berridge, "The Joyful Mind," *Scientific American*, August 2012, 42.

[17] Ibid., see accompanying illustration.

[18] John Seabrook, "Suffering Souls," *The New Yorker*, November 10, 2008, 72.

[19] Paul J. Zak, "The Neurobiology of Trust," *Scientific American*, June 2008, 88.

[20] Paul J. Zak, "The Trust Molecule," *The Wall Street Journal*, April 28, 2012, C2.

[21] Zak, "The Neurobiology of Trust," 89.

[22] Part of the ideas in Zak's research and writings.

[23] Jeffery Kluger, "Race and the Brain," *Time*, October 20, 2008, 59.

[24] E. O. Wilson, *The Social Conquest of Earth* (New York: Liveright, 2012), 193, Kindle edition, loc. 3119.

[25] O. J. Rando and K. J.Verstrepen (February 2007), "Timescales of Genetic and Epigenetic Inheritance," *Cell* 128 (4): 655–68. doi:10.1016/ j.cell.2007.01.023. PMID 17320504.

[26] Amy Arnsten, Carolyn M. Mazure, and Rajita Sinha, "This Is Your Brain in Meltdown," *Scientific American*, April 2012, n.p.

[27] "George W. Bush Quotes, http://www.brainyquote.com/quotes/ authors/g/george_w_bush_4.html#T7lsbVgSYkrFX3UM.99.

[28] Publius Syrus, *Moral Sayings*, 987, trans. Darius Lyman Jr., 1862, in Frank, *Quotationary*, 654.

[29] Amy Arnsten et al., "This is Your Brain in Meltdown." This article also emphasizes the role these elements of the brain play in a person having or not having stress.

[30] Tom Friend, "Elusive Gene Therapy Forges On," *USA Today*, February 24, 2003, n.p. Posted online on February 23, 2013.

Chapter 8

Bombs Awry

One man's terrorist is another man's freedom fighter.

Terrorism is a two-way street.

EGO was a popular program with the human race. It flourished through the arrival of the Cepees. The ILLS projects were engaged in a race against germs, diseases, and mental illnesses. They experienced astounding successes in prolonging life and decreasing misery. SANE put a capstone onto the the ILLS's mental programs.

Nonetheless, regardless of the successes of EGO, ILLS, and SANE, the ASSES programs would have been undertaken anyway, because the humans could not mitigate their killing propensities. They could not force themselves away from the Deadly Trinity (aggression, revenge, and the Law of the Instrument). In this chapter the Deadly Trinity is visited again in relation to the frightened and dangerous societies of the twenty-first century.

Before delving into these discussions, the time line is revisited. Figure 8-1 shows two more entries. As told here, during during the second and third decades of the twenty-first century humans used weapons of mass destruction (WMD) on civilian populations. Also, during this time, germ mutations created serious problems for the health of the race as the medical industry began to exhaust its inventory of cures.

By the second and third decades of the twenty-first century, the scientific community knew it had enough knowledge about the genome to use genetic engineering to make substantial modifications

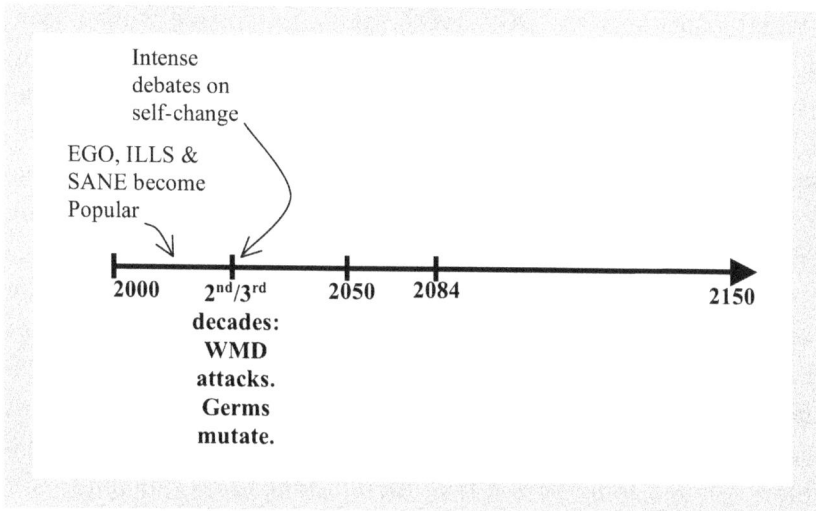

Figure 8-1. The time line, expanded.

to a human's behavior—including aggression and revenge. Thus, as noted in the figure, intense debates began on the subject of human self-change, the subject of Chapter 10.

This chapter is organized into two parts. Part I provides a profile of the individuals who used weapons of mass destruction on their fellow humans. Part II is a summary of how weapons of mass destruction came to be widely distributed.

Part I: Gunners and Bombers

The Eradicator Taxonomy

The subjects of the following three sections in this chapter are (1) demented loners, (2) demented dictators, and (3) disillusioned idealists.

Intrasocietal Mayhem, Courtesy of Demented Loners

Toward the beginning of the twenty-first century, many humans, especially those living in urban areas, began to suffer a common fear. They succumbed to a semiconscious, mass fright called the Drugstore Terrorist Syndrome, named after a man who visited several drugstores and doctored bottles of medicine with poison. The syndrome entered the picture when more than one innocent person discovered a trip to the drugstore might not be therapeutic. The result of these assaults was death or severe illness for those who were the unlucky victims of their own innocent headaches and the irrationality of a killer who struck against complete strangers having nothing to do with the killer's life.

The Drugstore Terrorist Syndrome became a catch-all phrase for other kinds of attacks, such as subway assaults, movie-theater maimings, and school slaughters. The effect of this syndrome was the inculcation into peoples' minds of a subtle, yet ever-present fear of engaging their society. Faced with the prospect of dodging a sniper's bullet, some people became reluctant to go shopping, take the train to work, go to the bank, attend a PTA meeting, show up for a college class lecture, or drive to a restaurant. Reasonably enough, for civilians who did not receive hazardous duty pay, these tasks became burdensome to their spirit.

In many cities it was unsafe to venture outside one's home at night. A common lament was, "We [are] scared every night. They will kill you for everything."[1] Or for nothing.

The emerging milieu was contrary to the humans' gregarious nature and their need for social engagement with other people. If the syndrome had been related to drugstores only, it would not have become such a pervasive problem. Caps on medicine bottles had been designed to detect any tampering. Unfortunately for the human race, the Drugstore Terrorist Syndrome exemplified other well-founded fears.

Increasingly, a human, acting alone, sometimes in concert with a few people, would stake claim to infamy by wiping-out groups of people. The Tylenol bottle poisonings, the Tokyo subway sarin nerve gas attacks, the Oklahoma City bombing, the DC/Virginia snipers, the Ohio freeway killings, the anthrax mailings, the slaughter of Russian school children, the murder of Amish students, the massacre of Virginia Tech students, the shooting of twenty children while they were attending an elementary school, the killing of Portland shopping mall customers, the slaying of movie theater patrons, the killing and maiming of athletes and spectators in arenas at sports events. These acts were accompanied by attacks on people at amusement parks, postal facilities, gambling casinos, and financial institutions.

Any public or private place became a potential killing field.[2] Even humans' homes, which the noted statesman Cicero declared to be more pleasant than any other place, were not protected from this chaos. Family members routinely polished off their relatives. Mom's dressing-down remark to a seething son about his dress habits had to be uttered with much more caution. The child might have a Glock stored in his sock drawer. Thieves would also kill residents in homes they robbed, often torturing them before leaving them dead.

Arming Schools. Regarding the assault on an elementary school mentioned above, the Cepee learns an organization named the National Rifle Association (NRA) proposed a solution to the problem: post armed guards at schools. At the time of this proposal, there were 98,817 public schools in America plus several thousand private schools. Rounding the number to a conservative 100,000, the proposal entailed hiring 100,000 armed guards. Many schools had multiple buildings. Many buildings had multiple entrances. Taking a conservative approach again, assuming 20 percent of these schools had two buildings, the proposal would have required 120,000 armed guards. Further assume 20 percent of these buildings had two entrances, the proposal would have required 184,000 armed guards. Again, these figures are conservative, so the figure is rounded to an even 200,000.

An armed guard could not stand guard an entire day without some help. At a minimum, another guard would be needed for relief and backup—now requiring 400,000 armed guards. Many public schools had night programs. Additional guards would be needed. Another conservative estimate would translate into well over one-half million armed guards manning the ramparts of education. The guards would not be protecting the walls of a military base, a bank, or a prison. They would be protecting educational institutions whose architectures were starting to resemble security stockades.

The NRA proposal was parodied by comedians, applauded by the gun industry, and praised by the security guard unions. While not put into law, the NRA proposal was put into practice. Heretofore unemployed (some unemployable) people would strap on their newly acquired semi-automatic pistols and report for work at the local kindergarten. The employment of over 500,000 of these citizens put a significant dent in America's unemployment rate, with the occasional side effect of innocent neighborhood strollers being felled by bullets from semi-trained, semi-skilled people.

The Cepee reflects: *What about school buses?*[3] *The children would have been even more vulnerable outside a school perimeter.* Sure enough, some school districts in America placed armed guards on buses. Other districts persuaded the local police to have patrol cars follow a bus. Some officers sat in their cars as the children boarded and de-boarded the buses. Others left their cars to personally watch over their flock as the tots made their way into the bus or into their homes and schools.

There were not enough personnel and patrol cars to protect each bus. The cops and killers played a game of school bus roulette. The police gambled the terrorists would not know which bus was under protection. The terrorists gambled they would find an unguarded bus.

Results. As the acts of urban killers became more frequent, segments of the population became accustomed to gunshots. The killing or maiming of groups of people living closely together in metropolitan areas began to take on the patina of the ordinary.[4] During coffee breaks at an office, instead of the heretofore usual banter about the local youth soccer league, the conversations came to focus on ways to lock down the local elementary school in hopes of keeping the youth inside the school safe from the outside world.

For many people, this Dodge City atmosphere became part of their daily lives, but at great cost to their psyches. They and their friends and relatives had become accustomed to living in secure and peaceful neighborhoods. Instead, they found themselves existing in an increasingly dysfunctional culture exhibiting violent traits. All the while, a phobic fear was instilled into the children about their homes and schools.

Intersocietal Mayhem, Courtesy of Demented Dictators

The demented loners, such as the attacks cited above, were a small part of the population in most societies. Without question, these people caused considerable trauma, pain, and suffering to the societies they attacked. But overall, their aggression toolbox contained a relatively modest inventory of pistols, rifles, and small bombs. As was mentioned, they usually acted alone or in concert with a small splinter group of like-minded people.

But there was another killer who existed in the humans' midst. This human manipulated other humans—often large groups, such as an entire nation—to promote his aggression. He and his followers employed deadlier tools than the urban assassin used, such as gasses, bombs, and firing squads.

The demented dictators fit into this group of sociopaths. They often controlled nation-states, such as Hitler's Germany, Stalin's USSR, Hussein's Iraq, Pol Pot's Cambodia, and Gaddafi's Libya. Their threats to the human race were far greater than the Drugstore Terrorists' acts. Fortunately, their onslaughts, easily traceable to their home turf, were met with counter aggression from alliances of other nation-states. These offsetting measures against a known nation kept the human race relatively safe.

Intrasocietal and Intersocietal Mayhem, Courtesy of Disillusioned Idealists

However, this situation changed when weapons of mass destruction became available to individuals and non-nation factions. Where once an individual (or a group) who possessed a modest killing toolbox could murder only a few people, this person (or group) could now kill thousands of people, all in one attack.

Unlike the situation of the demented dictator who ruled a country, vengeful retaliation was usually not an option, because the bombers were careful not to align their cause with a nation. They were vague, amorphous factions, usually identifying themselves by a firebrand name such as the Saved Sect, the Islamic Jihad Union, the Loyalist Volunteer Force, etc.

Unlike the urban psychopath or the head-of-state sociopath, most of these people were sane. Some were paranoid but not demented. Indeed, many were well educated, intelligent, and children of well-to-do families.

The most dangerous of this type of killer was the Islamic fundamentalist. One example was Ramzi Yousef, who established his Liberation Army. The purpose of the group was to carry out the World Trade Center bombing.

Initially, it was believed that members of these splinter groups were mentally unbalanced. However, later (and more accurate) findings claimed otherwise: "'Schizophrenics and sociopaths, for example, may want to commit acts of mass destruction, but they are less likely than others to succeed.' She [Jessica Stern, see endnotes] points out that large-scale dissemination of chemical, biological, or radiological agents requires a group effort, but that 'Schizophrenics, in particular, often have difficulty functioning in groups.'"[5]

Faults and Fault Lines

Then why would "the kind of guy you could have taken home to Mom" pull away from his supportive society in such a brutal way?[6] After hundreds of congressional hearings, interviews with terrorists, surveys of victims (those who were still alive), and Gallup polls, their reasons were understood. They were starkly simple: (a) moral outrage about their perceptions of injustices against their religion, (b) the American-sponsored Jewish colonization of their religious turf, (c) the audacity of the United States to tread on parts of Islamic religious turf (Saudi Arabia during the U.S. invasion of Iraq), and (d) their fervent wish to have the public know about their grievances as a means to justify their actions. The sidebar below provides a brief comparison between the demented loner and the disillusioned idealist.[7]

Sidebar. Demented Loner vs. Disillusioned Idealist.

Two eradicator taxonomy categories exhibited similar traits (with minor differences). The demented loner was often a bullied and/or alienated person. He was a social malcontent. In contrast, the disillusioned idealist was usually not bullied by his peers, nor was he alienated from them. He was a political/religious malcontent. Both had grudges, but the sources of their rancor were different.

Neither of these personality types had their actions triggered by "losing it." Their actions were not based on the ancient amygdala blocking the operation of the modern cortex. Indeed, their actions were far from snap judgments. They were well-planned.

They had persuaded themselves that their grand grievances would send a message to the world. They exhibited aspects of narcissism, ego-centrism, and grandiosity in believing they could teach the world a lesson.

Their acts became grander as the scope of the effect of their killings took-in more victims. Thus, they might have targeted specific people initially, but after a while, many of them began shooting indiscriminately, a deadly example of the Threshold Lowering Syndrome.

Their well-publicized actions lead to what pundits named the Hearse Carriage Effect. As more killers jumped on the bandwagon to copy other killers' actions, more corpses were piled into hearses for delivery to the local cemetery. These killings indeed had a bandwagon effect, accentuated by the Autocatalytic Effect.

The indignation of the political/religious terrorists was accentuated by proselytizing zealots, who were deeply bitter about their loss of an empire. Their once unassailable domain over vast areas of the world was now a distant memory, a faint reflection of the former greatness of their culture. The Muslims' intellectual, military, administrative, and political domains (turfs) had expanded into Europe (as far away as England), almost all of North Africa, Asia (as far away as Indonesia and the Philippines), parts of Tibet, and sections of East Russia. Between the eighth and thirteenth centuries, a period of intellectual darkness and economic regression in Europe, Muslim societies fostered science and scholarship:[8]

- Many caliphs "showered money on learning." This education was not just rote learning of the Quran, but critical thinking.
- For hundreds of years, the "Canon of Medicine" written by a Muslim was the standard medical text in Europe.
- Muslims created the principals of algebra, pioneered the studies of light and optics, and laid the foundations of modern trigonometry.
- Muslims did much to preserve the "intellectual heritage" of the Greeks, which scholars believe was a lynchpin to Europe's later scientific revolution.

But in the twenty-first century, their revered Caliph, who had formerly presided over an extensive empire, no longer existed. As well, where once the Muslims were leaders in the succoring of knowledge, by this time they had consigned themselves to the backwaters of intellectual advancement:[9]

- In 2005, Harvard University produced more scientific papers than the combined efforts of seventeen Arabic-speaking countries.
- 1.6 billion Muslims had produced two Nobel Prize laureates in chemistry and physics. Both moved from their homes and Muslim culture to the west and its worldly ways.
- The United States' 300 million citizens had produced 63 laureates in chemistry and 85 in physics.
- The Jewish community, laboring under a disproportionate population ratio of 1 Jew to every 100 Muslims in the world,

labored to produce 79 Nobel Prize winners to the two produced by the Muslim community.

These ratios—1:100 and 79:2—spoke to the heart of the matter. From the beginnings of recorded human history, the wealth and power of a population, be it a cluster of clans or an assemblage of tribes, was determined by the intellectual strength of that society. Mental muscle translated into the communal brawn, both in wealth and power.

Much of the Muslims' disillusionment was of their own individual making, or the collective fault of the country in which they were born and reared. The fact that thousands of young Muslims were unemployed and bitter was not the fault of anyone but their own failed nations and themselves.

In addition, growth and vitality were restricted in some Muslim societies that barred women from participating fully in the economic arena. The Quran was not the problem. It clearly stated man and woman were equal. But in practice they often were not.

The Cepee studying the Human Archives learns that scholars had differing views on how the Muslim empire came apart. No one questioned that the many invasions and wars with the Crusaders and Mongols sapped much of the Muslims' vigor. Later, especially in the twentieth and twenty-first centuries, one factor was starkly evident: the paranoid and intensified emphasis on religious scholarship with its associated repression of critical thinking. For centuries, the Muslims snuffed out the learning of much of anything but their holy book: [10]

- Rote learning of the Quran was considered the keystone of education. Learning how to apply the Pythagorean Theorem to the building of bridges—their passages to commerce—took a backseat to learning how to memorize spiritual passages—their bridges to paradise.
- If a scientific finding countered any passage in the Quran, the finding was rejected as being "scripturally indefensible."
- Apart from being anti-science, an utterance against the Quran or Prophet Muhammad could result in being killed. Counter

views that might lead to a tiny bit of enlightenment were forbidden. A Pakistani court sentenced a woman to death for committing an act of blasphemy against Muhammad. If she were pardoned, the Muslim clerics vowed to take to the streets, launch a jihad against the Pakistani government and the entire world, and kill all the blasphemers.
– If a thinker wished to stay healthy, he or she had to be careful about any critical comments that might reach the Muslim religious-thought police.

Essentially abandoned was the concept of *ijtihad*, the making of a decision independently of any Muslin school of law or any religious jurisprudence. Instead, religious experts (*mujtahids*) interpreted and made decisions (*taqlid*), often without the individual Muslim citizen examining the Quran. Many of these Islamic scholars were wise and practical. Others, such as the *Mutaween* in Saudi Arabia, were not scholars but doctrinaire-thought police.

The Cepee, who is growing somewhat accustomed to his ancestors' acts of ignorance and heartlessness, takes pause after reading this excerpt from the archives: On March 11, 2002, the Mutaween prevented schoolgirls from escaping a burning school.[11] Why? Because the children were not wearing headscarves and were not accompanied by a male. Result? The death of fifteen girls. Aftermath? The Mutaween, considered guilty of murder by some (including bystanders at the scene), went scot free with no taint on their resumes.

The Toll Is Taken. In the early twenty-first century, fifty-seven countries in the Islamic Conference spent 0.81 percent of their GNP on research and development. Fortunately for these countries, recent figures (late first and early second decade) showed an increase to 1.8 percent.[12] Still, that figure was paltry in comparison to other countries. America alone spent 2.9 percent. Israel, the religious enemy of the Muslims, spent 4.4 percent of its GNP on endeavors that would make the Jews an even more formidable opponent of the Islamics.

He Who Is Proud Eats Up Himself.[13] True to the lag effect, it took a while for the Muslims' once-mighty empire to decay. But what did not decay was Muslim pride and vanity. After all, they had carved out a majestic intellectual, governmental, and military presence that was equal to that of the Roman Empire. But as the American statesman Benjamin Franklin said, "Vain-glory flowereth, but beareth no fruit."[14]

As suggested by Mr. Franklin, humans' pride reared its self-defeating head. Consider Ahmed Omar Saeed Sheikh. He was a decent, peaceful man, one a daughter would be proud to bring home to meet her parents. But he became a lethal radical, a transition fueled by his "scrupulous moral outrage" at his perception of the United States and Israel waging an asymmetrical war against Islam.

His pride and the pride of his tribe had been compromised. In fairness to his plight, so had his place in life. As discussed earlier, the United Nations' and the United States' asymmetrical allocation of boundaries in the "holy land" for Jews and Arabs to occupy made no sense. With this exception, the actions made no sense to anyone but the Jews and their supporters. For others living in the area, the partitioning was an outrage.

Notwithstanding his faults, the faults of this tribe, and the ill-conceived U.N. partitioning of the Jews' and Muslims' holy turfs, Mr. Sheikh eventually resorted to self-defeating actions.

As he reached the end of his rope, he proudly proclaimed the righteousness of beheading any person who, however distanced from the source of his grievances, was aligned with the United States and Israel.[15]

Another disenchanted person was Osama bin Laden. The motivation for his terrorism had a lot to do with bruised pride. He was banished from his own home country (Saudi Arabia), then later forced out of Sudan. During these times, he regaled against perceived injustices against Muslims.

As stated, so did thousands of disillusioned young Muslim men throughout the world. Many were unemployed and had reached a dead end in their lives hardly before they had begun to live. They were easy pickings to become terrorists.

Usually, these once peaceful and idealistic men who became killers did not care about their own lives. The word *usually* is noted. The Human Archives documented instances of the terrorists' leaders vowing to their ignorant, idealistic subjugates that they would also strap an explosive tummy belt onto their own stomachs. This role reversal did not occur. The leaders remained on the back row of the chessboard to observe their pawns destroying others' pawns. Little did they know, as weapons of mass destruction found their way into their once secure back row on the chessboard, that their time would come.

If these martyrs died as a result of their acts, some believed they would be rewarded by their god with a place in paradise, populated with chaste maidens. But others were not looking for virgins awaiting them in a rapturous garden.[16] Their outrage and anger stemmed from their sense of discrimination and inequality. Their pride helped fuel their wish to build and live in a better world.

To balance the scales of criticism, the vast majority of young Muslim men did not descend into this fanatical fantasy world. Many of them attempted to bootstrap themselves into more humane and more secure lives. They remained idealistic. Their Arab Spring was a stunning and stirring demonstration of the better elements of human nature. But their noble initiatives were often undermined by a better organized and more heavily armed religiously fanatic minority, or a military establishment taking over when events started to veer from their vision of a country's "proper" behavior. Such "misbehavior" from these idealists might undermine the military's underground, illegal financial spigots.

The Cepee, who has been learning about the systemic failures of these societies, thinks: *It is impossible to move forward if one looks backward. These humans created cultures carved into stone, then blamed others for their inability to move away from their rigid inscriptions.*

Patriots or Terrorists?

The protestors in the streets of the Arab Spring nations were viewed as patriots by most people around the world, but as terrorists by the people they displaced. The fighters belonging to the Hamas contingent were labeled as freedom fighters to Palestinians but tagged as deadly insurgents by the Israelis. United States Marines were considered noble warriors to U.S. citizens but killer anarchists by many people who saw them repeatedly invade turf and dislodge the (former) turf owners. Hezbollah to Iran? Patriots. Hezbollah to Saudi Arabia? Terrorists.

George Washington, the ultimate patriot of the Americans, would have been labeled by King George and his English subjects—had they used such tags in the eighteenth century—by the disparaging descriptions shown in Table 8-1.

Table 8-1. George Washington as seen by King George.

Term	Definition
Terrorist	Uses violence or the threat of violence for political purposes.
Anarchist	Tries to overthrow a society's formal system of government.
Revolutionary	Committed to a political or social revolution.
Guerrilla	Committed to the overthrow of a government.
Insurgent	Involved in uprising against a government or ruler of a country.
Militant	Active in the support of a cause; engaged in fighting or warfare.

The humans' behavior revealed an instinctual and intractable problem, manifesting itself in the guise of political and religious philosophies: on and on, never-ending assemblages of opposing factions struggling to ascend their Human Tribal Hierarchies, never viewing a situation from another's perspective. What good would that do? While a human walked a few emphatic miles in his neighbor's shoes, the neighbor would be stealing the shoes of the empathizer.

Furthermore, what was noble to one faction was ignoble to another. True to the saying, "Where one stands depends on where one sits," these adversaries knew they had to use superior weapons and strategies if they were to scale the tribal hierarchical ladders that would result in the domination of their enemies.

Patriot or terrorist, in order for the tribe to succeed, even survive, it had to go to the jugular of its enemy. And it had to cut that jugular before the enemy had a chance to do the same.

Waiting for the enemy to strike first was tantamount to signing one's own death certificate, especially if the enemy had weapons of mass destruction. The other side believed it had to launch a preventive attack first: "We must bring the enemy to his knees before the enemy brings us to our knees." Simple logic really, it had been embedded into the humans' DNA centuries ago.

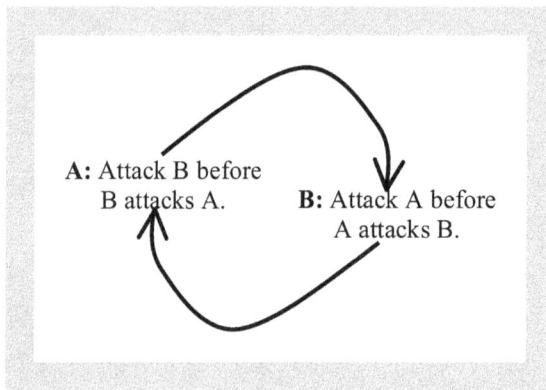

A: Attack B before
     B attacks A.   **B:** Attack A before
                          A attacks B.

Figure 8-2. The Preventative Attack Cycle.

The result was the Preventative Attack Cycle, seen in Figure 8-2. It resembles the Revenge Cycle (see Figure 3-4, Chapter 3), and the Aggression Cycle (see Figure 9-2, Chapter 9).

Consequences of Using Advanced Tools: A Review

It will be helpful to summarize a point made in Chapter 3 and amend an earlier illustration, shown in Figure 8-3. Thousands of years ago, the ancient humans' tools for destruction were limited. Clubs, knives, spears, or bows and arrows could not kill many people. Later, pistols, rifles, cannons, bazookas, flame throwers, grenades, TNT, machine guns, rockets, tanks, and other tools of the trade were added to the inventory of arsenals. The mayhem from these

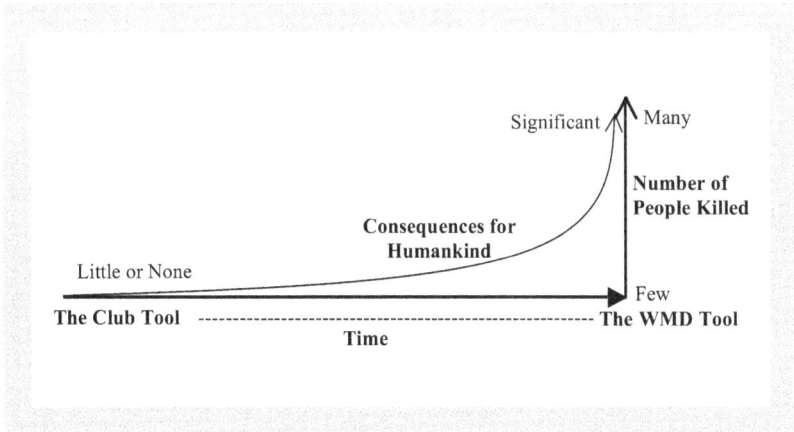

Figure 8-3. The Law of the Instrument in action.

weapons was also limited because, even though quite deadly, their killing power was limited to a few hundred humans.

With the invention of nuclear and biochemical weapons, accompanied by the increasing ease of their manufacture and distribution, the potential for a nation-state or a nationless sect to harm large populations became a harsh fact of life.

Two Forms of Attacks

The humans faced two related problems in dealing with weapons of mass destruction. One was the possibility of a nation-state attacking another nation-state. The other was a nationless faction attacking a nation-state. These two scenarios, both of which came about in the twenty-first century, unfolded as follows:

Nation States Attacking One Another. The possibility of one nation launching a nuclear (or biochemical) attack on another nation was real but somewhat remote, especially if both nations had these weapons. The aggrieved country could take revenge by launching its own missiles and gasses. This stalemate existed during the Cold War. It was a bizarre yet effective way of thinking: The possession of nuclear weapons kept nuclear weapons from being used.

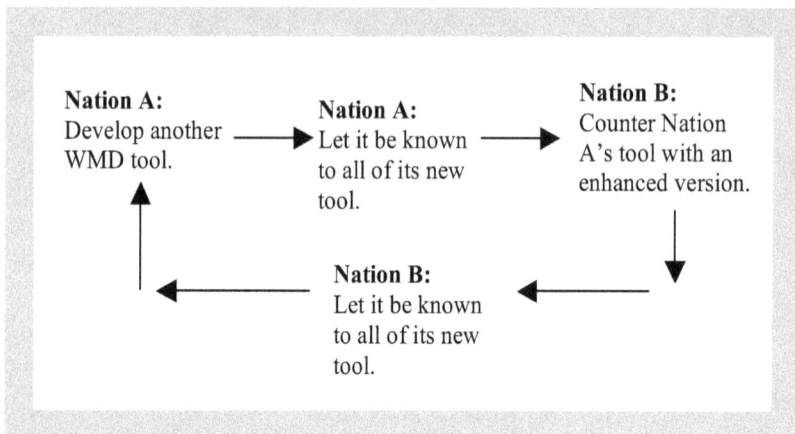

Figure 8-4. Overkill to avoid overkill.

But it was an expensive paradox, as shown in Figure 8-4. With each technological advance, a nation let it be known, usually through media leaks and other "unintentional" security gaffes, that it had developed improved nuclear and biochemical tools, instruments more capable than before of destroying any enemy who trespassed on its turf.

In the early twenty-first century, America's budgets for arming elementary schools, funding medical plans, and fixing infrastructure potholes began to eat into the budget for arming the country against its imaginary and real enemies. Enormous sums of money were needed to maintain America's status as the world's policeman. One program alone, that of a fighter plane named the F-35, ran into well over 400 billion dollars for 2,500 planes. Australia intended to buy 100 F-35s, but became a bit reluctant as the cost of each plane's purchase approached ninety million dollars.

Other countries that were climbing the rungs of Human Tribal Hierarchies had the same problem as the United States and Australia. Which was more important to a nation, a bomb or a bridge? A submarine or a school? An aircraft carrier or a fleet of air ambulances? The answers to these questions were slanted toward remaining secure from attacks from a foreign foe.

Bridges and air evacuations of an injured motorist (whose car had plunged off a rusty collapsing bridge) could wait until an enemy was defeated. After all, without bombs, submarines, and aircraft carriers, the enemy might never go away. The trouble with this approach: If enemy A went away, somewhere down the line enemy B cropped up. After all, a rung of the ladder of the Human Tribal Hierarchy for power was now available for someone else to climb.

Meanwhile, an enemy (publicly proclaimed, silently implied, real or imagined) could not afford to stand by idly while a potential attacker armed itself to the teeth. It had to build weapons and other measures to counter those the enemy had developed. Meanwhile, its infrastructure rusted away.

It was a never-ending cycle of the creation of overkill tools to avoid being killed by overkill tools, as seen in Figure 8-4.

While engaged in the cycle shown in this figure, Winston Churchill's "the romance of design," came to the fore, wherein a perfect weapon would make short work of the "nagging difficulties" of conventional warfare.[17]

Love of Weapons, Love of their Use. In addition to the fascination with better weapons, countries having sufficient tools in their armament toolbox looked for ways to use these weapons. The Law of the Instrument was once again on display. After the United States dismantled the USSR's iron curtain as well as the USSR, it had run out of contenders for its game of wartime chess. Only one nation appeared as a worthy competitor: China.

In the early twentieth-first century, China was fast becoming an economic powerhouse. Coupled with its sizable turf, large population, and past centuries of enjoying an exalted status, it began to take the position that it deserved to be treated as an equal to America.

But China's minority-status complaint was muted by its insistence that its wish for a new world order did not have to come at the expense of America's top notch places on the totem poles. It asked for "a new type of great-power relationship." To China, there was room for two in these hierarchies.

To America, a new type of great-power relationship was a threat to its hegemony and world-wide dominance. The Cepee pauses: *I've read about the British and other European nations forcing themselves onto a weak China during the Western world's imperialistic incursions into much of the world's turf; how these countries exploited and debased China with opium trade…my ancestors in action again. After decades of degradation from these Western powers for merely wishing to be left alone, China finally sought its rightful place among the family of nations.* The Cepee reads more.

Monks do not give up monasteries, voluntarily. Nations do not relinquish position and power, voluntarily. To do so would go against centuries of genetic and cerebral tilling-of-turf and empire-building. Yet, sharing of turf, sharing of hierarchies was possible in the later years of humans' times on earth. Unlike their ancient ancestors, the humans' physical existence and associated gene spreading were not at risk. But their pride was.

America began a slow, gradual, perhaps even unconscious campaign to protect its position on earth, and thwart what was a pragmatic and realistic assertion on the part of the Chinese. They went about these plans by:

- Asserting that China was ominously building up its military establishment. At that time, the United States' military budget was larger than the combined military budgets of all other nations.
- Questioning why China was engaged in cyberspace security snoops. At that time, America's NSA was routinely "snooping" into almost everyone's cyberspace, including that of China.
- Ignoring the centuries-old history of China not exercising military might outside the land and water that was not directly adjacent to it. At that time, America's ubiquitous military presence on earth earned it the moniker of U. S. E., for the United States of Earth, with "USE" interpreted as an action verb.
- Challenging China's motives for forming trade and military alliances with countries. At that time, the United States had established two major trade zones that surrounded China. But these alliances did not include China.
- Complaining China was not playing by the rules, those set by America and its allies for the past century.

This mentality was akin to a major stockholder of a company becoming a member of its board of directors, wherein his opinions and requests on changing some company policies were ignored by the older directors. Perhaps all they needed to do was engage in a bit of compromise here and there.

Perhaps not, how could they know the motives of this interloper? Like his Neolithic kinfolk, he might have come into their turf to stalk them. Better to stay "armed," better to stay prepared.

The Cepee thinks: *Yet, how could America know China's motives? If I place myself in the shoes of the United States and reflect on how the Western powers subdued and humiliated China during the eighteenth- and nineteenth-centuries; how Japan laid much of China to waste in the twentieth-century, I would have kept my guard up, too. With the ascension of China, the Revenge Cycle did not just suddenly disappear from the humans' behavior. Unlike the Americans, the Chinese did not have to invent an enemy. China's enemy had invented itself by its past behavior.*

However, my studies of the Chinese reveal they were subtle, indirect, and patient people. They adhered to a game called wei qi (go). The winner of this game did not go about engaging in a single battle, even a single war. The winner took his time. His campaign could be almost endless.

The humans' romance with weapons and enemies did not surprise the Cepee. The humans were merely carrying out their genetically ordained duties of expanding turf ownership and guarding their positions in their Human Tribal Hierarchies. However, the relatively sudden arrival of weapons of mass destruction in the *Homo sapiens'* toolbox, coupled with their revenge cycle, reinforced by the need to have a convenient enemy on which to apply their tools, accentuated by aggression gone awry, once again placed many ordinary humans in a precarious position. One not of their own choosing. One chosen by the players on the back row of the chessboard.

Nationless Tribes Attacking Nation-States. The second scenario was the use of weapons of mass destruction by disaffected, nationless individuals, or tribes. Take a pick for their moniker: They were terrorists or they were patriots. The term *terrorist* is used for this discussion.

A terrorist attack could target a vulnerable government establishment or a convenient civilian site. The attack was carried off with one of two tactics. For the first tactic, with little risk to this nationless tribe's diffused organization and its elusive leaders—but at "considerable risk" to the pawns carrying the explosives in a tummy pack—the enemy could be targeted with a bomb (usually a form of plastic explosive) that had the power to wipe out a block or so of an urban area.

With the second tactic, better-armed, better-funded, and better-organized terrorists could employ missiles and other aircraft to punish their enemy. Their explosives could wipe out an entire urban city center. With a nuclear warhead attached to the missile, an entire city could be decimated.

This type of terrorist did not sit idly on their turf waiting for the "preventive warfare" missiles from their enemy to strike. Initially, they positioned themselves in their homeland and fired their missiles from sites at home bases. But these sites were easily detected by their enemy, who then countered the attack by firing their own missiles into the terrorist's turf and surrounding neighborhoods.

The nationless terrorists were often at a disadvantage in this two-way exchange of missiles. They had fewer tools and the tools they possessed were limited in their destructive capacity. As well, most of their missiles could be shot down before reaching a target.

Consequently, with more than a tummy-tucked bomb in their possession, they migrated to the turf of their enemy, where they planted "preventive warfare" bombs and biochemical weapons in the cities and towns of their foe. They avoided confrontations with the enemy's military. Instead, they attacked nonmilitary targets or loosely guarded sites and avoided the enemy's armed forces. They became experts at asymmetrical warfare. They devised their own version of a foreign policy.

The militant Islamic fundamentalists did not expend efforts trying to penetrate and attack, say, airline security gates. Why bother? After earlier attacks, these gates were protected by security measures. Instead, other places were targeted, such as seaports, petrol refineries, bridges, railroads, storage tanks, and shopping centers, a process shown in Figure 8-5. Each time a terrorist attacked, for example a factory, the anti-terrorists then made the factory safe.

However, the attackers, being asymmetrical in their approach to warfare, selected yet another site, say a railroad yard. By the time the cycle finally terminated at "The world is safe" notation, many countries were spending a huge chunk of their resources on making an almost immeasurable number of sites terror proof.[18]

But the cycle never terminated during the humans' reign on earth. It never branched to "The world is safe." The Deadly Trinity, coupled with asymmetrical warfare and weapons of mass destruction, ensured planet earth would remain in a state of chaos until a wiser pedigree (the Cepees) could straighten out the mess.

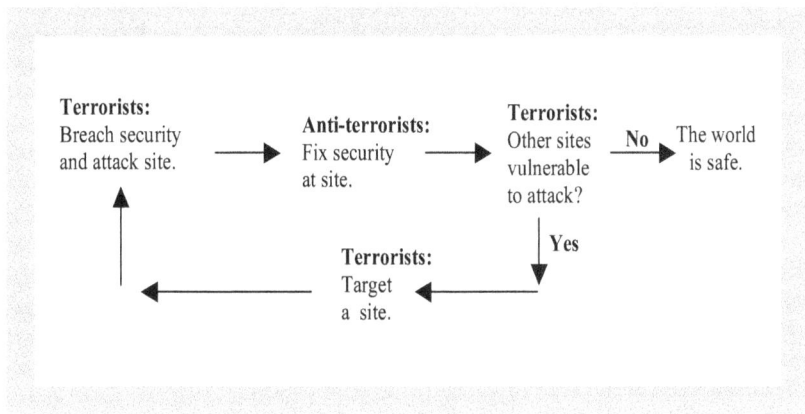

Figure 8-5. A closed loop.

Part II: Guns and Bombs

How did some humans, however small their population, reach a point where they could greatly influence the future of their race with only a few tools? What were the origins of their use of weapons of mass destruction? How did these weapons proliferate into the arms of these armed killers? The answers to these questions provide keys to understanding the effects of the Deadly Trinity. To set the scene, the Cepee studies origins of the use of chemical and biological weapons.

Chemical and Biological Weapons (CBW)

When the wind shifted on the afternoon of April 22, 1915, on fields near Ypres, France, the Imperial German Army ushered in a new age of warfare. World War I (1914-1918) had become a brutal standoff of opposing infantries fighting from fortified trenches. To break the stalemate, the German Supreme Command made a fateful decision to change strategy. At 5 p.m. German combat engineers opened 5730 cylinders of compressed chlorine gas. Blown by the wind, this vast yellowish-green cloud wafted across the battlefield toward the unprepared Allied lines.

Suddenly enveloped and choking from the mysterious gas, French and Belgian troops in the trenches turned and ran for their lives. Unopposed, but wary of the ominous cloud, the German infantry advanced a few hundred meters toward Allied lines and then dug in for the night.

The full price of developments in modern science began coming into view on this day. The science of chemistry had progressed steadily in the late 1800s and early 1900s, but it was on this day, in the blood-soaked fields of France, that newly isolated chemical agents (chemicals in a concentrated form) were first used for destructive purposes. The chemical weapons used in World War I were the first true "weapons of mass destruction" (WMD). Biological weapons of mass destruction would emerge in the 1930s, followed by nuclear weapons in the 1940s.

As chemical, biological, and nuclear weapons proliferated around the world and the technologies behind them advanced, they would together emerge as one of the most serious threats to human existence and international security ever produced by human beings. Scientific progress could bring knowledge and prosperity, but it could also provide new, ever-better tools for killing people or rendering lands uninhabitable.[19]

This narrative provided a fitting profile of a segment of the human population: creative, innovative, and deadly. As time went on, WMD became even more dangerous because the weapons could be disseminated as aerosols or liquids. Biological weapons were created from disease-causing microorganisms or toxins that were usually disseminated in vapors. Chemical nerve agents were designed to produce convulsions and death by blocking an enzyme needed to transmit messages in the nervous system. Lethal and little, a drop of toxin on the skin could kill a human in a minute or so.

Tables 8-2 and 8-3 provide a summary of prevalent biological and chemical weapons the humans had developed by the end of the twentieth century.[20] The Cepees, who retrieve and study this information, are once again astounded by the ability and willingness of their forebears to produce these tools of destruction.

Table 8-2. Biological Weapons Inventory (Not all inclusive).

Biological Agent	Effect
Anthrax	Brought on aches and pains, fever, fatigue, cough, chest pain. Inhalation was fatal.
Botulism	Affected central nervous system and interrupted nerve impulses. Impaired vision and speech. Brought on occasional convulsions, ultimately paralysis of respiratory muscles, suffocation, and death.
Salmonella	Could induce typhoid fever, food poisoning, abdominal pain, fever, nausea, vomiting, and diarrhea.
Smallpox	Skin rash developed on face, chest, back, and limbs. Rash developed into pus-filled pimples resembling boils. Death was common.
Tularemia	Caused chills, followed by enlarged glands.
Yellow Fever	Brought on high fever and jaundice, possibly death.

Table 8-3. Chemical Weapons Taxonomy (Not all inclusive).

Chemical Agent	Effect
Incapacitating agent	Incapacitated eyes and nose functions temporarily.
Choking agent	Attacked respiratory system.
Blistering agent	Created large skin blisters, with the goal of discomfort and infection.
Blood agent	Created convulsions and respiratory failure.
Nerve agent	Attacked central nervous system.

In the first part of the twenty-first century, several nations began the dismantling of their chemical and biological weapons (CBW) arsenal. But this operation ran into a problem. What was to be done with this material? The magnitude of the problem stemmed partially from the amount of CBW manufactured in the twentieth century. The United States stockpiled some 30,000 metric tons of chemical agents (although much of it was destroyed in the late twentieth-century). Russia produced at least 40,000 metric tons of CBW, with some estimates as high as 200,000 metric tons. Russia did not destroy its complete inventory. Thus, the problem did not go away easily.[21]

> Most other large states with chemical weapons arsenals pledged to destroy these stocks under the Chemical Weapons Convention (CWC), an international treaty approved in 1993. However, several states either boycotted the CWC or joined the convention but [were] still suspected of harboring clandestine chemical weapon programs. These states included China, Egypt, Iran, Iraq, Israel, Libya, Myanmar, North Korea, Syria, Taiwan, Vietnam, and the Federal Republic of Yugoslavia.

Burying the Past

What did the humans do to solve this problem? They buried it. They chose sites that were thought to be immune from earthquakes, volcanoes, and other topographical changing events. At these sites, they dug big and deep holes in which they placed *tons* of the most dangerous materials ever known to humankind, including nuclear waste.[22]

The sites were guaranteed by the companies that built them to be safe for thousands of years. If a site did not live up to this guarantee, say, one thousand years from the time it was constructed, the company that built the site could be taken to court, if the company was still around. The incongruity of this situation was not lost on the Cepee.

One site was located in cowboy country on the southeastern plains of New Mexico. This part of America was chosen because it was one of a few locations in the United States that was disposed to support uranium and nuclear weapons facilities. Thus, its population (a) had residents who were trained to deal with security challenges associated with these systems, (b) were accustomed to taking home a paycheck, courtesy of a controversial technology, and (c) were accepting of having radioactive elements in their backyard.

The plant's builders enticed prospective residents and workers to migrate and live there by advertising a rugged cigarette-carrying cowboy (a faded memory of that area) riding his horse over the ground containing tons of chocking agents. These buried materials were considerably more deadly than the chemicals in the cowboy's cigarette. In a touch of irony, the buried past was trodden over by a living past.

Nuclear Weapons

Sometimes, the best of intentions go awry. Who could have predicted the Cold War, followed by the humans' desire for cool air, large vehicles, and electrical gadgets would result, seven decades later, in the slaughter of hundreds of thousands of people, and the depopulation of thousands of acres of land?

In fairness to the humans, in many situations, they did not know their decisions would lead to long-term problems. They were not clairvoyant. The fearful consequences occurring in the humans' twenty-first century because of actions in the 1950s were beyond their comprehension. Their decision to build nuclear power plants was viewed by many people as a practical solution to serious energy problems. The results of their actions are shown in Figure 8-6 and described below.

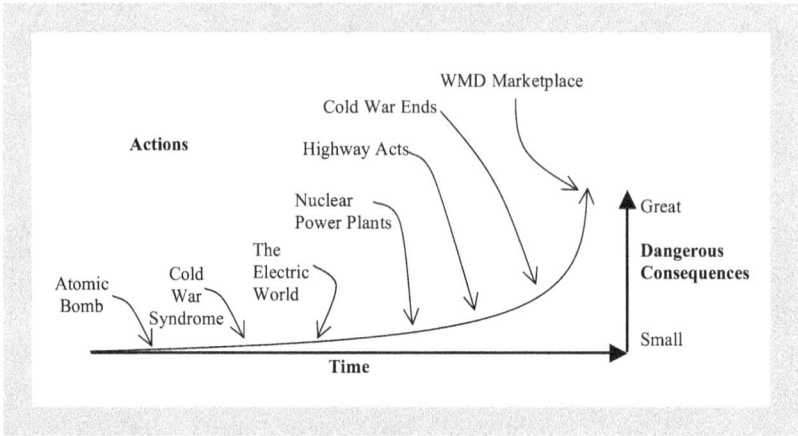

Figure 8-6. Unintended Consequences Curve for proliferation of weapons of mass destruction.

Atomic Bomb. The impetus to build a nuclear weapon came from a nation's fear of another country acquiring the weapon first and using it to dismantle that nation's societies. The problem was a real one. During World War II, it became clear that Germany and Japan had no reservations about whom they killed, in what way, or how many people died at their hands. The gas chambers, the sadistic eugenics experiments, the Rape of Nanking were chilling examples of these nations' brutality.

Thus, the race was on to build another war instrument as quickly as possible. The United States was the first country to have the bomb available, which it applied to the Japanese cities of Hiroshima and Nagasaki. The USSR followed in 1949 with its first successful test, followed by Britain in 1952, France in 1960, and China in 1964. This "group of five" took on the self-appointed job of the nuclear handmaiden for the world.

At that time, and at least for a while, these five nations had a monopoly on a powerful product. Naturally, they intended to keep it that way by preventing others from acquiring the weapon. Thus, the nuclear Non-Proliferation Treaty (NPT) was created and signed by "the group of five,' as they became known by other nations. A United Nations (UN) communiqué presented their view:[23]

> [The NPT] objective is to prevent the spread of nuclear weapons and weapons technology, to promote cooperation in the peaceful uses of nuclear energy and to further the goal of achieving nuclear disarmament and general and complete disarmament.

It took little imagination to see through this specious statement. Those countries who were outside the group of five knew they were being treated with disdain and disrespect. The UN statement was accurately read by every county on earth except five nations as (text within brackets are my additions to the statement):

> [The NPT] objective is to prevent the spread of nuclear weapons and weapons technology [to anyone except the group of five], to promote cooperation in the peaceful uses of nuclear energy [such as our bombs] and to further the goal of achieving nuclear disarmament and general and complete disarmament, [but with no timetable set for our group leading the way].

The Cepee reads, "It is said that a nation, or for that matter a person, once having its deception exposed, is thereafter suspected in anything it does." While this saying in the archives was likely overstated, the UN declaration by the group of five created long-standing distrust and animosity from other countries.

The closed club of five succeeded in containing the spread of nuclear weapons for a while. During this time, especially in the Cold War days, the possibility of mutual annihilation kept the nuclear weapons in their silos and wars contained, at least in comparison to the two world wars. So, there was positive aspect of having these weapons in existence.

But by 2006, the nations of India, Pakistan, North Korea, and Israel were armed with nuclear weapons and several other countries were thinking of going nuclear. Pandora's box was gradually being opened.

Cold War Syndrome. The Cold War confrontation between the United States and the USSR led to the eventual demise of the USSR. The Americans and Soviets kept themselves out of harm's way by arming themselves with massive armaments, including nuclear weapons. They confronted each other and backed each other down with the threat of nuclear force.

The Cold War led to five decades of military build up. The United States and the USSR armed themselves with every conceivable weapon. They also armed the armies of their respective allies. With a few exceptions, they kept nuclear weapons to themselves for their own toolbox.

At the end of the Cold War, hundreds of thousands of individuals owned modern weapons. By 2013, weapons were in every nook and cranny of the planet. Age played no factor in who had access to them. Children learned how to assemble and shoot machine guns and rockets. Old men utilized rifles for canes, crutches, and armaments. Land mines in some of the noble savage countries produced another mental malady: the Fear of Farming Syndrome.

The Electric World. During this time, the humans invented air conditioning to cool their habitats. The colder the better. Before long, most of the buildings in the non-noble savage countries were cooled down to a temperature requiring a person to wear additional clothes. It seemed the humans lost their understanding of the purpose of an open window.

The humans were either too hot or too cold. If they did not have their air conditioners turned on, they turned up their heaters. A sweater or light jacket would have done the trick but who wanted to walk around their house looking like a cast-off from a Charles Dickens' novel?

They also began to use other appliances that, as a whole, used substantial electrical power: TVs, dishwashers, clothes washers and dryers, vacuum cleaners, lights in every corner of a room, neon lights to decorate a city, lights on houses to celebrate Christmas, food and drink mixers, radios, shavers, saws, stereo sets, can openers, computers, phones—all in the envelope of cool, comfortable air conditioning.

Many people developed a fixation on driving large vehicles requiring tremendous infusions of petrol to keep them going. Some humans owned many cars and trucks, all with air conditioning and heaters.

The humans wished to be comfortable and enjoy their electrical devices. It was a reasonable desire, but they once again managed to carry their intentions to the extreme. For example, in the twenty-first century, total energy expenditures in the United States consumed about 10 percent of its gross national product (and 70 percent of its oil was used for transportation, see Highway Acts below).[24] Much of this energy was wasted.

As populations increased, many nations began to use more energy than was currently available. Some of the demand was met by harnessing the power of waterfalls, dams, and windmills, but other sources of energy were needed.

Nuclear Power Plants. The humans' solution to the energy problem was to build factories that generated electrical energy from nuclear energy. The first nuclear power plant began operating in 1954 in Obninsk, Russia.[25] Other countries followed suit in order to keep their citizens' record players (and later, iPods) fired up. All in all a practical solution, even though the radioactivity released during accidents could cause serious injury, deaths, and environmental damage. Another problem came into play: the possibility of the material at these plants being used to build nuclear weapons.

Highway Acts. The humans continued to procreate and with the exceptions of the unlucky nations populated with noble savages, many people became relatively affluent. Thus, they could buy more vehicles. To accommodate the growing populace and their increasing use of cars and trucks, the rich nations created highway acts. These laws were government-sponsored programs resulting in more roads and larger cars, requiring more energy and more highways, encouraging the purchase of still more cars, requiring yet more energy and highways. As stated above, the largest share of oil consumed in the U.S. was for transportation (70 percent).

The highway acts discouraged alternate forms of transportation and encouraged the use of motor vehicles. After all, what human would want to be transported in a bus, train, or streetcar when a private car was in the driveway, outfitted with enough accessories to resemble an ambulatory apartment? Indeed, the humans became so accustomed to their cars, they curtailed their use of bicycles, scooters, and even walking.

The motor vehicles (and many ships) of the world used some of the same fossil fuels as the electrical power stations, notably oil and natural gas (and coal for the older ships). Consequently, two huge users of energy were competing for the same rare commodity. However, if, as examples, ships and especially power stations could be redesigned to use nuclear power, the precious fossil fuels could be used for powering automobiles, trucks, and buses. So, the highway acts, which helped build the motor vehicle industry, also helped build nuclear plants.

End of Cold War and the Emergence of a WMD Marketplace. The Cold War came to an end with the dismantling of the Berlin Wall (1989) and the dissolution of the USSR (1991). These events should have had a positive effect on planet earth. The reduced tensions could have led to reduced armaments, resulting in reducing the human race's exposure to nuclear weapons.

After the Cold War, Russia's nuclear arsenal management practices began to deteriorate, a dangerous situation discussed in more detail shortly.[26] Recognizing the risks of this situation and its potential for catastrophe, the United States established a program aimed at securing the world's largest inventory of surplus plutonium and highly enriched uranium (HEU): the 600 metric tons located in Russia. The scope of the effort was vast. It encompassed several dozen research centers, even entire cities that had been fenced in containing over a million people. Some of these efforts were successful. Others were failures. The system was broken and no amount of aid, however well intentioned, could have prevented the stealing and/or selling of such a precious commodity.

Of course, no country whose leaders had intact minds would risk having their nuclear material associated with the production of an atomic bomb made by someone else. To do so would invite retaliation from the United States and/or Israel. But not all leaders had intact minds. A well-known seller of nuclear weapons was the Khan Research Laboratories, operating out of Pakistan, and also discussed in more detail shortly. It was caught in the act of trying to sell Libya a $100 million nuclear arsenal package. It was also accused of providing weapons information and nuclear weapons components to Iran, North Korea, and perhaps Syria and Saudi Arabia.[27] After being caught, its operator received a slap on the wrist from Pakistan's leaders.

The Warm War

After the Cold War was over, a neutral observer might have assumed the opposing factions would have dismantled their weapons. After all, a huge evil empire no longer existed that would warrant diverting a nation's wealth to a major conflict.

But the dismantlement did not occur. In keeping with the Monks Do Not Dissolve Monasteries Rule, generals did not dissolve pentagons, politicians did not dissolve military pork barrels, and military industrialists did not dissolve their industries.

The laws of human nature, with their thousands of years in creation and maturation, discouraged humans from dismantling the means by which they lived and thrived. How fatuous it was to think a person would give up his turf. Where was he to go? What was he to do?

Consequently, after the hot wars and the Cold War of post-World War II, much of the world settled into a warm war. This warm war consisted of occasional minor wars (a few thousand dead or maimed here and there) and occasional terrorist attacks (a few hundred dead or maimed here and there). But these wars were nothing on the order of the Great Wars. Just enough mayhem to keep the world armed to the teeth.

But why? After all, these huge drains on a country's resources, for nothing pertaining to roads, education, or bridges, made no sense. But it did, at least to a relatively few humans, the Disproportionate Ratio problem again. Those occupying the upper rungs of the power Human Tribal Hierarchy, such as generals, national politicians, and industry magnates, benefited from a never-ending conflict. A warm war was an ideal arrangement for them.

If ever so subconsciously, perhaps even unconsciously, these people adapted their behavior and machinations to sponsor and encourage conflicts with low enough casualties to keep mom and pop watching TV reruns of "I Love Lucy." But these conflicts also created enough casualties to keep mom and pop sufficiently concerned that they themselves might be casualties of a next, yet unknown attack.

Of utmost importance to warm war managers was to keep the government budget larders full enough to maintain a steady stream of money flowing into their bank accounts, as well as congressional pork barrel campaign contribution funds. Stock prices on these companies rose or fell in direct proportion to congressional fundings.

The very idea of closing a military base, of shutting down a trillion dollar weapons system, of sending soldiers home from Okinawa translated into lost jobs and citizen protests. The acronym of NIMBY, not in my back yard, became SIMBY—stay in my back yard—raised its head. America had become addicted to an economy revolving around a never-ending warm war.

It was subtle and unstated, perhaps not even on the conscious horizon of its adherents, most of whom were decent people, oblivious to their dependence on the warm war for their livelihood. They were too concerned about gaining their share of the booty to understand they were at odds with their long-term well-being. After all, they were not clairvoyant.

Nonetheless, it was there. Perhaps it was initially an unintended arrangement of mutual benefit among these collaborators. But it grew into an unmanageable association for all. Meanwhile, the average citizens of a country, thinking they would be fighting for the noble glory of a religious or political cause, volunteered their services for a deadly chess game in which they were the pawns on the front row of strife and sacrifice.

Thousands of low-level warriors died at the directions of their high-level leaders. Their pre-mortem reward was first, fighting for a cause, and second, receiving adrenaline rushes from killing the enemy or escaping death themselves.

Their successes often led to infusions of dopamine into their system. Acting as an intoxicant to their judgment, the culture conditioned many of these duped beings to want to stay in combat, to kill more, and to risk being killed. These soldiers of misfortune sometimes asked to be put back on the front lines of combat.[28] Once there, they savored the battles: "Fuck, I thought to myself, 'This is great. I fucking love this. It's nerve-wracking and exciting and I fucking love it.'"[29]

The Cepee pauses from his studies: *That quote came from Chris Kyle, the SEAL team sniper who killed 160 people during his assignment in Iraq. After he returned to the apparent safety of civilian life, he was killed by a fellow warrior, a veteran of the same war.* The Cepee goes to another section in the archives. He reads that Kyle was trying to help this man deal with his posttraumatic stress disorder.

The Cepee studies this part of the archives to learn his ancestors kept records on the most sniper kills snagged by one individual. The record was held by Simo Häyhä, a soldier of Finland. He shot 505 Soviet soldiers during the Russian invasion of Finland in World War II.[30]

Many of these men, if still alive from their wars with known enemies, descended into a netherworld of nightmares, drug abuse, and abuse of their loved ones. In Chris Kyle's case, he was murdered by a trusted comrade.[31]

Meanwhile, the manipulators of these frontline warriors, the collaborators, happy that the pawns had re-upped for another tour, continued to occupy the back row of the chessboard, safe from harm's way. They were privy to the spoils of their wars. They were also immune to the wreckage their actions had taken on their naive, trusting pawns who had watched too many John Wayne movies, played too many video killer games, and attended too many propaganda parades.

These pawns earned other rewards. They were given bonuses for enlisting as adolescents, sometimes without their parents in attendance, and before they had an ounce of knowledge about the realities of war. Even more, they knew they would have war medals placed on their chests for their heroic actions. Some generals and admirals displayed over *fifty* battle ribbons on their uniforms, for never having fired a shot in combat, or having faced a shot themselves. Ah, glory!

After the battles, the warriors were shuffled for a few moments through the news media's front door to advertise their fame, and to promote the insightfulness of the news media. Often as not, the same news media would publish in their obit section a short column about these warfare pawns' temporary residency at a funeral parlor.

Ultimately, their shuffle was through the back door of fruitless anonymity. They were a soon-to-be-forgotten contribution to the larders of those who were networked into the system. Their remaining virtual existence among the living were pictures on the walls of their loved ones, brief subjects of Memorial Day eulogies, and documentaries explaining the gallant causes for which they died.

But rarely were they dead for a noble reason. They were usually dead because the collaboration of the components of another Deadly Trinity had already sealed their fate.

The old days of plunder to gain gold, turf, slaves, and women were over. The modern war spoils of gaining lucrative campaign contributions, billion dollar defense contracts, promotion to a general, or hero worship were modern-day substitutions for ancient practices.

War Mongering

The Cepee is now studying a part of the Human Archives dealing with the second Iraqi war. He is dumbfounded to learn of America's leaders who led their country into this war, especially in view that they knew Iraq was not an *immediate* threat to the United States, of "selling" the war, of their politicizing intelligence and the intelligence agencies. These people treated war as if it were an ideological video game. The Cepee comes across these facts about his ancestors' behavior during this time:

- The presidential administration (George W. Bush) performed no extensive analysis to determine what to do with Iraq after the war was over. The war was launched for ideological reasons, without regard to the potential after effects on the Iraqi citizens and the American warriors. This lack of analysis showed its head when a high-level briefer to President Bush expressed reservations about starting this war. Condoleezza Rice, the President's trusted advisor, interrupted the briefing with, "Save your breath, Richard. The president has already made up his mind on Iraq."[32]

- The war that did matter, Afghanistan, was put on the back burner. The United States warrior pawns in Afghanistan found themselves playing a deadly chess game that was now considered of secondary importance to the leaders who had orchestrated the war. They sent these men and women to war with platitudes such as *I don't do quagmires*, when they themselves created a quagmire that killed and physically/mentally maimed their trusting hostages to misfortune.

- The Vice President of the United States (Dick Cheney) spoke with absolute certainty that Iraq had nuclear weapons. He was quoted as saying, "Simply stated, there is no doubt that Saddam Hussein [dictator of Iraq] now has weapons of mass destruction."[33]

The Cepee is astounded: *Wait one minute! If Iraq did have nuclear weapons, the very last option would be to invade the country. Left with no choice but to face America's overwhelming forces, Hussein would have unleashed his nuclear weapons on the American forces and Israel.*

- There was abundant doubt from the Department of Energy and the State Department. Nonetheless, the administration was guided by the neocons in their role in this scam. They said, "The administration sold it the way it sold it. That's history."[34]

– Paul Wolfowitz (Deputy Secretary of State), while attending an intelligence briefing on attempts to rout al Qaeda and catch Osama bin Laden in Afghanistan, interrupted the briefing, "Iraq. We must focus on Iraq—9/11 had to be state sponsored. [It was not, only by the tacit acquiescence of the Taliban to al Queda's presence in Afghanistan.] Iraq is central to our counterterrorism strategy [It was not. It was Afghanistan and Africa.]." Knowing Wolfowitz was inaccurate and attending the wrong meeting, the briefer thought, *What is this man smoking?*[35]

The Cepee thinks: *But these men were on the back row of war's chessboard and out of harm's way. Safe from the deadly battles they created, this cadre's actions resulted in the front row pawns going to a war for which there was no reason for a commitment of that magnitude, and certainly not an immediate commitment.*[36] *The debate was dangerously one-sided. The side that opted for war had America's vast intelligence pools from which to draw; intelligence pools whose information had been politicized to meet the goals of the administration. The doubters had only their innate skepticism, hardly an effective counter to a military-political-industrial complex of gargantuan power and influence.*

Thousands of people were killed, physically disfigured, and psychologically ruined. Veterans' hospitals could not handle the number of maimed bodies—mental and physical—that were carted through their doors. Iraq's infrastructure was practically destroyed. Before the war, Ms. Rice claimed Iraq was destabilizing the region. How so? The end of the war led to a Shia faction gaining control of the state, surely a destabilization unto itself. The Sunni nations warned of this danger. Where was the nuclear presence? North Korea and Iran. Not Iraq.

This neocon team repeatedly and falsely fed to the American public probable ties between Iraq and al Qaeda. In fact, Osama bin Laden detested the Iraqi regime and wished for its downfall, a truth known to any casual reader of the news.[37]

The rot went beyond the Iraq situation. Douglas Feith served as undersecretary of defense around this time. In dealing with the most important issue of the day, the Palestinian morass: "Feith's principal intellectual endeavor in the mid-1990s was to advocate a hard-line policy for Israel that would kill the peace process based on the Oslo Accords and have Israel indefinitely retain the occupied territories.[38]

Before he turned the archives pages on this subject, the Cepee reflects: *Where were the dissenters? They were shouted down by a vociferous few, who convinced an unwary citizenry for America to enter into what was a war of choice, an offensive war.*

Another Deadly Trinity

Figure 8-7 provides an illustration of a key aspect of the warm war: the interdependency and cooperation between the military, industry, and government. It was another Deadly Trinity. As with the other trinity, one fed on the other (the arrows were bi-directional). Military lobbyists greased the hands of the politicians. In turn, politicians voted for huge defense budgets. As mentioned, America's defense budget came close to or even exceeded the combined defense budgets of every country on earth.[39] Private industry made the weapons and made a killing on their resultant killings.

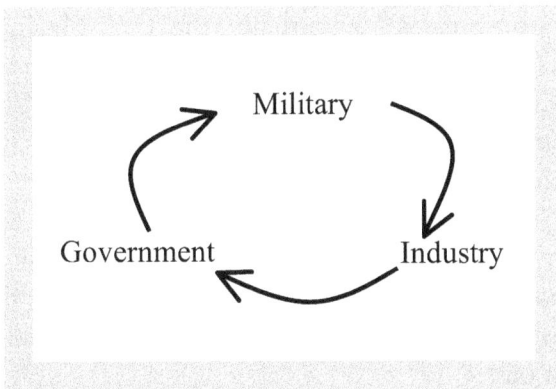

Figure 8-7. The military-industrial complex: another Deadly Trinity.

A former U.S. president and an exalted former army general warned of this trinity. He called it the "military-industrial complex." He asked America if one bomber was worth a school in more than 30 cities; than two electric power plants, serving each town of 60,000 people; than two fully equipped hospitals; than fifty miles of a paved highway?[40] What was America's response? "Of course! The bomber will save us from our enemies."

These enemies had no stealth flying bombers in the air, only stealth human bombers on the ground who were immune to air power. Sometimes, this system created virtual enemies who often were nothing more than creations of the military-industrial complex. As one example, Iraq's nuclear arsenal: a threat to mankind? Absurd, even laymen could see this falsity.[41] Yet an invasion took place. It did little more than upset a seesaw balance of power between Sunnis and Shias, to the detriment of the United States.

New Bully on the Block. After the dismantling of the USSR, the complex went about conjuring up another big country through which it could scare Americans and wring its citizens out of trillions of dollars. The new bad guy on the block was China.

But China did not take the bait. The smart Chinese knew better. They took over America's mantra of "the business of America is business." Their creed was "the business of Chinese business is America's businesses." Eventually, the U.S. Marine corporal stationed in Okinawa to save America and its minions from assorted threats to gerrymandering, Wall Street's too-big-to-fail/too-big-to-care socialism, congressional insider trading, and profligate lobbying became irrelevant.

Besides, unlike the Muslims, Jews, and Christians, the Chinese did not play chess, with its sudden actions, and abrupt stalemates and checkmates. As mentioned, they played *wei qi* (go), the game of protracted conflict. They, too had age-old scores to settle, but they could wait it out.

The Islamic fanatical elements were not as smart. Unlike the crafty Chinese, their idea of "making a killing" was to kill the people who might have given them the way to make a financial killing. Thus, it was not the self-franchised and patient Chinese who participated in the mayhem. It was the self-disenfranchised militant Islamics.

A bomber here, an aircraft carrier there. Before long, power plants were not being built; highways were not being paved. Bridges were collapsing. But bombers were being built to bomb imaginary targets and keep the cycle in Figure 8-7 in perpetual motion.

Before leaving this topic, it can be asked: Why weren't America's citizens outraged over these useless excesses? Why not divert America's immense resources toward solving their health care, financial security, and infrastructure problems? A Deadly Trinity unto themselves. Why did America not simply leave others alone to wallow in their own self-imposed misery?

The answer revolved around: (a) The country, since World War II, gradually evolved into thinking it was the world's moral and political policeman, responsible for the behavior and well being of others. (b) To insure its citizens were not disturbed by any possible war casualties, nor appalled by the size of the military establishment, the federal government increasingly resorted to the use of civilian contractors. Extended tours of duty began to be taken over by mercenaries. If a casualty occurred within this cadre, it was not a soldier, sailor, Marine, or airman. It was a voluntary private contractor. (c) To further distance the civilian from the military-industrial complex, many operations were secretly funded or not revealed at all. The complex became less accountable to the public.

In addition, America was at the top of the power hierarchy. No country came close to its position. It was against human nature to descend voluntarily down the rungs of any Human Tribal Hierarchy. On occasion, it happened, but not often.

Joe and Josephine Citizen went about their daily chores and watched their TV reruns. Meanwhile, a praetorian guard of political, commercial, and military assemblages watched over and isolated Joe and Josephine from the real and supposed dangers of the world. As long as Joe and Josephine paid their taxes and kept "American Idol" running, all was well.

Americans had become accustomed to their place on earth. It became part of their cultural DNA. An occasional hurrah about a victory over an Osama bin Laden sociopath soon gave way to cheering for the next contestant on "Dancing with the Stars." The hurrah for a military win was replaced with a ho-hum.

The Nuclear Club

For a half century, the human race had managed to keep its nuclear arsenal leashed and stored in containers, silos, and secure military installations. Even though the number of countries possessing nuclear weapons increased (see Table 8-4), the fear of mutual attack kept the weapons sheathed. If a nation used these weapons on another nation, it knew that it would, in turn, be attacked as well—behavior governed by the Revenge Cycle.

Table 8-4. Official Members of the Nuclear Club[42]

Country	Year Acquired	Number of Weapons[43]
United States (NPT)	1945 ("Triad")	10,640
Russia (NPT)	1949 ("RDS-1")	8,600
Britain (NPT)	1952 ("Hurricane")	200
France (NPT)	1960 ("Gerboise Bleue")	350
China (NPT)	1964 ("596")	400
India (non-signatory)	1974 ("Smiling Buddha")	30-35
Pakistan (non-signatory)	1998 ("Chagai-I")	24-48
North Korea (non-signatory)	2006	At least 2, likely 10
Israel (undeclared nuclear power)	Unknown (possibly 1979)	100-200

NPT: nuclear Non-Proliferation Treaty "group of five."
Non-signatory: did not participate in initial signing of NPT.

The column in Table 8-4 labeled "Year Acquired" also contains the nicknames that some countries attached to their first nuclear bomb explosion. Some were cast in irony, some seemingly inexplicable. India's explosion was named "Smiling Buddha." The word *Buddha* meant the awakening or the awakened one. That is, until this Smiling Buddah exploded over the bedrooms of sleepers. No awakening there. The French named their bomb "Gerboise Bleue," which meant blue "jerboa," the latter word described a desert rodent found in the Sahara.

Killing Power

The first atomic explosion occurred near Alamogordo, New Mexico, on July 16, 1945.[44] The blast was equivalent to 20,000 tons of TNT. Buoyed by this success, on August 6, 1945, the United States dropped the first atomic bomb on Hiroshima, Japan. A second bomb was dropped on Nagasaki, Japan, on August 9. Estimates vary on the casualties, but approximately 200,000 people were killed in these two attacks.[45]

Striving to stay on the top of the nuclear weapons pecking order, the United States developed a hydrogen bomb yielding 24 megatons (almost 24,000,000 tons of TNT)—more than 1,000 times the explosive power of the Nagasaki atomic bomb. Not to be one-upped, the USSR developed a bomb with 57 megatons of explosive power.

A megaton was the amount of energy released by 1 million tons (907,000 metric tons) of TNT. During the early part of the twenty-first century, most nuclear devices had yields of less than 1 megaton and large thermonuclear weapons were about 8 to 40 times as powerful as the Hiroshima bomb.[46]

The humans decided to manufacture a "clean" hydrogen bomb (CH-bomb), one that would kill but would kill cleanly with no excessive radiation. This bomb released significantly less radioactive fallout, yet maintained the same explosive power.[47] Consequently, the CH-bomb would have spared most of its victims the agony of radiation—that is, those victims who survived the initial explosion.

Another clean bomb, called the neutron bomb, was designed as a tactical weapon for use on a battlefield or cash-rich cities such as

Zurich. A neutron bomb rocket could penetrate tanks, ship hulls, and bank vaults, resulting in death or injury to nearby individuals, without spreading radioactive fallout on the bankers and especially their banknotes.

Proliferation of the Weapons

Previous discussions have provided details on why weapons of mass destruction came into existence.[48] Unanswered is the question: How did they fall into the hands of people who had little hesitation in using them? After all, for almost a century, the possession of nuclear weapons by two or more enemies kept these adversaries from using them out of fear of mutual destruction. What upset this (admittedly fragile) apple cart?

Resentment and Loss of Good Will. A. Q. Khan, a Pakistani scientist and a key player in this story, asked why Britain and America had appointed themselves with a "God-given authority" to explode bombs every month, yet if another country began a small program, the Americans labeled them as satans and devils. Khan's complaints were legitimate and widely held. The NPT was clearly discriminatory by stipulating five countries should have nuclear weapons only in their corner of the nuclear weapons boxing ring.

With one exception: Israel. A special exception was made for this country, the archenemy of Middle Eastern countries. This brazen action further alienated and enraged the have-not nations, many who saw the treaty as *further disarming those who were already poorly armed.*

The resentment ran deep. Some nuclear-rich countries began selling nuclear equipment to Pakistan. In spite of America's bullying, "the Europeans closed ranks. Their attitude toward the Americans was them against us." Along with this attitude was their belief that selling nuclear equipment and know-how to countries was a way to gain influence with those countries.

Security. Some countries stated: Because the United States had used the bomb already, the country might use it again…on them. Hiroshima and Nagasaki lingered in their minds.

The bitter relationship between Pakistan and India exacerbated the problem. Whereas India had the bomb, for a while, Pakistan did not. This situation was the same in the Middle East: Israel had the bomb (called the "Jew Bomb"), the Muslims did not. How could a country defend itself if it had no counter force to the bomb? It could not.

The group of five and their minions were living in a world of fantasy. Non-nuclear countries that were under threat from larger and richer nations had legitimate security concerns. As one example: Pakistan and India. As another example: Iran and Israel. The resentment of the Iranians was particularly severe. What gave Israel the right to illegally and secretly institute a nuclear weapons program without any blow-back? Without any sanctions? Without any threats from the Western powers? This injustice was not forgotten by Iran.

So, the idea of a "Muslim Bomb" took root. After all, there was a "Christian Bomb," a "Hindu Bomb," a "Jew Bomb," and a "Communist Bomb." It was only fair to even the playing field of bombs and their public relations monikers, for both security and pride respectively.

Pakistan thus decided to go nuclear. Their foreign minister declared the country's citizens would eat grass if necessary to have the bomb. Later, in mid-twenty-first century, other countries developed bombs.

Further Proliferation. Khan managed to steal classified documents while working for a Dutch engineering firm. Upon returning to Pakistan from Amsterdam, the Pakistani government set him up as head of a lab, where he gained enormous influence in the country's nuclear war materials programs.

After years of efforts, Pakistan had the bomb (1974). For the next thirty years, the nation enhanced its program while exchanging threats and insults with India. During this time, Khan sold and gave away nuclear weapons materials and knowledge of the technology. The extent of this proliferation was never made public. Principally through interceptions of Khan's "trade routes," these facts were revealed:[49]

U.S. agents had intercepted a German ship named the *BBC China* carrying parts for a Libyan nuclear-weapons-production program, and [as stated earlier] Libya, in subsequently renouncing its nuclear ambitions, had named Pakistan, and particularly the Khan Research Laboratories, as the supplier of what was to be a complete store-bought nuclear-weapons program. The price tag was said to be $100 million. At about the same time, it was revealed that the Pakistani-run network had provided information and nuclear-weapons components to Iran and North Korea, and had begun negotiations with a fourth country, perhaps Syria or Saudi Arabia.

The Cepee Human Archives reader is astounded to learn that the nation of Pakistan was a principal ally of the United States. The old adage was brought to mind, "With friends such as these, who needs enemies?" But America's policy makers believed the United States had no choice other than to support a less than friendly Pakistani regime. To abandon the country might have encouraged real enemies to take over the Pakistani nuclear helm.

Business Is Business

It was not only the danger of nuclear weapons finding their way into the hands of fanatics, there was also the danger of chemical weapons being stolen or bought by malcontents who were loyal to their cause, or financial opportunists who were out to make a buck. As one example, "...an Israeli businessman, a former decorated soldier named Nahum Manbar, had secretly sold Iran a full production line—twenty-four truckloads of equipment—to manufacture chemical weapons."[50]

In 1993, Manbar garnered a "finder's fee" of $16 million for finding and delivering mustard gas and the nerve agents sarin and tabun to Iran, an implacable enemy of Manbar's home country. All the while, his government looked on, and for years, did nothing.[51] In the meantime, he checked in with the intelligence agencies. This surreal protocol resulted in Israel's military granting former military officers wide latitudes in dealing with "pariah regimes."[52]

The Cepee could only marvel at the self-defeating duplicity of such a culture: *Some of the individuals in their military were interlocked into a short-range promotion of one another, even if the long-range consequences of their actions might be at the expense of their nation. Hmm, a new interpretation of Zionist faithfulness.*

Deceiving an Ally

For over two decades, Israel covered up its development of nuclear weapons (at a remote site in the Negev desert near Dimona). It even deceived its mentor, the United States, by lying to a succession of American presidents. The former Israeli Prime Minister Shimon Peres, in his final days in office, was fearful his pledge to the American President John F. Kennedy would be "unmasked as false." He had told Kennedy that Israel "…would not be the first country in the Middle East to introduce nuclear weapons."[53]

In a self-denying and patently counterfeit proclamation, Peres said, "What is wrong with the Iranians in addition to the nuclear bomb? This is the only country on Earth in the 21st century that has renewed imperialistic ambitions. They really want to become the hegemon of the Middle East in an age that gave up imperialism."[54] Meanwhile, Israel continued its imperialistic practices of building more illegal settlements in the West Bank.

Even during the early days of the Israeli nation, America was kept in the dark. Ben-Gurion was worried: "His worst nightmare would be that one of the superpowers discovered it, then confronted Israel and, with a show of force, demanded that it be dismantled or put under international supervision."[55]

When the United States did discover the sham, it did nothing. This brazen duplicity was not lost on the Middle Eastern countries who found themselves living next door to an nuclear-armed enemy. If Israel could do it, why couldn't they?

Russia's Leaky Weapons Filter

After the fall of the USSR, the security of Russian nuclear facilities deteriorated. Once guarded by elite military units, many sites came to be protected by the cast-offs of Russia's army. Underpaid, they often left their posts in search of food, drink, or entertainment. Personnel were subject to bribes from black marketers. The buildings fell into disrepair. Some that contained highly enriched uranium (HEU), the material for building a bomb, were only padlocked. Others had no security cameras and those that did, had no one looking at the film from the cameras.

The Western powers were concerned about the deterioration of the security surrounding the former USSR's nuclear facilities. They looked for ways to help Russia "secure its fissile materials:"[56]

> The first is a stop-gap measure called a "rapid upgrade." It involves bricking up the warehouse windows, installing stronger locks, fixing the fences, maybe hiring some guards. The second is a long-term fix called a "comprehensive upgrade." It often involves the full range of Americanized defenses, including crash-resistant fences, bombproof buildings, remote cameras and electronic sensors, bar-coded inventory scanners, advanced locks, well-armed and well-motivated guards, and all sorts of double- and triple-safe procedures.

These efforts were effective and helpful to the cause of containment. But as long as the group of five and the later club members strived to keep their monopoly intact and deny others a way of self defense, these efforts were like spitting into a nuclear wind.

Conclusion

The humans had changed little from the days of the cave dwellers, through the Crusades, the Inquisitions, Pizarro, the European and Cambodian Holocausts, to al Qaeda. Their age-old enchantment with the Law of the Instrument never changed, but the instrument itself surely did.

Pandora's nuclear weapons box was opened. Until the Cepees took matters under their control, the lid stayed off the box.

---

[1] Phillip Rucker, "We Scared Every Night," *The Washington Post*, July 24, 2006, B2.

[2] Richard A. Clarke, "Ten Years Later," *The Atlantic Monthly*, January/February 2005, 61-77. Mr. Clarke offered these opinions after I wrote this chapter. I include this source as a supporting assessment of my thesis.

[3] The day after the Sandy Hook shootings, this writer watched the local police in Hayden, Idaho, accompany a school bus as it made its rounds in the morning to pick up students. With the cops diverted, I wondered if the local robbers and other seasoned law breakers were aware of this window of opportunity.

[4] An example of the Threshold Lowering Syndrome.

[5] "The Sociology and Psychology of Terrorism: Who becomes a Terrorist and Why?" Library of Congress. A report prepared under an interagency agreement by the Federal Research Division, September 1999. The first quote is taken from the Executive Summary section of this report. The second quote about sociopaths is from: Jessica Stern, *The Ultimate Terrorists* (Cambridge,MA: Harvard University Press, 1999). Unless otherwise cited, this section relies on these two sources.

[6] Aryn Baker, "The Jihadi Next Door," *Time*, March 31, 2008, 81. Online edition is dated March 30, 2008.

[7] Ari N. Schulman, "What Mass Killers Want— And How to Stop Them," *The Wall Street Journal*, November 8, 2013, C1-C2.

[8] "The Road to Renewal," *The Economist*, January 16, 2013, 54. Also, http://www.economist.com/news/international/21570677-after-centuries-stagnation-science-making-comeback-islamic-world-road. Notes 8-10 use material thoughout this article.

[9] Ibid.

[10] Ibid.

[11] "Saudi Police 'Stopped' Fire Rescue," *BBC*, March 15, 2002. My account does not include the Committee for the Propagation of Virtue and the Prevention of Vice (the so-called thought police) stating its members (two mutaween) were at the scene only to assist in the rescue and protection of the girls. They claim the mutaween arrived after the girls had left the building.

[12] "Economic Cooperation and Development Review," Organization of the Islamic Conference 3, no.2, September 2010, http://www.sesric.org/files/article/422.pdf.

[13] Paraphrase of a quote from Shakespeare, *Troilus and Cressida*, 2.3, 164, in Frank, *Quotationary*, 654.

[14] Benjamin Franklin, *Poor Richard's Almanac*, April 1756, in Frank, *Quotationary*, 899.

[15] Baker, "The Jihadi Next Door," *Time*, 81. According to Baker, he "gleefully threatened a hostage with decapitation in 1994."

[16] The idea of access to virgins as a motivator to transcend to a paradise is discounted by some scholars as a made-up scenario fueled by tabloid TV and newspaper outlets. Ample online interviews are available of young men who proclaim this fantasy is indeed one aspect of their motivation to kill themselves.

[17] **(a)** For additional explanations on Churchill's fascination with a perfect weapon, see Andrew J. Bacevich, *The New American Militarism* (New York: Oxford University Press, 2005), 171. **(b)** For further explanations on a perfect enemy, see Mark Leonard, "Why Convergence Breeds Conflict," *Foreign Affairs*, September/October 2013, 125-135.

[18] Chas W. Freeman Jr., "National Security in the Age of Terrorism," Remarks by Ambassador Freeman to the Congressional Research Service Seminar for New Members, January 6, 2006. In 2003, the Department of Homeland Security listed 160 sites in the United States as likely targets for terrorists. Shortly, the list was expanded to 1,849 targets. By the end of 2004, the list had grown to 28,360 targets. By 2006, about 300,000 targets had been identified as potential targets, including such infrastructure treasures as the Indiana Apple and Pork Festival—a selection likely chosen as part of political pork barrel.

[19] A special note and thanks to the author for the information in this section, from which I quote directly. He is Richard A. Falkenrath, assistant professor of public policy at Harvard University's John F. Kennedy School of Government. Microsoft's Encarta Reference Library.

[20] Uyless Black, *Coming to You Live from the Dead* (Santa Fe: privately published, 2009), 13-1, 13-3.

[21] Falkenrath.

[22] By 2013, more than 65,000 tons of spent nuclear fuel were stored in 75 reactor sites in the United States, with 2,000 more tons produced each year. Source: Lea County (New Mexico) public documents and studies.

[23] "Treaty for the Non-Proliferation of Nuclear Weapons (NPT)," http ://www .un .org /disarmament /WMD/Nuclear/NPT.shtml.

[24] Elizabeth Kolbert, "Mr. Green," *The New Yorker*, January 22, 2007, 35.

[25] Microsoft's Encarta Reference Library.

[26] William Langewiesche, "How to Get a Nuclear Bomb," *The Atlantic Monthly*, December 2006, 80-98. The following two paragraphs also use material in Mr. Langewiesche's article.

[27] William Langewiesche, "The Wrath of Khan," *The Atlantic Monthly*, November 2005, 63.

[28] Sebastan Junger, *War* (New York: Hachette, 2010). Also, Dexter Filkins, *The Forever War* (New York: Alfred A. Knopf, 2008). See these two exceptional descriptions of this subject. The topic runs through many parts of both books, so I do not cite specific page numbers.

[29] Chris Kyle, *The American Sniper* (New York: Harper, 2012), 88.

[30] I searched the Internet for information on the "top ten sniper kills." The lists vary. Academic statisticians are not known to frequent these posts.

[31] As of this writing, the suspected murderer has yet to go to trial. Thus, the word allegedly is in order.

[32] Paul R. Pillar, *Intelligence and U.S. Foreign Policy* (New York: Columbia University Press, 2011), 28.

[33] Ibid., 37.

[34] Ibid., 30.

[35] Henry A. Crumpton, *The Art of Intelligence* (New York: Penguin, 2012), 188.

[36] Pillar, *Intelligence and U.S. Foreign Policy*, 66. Mr. Pillar also offers his opinion about the prevailing intelligence assessments at that time (the inaccurate NIE notwithstanding): (a) Intelligence did not guide the decision to go to war, (b) An invasion of Iraq was unwarranted and unwise, (c) Iraq was years away from acquiring nuclear weapons, (d) Any attempt to establish democracy in Iraq would be difficult and turbulent, (e) The war would boost political Islam. This writer adds: the war was a huge gift to terrorists' public relations campaigns.

[37] I wondered why indications of a nuclear weapons program were not in evidence (enrichment facilities, heavy water plants, the reactors, and other systems). Believing I did not have an inside track to this subject, I was persuaded by the administration's marketing. So were most Americans. In a nutshell, we trusted an ideologically tainted cadre of white collar intellectuals who had never put their life on the line for their beliefs— beliefs they sold to advance, not America's interests, but to buttress their ideologies. Even if we grant the idea of Hussein gaining a hold on nuclear weapons, it was clear to even the casual observer that he had no allegiance with Al Qaeda. As a layman bystander, it was obvious to this writer that Jihadist bin Laden and secular Hussein were natural enemies. Yet this issue was one of the biggest selling points for going to war, courtesy of the cadre surrounding George W. Bush.

[38] Pillar, *Intelligence and U.S. Foreign Policy*, 22.

[39] Andrew J. Bacevich, *Washington Rules* (New York: Metropolitan Books, 2010). This statement was taken from this source and several websites. The exact numbers vary, but all substantiate the fact that the United States is number one in the Human Tribal Hierarchy for building an armament establishment. Does one favor or disfavor this fact? The Cepee would state that it depends on one's political color.

[40] Dwight D. Eisenhower, "Quotes," http://www.eisenhower.archives.gov/all_about_ike/quotes.html.

[41] I have been taken to task by this assertion. One of my friends "worked" this issue while he was a U.S. Navy Captain and an intelligence officer. He tells me the evidence collected by the CIA, DIA, and other agencies pointed to a functioning Iraqi nuclear system. I disagree. Even as layman, it seemed remote that Iraq had in place the sophisticated and complex factories to produce nuclear weapons. I was dubious then, and I remain dubious. As a nontechnical observer, I wondered: Where were any evidences of nuclear reactors, milling plants, heavy water facilities, ore purification sites, uranium enrichment plants, research facilities, and delivery systems? Later evidence substantiates my suspicions. It is incredible that a nation would go to war, resulting in untold misery on its warriors, against a nation that posed absolutely no threat to that nation. Even if Iraq had the "bomb," how was it going to launch it into New York? So many other options were open to solve this non-problem. I remain astounded about the nature of my fellow man. But then, that is one reason I am writing this book.

[42] Federation of American Scientists. "Status of World Nuclear Forces," http://www.fas.org/programs/ssp/nukes/nuclearweapons/nukestatus.

[43] Federation of American Scientists, "Status of World Nuclear Forces," http://www.fas.org/programs/ssp/nukes/nuclearweapons/nukestatus.html. The estimates of the number of nuclear weapons held by these countries vary greatly. I have chosen this source as a representative example.

[44] Microsoft's Encarta Reference Library.

[45] David McCullough, *Truman* (New York: Simon & Shuster, 1992), 456 - 457. Estimates of the number of people killed in the two attacks vary widely. My source is McCullough. For Hiroshima: "In time, it would be estimated that 80,000 people were killed instantly and that another 50,000 to 60,000 died in the next several months." For Nagasaki: "Later estimates were that seventy thousand died...."

[46] George W.S. Kuhn, "Nuclear Weapons," *World Book Online Reference Center*, March 23, 2004, http://www.worldbookonline.com/training/pl_ref_center/

[47] Microsoft's Encarta Reference Library.

[48] William Langewiesche, "The Point of No Return," *The Atlantic Monthly*, January/February, 2006. Langewiesche, "The Wrath of Khan," 2005. Also, Langewiesche, interview by Elizabeth Dougherty, Oct. 10, 2005, http://www.theatlantic.com/magazine/archive/2005/11/the-world-in-which-we-live/304361/. For the information, statistics and quotes in this section, I have relied on exceptional pieces of journalism written by Langewiesche. See "Langewiesche," http://www.theatlantic.com. There, you will find examples that are models for what journalistic reports should be.

[49] "On the Trail of the Black Market Bombs," http://news.bbc.co.uk/2/hi/3481499.stm.

[50] Patrick Tyler, *Fortress Israel* (New York: Farrar, Straus, and Giroux, 2012), 358.

[51] In 1998, Manbar was finally corralled and sent to prison, five years after he was tracked by the Israeli intelligence service, Mossad. He was jailed for trading in chemical weapons technology.

[52] Tyler, *Fortress Israel*, 360.

[53] Ibid., 321.

[54] "Brainy Quote," http://www.brainyquote.com/quotes/quotes/s/shimonpere463605.html#sDX6OS3G6HVfR67k.99.

[55] Tyler, *Fortress Israel*, 101.

[56] Langewiesche, "How to Get a Nuclear Bomb, *The Atlantic Monthly*, December 1, 2006, http://www.theatlantic.com/magazine/archive/2006/12/how-to-get-a-nuclear-bomb/305402/2/.

CHAPTER 9

BOMBS AWAY

———

If the primitive Waorani someday do become fully Westernized,
they will have traded a life marked by the flight of a palmwood spear for
one measured by the parabola of a guided missile.[1]

The humans' nightmare finally became a reality. In the early part of the twenty-first century, ready-made nuclear weapons appeared on the black market in Central Asia. The world's intelligence services had suspected fissionable material, perhaps weapons, were being stolen or simply lifted from facilities in Russia and Pakistan and sold to the highest bidder who did not yet possess a nuclear tool kit.

Some people did not believe the terrorist network had sufficient technical knowledge to maintain or use nuclear weapons. A noted terrorist disavowed this view, "If you have $30 million, go to the black market in central Asia, contact any disgruntled Soviet scientist, and a lot of...smart briefcase bombs are available. ...They have contacted us, we sent our people to Moscow, to Tashkent (the capital of Uzbekistan), to other central Asian states, and they negotiated, and we purchased some suitcase bombs."[2] This claim was most likely an exaggeration at that time, because no nuclear attacks occurred in the first part of the twenty-first century. Shortly thereafter, the boast was to become a reality.

Influential scientists and persuasive high-level military personnel, those who yielded tremendous influence in their countries, added to the problem. They used their power to foster nuclear weapons proliferation. They operated in two ways: (a) For financial gain, they sold atomic nuclear material to a highest bidder, without regard to political or religious persuasions of either the buyer or the seller. (b) For ideological reasons, they gave the material away to Muslim brothers who were at war with their sectarian adversaries in the Christian and Jewish worlds.

After these acts, it was only a matter of time before the mantra for globalization, "transfer of technology" took on a new meaning.[3]

Part I: Intra-tribal Wars

Sunni and Shia

Religious tribes having differences within their factions had not been as damaging to the human race as inter-tribal disputes, such as the frequent battles between Christians and Muslims. However, after the post-World War II dismantling of ancient tribal boundaries and after the reconstituted Middle Eastern nations had formed associations with Western nations, several intra-tribal conflicts had major consequences.

A preponderant factor in these battles was attributable to the differences and related grudges between the Sunnis and Shias. Religious pride was part of the picture. So was the contest for power and influence, all leading to intramural animosities.[4]

Sidebar. A Religious Stalemate.

The conflict began many years ago. The Sunnis believed the founder of Islam, Muhammad, wished the Islamic leader to be chosen directly from the Muslim community. In contrast, the Shias believed Muhammad had chosen his son-in-law, Ali, to be his successor and only Ali's descendants were worthy to rule the Muslim world. These debates, which began as far back as 633, masked the facts that (a) Muhammad's initial successor was not Ali, but Muhammad's father-in-law, Abu Bakr, and (b) an ancient leader, from a branch of Muhammad's family known as the Abbasids, took over the Muslim reins and became the third Islamic

Caliphate.[5] These events created confusion and resentment among the Muslims.

Thereafter, the Sunnis and Shias fought each other on the issue of which tribe was best suited to control their religious turf. The Sunni "Arabs fear[ed] the rise of a 'Shiite crescent' from Iran through Iraq and on to Bekka." Whereas, the Shias were determined to vanquish the Sunnis.[6] Often, the fights became personal. If an "Ali" happened to drive into a security checkpoint operated by a "non-Ali" guard, Ali was often killed on the spot. The man was murdered because he pronounced a word incorrectly.

More often than not, each left the other alone to practice their beliefs. But on those exceptional occasions when one or the other did not, mayhem often followed.

The Cepee is studying the opinions of several human historians. They claimed the Shia/Sunni conflict came from the resurgence in religious fervor in Iran (during the latter part of the twentieth century) in advancing Shia credos.[7] To this time, Sunnis dominated the Islamic populations around the world (about 75 to 90 percent of practicing Muslims were Sunnis).[8] But two countries in the Middle East were predominately Shia: Iran and Iraq, as seen in Figure 9-1.[9] Also, Lebanon, Azerbaijan, and Bahrain were partly Shia, and Pakistan had the second-largest Shia population in the world.

Syria's rulers were now Alawites, who were part of the Shia faction. Even though Syria's population was predominately Sunni, the country was ruled by Shia Alawites, and the Syrian army was dominated by Alawites. In the past, before the Alawites gained power, the minority Shias (thus, including the Shia Alawites) were routinely mistreated by the Sunnis. Consequently, the Muslim brothers in Syria—the Sunnis and Alawite Shias—were not disposed to practice peaceful brotherhood with each other.

The Human Archives revealed Iran's Shia awakening, "led to a very violent Sunni reaction, starting first in Pakistan before spreading to the rest of the Muslim world." According to the archives, "two events created a sea change in the balance of power between Shia and Sunnis: the Islamic revolution in Iran and the American military intervention in Iraq."[10]

This latter event placed Americans on Islamic holy ground. These "heathen" interlopers included inadequately clothed females whose full faces, openly displayed in public, offended Islamic protocols. It did not matter that Sunni Saudi Arabia had invited the Americans to this land to possibly save the country from another Muslim country's invasion. (A Sunni cousin, no less, was the leader of Iraq.)

In the past, the Saudis had been considered by the Shias as sinful lackeys of the Americans. The action by the Saudis of allowing Christians onto sacred soil further reinforced the Shia view. Intra-tribal war swords were once again unsheathed.

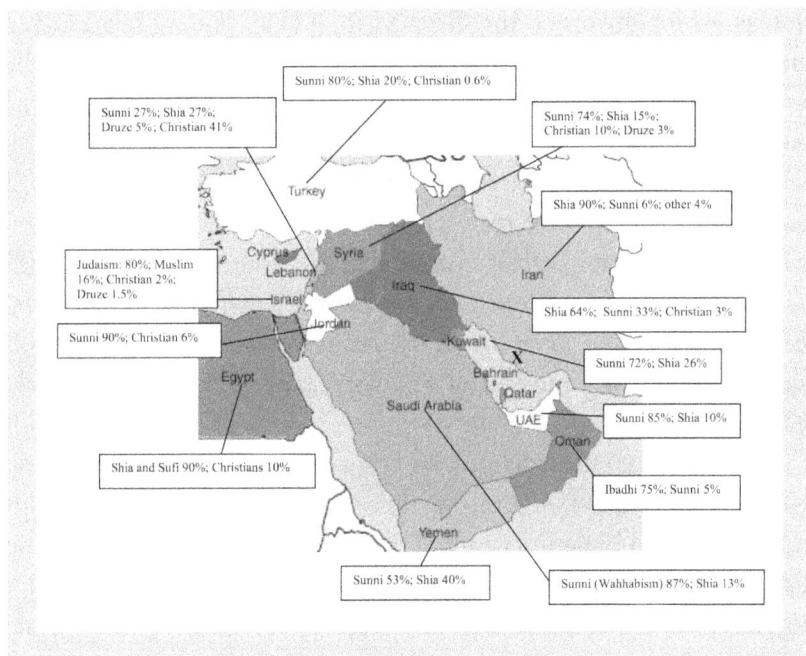

Figure 9-1. Religious alignments in twenty-first-century Middle East (small percentages are not shown).

That stated, it must also be said that Sunni and Shia swords stayed in perpetual readiness to be used against each other. As another example, Iran used its wealth and influence to foster Hezbollah, a militant Shia organization based in Lebanon. Syria, a collaborator with Iran, also helped Hezbollah inculcate its presence into Lebanon.

As introduced in Chapter 6, the foundation of Hezbollah came about after Israel invaded Lebanon in 1982. To the alarm of Sunnis, Hezbollah became a major force in the Middle East. It became a state within the Lebanon state.

While Hezbollah's initial public proclamations were focused on the ousting of Israel from Lebanon and the obliteration of Israel as a state, it was still a Shia tribe. Thus, for the Sunnis, Hezbollah was also bent on the destruction of Sunnis. If the Hezbollah had been a ragtag band of disorderly malcontents, the Sunnis would likely have paid them little attention. But they were not. They were disciplined, dedicated, and well-funded warriors. The Sunni faction called Hamas, which governed the Gaza Strip, had an uneasy relationship with Shia Hezbollah. To repeat, in order to help keep track of the actors on this stage: the Sunnis were suppressed in Syria by a Shia (Alawite) regime.

The Cepee pauses: *I recall reading that Hezbollah prided itself in championing the rights of the oppressed, so Syria's oppressive treatment of its Sunnis probably did not sit well with Hezbollah. Hmm. Hezbollah was aided by Syria (and Iran), but Hezbollah's reputation for protecting the underdog would have meant they would have protected a Sunni enemy! I think I'm going to need a player's card to follow this part of the archives.*

To add fuel to these flames, and more players for the Cepee (and us) to remember, the ongoing battles between the Jews and Muslims in Palestine and Lebanon resulted in thousands of Palestinians being displaced. In many instances, these helpless and hopeless souls were not allowed to return to their homes. Those who lived in Israel were restricted in how they conducted their lives. Tremendous resentment built up against the Jews for their actions against these homeless souls.

Saudis Form Ties

From a brief glance at Figure 9-1, it would appear the Sunnis would have had little worry about their place in the Muslim Tribal Hierarchy. They were dominant in most regions of the Middle East and most other parts of the Muslim world. They had enough power to be secure in their high position. But true to the Rules of Life, a tribe who thought enough was indeed enough also knew someone else inevitably considered this tribe's "enough" as being too much. Those on the downside of the scales sought to change the fulcrum point.

How could a tribe make certain it held on to its "enough"? Saudi Arabia took the path of many stable nations: make itself more secure by forming associations with other countries. In concert with the United Arab Emirates (UAE), Oman, Qatar, and Bahrain, the Saudis formed broad economic and military agreements. This group, named the Gulf Cooperation Council, later offered memberships to Jordan and Morocco even though neither country was located directly around the Persian Gulf.

Two parties who were feared by the Sunnis spurred the formation of the Sunni associations discussed above. One party consisted of the Shia Iranians (and their ally, Hezbollah) who (some experts believed) wished to export their revolution and become the preeminent power in the Middle East.[11] The other party consisted of Shias living in other countries who were working against Sunni regimes, sometimes under the guise of Arab Spring revolutions. Both threats were real. Both could lead to a sudden change in the balance of power:[12]

> Rulers have been forced from power in Tunisia, Egypt, Libya, and Yemen. Uprisings and protests have occurred in Bahrain and Syria, Algeria, Iraq, Jordan, Kuwait, Morocco, and Sudan, with minor protests in Lebanon, Mauritania, Oman, Saudi Arabia, Djibouti, and Western Sahara. Large scale riots against Bahrain's Sunni rulers were known to be led by the Shias.

The Saudi King told his Sunni brothers, "You all know we are the targeted in our safety and security." He added that whoever did not join in an alliance, "will find himself at the back of the caravan trail and be lost."[13]

Especially troublesome to the Saudis and Israel were ongoing dialogues between Iran and the Western powers about Iran curbing its nuclear weapons program. In the long run, even with Western countries' sanctions lifted from Iran, neither country believed Iran would forego "going nuclear."

Intra-Tribal Dissention Spreads to Inter-Tribal War. For the Sunnis, the war was conducted subtly. Several of the more powerful Sunni factions surreptitiously supported Israel's destroying the nuclear capabilities of Iran. Yes, Israel, the infidel imperialist. But it made sense to the Sunnis: Iran was the land of misguided Shias (Persians) and an anchor in the Middle East for the Shia worldwide minority. Besides, with Israel being a de facto fifty-first state of the United States, its continued existence was a given. Why bother trying to dislodge that which could not be dislodged in the first place?

Even more, what better way to remove heretofore intractable obstacles to the Sunni tribe's dominance in this region of the world than to have a hated Jewish tribe fight an equally hated Shia tribe? The two adversaries could contribute to each other's demise. As an added bonus, the battle would be joined by the Christian tribe in the United States. Brilliant. The Sunnis would not be a visible participant in this contest, nor would they participate in the ongoing Islamic verbal provocations against Israel and America. The jihadist war chants made no sense to the world-wise Saudis.

If only temporarily, a major challenger to the Saudis' Muslim position in the Middle East would be dismantled. As well, the Jewish thorn to its north would at least be dulled. Besides, in the end, it was not an Arab affair after all, but one between Persians and Jews.

Regardless of Iran's Islamic credentials, the Saudis wanted the Shias out of the picture. Iran had made far too many threats to the Sunnis in the past to be taken lightly.

For Israel, it was a dream come true. Regardless of the riots in Muslim countries that would ensue from the Israeli attacks on a Muslim nation, the Sunni powers that really mattered would remain on the sidelines.

Israel would have a free pass to solidify its evolution from a liberal and tolerant nation toward becoming an isolated, self-styled apartheid state. There would be diminished opposition to: (a) Palestine becoming an exclusive enclave of the ultra-orthodox Jews (explained shortly), (b) the extension of illegal settlements, (c) the building of more barriers between Jews and Muslims, and (d) a continued discounting of the Saudi Arabia olive branch (which offered a means to recognize Israel and establish Palestine as a formally recognized nation). As an added bonus, Israel would remain the only country in the Middle East possessing nuclear weapons.

For icing on the cake, the United States would not—could not—remain passive. Overwhelming the moderates, its brigades of Christians Soldier Crusaders would laud the Israeli attack on Iran. America might once again put boots on the ground in the Middle East.

The Cepee pauses: *What is left unsaid in these archives seems to be a given, not mentioned to any significant extent: The principal benefactors of that war, and so many others, were two sets of tribes, powerfully aligned. They were the armaments industry and their allied politicians.*

The Cepee pauses once more: *The archives tell this story time and again. These benefactors never placed themselves onto the front row of the battlefield chessboard. Of course not! That would have violated the humans' unwritten Rules of Life as well as Darwin's slide rule. There was nothing to be gained at the front lines. That's where dismemberments took place. The back row was the place to be. That's where disbursements occurred.*

But these entries in the archives have led me to these same thoughts before. As the humans liked to say, it appears I'm beating a dead horse…or dead human.

Secular vs. Ultra-Orthodoxy. The Israeli Jews themselves were not one happy family. One group, known as the ultra-orthodox, was not required to serve in the military. They enjoyed special privileges pertaining to child care, education, and housing. Nice work if you could get it, and the blacks, as they were called (from their attire), found the situation to their liking. They increased their share of the population in Jerusalem to 31 percent, roughly the same as secular Jews (those who took religion less seriously) and in comparison to the 35 percent Palestinian Muslim population.[14] The ultra orthodox

Jews' population in Jerusalem was growing rapidly. They were taking up more of the landscape.[15]

Why was this part of the Jewish society a problem? Because, according to the secular Jew, the blacks (a) originated from a sect who rejected the "age of reason," (b) separated girls from boys as early as nursery school, (c) barred smart phones, (d) forbade many Internet sessions, (e) had their women sit in the back of public buses, (f) called young girls "whores" for wearing the wrong clothes (inappropriate dresses), and (g) set the conquering of "their" holy land as one of the most important missions in life.

For the overall Jewish population in Israel, almost half claimed to be moderate and identified themselves more with the nation than with its religion. But the growing population of ultra-orthodox and especially messianic, hawkish fundamentalist Jews did not auger well for the stability of this region.

Consequently, the die-hard Islamic militant was fighting an equally die-hard Jewish militant. The Islamic die-hard, who was even more radical than his Zionist predecessor, was increasing in number and influence. They were growing to take over the Holy City. They were moving into the suburbs, pushing outward farther into the land settlements. Their teachings were finding their way into the "much broader swatches of Israel's politics and culture."[16]

These events, accelerating in their effects during the first quarter of the twenty-first century, were not lost on the observing Muslims.

The Sunnis' Tacit Deputies

If Jewish Israel did not act openly as a proxy for the Saudis, it can be said that the Jewish military was surreptitiously deputized by the Arabs, tacitly assigned to be the stand-in. Several political leaders of Iran had declared the goal of Islam should be the destruction of Israel, a proclamation considered by even die-hard anti-Jews to be a blatant and stupid provocation. By making these statements, the Iranians were inviting aggression from the Jews against Muslim states, especially Iran.

Given these calamitous threats from an increasingly well-armed enemy, Israel was convinced it had no choice but to protect itself. It could not afford the luxury of withstanding a first strike, not when that first strike might be with nuclear warheads.

It mattered little that thousands of Iranian citizens were against religious and national extremism; that they were members of an intelligent, sophisticated culture; that many of them were resigned to a live-and-let-live existence with Israel. But their society had been hijacked by religious extremists. And in fairness to the Iranians, they had been deceived in the past by the duplicitous dealings of America (and Britain). These countries had contributed to the overthrow of an elected leader, then installed their own puppet autocrat. Small wonder the Iranians did not trust the Western nations.

On the other side of the chessboard, it mattered little that hundreds of thousands of moderate Jews and Gentiles throughout the world opposed the extremism of Israel's colonial-style land grabbings. However, in America, Jewish votes accompanied with lobbyists' leverage, and whetted by Christian Soldier Crusader zeal, kept the U.S. Congress and executive branch at bay.

It mattered little that the president of the United States gave a speech identifying the problems and laying the blame on both sides.[17] He informed the Arabs they could never take over Israel because the United States would not allow it. But he also informed the Israelis they would not survive if they did not embrace and help create a Palestinian state. He made a dent in the moral armor of both parties, but not enough to curtail the Deadly Trinity.

He shied away from addressing the thorny problem of Jewish illegal occupation and related justifiable eviction of the Jews who had confiscated the Palestinians' turf. How could he be so eloquently maze-dull? Because he was maze-bright. He knew the futility of demanding America's fifty-first state to give up turf where over one-half million Jewish settlers had established their homes. Where were they to go?

In spite of the president's speech—one of expressing empathy and support for the displaced Palestinsians—the Iranians who were in control of Iran's international policy were not moved. They believed Isreal and its appendage America were seeking, if not to disembowel a cultural and religious Iran, then certainly to disembowel a military and economic Iran. Based on past experiences, Iran's suspicions were well-founded.

The fears of both parties were real. The Jews (with Israel as their icon) feared and hated the Muslims surrounding them. The Muslims (with Iran as their surrogate) feared and hated the Jews.

As a consequence of these fears and hatreds, the nations set off another version of the Aggression Cycle, introduced in Chapter 3, and shown with an altered picture in Figure 9-2. Other than the cast of players in the old and new shows, the scenes and acts of the play remained the same. The settings in the acts were also different. Earlier, the backdrop was thousands of arrows coming down on an enemy, often causing causalties numbering in the hundreds. Later, the scene was set with hundreds of missiles, also coming down on an enemy, but often causing casualties numbering in the thousands.

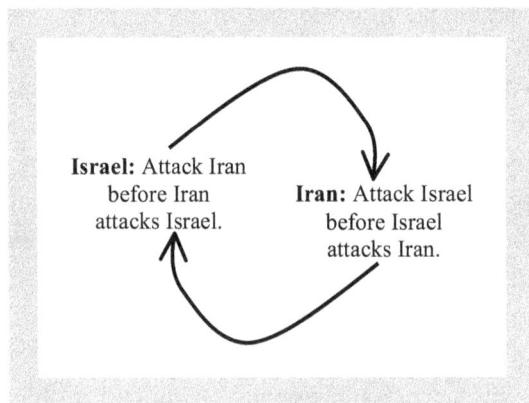

Israel: Attack Iran before Iran attacks Israel.

Iran: Attack Israel before Israel attacks Iran.

Figure 9-2. The Aggression Cycle drama: different players, different sets, same acts.

Damage "Control"

The Iranian Bushehr nuclear power plant was one the country's supposed proofs that the Iranian government was building nonmilitary nuclear facilities. (See Figure 9-3 for the location of this plant.) But to a world that was worried about Tehran's intentions and especially its threats against Israel and Sunnis, its nuclear program was seen to be aimed also at securing an energy source for nuclear weapons.

Depending on the political climate, Iranian leaders wavered in their vow to annihilate Israel. But with their on-going antipathy toward Israel (and America), it did not take much thinking to understand the means for this annihilation could be achieved only with the use of nuclear weapons.

Other instruments took too long to become effective or had unmanageable logistical problems in their dissemination and use. To the chagrin of special sectors in the military-industrial complex, most of the chemical and biological weapons went to waste and to waste dumps, because they were too complex to deploy. But not all of them were put to rest. As described shortly, some were used by a Muslim faction on a cousin Muslim faction.

While Bushehr was not considered a major weapons proliferation risk by Western states, it was one among several Iranian sites that was creating weapons-grade uranium, and thus of great concern to Israel and its allies.

The American public was divided in its stand on U.S. intervention in Iran. Some polls showed the favoring of bombing Iran's nuclear plants. Others showed disapproval. The majority of Israelis were not in favor of their country attacking Iran's sites, *unless* the United States was an active partner to Israel in the battles. Other nations joined in one way or another, depending on their ties to Israel and their dependence on the United States.

The estimated casualties gave all parties pause.[18] Studies forecast the highest level of environmental damage would be caused by strikes on reactors, spent fuel storage facilities, and reprocessing plants. Attacking the Bushehr nuclear reactor might release lethal contamination into the air.

Bahrain, Qatar, and the UAE could be contaminated by the fallout released from a Bushehr attack. The strike on this reactor could possibly cause the death of thousands of people living in or adjacent to the site, and thousands might die of subsequent cancer.

That is, unless a surgical strike (a set of targeted strikes) could be mounted in a more limited and piecemeal fashion. The Christians and Jews knew the locations of many of the Islamic nuclear sites, as seen in Figure 9-3.[19]

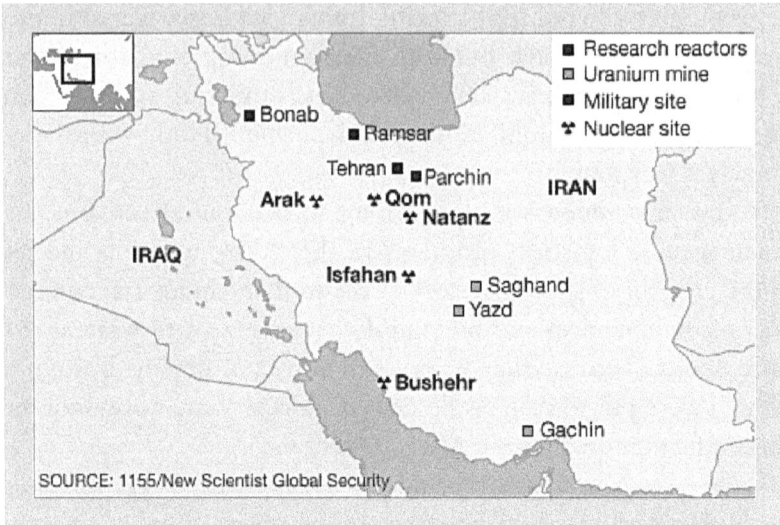

Figure 9-3. Key nuclear sites in Iran.

Thus, the Deadly Trinity of the twenty-first century unfolded as follows:

The Palestinian two-state situation was never resolved to the satisfaction of the Jews or the Muslims. The Christians, standing somewhat on the sidelines, wanted their share of the holy land, but not as passionately as did the other contenders. Nor was the nuclear stand-off with Iran resolved. With international agreements, Iran continued building nuclear facilities, and Iran's adversaries, not believing in these agreements, threatened to bomb the facilities.

In another touch of irony—a feature common to humans— the contending parties sensed the danger they faced if these issues were not resolved. A subconscious fear clashed with a conscious denial that factions of the Muslim camp would eventually resort to the use of unconventional weapons. In retaliation, so would the Israeli camp.

Some exchanges of land held by Israel in exchange for a few Muslim peace vows took place during the second decade of the twenty-first century. But in comparison to the magnitude of the problem, in which several thousand Jewish settlers lived in the West Bank and Gaza, the Arabs felt cheated.

Iran found itself (and its struggling ally, Syria, along with Hezbollah) isolated from the west. But they were accustomed to this reality. Some countries, such as Russia, did not trust America's motives, and sided with Iran. Iran recognized the hypocrisy of America's foreign policy toward them in relation to Israel's illegal nuclear program. As mentioned, Iran also remembered America overthrowing an Iranian government head-of-state who had shown trust and believed in the United States (Mosaddeq, who made the mistake of nationalizing the West's oil companies), and replacing the man with a despot (the Shah, who brought the oil companies back in). And Americans were puzzled why the CIA operatives were called devils! In any case, the sabers were being drawn. China, always the astute silent one, let the course of events take its own path.

Israel faced these problems and options: (a) To placate the die-hard faction in the Muslim camp, Israel could have abandoned all its illegal colonies, which likely would have created revolts among many Israeli citizens. (b) As part of this resettlement, it could have entered into a two-state solution with the Arabs. (c) It could have accepted that other nations in the Middle East had a right to possess nuclear weapons.

Two states or not, some Muslim factions had vowed to destroy Israel for just being Israel. But the tide could have been turned. The Arab Peace Initiative represented an olive branch to the Israelis from several Muslim nations in the region. Consequently, the stage, however modest, was being set for resolution of the Palestinian problem.

However, the Palestinian situation was not a direct part of the Iranian nuclear weapons problem, and the continued evidence of Israeli colonization led to lingering animosities on the part of the Muslim parties. The situation further encouraged many Muslims in the region to arm themselves against their Jewish enemies.

Toward the end of the second decade of the twenty-first century, Iran was well along in its nuclear weapons aspirations. By this time, the nation considered three options in dealing with its Jewish and Sunni enemies: (a) abandon its nuclear weapons aspirations, (b) go full speed with their deployment, (c) continue to dither and play for time, while gradually building up its arsenal. If Iran had opted for option (a) and had not proclaimed the annihilation of Israel (not to mention the killing off of Sunni brothers as well), it could have backed-off into safety. But it did not. Its leaders were hard-wired through centuries of turf battles to plow ahead.

With option (b), it would have been only a matter of time before Iran was attacked. (This option would have afforded the militant, radical Shia camp a satisfying sip from the cup of revenge before they paid their final conscious call to Allah.) With option (c), Iran could continue leading Israel and America down the primrose path of delay, while attempting to weaken the Sunni presence in the Middle East.

Opting for (b) or (c) was obviously courting the likelihood of disaster. But option (c) if strung out long enough, who knew what might happen? At least it was a more gradual form of suicide.

Regardless of these options, in a surreal twist of irony, two age-old enemies (Jews and Arabs), combatants almost from the time Jesus and Muhammad walked the earth, entered into a military alliance with the purpose of ridding the Middle East of another enemy bloc. Ancient scripts were being played out again. The only changes were the roles played by the characters on the stage and the deadliness of their weapons.

The genie came out of the bottle, followed by a multitude of fights for revenge, pride, and turf. The battles began with Israel bombing several Iranian nuclear sites.

Iran immediately retaliated with air strikes aimed toward Tel Aviv. The strikes were partially intercepted by anti-missile rockets fired from Israel and U.S. attack fighters stationed on carriers in the Mediterranean Sea. But many missiles hit their targets.

The United States was in, hook, line, and sinker. It was political suicide for an American politician to go pacifist on this battle. America's fifty-first state was in danger. Its sea-based planes attacked Iran's defenses and sunk most of Iran's navy.

Pandora's box was open. Iran and its Shia minions were now in the heat of a war. Taking advantage of this diversion, Sunnis went on the attack. In most parts of the Middle East, where the two religious cousins co-mingled, they fought to right centuries of wrong-doings.

Yet another battle took place in the Middle East. The Hezbollah in Lebanon, acting in concert with the embattled Syrian government, joined in their own war with the hated Jabat-al-Nusra Sunnis.

The actors' cast for these tragicomic plays seemed to never end. The knives had left their scabbards. Guns, grenades, and bombs left their hiding places. In several of these confrontations, the instruments for hammering were far more lethal. Deadly chemicals left their storage tanks and found their way into thousands of people's lungs. The warriors themselves could not be singled out for these killings, as they used their noncombatant cousins for (futile) cover and protection. Nerve agents did not distinguish between soldier and civilian.

In many countries around the globe, anti-Jew, anti-American, anti-Muslim, anti-Shia, and anti-Sunni riots broke out. But their protests did little good. They were little more than noise in the spectrum of overall global violence.

But the battles were not done. While the toll of this conflagration on mother earth and its inhabitants was immense, the Deadly Trinity had yet another cycle of revenge left in its inventory.

Part II: The First Bomb

The societies of the United States and other democracies had evolved over many years to be open to its citizens and visitors. Public buildings were well named, as they were open to all. Tourists could even visit several corridors of the Pentagon. Travel was largely unrestricted, and law authorities were not allowed to stop or detain a citizen or tourist without due cause. Unfortunately for the citizens of these free societies, they could not close their communal milieus soon enough to barricade themselves against the onslaught of attacks from terrorists.

Washington, D.C. was a prime location for a nuclear attack. The reason was easy to understand. To its citizens, Washington, D.C. was the citadel of freedom, democracy, and capitalism.

In addition to being the capital of the United States, the city was famous and respected for its championing the rights of the downtrodden.

To the enemies of America, Washington, D.C. was the fortress of apostates. It was a bastion of perverted heretics who practiced the wrong religion and inserted themselves into affairs around the globe that were none of their business. In addition, many of the city's inhabitants created the policies leading to the invasion and desecration of the Muslim holy lands—their religious turf. What was more, Washington, D.C. symbolized the material despotism of affluent, perverted Western societies. In addition, Washington, D.C. and its citizens occupied far too many upper levels of the human pecking orders. It held too many aces. A reshuffle of the cards was in order.

Bombs Away

As best the experts could estimate, the detonation was a one megaton blast. No one predicted a bomb of such strength could have been acquired, assembled, and ferried into the Nation's Capital. But then, no one predicted Hitler's first invasions in Europe, the Pearl Harbor attack, the North Koreans invading South Korea, the Chinese attacking across the Yalu River, the Russians invading Afghanistan, Hussein attacking Kuwait, 9/11, the Madrid railway explosions, and many other assaults.

A "tour" bus carried the device. The vehicle made its journey into the city from Arlington, Virginia, passing by the Pentagon, where it was captured on film by several bomb-proof cameras. The bus was parked on Constitution Avenue, three blocks from the White House to the north and two blocks from the Washington Monument to the south. Figure 9-4 provides a view of the area, where the X identifies the position of the bus and bomb.

The explosion began with an instantaneous fireball formation of dust and hot gases. A few milliseconds after the explosion, the gases expanded to form a shock wave, which traveled about 12 miles from ground zero (the bus) in 50 seconds. Tremendously strong winds accompanied the blast wave, reaching speeds of 400 miles per hour two miles from ground zero.

The blast left a center crater 200 feet deep and 1,000 feet in diameter.[20] Nothing recognizable remained within 3,200 feet (0.6 miles) from the center, except a few building foundations. The White House and the Washington Monument were leveled. At 1.7 miles, only a few buildings were left standing. Ninety-eight percent of the people in this area were killed. Those who survived wished they were dead.

Figure 9-4. The nuclear bomb attack.
(dashed lines show an approximate three- mile radius from ground zero).

The blast destroyed everything within a 2.7 mile radius, including the Capitol, other buildings along Pennsylvania Avenue, the Lincoln and Vietnam Memorials, the Pentagon, the Federal Reserve buildings, the Arlington National Cemetery, parts of Georgetown, the Einstein Memorial, and Reagan National Airport…among others. Fifty percent of the people in this area were killed instantly. Forty percent were injured. Miraculously, 10 percent of the population were not injured immediately from the detonation, but many of them eventually succumbed to radiation poisoning.

Part III:
Aftermath, the Second Bomb, Assessment

Aftermath

The militants who committed these acts against America's capital city considered their deeds successful, worthy of admiration from their family, friends, comrades, and fans. However, in their zeal for self-expression, they disregarded the Deadly Trinity. The Revenge Cycle Token had now been passed to the other party. Did these people think their families, other loved ones, and comrades would be immune from retaliation? Even though they were not geographically fixed, not subject to a set place on earth, the intelligence services knew the locations of many of their camps, other members of their throng, and in some instances, the nation-state that had furnished the weapons to them.

What made them believe their treasured cultures and holy sites would be immune from the Deadly Trinity? How could they remain oblivious to inevitable retaliations? Because the terrorists had explained their motives and intentions: *We desire death more than you desire life*.

They did not care who died. Friend or foe, it made no difference to them. If a relative died at the enemy's hands, the relative also went to paradise. Of course, not all relatives were consulted about this matter. Small wonder why the ASSES programs gained such momentum in the humans' twenty-first century.

In a final twist of tragedy and irony, the humans' fear of a Cold War nuclear slaughter proved to be unfounded. Their statements, "The Cold War is over. Everyone can come out of your bomb shelters!" was a premature proclamation.

The Second Bomb

As a consequence of these attacks, the terrorist became the object of his own terror. The terrified became the terrorist. Shortly after these bombings, the United States and Israel launched retaliatory attacks on the attackers. They used bombs and assassination squads, greatly aided by increasingly intelligent drones, to kill their opposition in selected targets in Kabul, Islamabad, Tehran, and other areas known to house anyone associated with the bombings.

Washington, D.C. had to be revenged. Blood for blood. Bomb for bomb. Thus, the United States placed a modern Enola Gay into the air and delivered a bomb whose devastation was twice that of the bomb that leveled America's capital. Millions perished.

Revenge was had by both sides. Was the Revenge Cycle to be repeated? No. This time the Law of the Instrument and its hammer had pounded the humans into a self-imposed submission. The humans came to realize a hubristic arrogance had only succeeded in their defeating themselves.

The Cepee pauses: *So, it finally happened. I suppose it was inevitable. I've been expecting this from the very moment I read about White Sands and the five original possessors of the bomb. I wonder what happened then that led to my being here now…without the humans and their assorted hammers?* The Cepee reads on.

Assessment

The nuclear and chemical attacks, the resulting counter attacks, the ongoing wars between nation-states and nationless factions, the fratricidal blood lettings between the Sunnis and Shias, as well as countless other inter-tribal killings around the globe eventually became the proverbial straw that broke the camel's back. The camel had been the refusal of many humans to accept or support radical genetic engineering or brain bioengineering. The straw was the death of millions of humans, with the expectation the mass slaughters and resulting chaos would never stop.

In the Washington, D.C. attack alone, about one-half million people in northern Virginia, southern Maryland, and the city itself were killed almost instantaneously. Another 300,000 succumbed later to radiation poisoning. In the other nuclear strike against a major city in the Middle East, the death toll was well over one million. For decades, these parts of planet earth were as toxic as a leaking nuclear plant.

Part IV: 2084

After this destruction, it was a relatively brief time before the world's leaders, both friends and enemies—of course, any still standing—assembled. There was a lapse of time before the parties got together, because they met at the scenes of their respective holocausts. This interregnum was needed for the nuclear clouds to drift away from the meeting sites to settle somewhat. For the first bomb, into the valleys of nearby Shenandoah Valley, and for the second bomb, onto the hills of the former Fertile Crescent. ...It took a while.

Had a Biblical Armageddon come about? Not to the magnitude written in Revelation 19:18. The attacks and counter attacks did not "...eat the flesh of kings, and the flesh of captains, and the flesh of mighty men, and the flesh of horses..." But the Bible was prophetic in that these wars with weapons of mass destruction affected the minds of many people, both free and bonded, both small and great.

Even though the nuclear and chemical destructions did not reach all parts of the earth, most people responded to this modern Armageddon. Geiger counters showed trade winds from the Washington, D. C. attack carrying nuclear particles into Europe, across the terrain of Russia, and back to the west coast of America. With each mile of riding these winds, the deadly residue diminished in its intensity. Nonetheless, it made its presence known to a vast population.

The nuclear airborne residue from the attack in the Middle East caught the winds coming from the east. They carried their deposits across north and mid-Africa, over and into the Atlantic, and across the northern terrains of South America. China was not directly affected, but its trading partners were, greatly diminishing its once accelerating economic growth.

An aberrant neighbor of China, North Korea had the bomb. India was not directly affected by these attacks, but its nemesis, Pakistan, owned a huge nuclear arsenal. India possessed the bomb as well, a fact keenly on the minds of Pakistanis. Second thoughts prevailed among these people: *If it can happen there, it can happen here.*

The citizens of the once supposedly secure enclaves in the southern hemisphere—South Africa, southern South America, Australia, New Zealand—realized the equator and its associated trade winds, would not keep them from eventual harm. The changes that were blowing in the wind could very well have the wind shift.

Thus, Jew, Gentile, Muslim, atheist, terrorist, or patriot: All came. Their exterior handles no longer mattered. With further use of nuclear and biochemical weapons, all knew they were facing the self-destruction of their cultures, themselves, and for a few centuries, the desolation of the earth.

As they assembled, they knew their clans were at risk. Their tribe—be it of the Baptist or Shia persuasion, of the Catholic or Sunni belief—became less important. When all was stripped away, it was not the tribe that mattered. It was the clan, the family.

The notable assemblages met twice, once in North America, and once in the Middle East. On both occasions, they toured the scenes of destruction. Careful not to become part of the scene, they donned anti-radiation gear.

Two speeches were given during these meetings. One was delivered in Washington, D.C. The other speech was presented at the site in the Middle East that had tasted America's revenge. Both speeches were given by two esteemed leaders. One was of the Christian world. One was of the Muslim world.

The leader chosen to deliver the address to the chastened Christian assemblage in Washington, D.C. decided to base the address on United States President John F. Kennedy's speech to the American people about placing a person on the moon before the end of the decade of the 1960s.[21] As did President Kennedy, the idea of the speech was to turn the world toward a common goal, one to be met at a specific time in the near future.

The address took place at the site of a former college, which was once located a short distance from the polluted Potomac River. Delivered before a limited radiation-proofed audience, but seen by the world, the speech went as follows:

Presidents, Vice Presidents, Patriots, Victims, Governors, Congressmen, Senators, scientists, distinguished guests, ladies and gentlemen:

We are saddened to be here, because we ourselves, our race, set the stage for this occasion.

We meet at a college once noted for knowledge, in a city once noted for progress, in a state once noted for strength, and we stand in need of all three, for we meet in an hour of change and challenge, in a decade of hope and fear, in an age of both knowledge and ignorance.[22] The greater our knowledge increases, the greater our ignorance unfolds, as you see before you. (As the audience bends around in their protective suits to behold the devastation of a former place of learning.)

We need only look over our shoulders to see the surrounding landscape to understand the magnitude of our collective incomprehension…incomprehension of this now startling fact: With our present composition, we humans cannot control ourselves. And if we do not somehow find a way to put a rein on ourselves, earth itself will come to resemble this college, this city, this state.

No man can fully grasp how far and how fast we have come, but condense, if you will, the 50,000 years of man's recorded history in a time span of but a half-century. Stated in these terms, last month electric lights and telephones and automobiles and airplanes became available. Only last week did we develop penicillin and television and nuclear power. Yesterday, we came close and are still in danger of annihilating ourselves.

The Cepee pauses from his study of this speech: *It appears my ancestors had finally begun to understand the consequences of their Autocatalytic Cycle and the Threshold Lowering Syndrome. …Too little too late? Hmm. Even though they are not here, I am. So, something happened leading them to fix themselves that led to me. I'll read on.* As he does:

This is a breathtaking pace, and such a pace has created the ills we have just witnessed. We have not been able to control our own creativity. We have lost control of ourselves as a race. We humans have allowed ourselves to let the circumstances of what we created take control of what we do with those creations.

If this capsule of our recent devastation teaches us anything, it is that modern cerebral man, in his quest for knowledge, progress, and yes, domination, is not accompanied with an equally modern genetic partner that counsels caution and restraint.

We have known for a while, and fully realize after these wars that there is a great mismatch between the inclination toward violence in our primitive makeup and inclination toward nonviolence in our modern makeup. Yes, we *have* known, and have known for many years, but we have not had the moral courage to face the stark fact that we humans are wired for Orwellian perpetual war.

In our ancient times, this wiring led to launching a spear to kill one person. Now this wiring leads to launching a nuclear rocket to kill an entire culture…a culture that, not so long ago, lived on the land where you and I are standing.

If our race is to survive, if our race is to once again flourish, we have no choice but to overpower those parts of us that led us to perpetual war.

We know this behavior is leading us to the road of chaos and misery.

We must now set sail from this place of our own making, and onto a new sea. We cannot stay at our present shore of mutual annihilation. But we *can* reach another shore, a shore of mutual acceptance of one another, and leave this deadly legacy behind us. If *we choose not to reach* this shore, we are destined to repeat the wars we have recently endured. We will perish in a sea of ignorance, revenge, and aggression…all of our own making…all to our own demise.

Many years ago the great British explorer George Mallory, who was to die on Mount Everest, was asked why he wanted to climb it. He said, "Because it is there."

We must answer the question of why we should climb a different Mount Everest of much greater difficulties with, "Because we have no choice."

Therefore, in honor of George Orwell, who in 1984, laid down the gauntlet for humans to end perpetual war, we are placing 2084, a century after his book became known, as the year that we will have transcended the Orwellian world of 1984.

For now, we pick up his gauntlet and declare: We shall succeed. We shall purge from our societies, the deadly weapons, and from ourselves, we shall purge those twins of our own potential destruction: revenge and aggression. We will purge this Deadly Trinity from our societies and our souls.

But let us have no illusions. If we do not find a way out of the Deadly Trinity, we might go to our own heaven, so might our children. But our children's children will not. They will not go to heaven, nor will they come to this earth, for they will never have the opportunity to exist. Our race will no longer be present to extend our legacy on this earth.

The Cepee pauses: *A pebble of sense from a mountain of past denial.*

The Islamic leader's speech took a different turn. It did not dwell on the more-or-less biological solutions to humankind's problems. It spoke of forgiveness. The speech went as follows:[23]

We find ourselves today being tested as we have never been tested before. In days past, our ordeals, more often than not, had us pass our tests with assertions of pride and revenge. On this earth, we are far from alone. Like all of us on this planet, how often have we declared ourselves to be merciful, joyful? In the end, we have declared: "Blood calls for blood."[24]

But today is different. Today makes these boasts irrelevant, even disdainful of our heritage. For I say to you, we are in danger of our heritage being lost. Our culture and religion are tottering on a cliff's edge of vengeful hatred.

A few, *very few* it must be said, of our brothers have taken the reins of our religion away from the many of us. They have led us to, if not ruin, then near-ruin. It is now up to us to take back those reins. We *can* regain our heritage of respect and influence in the world.

If we do not, we will simply cease to exist on earth. This goes for everyone, including America. "Enola Gays" have become common property.

Certainly, these Enola Gays might consign us to Paradise, but what about our legacy here on earth? It will be no more.

How can we solve our problems? Let me read to you a passage:

> "Allah subhanahu wa ta'ala has granted intellect to human beings. The intellect entails responsibility. The more intellect a person has the more he/she is responsible. …However, part of our being human is also that we make mistakes. …As human beings we are responsible, but we do also make mistakes and we are constantly in need of forgiveness."

Allah subhanahu wa ta'ala is the most forgiving, but I fear some of us have forgotten that the Qur'an speaks of forgiveness often. Yet, some of us have chosen to ignore these wisdoms and have focused on aggression and revenge.

The Cepee pauses: *Aggression and revenge? But I have learned many humans who practiced Christianity had come to believe that Islam was focused only on advancing vengeful wars. I suppose it was not unreasonable to think so. Muhammad, unlike Jesus, was not much of a pacifist. Let me surf the archives for this subject.*

The Cepee finds these entries in the Qur'an on the subjects that make reference to acceptance and forgiveness (over two hundred times): Al-Ghafoor, Ghafir, Ghaffar, Al-'Afuw, Al-Tawwab, Al-Haleem, Al-Rahman, and al-Rahim.

The Cepee returns to the speech of the Islamic leader.

Islam emphasizes justice and punishment of the wrong docrs, but it equally strongly emphasizes mercy, kindness, and love. We must keep in mind that as much as we need Allah's forgiveness for our own sins and mistakes, we must also practice forgiveness towards those who do wrong to us.

If our religion is to survive, if our religion is to once again flourish, we have no choice but to overpower those parts of us that led us to these continuous, vengeful wars.

We know this behavior is leading us to the road of chaos and misery. Look around you. (As the audience bends-around in their protective suits to behold devastation.)

We must now depart from this place of our own making, and place ourselves into a renewed oasis. We cannot stay at our present land of mutual annihilation. But we can reach another ground, a place of mutual acceptance of one another, and leave this deadly legacy behind us. If *we choose not to reach* this refuge, we are destined to repeat the wars we have recently endured. We will perish in a desert of ignorance, revenge, and aggression…all of our own making…all to our own demise—which is quite close to what we are doing now.

The Islamic leader did not go into Kennedy-like metaphors. His message was elegantly simple.

But let us not deceive ourselves. Our revenge, our aggression, our fixation on religion to right all wrongs has led us into a deadly trinity. If we do not find a way out of this trinity…yes, we will go to Paradise, but we will be the last ones to go. We will no longer exist to extend our legacy on this earth.

But let us also come to accept that we need not alter our beliefs. We need to alter how they are practiced.

The Cepee thinks: *A grain of sense from the sands of past denial.*

To Change or Not to Change?

As a result of these wars, the resultant speeches, and the unprecedented cooperation among admittedly severely damaged societies, the problem solvers got together. As noble and invigorating as these speeches were, and if heeded, would have fixed a lot of problems with the human race, it was still wired for self-destruction.

But with unprecedented funding, genetic engineers and cerebral surgeons entered the stage and began in earnest to "disinfect" the human of his deadly aggressive behavior. The magnitude of the attacks, the number of dead humans or those with radiation sickness, the burying of friends and loved ones (those who could be found), and the knowledge that more attacks would follow, spurred the humans to fix themselves.

As stated in the speeches, the humans had no choice. The two principles for eschewing human self-change fell into disapprobation. Critics of these principles, who now included a majority of the human race, called them, "The Flotsam and Jetsam of Self-Change Taboos." The first principle for leaving the human alone, to evolve naturally as it had for centuries, was cast aside as academic flotsam.

The second principle, the argument for keeping the mind unaltered and available for housing God's soul, was debunked as religious jetsam. Most religious leaders came on board to declare the heretofore forbidden self-changes to the human were indeed part of God's will.

Regardless of the religious implications (and the associated debates, a subject for Chapter 10), the first extensive use of weapons of mass destruction since World War II altered the self-change or no self-change debate. The no self-change philosophy was now viewed as a sophistic mockery of reality. The ideas are reflected in a more detailed time line, shown in Figure 9-5.

Intense
debates on
self-change

Continued germ
attacks. Aftermath
of wars of mass
destruction

The goal for the
defeat of the Deadly
Trinity is set

EGO, ILLS,
SANE become
popular

2000   2nd/3rd   3rd/4th   2084   2150
        decades: decades:
        WMD   ILLS and
        attacks.   SANE
        Germs   declared
        mutate.   vital.
                ASSES
                declared
                critical.

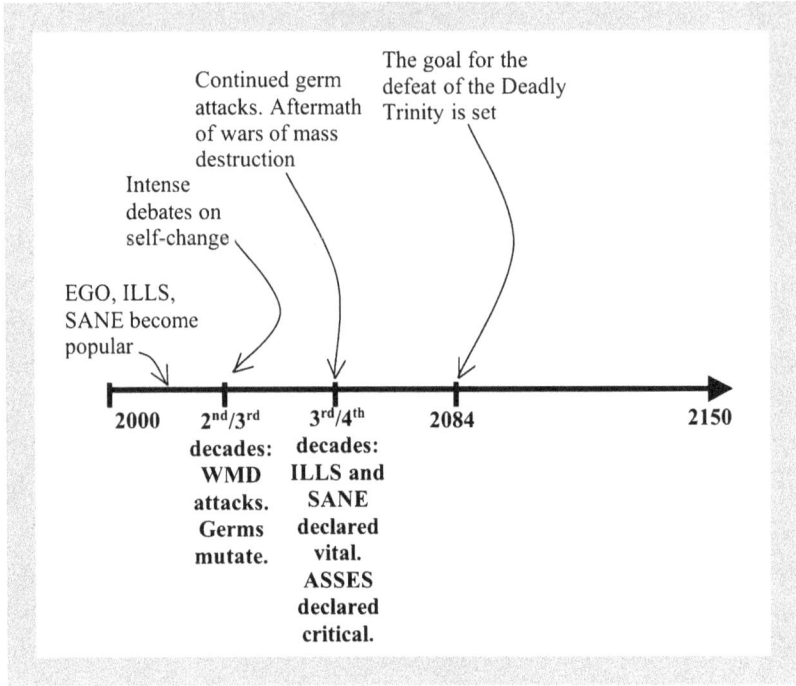

Figure 9-5. The time line again.

Notwithstanding this increased effort and focus, the task was not easy. Just as there was no smart gene, there was no aggression gene. Multiple genes contributed to the humans' aggressive behavior, and each gene yielded "several thousand expression variants."[25] Finding the genomic basis entailed a more extensive search than a simple elimination of non-participating gene markers. Some scientists were skeptical of the ability of the human to discover and treat the genetic causes of deadly aggression.[26]

Part V: Nature or Nurture?

The pathological behavior residing in a segment of the humans' population was not solely a matter of nature dictating the course of events. Nurture played a significant role as well. In the early years of the twenty-first century, the humans came to understand that through the interaction of genes with the environment, including the humans' cultures, the race unconsciously developed epigenetic rules to function, and survive—even thrive—in different environments. The seemingly unintelligent cells in the human's body and mind proved to be amazingly prescient.

These rules were inherited changes in gene expression that could be passed down from generation to generation. Events occurring, say, in the 1960s through the 1990s created physiological mechanisms in later generations that were played out with pathological aggression. As expressed by a twenty-first century scientist: "[These rules are] caused by mechanisms other than the underlying DNA sequence…. These changes may remain through cell divisions for the remainder of the cell's life and may also last for multiple generations. …Non-genetic factors cause the [human's] genes to behave (or 'express themselves') differently."[27]

This relationship resulted in the possibility (even likelihood) of humans' behavior being partially established, not only by genes, but also by external factors that affected the behavior of the genes. Modifications could occur to the genome without a change in the arrangement of the DNA components.[28]

Consequently, humans were by no means genetically hardwired to the extent they had no control over their behavior. Non-genetic factors, such as a social environment, food intake, extended assignments in war zones, and prolonged periods of no human contact could cause the human's genes to express themselves differently. "Those who possess the genes are not absolutely condemned to acquire the trait, but in certain environments they are more likely than the average person to do so."[29]

From ancient to modern times, the epigenetic rules pertaining to pathological aggression were derived from the humans' social acculturations. This cultural evolution resulted in the rules themselves changing. These rules defined "cultural experiences that could change genetic selections."[30]

The discovery of epigenetic rules was a step forward in this understanding (see Figure 9-6): Humans' cultures affected gene behavior, and gene behavior affected the behavior of humans' cultures.

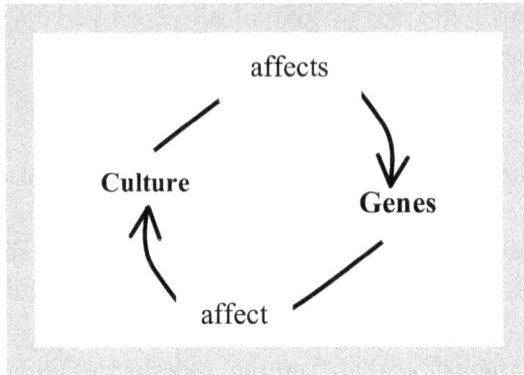

Figure 9-6. Epigenetic rules for human behavior.

The humans came to understand that the frequent killing of students on a campus or diners in a McDonald's was more than mere mimicking. A gradually emerging culture of gratuitous violence that had emerged in the latter twentieth and early twenty-first centuries created a set of epigenetic rules in a limited number of people who already had a dysfunctional mental makeup. With practically no control over who could own armaments, epigenetically disturbed killers made their way into elementary schools and shot at point-blank-distance six- and seven-year-old children.

The learning about epigenetics brought forth different schools of thought about the effects of nature and nurture. As examples: Where was the line to be drawn between a marginally functioning or outright insane person, especially when behavior might be subject to changing environments? What happened (if anything) to people's gene- and culture-based epigenetic rules (and their genetically related offspring) who watched violent movies and computer games simulating the knocking-off of fellow humans? What was the effect of live games that marked the emulated dead people with paint spots?

Some experts said that daily doses of TV violence, common as an advertisement, helped stoke the epigenetic rules.

Others said having guns around the house meant they would inevitably be used on humans. Opponents of this view cited examples of ranchers keeping shotguns, rifles, and pistols in an open cabinet in their living rooms. Physically, their children had open access to them. Psychologically, the young ones had been taught (conditioned by their environment) that the cabinet had a mental lock on it.[31] Even more, guns were part of these people's way of life, part of their existence, part of their identity. These gun-totters had no intent to use the weapons on humans. Nonetheless, gun ownership continued to increase up to the Cepee times, because people believed they had to bear arms in order to protect themselves from other people.

Regardless of these debates, the realization that the killers' sicknesses were partially created by humans' increasingly violent culture was not to excuse their behavior. It was to understand their behavior. And in knowing their makeup, in understanding how and why they behaved, the human race could more readily confront the sociopaths and psychopaths in their midst and address the root causes of their maladies.

Finally, the nature vs. nurture debate was laid to rest. Human behavior was determined by both, and nature and nurture were determined by each other.

Altering Nature

Therefore, it was accepted that genetic engineering, brain bioengineering, and environmental engineering were the three keys to altering the humans' aggressive behavior. In spite of protests from social workers, psychologists, spiritual therapists, and preachers, nature began to take a side seat next to nurture. One example was the discovery of the genetic basis for sexual fidelity or infidelity, first in rats, later in humans.[32] What could be more convincing about the interplay of nature and nurture than an operation that successfully altered the gigolo's genes to make this former Lothario a hearth-side homebody?

After exhaustive research, scientists began making inroads into understanding the nature side of revenge. Previously, self-help groups, feel good pundits, and social workers blamed revenge on nurture. While environmental conditions certainly affected revenge, doctors at the University of Zurich discovered it also had cerebral foundations in the part of the brain structure called the caudate nucleus.[33]

Further studies revealed that religious, racial, ethnic, and political beliefs, as well as biases and prejudices, resided in several parts of the brain that processed emotions, conflicts, and judgment. During the assembling and processing of events relating to political or religious subjects, the part of the brain associated with reasoning was quiescent. Later, after the political or religious decision had been made, yet another brain part associated with reward and pleasure became active.[34] The task at hand became obvious. Among other alterations, one job was to suppress the cerebral attributes that encouraged aggression and revenge and amplify the attributes that processed reasoning.

Regardless of the skeptics, regardless of the diminishing cries from ethicists, and with help from the ongoing EGO, ILLS, and SANE programs, the race began in earnest to engineer aggression out of the humans.

The goals were twofold: (1) Eliminate the eradicators' penchant to use weapons such as AK-47s and Glocks on citizens in schools and malls. (2) Eliminate the eradicators' penchant to use weapons such as chemicals and nuclear bombs on cities and nations. These two sets of killers varied in that the former was usually a lone individual, bent on local destruction, and the latter a group of individuals, bent on regional and national destruction. While their phenotypes (observed behavior) were different, their genotypes (genetic makeup) were closely matched, at least close enough to allow genetic engineers to address both phenotypes with similar treatments.

Regardless of phenotype differences or genotype similarities, the ultimate goal was to make the transformations before aggression with Glocks and nukes destroyed the civilized fabrics of the human race.

Aggression Anonymous (AA)

The assaults upon many urban areas did extensive damage to these cities' social, financial, and technical infrastructures, but the explosions and radiation did not physically destroy outlying parts of these urban areas or other parts of earth. After all, the gears of humans' societies were far flung. Governments, banks, and military installations adhered to the dictum of distributed processing: spread the risk of attack into multiple locations. Additionally, the Internet, the central means of communications for these societies, was too spread out to be taken down with a few bombs.

Nonetheless, the damage and trauma were so severe the human race finally recognized it could not control itself. Like an incurable alcoholic who must radically change his life's patterns, the humans decided they had no choice but to radically change their cerebral, genetic, and epigenetic compositions. Lucky for them, EGO, ILLS, and SANE were well underway by this time, and the human had already begun to become a different being. ASSES was icing on the genetic and cerebral cakes.

Conclusion

The humans had changed little from the days of the cave dwellers, through the Crusades, the Inquisitions, Pizarro, the European and Cambodian Holocausts, to al Qaeda. Their age-old enchantment with the Law of the Instrument never changed, but the instrument itself surely did.

Their fixation on the Deadly Trinity persisted until their urban societies began to disintegrate. Finally, the nuclear and chemical attacks on segments of the humans' populations changed the rules regarding human self-change. The need to eliminate violent aggression overwhelmed previous ethical and moral taboos, as well as religious proscriptions.

----

[1] Richard Wrangham and Dale Peterson, *Demonic Males* (New York: Houghton Mifflin, 1996), 80. Also, http://www.sfgate.com/news/article/Al-Qaeda-bluffing-about-having-suitcase-nukes-2776832.php Note: Online citations of a 1997 publishing date are in error. The Waorani is a tribe who live in the Amazon rainforest, in parts of Ecuador.

[2] "Al Qaeda May Have 'Briefcase' Nukes," *The Spokesman Review*, March 22, 2004, A1. The quote is from Ayman al-Zawahri, al Qaeda's second in command when he made this statement.

[3] The scenarios presented in the first part of this chapter pertain to conflicts in the Middle East, the details about wars using unconventional weapons, as well as several alliances and schisms among religious factions, ethnic groups, and nations. They represent a few examples among a vast array of possibilities that could unfold. Indeed, the odds do not favor these scenarios taking place exactly as I describe, because of an almost limitless combination of credible possibilities.

These scenarios were chosen because they are plausible and serve as a foundation for illustrating the complex state of affairs that exist in this part of the world. Whether or not these scenarios emerge is not germane to my central thesis: If humans do not deal with the current problems, we face the stark probability that weapons of mass destruction are likely to be employed in this part of the world, and in parts of the world closer to home.

The Cepee would likely offer: *Knowing the history of my ancestors, resolving these problems would require the casting aside of pride, innumerable prejudices, countless intransigent attitudes, as well as a willingness to step down a notch or so in the Human Tribal Hierarchy.*

[4] "Religions," CIA, *The World Factbook*, 2010. https://www.cia.gov/library/publications/the-world-factbook/fields/2122.html. "Islam," *Encyclopædia Britannica Online*, 2010, http://www.britannica.com/EBchecked/topic/295507/Islam.

[5] William R. Polk, *Understanding Iraq* (New York: HarperCollins, 2005), 39-49.

[6] David Remnick, "Danger Levels," *The New Yorker*, July 31, 2006, 22.

[7] "Sunnite," *Encyclopædia Britannica Online*, 2010, http://www.britannica.com/EBchecked/topic/574006/Sunnite.

[8] "Mapping the Global Muslim Population: A Report on the Size and Distribution of the World's Muslim Population," *Pew Research Center*, October 7, 2009, http://pewforum.org/Muslim/Mapping-the-Global-Muslim-Population%286%29.aspx.

[9] The statistics represented in Figure 9-1 vary, depending on the source. These data reflect tabulations based on The Pew Forum, http://www.pewforum.org/Muslim/Mapping-the-Global-Muslim-Population(6).aspx.

[10] Oliver Roy, *The Politics of Chaos in the Middle East* (New York: Columbia University Press, 2008), 106. Note: some web sources cite p. 105 for this source.

[11] Seth G. Jones, "The Mirage of the Arab Spring," *Foreign Affairs*, January/February 2013, 62.

[12] Extracted from various websites, *Time, The Economist, The Wall Street Journal*.

[13] Ellen Knickmeyer and Alex Delmar-Morgan, "Gulf States Balk at Regional Union," *The Wall Street Journal*, May 14, 2012, A10.

[14] Karl Vick, "The Ultra-Holy City," *Time*, August 13, 2012, 48.

[15] Ibid., 49.

[16] "More Jewish than Thou," *The Economist*, July 28, 2012, 9.

[17] Barack Obama, President, March 21, 2013. Aired on major television stations.

[18] "Estimated Causalities," http://csis.org/files/media/csis/pubs/090316_ israelistrikeiran.pdf. Also, http://www.globalsecurity.org/wmd/world/iran/ karaj.htm.

[19] "Iran: Foreign Policy Challenges and Choices," November 2006, http:// www.david-kilgour.com/2008/pdf/iran/Iran%20Report.pdf. A report sponsored by DLA Piper US LLP. The map in Figure 9-3 is courtesy of New Scientist Global Security. It is a simplified version of the map on page 2 of the report cited above.

[20] "The Effects of Nuclear War," Washington, DC: Office of Technology Assessment, Congress of the United States, 1979, http://www.pbs.org/wgbh/ amex/bomb/sfeature/1mtblast.html. All estimates of nuclear destruction are sourced from this document with ancillary information sourced from http:// www.aolsvc.worldbook.aol.com/wb/Article?id=ar396520&sc=2#h5.

[21] John F. Kennedy, "Man on the Moon," A Special Presidential Address to Congress on the Importance of Space, May 25, 1961, http://www. homeofheroes.com/presidents/speeches/kennedy_space.html. I have taken the liberty of integrating parts of President Kennedy's speech with the speech the world leader made at the D.C. site. If you wish to know which parts are those of JFK, see "Man on the Moon" speech on the web.

[22] I trust the reader will overlook the reference to the District of Columbia being a state.

[23] "Forgiveness in Islam," Summary of a Friday Khutbah, April 14, 2000, http://www.pakistanlink.com/religion/2000/04-14.html. As with the Kennedy speech, endnote 21, I have also taken the liberty of mixing parts of the world leader's thoughts with this essay. For its original content, see "Forgiveness in Islam" on the web.

[24] CBS program, "Face the Nation," aired July 30, 2006,

[25] Paul H. Silverman, Letters to the Editor, *The Atlantic Monthly*, June 2004, 14.

[26] Ibid. This writer may be reading in too much pessimism on the part of Dr. Silverman and his letter, cited in note 25. Nonetheless, I think pioneers in genome and stem cell research, such as Dr. Silverman, will grant that

we humans will transform ourselves in radical ways during the next few decades.

[27] Philip Hunter. "What Genes Remember." *Prospect Magazine*, no. 146 (May 2008); Web.archive.org. 2008-05-01; http://web.archive.org/web/20080501094940/; http://www.prospect magazine.co.uk/article_details.php?id=10140.

[28] Adrian Bird, "Perceptions of Epigenetics,"*Nature* 447 (7143): 396–8, doi:10.1038/nature05913. PMID 17522671.

[29] E. O. Wilson, *The Social Conquest of Earth* (New York: Liveright, 2012), 203, Kindle edition, loc. 3288.

[30] W. Reik, "Stability and Flexibility of Epigenetic Gene Regulation in Mammalian Development," in *Nature* (May, 2007); http://www.ncbi.nlm.nih.gov/pubmed/17522676.

[31] In my youth, our family ranch-house living room had such a cabinet. I recall it contained two gauges of shotguns, several .22 rifles, pistols, and a nifty lever-action .30-.30 with a six-sided barrel. At my discretion, I could use the .22 rifles for hunting. But the other guns in the cabinet were cerebrally-lockup. Perhaps family epigenetics came into play, as I never broke that mental lock on the cabinet.

[32] Elizabeth Weise, "Report: Rodents May Offer Insight to Monogamy," *USA Today*, June 16, 2004, 2A. Taking writer's license, I fast-forwarded this technology from the rat's genome to that of the human.

[33] David Brown, "Joys of Revenge Documented," *The Washington Post*, August, 29, 2004, A13. Note: Online copy lists Juliet Eilperin with a byline. The hard copy cites only Mr. Brown. In addition, hard copy is dated August 30, 2004.

[34] Michael Shermer, "The Political Brain," *Scientific American*, July 2006, 36.

CHAPTER 10

ISSUES AND QUESTIONS

—✦—

Cogito cogito ergo cogito sum.[1]

Looking backward is easier than thinking forward.

It is because of them that I am I.
Their whole is a part of me.

The process of changing the human into the Cepee was undertaken initially to enhance the lifestyle and health of the human race and to combat increasingly dangerous germs and associated diseases. Later efforts were directed toward making the human less prone to engage in pointless aggression.

Initially, these changes were not made with a long-range plan in mind. During the twentieth and the first part of the twenty-first centuries, most of the human race still labored under the Immediacy Syndrome and had no long-range vision about their eventual constructions. However, as the humans made their way through the twenty-first century, and as brain bioengineering and genetic tailoring became realities, the changes underway on their bodies and brains were recognized to be of far greater consequence and complexity than rearranging skin or propping up sagging buttocks.

Consequently, the later generation humans, recognizing the possible consequences of these alterations, began to assess the implications of what their technologies had brought, and might bring to the human race in the future.

Their philosophies, biases, and prejudices complicated matters, creating a profusion of roadblocks for many of the changes. Alterations to the brain affected the very essence of what constituted a human being. The changes could possibly interfere with the workings of free will, the concept of self, and the revered soul. Thus, brain bioengineering was fraught with moral, ethical, and religious uncertainties. The questions surrounding these issues had no clear answers. It often came down to the simple fact that humans were afraid to make changes to themselves, yet afraid not to.

Many debates occurred about the kinds and degree of changes the humans might make to themselves. Deliberations and arguments sprang forth from street corner saloons, pulpits of churches, bully pulpits of legislatures, and halls of academia. While the tone, context, and intellectual level of these debates varied, they were infused with the same themes.

To gain an appreciation of the complexity and intensity of these issues, a debate about the subject is re-enacted. The debate took place between a proponent and an opponent of human self-change. It took place in the early part of the twenty-first century.

Opening Remarks

Moderator, "Good evening. We are pleased to present a debate on the thorny issue of humans changing themselves through genetic tailoring, biosynthetic surgery, organ and limb replacements, and brain engineering. The panelists represent two groups: One is opposed to self-change and the other is in favor of using these technologies in any manner to, as this group claims, 'improve' the human race."

The change proponent is asked to begin the debate, "Thank you. I will start by asking some questions. Why should we humans remain as we are? We did not begin our life on earth as we are today. Throughout our time on this planet, through thousands of years, we have evolved, never remaining static. Why should we remain fixed now? Should we change the equation of change itself? What right do we have to halt the evolution of our species, to ossify ourselves inside a time capsule, immune to transformations?"

The change opponent responds, "Because our actions will not be part of the evolutionary process. The changes to humans, from our very creation to what we are now, occurred through a natural course, and without direct, intrusive human intervention. We recognize the human will change. We accept this fact. The question you ask is who will make these changes? You are saying we humans should alter ourselves. This action would be a break from the past. It would not be natural selection. It would be unnatural selection."

The change proponent disagrees, "We have intervened directly in our lives for thousands of years. Altering our hunting habits led to a change in the shape of our jaws, eventually the size of our brains. Changing the foods we ate led to our becoming a fitter race. We made these changes as part of our natural process. Who is to determine what is natural or unnatural and who is to determine if we humans make these changes? I say it is we humans who should make this determination."

The change proponent continues, "If we humans are clever enough to find ways to improve our brains and our genome, why not do it? After all, this approach is nothing more than the next step in our evolution. Furthermore, if we know how to enhance our species, yet do not perform this task, then we are committing an unnatural act, one that goes against nature itself."

Religion Enters into the Debate

Change opponent, "I suspect our small jaws and large brains came from our need to adjust to a changing environment and not from our own volition—points for a future debate. Anyway, your questions are easy to answer. We stay true to God's intentions as established in the holy book. God establishes the natural process. What right do we have to interfere with nature?"

Change proponent, "Which God? Which holy book? And nature? God's nature can be very cruel, yet you continue to mask your God in gentle benevolence with a grand cosmic plan. But when you are dealt a bad hand by God's nature, you blame yourselves because you are unworthy sinners, thus deserving of your misfortune. You say a landslide is the result of humans' sins; a tsunami rolled ashore because of our religious transgressions; a volcanic eruption spurted forth because of our vices; New Orleans is under water because

Bourbon Street poured too much Bourbon. If you don't blame our race for evoking 'nature,' you somehow exempt your God from the catastrophe. Your approach is insulting to our race."

Change opponent, "I've heard these kinds of remarks many times. You and your school of thought proclaim, 'How can there be a God if that God allows painful deaths? If that God allows children to die? If that God allows murders to occur?'

"Yet you fail to consider that you are alive in the first place! While you construct your criticisms of death, you ignore the fact that you are living. You have been given the gift of life, yet you treat your place in our universe as if it's an entitlement, as if God is required to consign you a place on earth."

Change proponent, "Entitlement? We humans have been trying to insulate ourselves from nature's 'entitlements' and the physical whims of nature's God from the time we could think! I submit that nature, in how it treats humans, is not a grand design at all. Nature is imperfect. So are humans, and imperfection is not a grand design.

The Natural Process Is Not Working

"Look where this supposedly 'natural process' has taken us. Our planet is out of control. Let's go down the list. We have not solved the problems of distributing our wealth to other members of our race. More people in the world are abjectly poor. While many of us dine on steaks, others in our species are starving. Those who manage to avoid starvation may die from drinking too much toxic water or not having enough water to drink. We are murdering ourselves with increasing frequency and efficiency, yet we have not found a way to obey a fundamental law of our race that a human shall not kill another human."

The change proponent advances another point, "We have evolved into a species that appears incapable of taking care of itself. The stratifications of our societies into groups of 'haves' and 'have-nots' have placed us into a position in which we are slowly but surely creating a vast population of underclassed humans. These have-nots have no control over their lives. They have no opportunity for social engagement. They constitute a sub-race, little more than members of the walking dead.

"In the long run, we have no choice. Either we alter our genetic makeup and mental properties or we continue to spiral down the road to more inequities in our race, more killing, and a more chaotic existence. We might continue to limp along through all this mayhem. But why should we do so? We have the power to change our mental and physical constitutions. We have the power to change the despairing, often deadly qualities of our behavior.

"Certainly, we are not living in Voltaire's imaginary 'best of all possible worlds,' far from it. Yet we have the capacity to alter the miserable lot of Candide's human race. How can you deny these opportunities to the less fortunate of our species?"

Eugenics Enters into the Debate

The change opponent responds, "Then tell me, how do we decide about changes made to the brain? How are we to reconcile the ethical issues of altering our memory capabilities, our consciousness, and our awareness? Will the changes have an effect on our moods; should they?

"How about our humor? Our intellect? Who is to be gifted with high intelligence? Who is not? As a practical matter, how do we maintain our individual identity and the integrity of our intelligence if our brain is fitted with off-the-shelf components?

"Furthermore, which of us is to be a lucky person to be gifted with all these life enhancing and life prolonging treasures? Will it be determined by who has more wealth, more power? If so, those less affluent and less powerful among us will essentially be pushed off the gangplank of life. So will their descendants. Eventually, they will simply die out sooner than their altered competitors.

"Shall the government take over? Shall there be a lottery on who gets the next gene sequence overhaul? How can we humans hope to achieve any degree of control over these scientific nightmares? It's unnatural!"

Change proponent, "I am certain these issues will be addressed as the scientific community encounters them. They are of scientific origin. Science can deal with them."

Change opponent, "Science! Science gave us the neutron bomb, nerve gas, and warfare viruses! Science also gave us Charles Davenport, the father of eugenics.[2] The pseudo-scientific misconceptions of Davenport led to the forced sterilization of 40,000 women in the United States in the early 1900s. The U.S. government attempted to control this gene pool until the insane policies fell into disfavor."

The change opponent continues, "After this abominable program, then came Hitler, the supreme eugenics practitioner. As eugenics and sterilization fell into disfavor in America, they raised their heads in Germany, leading to atrocities the world could hardly imagine. All in the name of 'improving our race.'"

Change proponent, "But science also gave us the polio vaccine, bypass surgery, and organ transplants. Moreover, you mistakenly criticize science for the ills of society. I am disappointed you have brought Davenport and Hitler into this debate. We humans have learned from these men. We will not repeat their mistakes. They were anomalies, aberrational blips on the humans' scope of life."

Change opponent, "I disagree. These men represented a very real segment of our population. These kinds of people still exist and are eager to ply eugenics on our race when they have the opportunity."

Life, Maybe Death, Maybe Not

Moderator, "Sir and madam, we must move on."

Change proponent, "I believe it is my turn?"

Moderator, "Correct."

Change proponent, "During the past few decades, we have made startling discoveries that have led to the prolongation of life. Noted scientists declare that someday we humans might never die, that we will have an everlasting life. It is evident that many of your views are based on your religion. How do you square your beliefs about death, a subject integral to many religions?"

Change opponent, "Including mine. First, your question was not complete. You made no mention of an afterlife. Second, Jesus Christ died and was resurrected. He is our model. After the resurrection of the dead, we will indeed have an everlasting life, but one that will come from the hands of God and not the hands of humans."

The change opponent continues, "It is quite clear, just read John 3:16, from which I will quote: 'For God so loved the world that he gave his one and only Son, that whosoever believes in him shall not perish but have eternal life.' "

Change proponent, "But John 3:16 says nothing about death! The quote of 'shall not perish' coincides with the views of many scientists (and mine). And while we are on the subject of John, here's another passage from John 10:28: 'And I give unto them eternal life, and they shall never perish, neither shall any man pluck them out of my hand.' No dying there, no Jesus-like resurrection. You choose to quote the Bible to refute my stand on humans dictating an everlasting life, and then cite passages that refute your own argument."

Change opponent, "The Bible clearly states the living *will indeed* die, but they will be resurrected and have an everlasting life. You can't conveniently select single passages from the Bible to make an argument."

Change proponent, "I say the same to you."

Manipulation of the Mind

Moderator, "We must move on."

Change opponent, "I agree. I think we have reached a stalemate on the issue of eugenics and death. I have the turn, so I will state that I have another objection to intervening in our mental and genetic makeup. What about the consequences of erasing one's memories? If your philosophy is allowed to prevail, we are certain this procedure will be carried out. We humans already have methods, with pills and surgery, to erase remembrances of events in our past, and we are now using these techniques on parts of our population. We opponents of change state unequivocally: Our memories make us who we are. The awareness of our past makes our present meaningful."

Change proponent, "But why shouldn't we condition our minds to consider the past irrelevant to the present? What would be the harm of living in the 'today,' forsaking the debilitating 'yesterdays?' Why shouldn't we cast aside unpleasant experiences and memories?

"I am not suggesting all our recollections should be subject to manipulation, to change, to erasure. I am suggesting we should have the decency and empathy to make changes to our brains if change will help the mental well-being of humans who have been traumatized by horrific events in their lives such as rape, incest, and assault."

Change opponent, "We change opponents think your view is a spurious argument. Negative, painful experiences are part of the human process, an inevitable consequence of being born with a highly intelligent and facile brain. If we cease to remember traumatic, stressful experiences, we believe the human will become stunted. After all, unpleasant, even terrible experiences are known to contribute to the growth of a person's psyche. It could turn out our painless memories will lead to a mentally impoverished person, perhaps to a stunted mentality. But we don't know! So why take the chance?"

Change proponent, "I am not saying we won't continue to experience painful experiences. We just won't remember them. I quote a passage about this issue."[3]

> ...a person crippled by memories is a diminished person; there is nothing ennobling about it. If we as a society decide it's better to keep people locked in their anguish because of some idealized view of what it means to be human, we might be revealing ourselves to be a society with a twisted notion of what being human really means.

Change opponent, "I cannot deny we should undertake *curative* changes to our minds and genome. But you miss my main point: The human race does not have the ability to draw the line and say, 'No more!' We have not been able to constrain ourselves in the past. Why should the future be different?"

The Slippery Slopes of Science

The change opponent continues, "Furthermore, you say the scientists will find answers to these questions. We think the opposite. Time and again, scientists supposedly make their science safe, but inevitably they become so excited with their discoveries, they lose sight of the consequences of their findings and forge ahead to the next discovery. Scientists are scientists. They are grounded in research and discovery. And some scientists simply do not care about the moral or ethical consequences of their work. That is not their job."

The change opponent thrusts again, "You're on a slippery slope. Your scientists will make genetic alterations that have unintended consequences. It is well known that many genes are pleiotropic: having multiple effects, perhaps on unrelated human traits. Thus, we do not know what the effects of genetic engineering may be over a long time span. Equally dangerous is the problem of alerting a gene to eliminate a problem, when that very same alteration will also eliminate a benefit. This type of tampering is not the domain of the human."

The change proponent parries, "I disagree. We recognize we are currently at the tip of the genetic iceberg, at its visible point. But science will learn about pleiotropic genes and learn to control their effects."

Packaging Gene Combinations

The change opponent changes the subject, "That brings me to my next point. I have another issue to put on the table. We opponents to self-change do not believe the greed and avarice inherent in our race will allow humans to rein in their desire for monetary rewards for genetic engineering, as well as brain engineering discoveries and inventions. The capital markets are not constructed on ethical and moral foundations. Quite the opposite, they are neutral about the matter. If someone can make money on a discovery or an invention, that person will do so, and the capital markets will reward the person."

Change proponent, "Not entirely. The capital markets are largely self-healing and self-regulating. If left alone, they will take care of themselves. The leaders in the industry will certainly know when and where to draw the line."

Change opponent, "Is that so? Capital markets are run by humans, which is precisely why they are not self-regulating or self-healing. Scores of venture capitalists await the creation of the first human cloning company in order to add this company's portfolio to their initial public offering (IPO). Hundreds of insiders eagerly await the next IPO that 'advances' humankind with self-change technologies. Thousands of eager buyers, thumbing and fingering their iPhones and iPads, are waiting to snap up the next offering for a genome-enhancing stock. The human self-change gold rush is on."

Change proponent, "So what? Besides, the Supreme Court has ruled against gene patenting. There is nothing wrong with this 'gold rush.' We must look beyond our current human experience. We will not resolve these issues if we continue to think about the problem with our conventional approaches to problem solving. We must try to conceive solutions that are not apparent in everyday life."[4]

Cloning

The change proponent changes gears, "You brought up the subject of human cloning. I suspect you don't support it?"

Change opponent, "Support it? I abhor it. I will oppose it to my death."

Proponent, "Cloning has been going on since humans first walked the earth. After all, Eve was cloned from Adam's rib.[5] She carried a carbon copy of his DNA, exactly like modern DNA replicas do. Adam described Eve as, "Bone of my bone, flesh of my flesh."[6]

The change opponent counters, "Adam and Eve were God's work."

The Religious Argument Is Resurrected

Change proponent, "I figured you would put God back into this discussion. I submit that God, if God exists, does not forbid humans to undertake these changes. We humans are doing nothing more than speeding up what nature has been doing for millions of years. Nature has changed the human. We are acting as partners to nature in making these changes. Surely, your God, my God, anyone's God would not object to our quest to make ourselves better."

Change opponent, "I can quote scripture from the holy books refuting your claim."

Change proponent, "Of course you can. And I can use the same books to substantiate my views."

The Cepee reflects: *True to my ancestors' behavior*; "Where you sit is where you stand on a subject."...*including their holy books.*

Change proponent continues, "If we don't play God, who will?"[7]

Change opponent, "God will."

Moderator, "We are out of time. I wish to thank our distinguished program participants for expressing their views about the thorny issues surrounding human self-change. In spite of the discussion, these issues remain troublesome and unresolved. Until next time, good evening."

The Disproportionate Ratio at Last Comes to the Rescue

Humans had difficulty executing many of the self-change technologies because of differing views on what constituted normal behavior, or for that matter, what constituted a normal brain. Consider insanity, for example. This illness was clearly not an attribute the change proponents thought should be retained in the human. But the task of eliminating insanity from the model was not as easy as simply altering the humans' DNA. Indeed, the humans discovered illnesses such as schizophrenia and manic depression were caused by more than one gene.[8]

The human's mind was meshed with behavioral attributes that interspersed normal and abnormal behavior. Many of the brilliant minds of the human race were also tainted with mental illnesses. Should the genetic surgeon have cured a Van Gogh of his mental madness, a cure that might have denied the world his art? In whose interests were such decisions made, the individual or the individual's society? Did the Van Goghs of the world have the right to make their own decisions about someone cutting into their brain? The humans never answered these questions. They just kept on making changes to their minds and bodies.

To complicate matters, the concepts of normalcy or abnormality were open to interpretation, such as suicide. Some people thought it was normal, even honorable if performed for a patriotic or religious cause. Others were less enthusiastic, declaring persons who killed themselves to be mentally ill. Such an environment made it difficult to come to terms with the issue of humans changing themselves. Nonetheless, these changes came about, not through the ironclad evolutionary process, but through the humans' revolutionary interventions.

At last, we encounter a positive example of the Disproportionate Ratio: In relation to the human population of over seven billion people, a relatively few humans, numbering in the tens of thousands at the most, were instrumental in rescuing the human race from itself.

They excelled in diverse fields such as genetics, behavioral science, synthetic biology, neuroplasticity, psychology, ethics, and organ growth. Their lifelong dedication to mastering a specific treatment, be it restoring sight to the blind, healing a mentally damaged war veteran, or altering a gene that caused jaw tumors, became a tiny but vital part of a whole. It was this "whole" that transformed the human race.

With the exception of a small segment of the human population who were pathologically violent, we can now ask if the humans of 150 years ago in the early twenty-first century were on a moral and ethical plane similar to those who now inhabit the earth (the year 2150)? But how can we? We are not around in 2150. So, we must leave this judgment to the Cepee.

The Cepee closes the Human Archives. *I know the answer. It is because of them that I am I. Their whole is a part of me.*

---

[1] A paraphrase of Descartes' Cogito ergo sum, "I think, therefore I am." This rendering is translated as "I think that I think, therefore I think that I am." Microsoft's Encarta Reference Library.

[2] "DNA," Howard Hughes Medical Institute, Alfred P. Sloan Foundation, Films for the Humanities and Sciences # 32869, Princeton, "Pandora's Box," 2003.

[3] Robin Marantz Henig, "The Quest to Forget," *The New York Times Magazine*, April 4, 2004, 32-37.

[4] "DNA," Films for the Humanities and Sciences # 32869, "Pandora's Box," 2003.

[5] Thank you Sylvia Gann Mahoney for this idea.

[6] In Hebrew writings.

[7] James Watson's often cited comment.

[8] "DNA," Films for the Humanities and Sciences # 32869, "Pandora's Box," 2003.

CHAPTER 11

CHANGING THE HUMAN

———

Procrustes in modern dress...there will have to be some stretching and a bit of amputation...only this time they will be a good deal more drastic than in the past.[1]

A *Brave New World* character said, "I am I, and wish I wasn't." In the world beyond 2084, this character could become what he wanted to be.[2]

Just as the humans did with the Neanderthals, the Cepees did with the humans: *They were bred-out and genetically over swamped.*[3]

The cells knew what to do. It was as if they possessed an invisible and undetectable intelligence of their own; that their simple structure contained a cerebral astuteness of their own making and under their control.

The humans' trip to self-constructed obsolescence began in the late twentieth century and accelerated rapidly thereafter. Some 100 years later, they were a significantly altered race. The time line for this process is shown in Figure 11-1.

Toward mid-twenty-first century, the humans experienced attacks from terrorists and diseases, recounted in past chapters. With solutions to these problems emerging in the genetic and brain engineering labs, the debates about human self-change declined. While a few opponents of self-change persisted, principally in religious circles, the majority of the species were eager to extend their life, improve their appearance and health, and rid themselves of the Deadly Trinity.

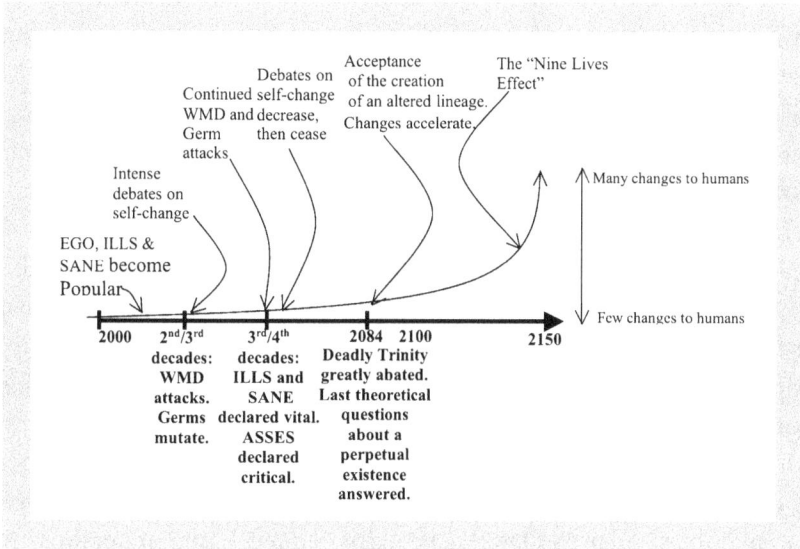

Figure 11-1. The complete time line.

By 2070, those humans who were born in the later part of the twenty-first century could expect to live twice as long as those born in 2000. Many humans lived into their 160s.

1984 and 2084

Toward the end of the twenty-first century, the rapidly changing human race chose the year of 2084 as one of great symbolic significance. Because of Orwell's influential book *1984*, the year of 2084—a century later—became a year of celebration. As shown in Figure 11-1 and discussed in this chapter, in less than a century, the strides made in genetic engineering and the creation of organic/synthetic brain and body parts had altered the human significantly. Notable progress had also been made in identifying the genetic and mental underpinnings of pointless violent aggression. This advancement was a landmark achievement because it led to the decline of the conditions associated with the Deadly Trinity. The semi-humans/semi-Cepees were culling their killing tendencies as well as miscellaneous antisocial traits, and by mid-twenty-second century, the process to achieve perpetual life was complete.

In making these changes, humans began to believe their genetic engineering feats were changing the ancient natural selection paradigm. It was now one of un-natural selection. Or was it? As discussed in Chapter 12, the argument could be made that the intervention of the humans into their own DNA sequencing was nothing more than a series of mutations with associated natural selection processes then taking the reins.

These issues aside, the dystopian world of George Orwell's *1984* did not come about, although aspects of Orwell's world seemed frighteningly close to reality in the late twentieth century and the early to mid-twenty-first century. For a while, totalitarians continued to terrorize their citizens and citizens of other countries. Most of the world seemed to be at perpetual war. Hate crimes could be brought against someone who uttered his/her thoughts too plainly, similar to Orwell's thought crimes. Cults of personality and "Big Brothers" continued to exist.

Nonetheless, Orwellian dystopia was yielding, perhaps not to utopia, but to a decidedly more pleasant and less dangerous existence. A world was coming about in which Orwell's satirical and repugnant ministries of peace, plenty, love, and truth, ironically came to mean what their names implied. Except with one exception: The Cepees never found it necessary to construct such institutions in the first place.

How was the Orwellian world defeated? By the humans choosing to change themselves, as discussed in this chapter.

Benchmarks: The Nine Lives Effect

Thus far, this narrative has made passing references to the alterations the humans made to themselves during their journey to becoming the Cepee. In this chapter these changes are examined in more detail.

For illustrative purposes, nine major events are examined in the humans' self-change endeavors. These events represent a very small sampling of thousands of changes made to the human, but they provide cogent examples for this study.[4] They were collectively called the Nine Lives Effect in deference to the adage about a cat's nine lives and to scientists' sense of humor. Of course, the term was inaccurate because the Cepee could have an eternal life. The phrase was uttered in jest by genetic engineers and neurosurgeons who used it to somewhat self-mock their increasingly astounding accomplishments.

Table 11-1 will aid in this discussion. It lists nine events broadly categorized into these nine lives. While reviewing the cerebral, genetic, and bodily changes described in this chapter, it will also be helpful to recall the Autocatalytic Process and the Threshold Lowering Syndrome. The events associated with the Nine Lives Effect fed on one another in increasingly rapid succession and more frequent occurrence.

Table 11-1. The March to the Cepee: Benchmark Events.

Event	Event Description
1	Stems and Synthetics
2	Digital 3-D Fabrication and Bioprinting
3	Enhancing and Replacing Body Parts
4	Growing Body Parts
5	Beyond Plastic Surgery
6	Brain Implantations and Enhancements
7	Human Cloning? The NEAR Programs
8	Genetic Engineering
9	Epigenetic Engineering

What Does the Cepee Look Like?

Because of a terse description in Chapter 1, you may have been wondering what the Cepees look like, as only passing references have been made about the subject. Do they have an enlarged head and a bigger brain for their wonderful cognitive skills? How many thumbs do they have? The humans believed their thumbs gave them special status over other mammals. After all, no one ever witnessed a chimpanzee cocking the hammer of a gun with only one hand. Perhaps the humans thought, "The more thumbs, the better. Let's graft more of these useful digits to our wrists."

But no, the Cepee's cranium remains a similar size and each hand continues to house one thumb. The same approach applies for the number of arms, ears, legs, fingers, toes, buttocks, penises, and breasts. Let's see why.

Conjure in your mind an attractive being. Think about the beautiful people on the front pages of glamour and health magazines. Visualize the person you would like to be. The fanciful image you have in your mind might well be the Cepee.

As the human race geared up in the latter part of the twenty-first century to accept that they were becoming a greatly improved and better looking lot, a reporter in the news media predicted the humans' beauty contests would become obsolete because all candidates would tie for first place.

Notwithstanding this appealing countenance, the later generations of humans and the early Cepees did not change their external architecture. After all, the process of changing a human into a Cepee took 150 years, and the designers could not arbitrarily increase the size of the cranium, add an arm or leg, or create a hand with two thumbs. Such acts would have relegated the upgraded human to the back seat on society's bus. Not to mention the impossibility of making such rapid and radical alterations to what nature took millions of years to create.

Nonetheless, the Cepees are a delight to view. Of course, there are differences in the Cepees' looks. They are not replicas of one another. Some have larger noses than others, some have longer legs. Nonetheless, in their own way, the Cepees are fine looking creatures.

The remainder of this chapter provides a summary of several of the many changes humans made to themselves during a period of 150 years.

Benchmark 1: Stems and Synthetics

Many of the feats explained in benchmarks 2 through 9 made use of stem cells and the manufacturing of synthetic biological components for the body. The latter was called synthetic biology. Even though these two procedures were not dependent on each other or related in how they were used by the humans and later Cepees, they were often used in conjunction to support the many procedures described in the other benchmarks. They are placed in benchmark 1 to lay the groundwork for later explanations. (Had this writer placed them in separate benchmarks, the result would have been the Ten Lives Effect, which would have disappointed the scientists who coined the Nine Lives Effect term.)

Stem Cells. Stem cells could divide to become diverse specialized cell types. This capability was identified by the term *pluripotent*. They could regenerate to produce more stem cells. In adults, stem cells (and other cells) acted as a repair system for the body and could replenish tissues. In an embryo, stem cells could make themselves into specialized cells, such as those for the nervous and circulatory systems.

Research and resulting treatments focused on specialized cells that yielded treatments tailored to individuals, as well as the ability to grow new tissue and organs from a person's own body (called autologous cells). These cells could be taken from bone marrow, adipose tissue, and the blood, including but not restricted to umbilical cord blood.

Stem cell research led to treatments of a person's depleted immune responses to such diseases as HIV, cancer, macular degeneration, Parkinson's disease, glaucoma, and multiple sclerosis. This research also led to the growing of body parts, such as windpipes and organs. The success of this technology was a landmark achievement in the EGO and ILLS programs. Several examples of the use of stem cells are provided in this chapter.

Synthetic Biology. In 2003, researchers at the J. Craig Venter Institute created a life form that lived on "artificial genetic instructions."[5] Scientists built a fully synthesized genome from scratch and used it to transform one species to another. The headlines in the newspapers proclaimed life had been created in the laboratory.

The Venter team created man-made versions of various combinations of base pairs of DNA (A, C, G, T) from the genome of the *Mycoplasma mycoides* (bacterium). The resulting genome consisted of about 1.1 million base pairs. They assembled this genome inside a yeast cell and later inserted this synthetic genome into a closely related species, the *Mycoplasma capricolum*. In a few days, this bacterium was thriving as a colony of cells living as the synthetically driven genome. "After the newly made cell had divided, the cells of the bacterial colony that it formed contained only proteins characteristic of *M. mycoides*."[6]

The potential for synthetic biology was enormous. Genetic instructions could be embedded into foreign cells causing those cells to express protein from the synthetic source. Those proteins could then build "new functioning copies of the life-forms whose instruction manual is in the embedded sequences."[7]

The scientists at Craig Venter called this process, "software that creates its own hardware."[8] Yes, and its own organic Internet. As implausible at it might seem to a casual observer, engineers added "watermark sequences" to distinguish a derived version from the original version. These sequences contained Internet-based URLs, email addresses, and other identifiers for future use. The Cepee wonders if these initial efforts were forward-thinking enough to have included Internet port and socket numbers in the watermark. He consults the Human Archives and discovers the answer is yes. After all, these identifiers were also essential for an organic website.

Eventually, these genetic software systems were creating microbes that made materials for the creation of other organisms. They were creating microbes (with resulting viruses) that could, if necessary, disable portions of the brain. This action was akin to debugging faulty software code or bypassing a failed Internet node.

Benchmark 2: Digital 3-D Fabrication and Bioprinting

Imagine that a computer, such as the one you likely have on your desktop, is running software that directs a printer's output. The output is routine. The ink jet images from the printer are formed on the paper. Next, imagine a computer using decidedly different software directing the output of a markedly different printer. This printer is not using ink to produce an image. It is using living cells. The Cepee reads about the history of this technology from the Human Archives. He learns:

Laser printing nozzles forced out solutions composed of different cells' structures, such as a heart valve or patches of a cardiac muscle. This extrusion process created 3-D building blocks of cells. This initialization procedure was then turned over to the cells to do most of the work. As one engineer said, "The cells do all the finishing touches themselves."[9]

These systems became commonplace in the early part of the twenty-first century. One set of frequently used applications was a printer/computer/software setup that could construct tissue structures. By repetitively "printing" layer after layer, this arrangement could create any 3-D shape programmed into the software, such as blood vessels, cartilage for joints, or patches of muscle and skin.[10] The systems were capable of printing three dimensional human tissue that was living and fulfilling its genetic duties.

As an added bonus, a design created at one place could easily be sent via the Internet to anyplace in the world that needed a component and had the parts and printer. "Need a kidney in Toledo? Here comes the download." "Need a windpipe in Chicago? I've just hit the send key."

Shipping industries went bankrupt. Trucking companies hit the skids. After all, a 3-D printer, even if it cost millions of dollars to build, easily paid for itself in relation to those 18-wheelers pounding the highways and sucking up petrol day after day.

Printing 3-D Body Parts. Inkjet technology was used because the printers printed images with small ink droplets with multicolor inks with a high resolution. "These characteristics [were] considered advantageous for arrangement of cells and biological materials," permitting the arrangement of various cells, the fabrication of huge structures, and the micropatterning of biomaterials.[11]

The process followed these steps:[12]

— One printer nozzle deposited drops of cells while a second nozzle deposited a hydrogel that acted as a mold to shape the tissue.
— The printer built up the cells and mold layer by layer, creating a 3-D structure.
— After printing, the cells naturally knit themselves together to strengthen the tissue structure. *They knew what to do. It was as if cells possessed an invisible and undetectable intelligence of their own; that their simple structure contained a cerebral astuteness of their making and under their control.*
— The support hydrogel mold was removed, leaving a structure made solely of living tissue.
— The tissue was bathed in nutrients and kept alive in a bioreactor. After about three weeks, the tissue gained its full strength as the cells built bonds among themselves.

Initially, bioprinting was restricted to relatively simple cell structures a few hundred microns thick (not the fanciful kidney destined for Toledo). Larger printed tissues, such as cartilage, were not strong enough to stand on their own, nor were these prototypes as strong as their natural counterparts. But in a few decades, bioprinters were producing thigh bones that would have put Arnold Schwarzenegger's leg to shame.

The Autocatalytic Process in Action. In 2013 alone, and as a very small sampling, scientists and their manufacturing partners succeeded in successfully printing custom-made track shoe spikes based on each runner's profile, as well as football cleats, different types of wrenches, parts of ears, nose cartilage, skull replacement parts, etc.

In one of the most startling 3-D print jobs, scientists in Scotland printed a collection of human stem cells made up of "ink jet" droplets of organic components, including an embryonic kidney.[13] The printer nozzle was only .002 inches wide and printed the organic ink in droplets less than one billionth of an ounce.

The Scots reported that, "…between 70 and 95 percent of the cells survived past 72 hours, and three days after, the cells tested positive for pluripotency, and seemed to be growing."[14]

In harmony with the Autocatalytic Process Rule of Life, 3-D innovations happened more rapidly and inventions increased exponentially. Hardly a science, industry, or technology was bypassed by 3-D printing.

In a touch of humility, humans realized their digitizing the creation of organs and other body parts had been done long before their successful efforts:[15]

> The digitization of material is not a new idea. It is four billion years old, going back to the evolutionary age of the ribosome, the protein that makes proteins. Humans are full of molecular machinery, from the motors that move our muscles to the sensors in our eyes. The ribosome builds all that machinery out of a microscopic version of LEGO pieces [and] amino acids, of which there are 22 different kinds.

The Cepee pauses and reflects: *The humans came a long way from their molding Plexiglas windows.*

Benchmark 3: Enhancing and Replacing Body Parts

With a few minor exceptions, the enhancements and replacements of body parts did not create controversy among the humans. Religious or ethical taboos were rarely a deciding factor in this matter because these alterations did not include the brain, which in the view of many religious circles, was the seat of the soul.

The thousands of procedures associated with the humans' body parts enhancements and replacement programs are beyond the scope of this narrative. Several examples are selected to illustrate the progress the humans made to amend and rectify their body parts.

Bones and Appendages. New arms, legs, fingers, and toes were considered to be positive enhancements to a damaged human body. Some of these body parts took on the characteristics of the originals.

For example, through a process called osteointegration, a titanium rod could be inserted into the femur of the leg in which the lower part was missing because of an illness or accident. The rod eventually fused with the bone matter. A false leg was then screwed into the rod, providing a stable, non-painful appendage.

The process was so effective some patients experienced osteoperception: The upper leg took on the ability to sense the false (lower) leg's environment, such as walking on grass or pebbles, and riding a horse or bicycle. The surgeons thought the bone was capable of relaying messages to a part of the brain that had atrophied. This part of the brain "woke up" and began functioning once more.[16] Time and again, the surgeons were surprised and amazed to discover how effectively the brain could adapt to changes to body parts.

Another problem and challenge pertained to the repair or replacement of deteriorating bones. Like most parts of the body, human bones decayed and lost their strength. Osteoporosis was one of the most serious problems facing humans as they reached old age.[17] Because the problem was gene related, it could be attacked with gene therapy. As events unfolded and progress led to more progress, osteoporosis became history as the humans indemnified their once fragile bodies against the perils of aging. By mid-twenty-first century, bone problems had been relegated to the humans' skeleton closet.

Restoration of Sight. In 2013, regulators approved a technology called the artificial retina. It helped to partially restore a human's sight.[18] A sheet of electrodes was implanted into the damaged region of the retina. Along with a tiny camera, attached to glasses, a microprocessor allowed visual signals to bypass that part of the retina. The signals were sent directly to the brain.

The people who used the artificial retina were overjoyed. Some could now walk on city streets. They were able to distinguish dark and light shapes, locate bus stops, and spot their homes and apartments from a taxi. A Rod Stewart fan was elated to discover she could distinguish the performer's "white-blond" hair under the stage lights. Unfortunately, she had less luck watching a James

Taylor show, saying his "low key clothing created no contrast for the artificial retina to register. Alas, Ms. Campbell said, 'He wasn't so sparkly.'"[19] While just a beginning, the artificial retina led to other projects that treated other problems, such as spinal paralysis and bladder disorders.[20]

Replacement of Limbs. By the mid-twenty-first century, many parts of the humans' legs, feet, arms, and hands could be repaired or replaced. These efforts were landmarks in the first part of the century. As one example, doctors attached a hand from a cadaver to a man, whose own hand had been blown off in a fireworks accident 13 years earlier.[21] The surgery was controversial because several doctors and medical ethicists questioned if sufficient research had been conducted on hand transplanting procedures. But the hand did its job just fine. The handler of this new hand was elated, which led to more successful efforts of increasing sophistication.

The humans' organic peripherals, such as a hand, wrist, arm, and elbow, were complex. Replacing them with a prosthetic peripheral was a huge undertaking. First, while both kinds of appendages used electrical signals to direct, say, picking up a pencil, these signals differed. For the human it occurred with the "depolarization of cell membranes and the release of signaling chemicals in the gaps between nerve cells."[22] Computer semiconductors employed the movement of electrons across conductors. The fanciful images of electrical lightning bolts activating the neck and head of a Frankenstein were fine for late night TV, but they were not relevant to the real world.

The difficulty came from a human's extraordinary proprioception (the sense of bodily positions, pressures, and movements) and the difficulty of emulating these sensory and motor signals. If not done properly, the effort needed to, for example, tie a shoelace would mentally and physically exhaust a human. The goal was to create an interface between the central nervous system (the human's mainframe) and a prosthesis (an artificial peripheral). Such an interface would sense the electrical signals in the brain, have them analyzed by software, and signal the desired movement to the prosthetic limb. The neuroengineers called this system a "neuromechanical" interface.[23]

The complexity of the brain giving directions to an appendage and the complexity of the appendage's movements could have discouraged the humans. But they were aided by that extraordinary organ, the brain:[24]

> In performing [for example] hand transplants, surgeons cannot possibly connect every last nerve fiber correctly from host to a transplanted hand. Such precision turns out to be unnecessary, however. The brain essentially redraws its own internal map of which motor neurons to do what, allowing it to eventually gain control of the new hand. Similarly, driving a robotic hand that is linked to the central nervous system will probably require extensive retraining of the brain.

By mid-twenty-first century, worn-out or severely damaged appendages were replaced in a rather routine way with a "living bridge between the human nervous system and an artificial limb."[25] Laboratory-grown nerves were directed to grow at the edge of electrically conductive microfilaments that were connected to the mechanical limb. At the other end, neurons of these lab nerves were "gently pulled apart," which allowed the human's host nerves and axons to bridge across this interface. Thus, signals could flow back and forth between the brain, the spinal cord (where the human's axons were connected), and to the artificial limb. The software engineers on these projects were well paid.

Organ Replacements. Humans had been replacing their organs for many years. As they refined their methods, it became a common occurrence for an organ or organs from one person to be donated to another. For example, a six-month-old baby had eight organs transplanted into her body because she was born with smooth muscle disorder, a malady preventing the normal functioning of her stomach, intestines, and kidneys.[26] Left untreated, her condition was fatal.

This twelve-hour operation was the first eight-organ transplant, earning the feat an entry in the a book of records for most organs transplanted with one continuous surgical procedure: (1) liver, (2) stomach, (3) pancreas, (4) small intestine, (5) large intestine, (6) spleen, and (7, 8) two kidneys. However, some critics, those vying for top place in the pecking order for Most Organs Transplanted in the Human Body, claimed the operation was only a seven-organ affair because other facilities recorded the stomach and the small intestine as one organ.

Benchmark 4: Growing Body Parts

Liver disease allowed few of its suffers to escape. Those with cirrhosis experienced increasing difficulty with their liver fulfilling its role of filtering toxins. For many years, the only solution to a near certain early death was a liver replacement, a transplant. However, in the early twenty-first century in America, there were only 6,000 organs available for some 100,000 patients in any given year.

To address this shortage, a development team at the University of Pittsburgh discovered how to turn a lymph node into an incubator that could grow an entirely new liver.[27] Lymph nodes (some 500 of them in the human body) acted as filters for fighting off viruses, bacteria, and other sources of sickness.

The team implanted liver cells of mice *away* from its diseased organ. The cells that were implanted into a kidney or spleen died. However, when they were placed into the belly, they survived. To the surprise of the team, the cells then migrated to lymph nodes, where they flourished.

In yet another example of the astonishing astuteness of the human body, it was shown that the injected liver cells in the lymph node (the hepatocyte cells) picked up signals released in the bloodstream from the dying liver. These signals were proteins conveying "essentially SOS signals to grow."[28]

In a nutshell, the diseased liver was communicating with the new liver. The Cepee reflects: *What a legacy the humans passed to us. Not just their minds, but their bodies as well.* Later, the Cepee learns that livers were grown in pigs. Before long, they were grown in humans. Cirrhosis died out, leaving thousands of otherwise dead humans alive.

Outgrowths of Prototype Growths. From the initial landmark experiments in laboratories, the humans learned to grow artificial organs and other body parts. One of the first body parts was a windpipe.[29] A patient in Sweden had his cancerous windpipe removed and replaced by an artificial trachea grown from his own stem cells. The trachea was created in only two days:[30]

— Bone marrow was removed from the patient, filtering out certain cells.
— The filtered cells (mononucleocytes) morphed into cells that formed the ring of the trachea.
— A matrix (essentially, a mold) was made that replaced the cancerous portion of the windpipe.
— This matrix and the cells were placed in a solution of nutrients in a bioreactor.
— The matrix was repeatedly rotated and dipped into the "cell broth," coating it and exposing it to living cells of oxygen.
— Within 48 hours, the windpipe was ready for implantation.

These forms of regenerative medicine led to growing bladders, muscles, digits, and eventually, human limbs. The first successful limb growth came from the pioneering work done on the lowly salamander.[31] For this work, researchers learned to control a human's wound healing to mimic the salamander's regeneration process.

Benchmark 5: Beyond Plastic Surgery

Chapter 7 introduced the humans' use of cosmetic plastic surgery. Benchmark 5 continues this discussion, with the emphasis on therapeutic surgery. During the time a person was recovering from loss of skin because of a wound or burn, human cadaver skin was sometimes used as a covering to the afflicted area. This solution was temporary because a patient usually rejected cadaver skin within twenty days of the surgery. The long-term solution was engineered skin (ES). The basic idea involved making the skin in petri dishes. The dish contained a liquid nutrient that stimulated the growth of the ES by impersonating the skin's natural environment.[32]

Initially, the process was bootstrapped by using the foreskin of a human, usually that of an infant after a circumcision. On occasion, the foreskin of an adult was obtained, usually a male who had changed religions or decided he wanted a different sexual countenance. Unless asked, the recipients of these skin grafts were not indoctrinated as to the origins of the synthetic skin that was to be part of their body.

In the earlier procedures, the petri dish technique had the lab technician spread dermal cells over a matrix of collagen, taken from cows, which formed the lower layer of the skin. What self-respecting human would want its epidermis to be constructed with cow gelatin? The answer: a human who had no epidermis.

The petri dish approach was slow and cumbersome. Before long, engineers had developed a method to grow skin in chambers called bioreactors. These machines allowed various nutrients to flow across the foreskin cells, causing them to multiply and grow into functioning synthetic skin. The bioreactor was controlled by computer-based sensors, which insured the chamber was kept at the proper temperature and humidity.

The bioreactor concept was expanded to support the building and growth of cartilage. This operation was a more complex procedure than skin replacement technology because the original human's cartilage was three-dimensional. Nonetheless, the bioreactor also allowed the creation of cartilage scaffolds, which permitted the tailoring of specific 3-D cartilage sizes and shapes. This advance was a key component in operations that yielded joint replacements in athletes, accident victims, and older people.

It was only a matter of time before synthetic skin became an off-the-shelf commodity. It was produced in mass quantities and made available to technicians who, mostly using robots, repaired or replaced a human's outer covering.

Like the synthetic skin industry, the cartilage replacement market also became commonplace. Both procedures, considered to be extraordinary technologies at the beginning of the twenty-first century, became as common in the mid-twenty-first century as a face lift had been in the mid-twentieth century.

Face Transplants. In some instances, plastic surgery was insufficient to restore a badly disfigured part of the body, for example, the face. But during the early part of the twenty-first century, techniques were developed to transplant faces from one human to another.

The first successful face transplant took place in France when surgeons removed facial tissue from a brain dead donor and grafted it onto the face of a woman who had been mauled in a dog attack.[33] The nose, lips, and chin of the "skin fragment" were sewn onto the patient's face. All necessary vascular connections were made in only four hours.

Even though the patient was satisfied with the outcome, she took drugs for the rest of her life to combat the possibility of graft rejection. The skin was a human's first defense against germs. Thus, epidermis was designed to reject foreign intruders. To reduce the danger of rejection, the patient was injected with stem cells taken from the donor in order to "instruct" the patient's "immune system to tolerate the graft." During the twenty-first century, face transplants, enhanced with lab-grown epidermis, became commonplace.

Benchmark 6: Brain Implantations and Enhancements

The most difficult part of the human body to modify or replace was the central nervous system, the human's mainframe. This aspect of the Cepee development proceeded more slowly than other operations, such as parts replacement and plastic surgery. Nonetheless, at the beginning of the twenty-first century, a landmark brain operation paved the way for many subsequent brain modifications.

This operation represented the installation of the first brain prosthesis.[34] Unlike devices such as ear (cochlear) implants, which stimulated brain activity,[35] a silicon chip implant performed the same functions as the damaged part of the brain it replaced. The hippocampus was selected for the prosthesis because it was an ordered, structured, and well-known part of the brain. Its function was to encode and store short-term experiences for their subsequent storage (elsewhere in the brain) as long-term memories.

This first successful effort to implant computers in the brain that performed the same functions of a part of the brain was an important event. The inventors of the prosthesis had a formidable task before them: First, they had to model (mathematically) all the operations of the hippocampus. Next, they had to translate this model (program it) into a silicon chip. Then, they had to interface the chip with the brain.

The task to model the actual operations of the hippocampus was impossible to accomplish, because no one understood how the hippocampus encoded the information it received. However, the team was able to emulate its behavior by stimulating slices of a rat's hippocampus millions of times until it was known which electrical input produced which electrical output. This approach allowed the team to construct a mathematical model of the hippocampus.

The model was then programmed into a chip. It communicated with the brain through two arrays of electrodes, placed on each side of the damaged part of the hippocampus. The chip acted as a relay unit: It received and recorded signals coming in from the brain and sent signals back out into the brain.

From this pioneering work, it was a short time before interfaces were built between computer chips, the hippocampus, and other parts of the brain. The interfaces were constructed to create artificial synapses, the junctions between nerve cells. By 2003, a working synaptic chip had been produced and computer/brain interfaces became common by the middle of the twenty-first century.

Suppressing and Activating Brain Parts. Armed with this knowledge, brain surgeons, working in conjunction with genetic engineers, developed procedures to enhance the functioning of the dorsolateral prefrontal cortex, a brain part associated with reasoning. Other procedures altered the operations of the orbital frontal cortex (emotions), and anterior cingulate (conflicts). An active dorsolateral prefrontal cortex and/or a quiescent orbital frontal cortex would stimulate the ventral striatum, a brain part related to reward and pleasure.[36] With such operations, the human brain was gradually altered to diminish or eliminate synapse firings associated with anti-social and other unreasonable behavior.

Of course, what constituted unacceptable behavior was the subject of intense debate. The humans were finally able to agree that this type of cerebral tweaking would at least be used to allow a person to look at another point of view on a contentious issue, an alteration that led to significantly reduced conflicts between formerly fractious tribes.

Neuroplasticity. For most of the life of the human race, it was accepted that the brain, after its growth in childhood and puberty, was fixed in its functions and even in its composition. In hindsight, this idea was preposterous. Otherwise, how could a human learn something new? Nonetheless, the view was that a brain kept its physical structure while somehow learning new tasks.

In the early twenty-first century, it was determined that changes to a person's environment (such as stress, exercise, and rote learning) resulted in physical changes in the brain. These changes included the "connections between existing neurons … in the hippocampus and other parts of the brain, including the cerebellum."[37] In Chapter 3, an example was provided of musicians' brains (the cerebrum) being altered naturally because of the musicians playing a violin regularly.

Surgeons and other brain specialists developed methods to aid the brain in "rearranging" its functions. One example was a machine that aided a patient to regain her damaged balance system by sending signals from her tongue to her brain. Eventually, her brain did not need these signals, and the woman regained her balancing functions. The boast of "her balancing act days are over" rang true.

The humans later discovered that prolonged meditation could alter the cortical thickness or density of gray matter. Exercise was shown—especially vigorous exercise—to improve cognitive responses to stress.[38] These researchers concluded the brain had rewired itself to accommodate these challenges.

Mind over Matter. Yet with all these brain alterations, the Cepees have not solved the mystery of the mind. They know many facts about the brain, but they do not know how the mind functions or how the brain might be the enabler of the mind. Earlier, using brain scans and brain taps, human neuroscientists were able to trace and correlate a multitude of mental thoughts to their associated physical actions. Eventually, the brain's regions were as well known as a map of a city, and the "behavior" of its transmitters/receptors was often altered to control a mental state and physical action.

Even with this knowledge, the Cepees cannot account for the mind's role in determining a wide range of mental traits, such as ethics and altruism. They know these attributes are usually species-enhancing, but they have never learned the mind's enabling mechanisms for their existence.

As related earlier, many of the genetic and cerebral underpinnings of (first) human and (later) Cepee behavior were revealed and manipulated. Consequently, the Cepees have tinkered extensively with their central nervous system. They have enhanced memory with medicine and gene therapy, created biosynthetic computer chips to aid in problem solving. They have discovered methods for relieving or curing many mental illnesses.

But in the end, the Cepees are wise enough to leave well enough alone. Concluding the mind has a mind of its own, they undertake changes to the central nervous system based on their belief that even their advanced neuroscientists cannot find a brain correlate for the ephemeral mind.[39] Nor do they attempt to find a brain correlate for a soul, much to the satisfaction of the Cepees who are believers.

Benchmark 7: Human Cloning? The NEAR Programs Non-Human Cloning

Cloning occurred before humans themselves were almost cloned. First there was Dolly the sheep, cloned by Scottish scientists in 1997. In short order, mice, pigs, goats, and cattle were cloned, all within five years of Dolly's cloning. In 2003, researchers at the University of Idaho added mules to the collage of cloned critters by using a cell from a mule fetus and an egg from a horse. This specific event drew considerable attention because hybrids from these animals were sterile and not able to reproduce.

Earlier, in 2001, scientists at Texas A&M University successfully cloned a cat, and named it cc, for carbon copy. As expected, the announcement of cc to the world drew cries of protest from special interest groups. Animal rights activists were especially upset that a pet owner might consider cloning a dead pet, when thousands of potential pets sat unloved in animal shelters.

Inevitably, the successful cloning of mice, pigs, goats, cows, cats, mules, etc. led to pressure from other special interest groups to expand into human cloning. After all, once an instrument (cloning) had been invented, the Law of the Instrument ordained the human race to use it.

Nonetheless, the artificial creation of a copy of a living human created considerable controversy. As recounted in Chapter 10, the opponents to human self-change said humans were not supposed to change themselves. They believed human change was not in the humans' job description, but ordained by God.

Despite these ethical and moral issues, several laboratories initiated cloning operations in the late 1980s. In 1988, a research team from South Korea announced it had cloned a human embryo, even though the embryo had only four cells. In 2001, an American team claimed a cloning procedure yielded six cells before dying. Detractors argued these experiments were not valid because—unlike real embryos—they did not double their cell quantity every 24 hours.

After these initial efforts, many countries banned human cloning to produce children. The complications associated with this procedure were so intractable that scientists, ethicists, and others declared that the cloning to produce children was not allowed.

The problems of identity, individuality, family relations, and the overall effects on society outweighed many people's desires to allow infertile couples to have genetically related children, or to permit couples at medical risk to have a cloned child. Some humans lobbied for cloning "above average people" in order to improve the gene pool, but these views did not prevail in mainstream societies.

A few nations were not governed by people who cared about or adhered to international tribunals. Renegade scientists and doctors bribed these governments to provide a safe harbor for their human cloning operations. However, mainstream governments and their societies forbade human cloning, so the practice did not find sufficient supporters for it to become a factor in humans' lives.

NEAR

We now take a closer look at the humans' approach to this issue, which was carried over to the Cepees. The humans modified DNA in existing adults, which affected the behavior and traits of their offspring. These procedures were called NEAR, an acronym for NEarly A Replica.

This handle was not accepted by all humans. Scientists said the acronym should have been FAR: Far from A Replica. After all, with each generation, the offspring possessed fewer and fewer traits of their ancestors. In the end, the NEAR acronym won the naming battle because it had a more positive ring to it.

The majority of governments around the world came aboard to support the NEAR programs. Some countries were victims of nuclear attacks, others were casualties of biological and chemical warfare; still others suffered rifle and bomb attacks on their citizens. But in the final analysis, most folks just wanted to improve their lot in life and that of their children.

Humans began to understand how to engineer the genome to "fix and repair" DNA problems. Thus motivated, they acted to make NEAR a success. Laws were passed defining how the programs were to proceed. A new breed of moralists and ethicists created, debated, and smoothed out a new paradigm. These apologists sprang from the largesse of government grants and a reinterpretation of the holy books.

There were hold outs to NEAR. Many of the disenfranchised noble savages, eking out their meager existences in earth's backwaters, were ignored. Eventually, as time went on, they fell off the scope of life. Some countries, such as China, viewed NEAR as an extension to their existing genetic engineering programs and tacked on additional genome altering procedures as part of their national health plans.

Some mothers and fathers in the affluent parts of the world refused to submit to the new laws and resorted to home birthing. But these people were in the minority, and most of them had changes already made to their DNA and brain over the past decades, courtesy of EGO, ILLS, SANE, and the Threshold Lowering Syndrome. Eventually, as 2150 rolled around, the NEAR recalcitrants in the population were little more than white noise in the human self-change spectrum.

This quote explains, in a general way, the bioengineering aspects of NEAR. The text is part of a report prepared by the U.S. government.[40] The type within brackets represents the modifications made to the natural birthing process with NEAR.

> In sexual reproduction each child has two complementary biological progenitors. Each child thus stems from and unites exactly two lineages, lines that trace backward in similar branching fashion for ages. Moreover, the precise genetic endowment of each child is determined by a combination of nature and chance, not by human design. [NEAR changed this relationship.] Each human child naturally acquires and shares the common human species genotype [As influenced by the NEAR-altered genotype.], each child is genetically (equally) kin to each (both) parent(s), yet each child is also genetically unique. [As aided by NEAR.] Cloning-to-produce-children departs from this pattern. A cloned child has unilineal, not bilineal, descent; he or she is genetically kin to only one progenitor.

As stated, NEAR did not clone humans. Rather, it altered the genome of existing humans, which had the effect of altering the genome of these humans' offspring. Furthermore, it allowed additional modifications to the offsprings' DNA, leading to an increasingly different human.

"If it is understood, it can be controlled."[41] This quotation represented the fundamental assumption humans made about their bodies and minds. Consequently, after altering their philosophy about self-change, after hundreds of thousands of experiments, after searches for relevant gene markers and marker combinations, the humans won the race to make NEAR a reality. They finally understood the genetic underpinnings of aggression and aging, which in the end, allowed them to control these human traits.

Following their conquering the "nature" side of aggression, attacking the "nurture" side was the next task. Without question, environments and milieus, cultures and societies were important variables in the aggression equation. As the humans made inroads into their knowledge of the genome, they discovered human behavior was explained both by nature and nurture—thus subject to manipulation with gene engineering (Benchmark 8) and epigenetic engineering (Benchmark 9).

Benchmark 8: Genetic Engineering

Benchmark 8 deals with more sophisticated and refined procedures for altering the human genome. As stated in Chapter 1, humans and later Cepees were careful about engineering the genome because of its complexity. "Genes usually perform more than one function; conversely, functions are usually encoded by more than one gene. Because of this property, known as pleiotrophy, tinkering with one gene can have unintended consequences."[42]

The organization for this discussion is as follows. (This arrangement is made to ease the analysis. Some subjects are necessarily overlapping.) (a) Curative Gene Therapy, (b) Hormone Enhancement, (c) Computers, Software, and Robotics, (d) Boolean Biology, (e) Programmable Chromosomes, (f) Mediating and Stimulating Friendly Behavior, (g) Unnatural DNA, (h) Anti-Aging, and (i) Reverse Engineering of Anti-Aging Procedures.

(a) Curative Gene Therapy. After DNA was discovered and the human genome mapped, thousands of scientists devoted themselves to finding the genetic origins of disease. The goal was to find the gene (or genes) contributing to a disease and then develop a cure.

A landmark project provides an example of gene therapy: the cause (and cure) for inherited breast cancer.[43]

In the latter part of the twentieth century, the humans discovered mutated genes could cause cancer. Several scientists noticed how breast cancer ran in families, leading to the conclusion that a class of diseases was inherited. One of these pioneers devised the idea of a gene marker. She examined the DNA code and looked for markers *not* shared by all the diseased members of the family. These people were no longer part of her study, and all others were possible suspects. She then looked across families and eliminated markers not shared between families. Therefore, she honed in on a marker shared by all diseased individuals of the families under study. If a marker was always inherited by all, the marker had to be in the same region of DNA as the diseased gene.

After 17 years, Dr. Mary Claire King discovered the DNA damage that caused female breast cancer. It was located on chromosome 17. The search continued until the gene was found. The scientists eventually found a way to fix it, resulting in finding a cure for genetically based breast cancer.

As notable as this feat was, the fact remained that most cancers were not inherited. The human picked up damage to its DNA in everyday life, such as the inhalation of smoke, the consumption of toxic fish, and the drinking of polluted water.

Nonetheless, as the twenty-first century rolled into the twenty-second century, these advances enabled doctors to identify all cancers and their genetic variations. Using the adage, "If you understand something, you can control it," they learned how DNA was damaged. Therefore, they learned to cure it. By the middle of the twenty-second century, genetically based illnesses and diseases were history.

(b) Hormone Enhancement. Hormone enhancement entailed procedures to cure illness and to save lives. Hormone manipulation was also employed to feed the human's ego and caused many confrontations between humans who had differing views on the use of hormones.

One court case involved a boy who was considered to be too short by his mother but just the right height by his father. The mother had taken the case to court to force the child to take growth hormones and the father to pay for them. The ruling was in favor of hormone therapy even though the child's parents were quite short, and he had inherited his small stature from them.

On a more serious level, during the early part of the twenty-first century, scientists began to experiment with hormones and their ability to activate or deactivate specific genes.[44] They learned how to bind a hormone to a receptor in the cell's cytoplasm—specific sites in the deoxyribonucleic acid (DNA), the repository for individual genes. They learned how to use hormones to activate or deactivate some genes. The effect was to alter the cell's activity, an extraordinary achievement.

(c) Computers, Software, and Robotics. Synthetic robots became a key component in the latter-day human's physical makeup. Ultimately, the difference between a corporal constituent of the human/Cepee (such as a finger) and its artificial equivalent was considered irrelevant because synthetic and organic components eventually fused with each other.

These parts of the soon-to-be Cepee became melds and mixtures of chemicals and computers. They took on the characteristics of biological binary circuits, strewing their 0s and 1s, their Boolean values, through and around cells as if the being were an ambulatory Internet. Before long, the devolving human could not tell the difference between his or her artificial parts and the real ones.

Scientists in North Carolina built a brain implant that let monkeys control a robotic arm with their thoughts, marking the first time mental intentions had been harnessed to move a mechanical object.[45] The technology later allowed people with paralyzing spinal cord injuries to operate machines or tools with their thoughts as naturally as earlier generations did with their hands.

The experiment involved teaching a monkey to play a video game with a joy stick. The animal received a drink of apple juice each time it executed a successful transaction in the game. While the game was being played, receptors placed in its brain captured the brain's electrical signals and recorded them in computer memory.

Next, unknown to the monkey, the joy stick was disconnected, but its brain interface was connected to the video game. The monkey was able to play the game successfully with only its thoughts. Eventually, the monkey discovered it did not need to manipulate the joy stick and stopped using it, thus gaining gulps of juice by just thinking about the game.

Success led to more success. Before long, scores of programs sprang forth that integrated nanosize biosynthetic robots with the human mind to assist with mental processing activities such as memory retention. By the end of the twenty-first century, robotics was an integral part of the human/Cepee's mental activities.

However, the Cepees draw a line in the cerebral sand about the extent that biosynthetic hardware and software can influence their brains. After evaluating thousands of human experiments that simulated or emulated brain functions, the Cepees came to realize some of these artificial mechanisms were *too* human-like. Their concern was well founded, because robotics specialists had begun to create life-like robots.

These androids displayed human-like motions, such as moving ears, downcast eyes, beguiling smiles, and wrinkles in the forehead— all in response to a human's interaction with them. They were mesmeric creatures for sure, because they seemed human. But they were nothing more than sands of silicon, computer logic gates, and lines of software code, camouflaged under a veneer of plastic skin, synthetic hair, and glass eyes. Their "social interactions," their "relating to people" were clever executions of computer programs.[46]

Humans created many kinds of robots. For example, they manufactured a robotic dog, barking and otherwise behaving as if it were a dog (less the body emissions). Should this have been a concern? And to whom? To the child who thought the robotic toy poodle was a real toy poodle? To the old-age home resident, thankful for rare, unsolicited affections, even if they came from a computer in the guise of Snoopy? How did one counter the well-intentioned naïveté of the robotics experts? After all, they believed they were creating something capable of showing emotions and feelings, all to the benefit of humankind.

After viewing the humans' feel good robots, the Cepees declared, "When needed, we will use real dogs, not appliances, to cheer us up." This idea is the practice for their use of robots in general. Thus, the Cepees' mental robotics programs are a complement to their mental functions, but not a replacement.

(d) Boolean Biology. Because genes and computers were constructed of different components, integrating computer technology into the genome was a monumental task for latter-time humans as well as for the early Cepees. This discussion focuses on the human endeavors.

The genes of the *Homo sapiens* were constructed of chemical components—pieces of the humans' biologic mucilage. They were rendered into a four-letter alphabet representing the basic building blocks of DNA (adenine, thymine, cytosine, and guanine, noted earlier as A, T, C, and G). The many combinations and sequences of successive four letter codes on the DNA controlled who the humans were and what they were able to do. Their many code combinations were translated into the flesh and blood of the human.[47]

In contrast, computers were constructed of iron ore, silicon, antimony, arsenic, gallium, indium, mirrors, and glass; foreign elements to the human body. Computers also executed software, all for the sake of processing 0s and 1s. However, from this simple model of binary math, a myriad of Boolean constructs of AND, OR, and NOT gates could be created to produce machines of astounding power and intelligence. *Any* computer computation could be performed with these Boolean operators. The challenge was transferring this technology into the human.

All true. But what if the condiments of biologic and computer matter could be mixed? Not the mechanistic brain prosthesis described earlier, but an integrated assemblage of the chemicals that made up these seemingly disparate systems. What if the organic matter in the human's genome could take on the characteristics of

Boolean logic? What if software could become as natural to the human as soft tissue?

The implications of such an achievement would be far-reaching. This achievement would provide a vital key to genetic tailoring. And of course, this problem was just the sort of challenge the humans liked to undertake: seemingly impossible, but if accomplished, leading to fame and fortune.

Efforts began in the early part of the twenty-first century to create libraries of programmable DNA parts, a discipline introduced in Benchmark 1 and called synthetic biology.[48] The goal was to create general components that could be used in more than one DNA application. These plug-and-play parts would be like a generic capacitor used in electrical hardware circuits, or a generic perpetual calendar routine used in accounting software packages. Pundits dubbed this technology, "BioBricks."[49]

The first efforts focused on assembling Boolean logic gates in certain microbes, those that could detect dangerous chemicals, such as TNT or carcinogens. To cite one example, a microbe was designed that not only located the substance but glowed as it announced its discovery, thus signaling it had found a land mine or a dangerous part of a land fill. The systems could operate inside living cells, deriving their energy from their hosts. Some of them could move and reproduce.

In addition to the TNT and carcinogen "sniffers," other early synthetic biology devices were made of artificial amino acids and removed heavy metals from wastewater. Later systems removed plaque from arterial walls. Some performed binary logic, an application of great interest to the scientists because of its relationship to computer architectures. This part of the technology is examined in more detail.

At the simplest level, a protein (coded by another gene) was input into a distinct section of DNA to produce (say) a NOT operation. An inverter gene would produce a protein *output* if it had no input and, conversely, produce *no output* if it received input—just like a computer.

It was that simple, as well as astounding. The humans were on the road to creating computers made from human material. Material not from the earth, such as silicon, but material from the human, such as protein.

It was also complex. It took many years to refine the process that created biologic binary circuits. These circuits consisted of Boolean gates, the vital foundation of a computer's architecture. The task was daunting. For example, the engineers had to cope with the fact their living machines often mutated as they reproduced. Nonetheless, by mid-twenty-first century, biological engineers had produced a wide variety of plug-and-play components, all stored and ready for use in Biological Computer Mucilage (BCM) libraries. As a result, like conventional computers, hundreds of thousands of protein-based Boolean gates were assembled in many combinations to produce BCM libraries of astounding power and intelligence.

In the end, biologic and computer matter became partners to aid the humans in their unintended race to become the Cepee. Eventually, the machines' output of protein was used to grow organs. Later, the engineers discovered how to control the genes involved in the organ creation, how to determine their behavior and personality.

The Cepee has been studying the humans' newspapers published in the early twenty-first century. He pauses: *If I imagine myself living in my ancestors' early twenty-first century, I am certain I could not have envisioned machines embedded into my body and brain. Certainly, they had some machines internal to their bodies working on their behalf, such as pacemakers, pain medicine injectors, and ear implants. I've learned they had also succeeded in placing primitive computers in the hypothalamus.*

But organic computers, constructed from humans' parts! Computers that helped keep their non-computer parts functioning; computers that monitored their bodies and took remedial actions when something was amiss.

My forbearers not only prolonged their lives with their inventions, they invented marvelous preventative mechanisms to make their ongoing lives less painful and more pleasant.

Yet, could they possibly have imagined what their creativity would lead to? Of course not. My ancestors of the eighteenth-century could only have had fanciful imaginations of their going to the moon. After all, space ships were on the drawing boards of only rare visionaries.

Yet, for my ancestors, I am sure some of them held to their hearts their visions leading to us Cepees. One of their poets, William Blake, said it well, "What is now proved, was once only imagin'd." The Cepee returns to the archives to learn about other aspects of humans' computers and human computers.

(e) Programmable Chromosomes. The logical next step to the Boolean Biology technology was the development of programmable chromosomes.[50] The efforts, a form of synthetic biology, were directed to the creation of an extra chromosome, one that could be programmed with Boolean and therefore, computer logic. In this manner, humans (and later) Cepees could be upgraded, downgraded, or otherwise changed.

As examples, a Cepee with attributes dealing with facial muscles, hair color, or the shape of the nose does not have to pass these characteristics to a later generation Cepee. The programmable chromosome can be changed. What is in vogue at one time may not be in vogue a few years later. The programmable chromosome allows a fad or trend to be reversed. Moreover, as the Cepees make new discoveries, the programmable chromosome (as well as the other chromosomes) can accommodate the associated changes.

(f) Mediating and Stimulating Friendly Behavior. In the early part of the twenty-first century, researchers discovered people who suffered from Williams Syndrome were missing a small piece of chromosome 7. These people were, "...weirdly, incautiously friendly and nice—and unafraid of strangers."[51] Thus, the scientists demonstrated a genetic underpinning for friendliness. They showed this human trait was, "...indeed as primal as ferocity."

It was only a matter of time before genetic engineers began to manipulate part of chromosome 7 in efforts to make this segment of the population in the species *more* contentious. The results (for this small population) led to a less harmonious human, but one who possessed better defense mechanisms against humans who were pathologically unfriendly and who preyed on those naive creatures who suffered from this syndrome.

Most humans were hardwired for what scientists called the "optimism bias."[52] MRI scans revealed the amygdala was central to the processing of emotion. Scans also revealed that the rostral anterior cingulated cortex (rACC) modulated emotion and behavior. In depressed individuals, these parts of the brain showed abnormal activity, just as they did with people who had a short fuse, suddenly lost their tempers and became violently aggressive.

Finding treatments to kindle optimism as well as to hold back depression was not just an EGO program. It was well documented that optimistic humans worked longer and tended to make more money than pessimists. They also exhibited an inclination toward not killing people. Culling out of the humans' DNA or carving out parts of the brain to lend a hand to the optimism bias was much more than a Dr. Phil-Good palliative. It was instrumental in addressing some serious deficiencies in the human race.

Notwithstanding these success stories, the problem with segments of the human population was not too much trust, it was too little. Why should this aspect of the human have become a problem? After all, caution and associated mistrust of other humans led to a better prepared and more fully armed human. The answer returns to the discussion in Chapter 3 about the critical aspect of member cooperation within a tribe. Tribes composed of cooperating, trusting, and even altruistic members fared better than tribes whose members were uncooperative and mistrustful of one another.

As the human race evolved into that of national tribes, it was discovered that "trust [was] among the strongest known predictors of a country's wealth; nations with low levels tend[ed] to be poor."[53] Consequently, finding a way for humans to naturally exhibit trust was not an academic exercise, it had powerful practical ramifications.

The researchers found that a primeval neurotransmitter (chemicals enabling signals to be sent across cells) named oxytocin played a major role in the human brain's determination of whom to trust or distrust. Oxytocin, composed of just nine amino acids, played several roles in the human body. One was trust.

Oxytocin was nicknamed the "cuddle hormone" because levels of it spiked in men and women during a sexual climax and lingered in their bodies after their breathing eased. It stimulated milk flow in nursing women. It played a role in inducing labor. And for this discussion, it influenced cooperation and trust among humans. In dysfunctional conditions, a human body's inability to be responsive to its own release of oxytocin led to personality traits resembling "those of sociopaths, who are indifferent to or even stimulated by another's suffering."[54]

Thus, as part of the ILLS and ASSES programs, oxtytocin enhancers were invented to aid other therapies in combating aggression and depression.

However, it is noteworthy that the treatments described in this section had to be applied judiciously. MRIs also revealed the amygdala, as well as the anterior cingulate cortex and the dorsolateral prefrontal cortex, were instrumental in keeping the human alert to dangers.[55] Their proper functioning was essential for survival. Excessive treatment to enhance optimism and trust could make the human too laid back, perhaps at the risk to his well-being, "My, that is a lovely avalanche coming down the mountain toward me."

Significant progress was also made in curbing the number of public massacres that were taking place in the twenty-first century (As described in Chapter 8, see "Sidebar. Demented Loner vs. Disillusioned Idealist): The humans simply curtailed the media coverage on the events. By restricting these killers' press releases, they eliminated one of the major reasons they killed in the first place: for publicity. When the mass murders were reported, the killer's name, picture, history, and any possible "propaganda" he might have written was kept from public eyes. Instead of stories lamenting his plight, stories were published about his victims. No gory details were provided.

Granted, the news media had some of its rights curtailed, but the restraint was voluntary because research demonstrated that the loss of press led to a reversal of the Hearse Carriage Effect: fewer people jumped on the killer bandwagon.[56]

(g) Unnatural DNA. For billions of years, earth's organisms were composed of the same molecular ingredients that made up DNA, RNA, and the 20 amino acids.[57] Life (and the associated chemical reactions in cells) was constrained by these components and how they interacted with one another. This ancient legacy changed in 2001 when scientists succeeded in adding to bacteria the capability of decoding a certain DNA sequence into an unnatural amino acid. Later, cells were modified to allow them to synthesize artificial amino acids and string them together to form proteins that had *never existed* on earth, again a topic introduced earlier in this chapter (see Synthetic Biology).

(h) Anti-Aging. The devolving humans could not master the art and science of metamorphosing all parts of their bodies and central nervous systems. The evolving Cepees were faced with the same problem. Neither lineage came close to building these systems from scratch. For example, the complexity of the brain militated against procedures affecting perhaps the changing of billions of cells on an individual cell basis. To add to this complexity, the firing of a single neuron in the brain brought many gene products into play, perhaps hundreds of them. Usually, the best that could be done was to emulate, enhance, and sometimes alter the brain's chemical and electrical behaviors.

As another example, aged and worn-out cells, leading to the death of the cells and their associated functions, had been built into the human genome millions of years ago. It was folly to assume a couple hundred years of effort could lead to the reversal of a process that had evolved over eons. Brilliant as the humans were, the more modest and realistic members of their race were content to accept Mohandas Gandhi's advice, "Satisfaction lies in the effort, not in the attainment. Full effort is full victory."[58]

Consequently, as advanced as the emerging early twenty-second century Cepee was, it could not overcome the challenge of continuous biosynthetic regeneration and replacement of billions of its cells. Some method—for certain, an advanced technology—had to be found to prevent cells from dying. Otherwise, the vaunted idea of an everlasting life on earth would come to naught.

The problem was compounded by the complex blend of the problem. The Cepee race had been created from both human organic matter and biosynthetic components—all mixed together into an impressive array of polymerized parts. Examples were organic Boolean circuits, synthetic synapses, natural cells, and lab-grown skin. The surgeon could not treat these assemblages as if they all followed the same rules for their existence and behavior.

However, because many of the Cepee's parts were designed and created in less than two centuries by the disappearing humans and the emerging Cepees, they were more easily understood. Thus, they could be more easily manipulated than the millions-of-year-old parts that were created and fostered by mutation and natural selection. Nonetheless, a being containing parts that were naturally selected and parts that were "unnaturally" manufactured made for a complicated set of peripherals and mainframe.

The organic cells' aging problem was eventually solved. First, scientists discovered a normal human cell had a finite lifetime span. It divided about 60 times before dying. This bound was called the Hayflick Limit, named after the biologist who discovered it. Each time the cell divided, a part of the cell's chromosome, named telomeres, became a bit shorter.[59] Scientists eventually concluded that telomere shortening was a leading cause of cellular aging and death.

During this time many projects complemented the telomere research. As one example, scientists discovered several genes that could be manipulated to improve health and prolong life. They came to understand:[60]

> By optimizing the body's functioning for survival, these genes maximize the individual's chances of getting through a crisis. And if they remain active long enough, they can also dramatically enhance the organism's health and extend its life span. In essence, they represent the opposite of aging genes—longevity genes.

Later, researchers discovered techniques for inserting genes that blocked telomere shortening. The process was quite difficult to carry out because some genes frequently transmuted into unplanned reactions. For example, during the humans' times, one genetic operation created a process in which calcium was deposited more rapidly into bones, making for very healthy skeletal frameworks. Unfortunately, the same operation also resulted in excessive calcium deposits in arterial walls, making for very unhealthy cardiovascular systems (and dead humans with wonderful skeletons).

Another successful project discovered aging (senescent) cells produced a molecule called p16^{INK4A}. It was one control mechanism that brought cell division to a halt when the Hayflick Limit was reached. These kinds of cells accumulated as an animal aged. Some biologists believed they had a great influence on life span.

In an experiment with mice, a drug was used to kill cells that had reached their Hayflick limits. The procedure was conducted as follows: A second gene was inserted into the mice's DNA, near the gene for p16^{INK4A}. This "drug" killed cells that had reached their limit. The theory of this lab test was that aging cells had adverse effects on other healthy cells, and if they could be removed, the animal's life would be prolonged. The results were astounding:[61]

> Cells producing p16^{INK4A} were killed and cleared away as they appeared. ...Mice given the drug every three days from birth suffered far less age-related body-wasting than those which were not. [They] lost less fatty tissue. [Their] muscles remained plump [and according to treadmill tests, effective].

Expressing hope for this work, the researchers offered, "The wasting and weakening of the tissues that accompanies senescence would be a thing of the past, and old age could then truly become ripe."[62]

With these successes and many others, after decades of human research and experimentation, and still later, after many hits and misses from the Cepees, aging was aged-out of the Cepee.

(i) Reverse Engineering of Anti-Aging Procedures. This last entry of Benchmark 8 moves this narrative from the human era into the twenty-second century and the Cepee era. Millions of humans had been devoted to their religions. Many of these people fervently believed they would die, but would rise from the dead, and thereafter enjoy a permanent afterlife. The human's view was a variation—but similar in spirit (so to speak)—to the Cepee's perpetual life.

The transition of a human to a Cepee did not necessarily result in the Cepee no longer believing in a God. Nor did it automatically result in the acceptance of a Cepee's permanent residence on earth as a substitute for a Cepee's permanent place in Heaven.

Certainly, a substantial number of Cepees were happy and content (and relieved) with their guaranteed lock on life, courtesy of EGO, ILLS, SANE, and ASSES. After all, Matthew 24:35 proclaimed that heaven itself "shall pass away." Even the believers took pause when they read this passage. But some of the more ardent believers interpreted the passage to mean their metaphorical, cloud-filled heaven was earth itself, courtesy of EGO, ILLS, SANE, and ASSES.

Notwithstanding the confusion surrounding Matthew 24:35, how could an honorable and moral race force one of its own kind to go against his or her religious beliefs, especially beliefs that were accepted by many members of the species? These beliefs had been integral to the mores of the Cepees' ancestors. How could an ethical society discount such a profound and important legacy? After all, when viewed dispassionately, it was simply a matter of choosing one form of permanent existence over another.

After much debate, the Cepees decided they would honor the legacy of their forebears with a simple approach: Upon reaching a certain age, the "believer" Cepee who wished to follow his/her own religious path of a permanent existence (afterlife) was taken through some genetic reverse engineering procedures pertaining to telomeres and the Hayflick limit. In contrast, those who opted for the scientific path of a permanent existence (neverdeath) were left intact.

Benchmark 9: Epigenetic Engineering

The human body had some 300 different types of cells. One part of the body might consist of more than one cell type. As examples, there were seventeen different kidney cell types, eight different hair cell types, numerous blood, bone, brain cell types, and so on. Each cell type had the same DNA, but could be differentiated with the presence of epigenetic marks.[63]

As introduced in Chapter 3, epigenetic marks that sat atop cells offered instructions to the cells. This cellular material was called the epigenome. In the mother's womb the emerging cell's epigenetic marks activated or silenced certain gene sequences, and accentuated or lessened its effects.[64]

Chapter 3 also introduced the idea that factors such as stress, smoking, over eating, and successful battles using weapons could create the epigenetic marks, which would then influence the children who had the marks passed to them by their parents. Thus, epigenetic changes represented "a biological response to an environmental stressor." The changes did not alter DNA code. The removal of the environmental stressor would result in the fading away of the epigenetic mark, and the DNA code would "begin to revert to its original programming."[65]

The human genome contained roughly 25,000 genes. Each cell type had a different pattern of epigenetic marks. These patterns of epigenetic marks numbered in the millions.[66] The complexity and scope of first, mapping the epigenome, second, understanding the implications of the map, and third, altering the map to change the human was staggering. But the humans thrived on these kinds of challenges. Even more, the results could lead to enormous improvements to the humans' bodies and minds. But the task was enormous, as explained below.

Changing a Gene's Expression. A key component of epigenetics was a methyl group, a basic unit in organic chemistry. The group, labeled CH_3, contained one carbon atom bonded to three hydrogen atoms. Through DNA methylation—the transfer of the methyl group to a specific spot on the gene (chemically speaking, the transfer to another compound)—the gene's expression could be changed.

The importance of DNA methylation was revealed in 2003 during an experiment at Duke University.[67] By consuming a rich input of folic acid and vitamin B_{12}, mice that were fat and diabetic produced healthy offspring that had no diabetes and were of normal weight. Another experiment exposed fruit flies to a drug that resulted in the flies showing unusual outcrops on their eyes. No change in DNA occurred in generations 2 through 13, yet the offspring carried the unusual outgrowth.

Since those times, epigenetic drugs began to appear in the marketplace at an accelerating rate. Cancer, autism, Alzheimer's disease, sociopathy, psychopathy, and other forms of schizophrenia came under the surgeon's computer and petri dish to lead to an increasingly robust human—both physically and mentally.

These drugs had the effect of regulating the genes' behavior through changing the association of DNA and related proteins (called histones). The drugs remodeled chromatin (the combination of DNA and proteins making up the nucleus of a cell). They did so by altering the way DNA was "wrapped around" the histones. In so many words, certain kinds of wrap-arounds would render the gene inactive. Others would cause the gene to be activated.

And while the task of epigenetic engineering was difficult,[68]

> ...the potential is staggering. For decades, we have stumbled around massive Darwinian roadblocks. DNA, we thought, was an ironclad code that we and our children and their children had to live by. Now we can imagine a world in which we can tinker with DNA, bend it to our will. It will take geneticists and ethicists many years to work out all the implications, but be assured: the age of epigenetics has arrived.

Some humans argued that epigenetics did not change human nature. It gave human nature temporary fixes with temporary rules.[69]

> These rules are the genetic biases in the way our senses perceive the world, the symbolic coding by which we represent the world, the options we automatically open to ourselves, and the responses we find easiest and most rewarding to make. ...epigenetic rules alter the way we [see things]. ...They lead us differentially to acquire fears and phobias concerning dangers in the environment, [to communicate, to form expressions, to bond, to have sex].

All true, but this temporary fix also led to a dramatic change in the humans' overall gene pool. For example, if a person died at an early age because his parents smoked, this person's genes did not have as much a chance of contributing to the humans' genetic pool than if the person's parents were nonsmokers.

From Eugenics to Liberal Eugenics to Preventive Eugenics to Inventive Eugenics

Were the accomplishments described in this chapter indicative of constructive strides made in the evolution of the human race? Or were they to be avoided because they were a violation of longheld taboos against eugenics?

During the first half of the twenty-first century, the responses to these two questions usually depended on who was answering them. If the person responding did not need their preventive and curative powers, the answers varied. If the person responding needed these cures, the answers were almost always yes and no respectively. The survival instinct kicked in, rendering the discussion irrelevant.

By the latter half of the twenty-first century, almost all members of the human race had come to accept and even embrace the changes described in this chapter. Those who did not were left behind. They never got on the self-change bandwagon, so the bandwagon left the station without them. Their increasingly inferior minds and bodies— in relation to those who were being transformed—relegated them to the evolution's backwaters. Regardless of their views or anyone else's interpretation of eugenics, inventive or otherwise, their decreasing numbers rendered their views to be unimportant. Just as the humans did with the Neanderthals, the Cepees did with the humans: They were bred out and genetically over swamped.[70]

From Nurture or Nature to Nurture and Nature

The evidence could not be disputed. Unless a person was shackled by the Ignorant Therefore Doctrinaire Law, most humans came to understand that both environmental and physiological factors drove the human's mental engine and physical wheels. Returning to oxytocin, the cuddle hormone, these two factors.[71]

> …also indicate that our life experiences may "retune" the oxytocin mechanism to a different "set point" and thus to different levels of trust throughout the course of life. Residing in a safe nurturing environment may stimulate us to release more oxytocin when someone trusts us—and to reciprocate that trust. Stress, uncertainty, and isolation all work against the development of a trusting disposition.

Semi-Heaven on Earth

The individual Cepee was not completely immune from destruction. After all, the planet's volcanic eruptions, tsunamis, earthquakes, blizzards, avalanches, tornadoes, forest fires, floods, mudslides, and hurricanes did not just go away. Indeed, these natural events continued fulfilling their job descriptions on the humans' replacements.

Thus, Cepees disappeared into tsunami surges in the Indian Ocean; they vanished beneath gigantic hurricane waves in the Caribbean; they fell into earthquake cracks in Japan; they decomposed under mudslides in Peru; they disintegrated inside tornado funnels in Kansas; they were swept out to sea, courtesy of flooded cul-de-sacs in southern California; they evaporated under volcanic flows in Mexico; they broke apart from avalanches in Colorado; their frozen bodies were pinned down by Montana's ice storms; they burned away in forest fires in New Mexico.

The Cepee had been added to the list of potential recipients of Mother Nature's gifts, and planet earth continued to perform its ageless population-control rituals, accentuated by the effects of global warming.

Results

Notwithstanding the Cepees who succumbed to Mother Nature's specters, as time went on, an array of novel genes and proteins became available to aid this being in enhancing its genome and curing its diseases, as well as proportioning the aging process to fit the Cepees' desire for a disease-free, everlasting life.

The mapping (and understanding) of the multifarious effects of multifunction genes was completed, thus allowing genetic surgeons to orchestrate the genes' behavior in relation to the body and mind. Bodily peripherals, such as legs, arms, and ears that were damaged from accidents or excessive wear, were replaced by brain-driven prosthetics or by growing another peripheral.

Eventually, *anything* in the human that was defined by its genome and brain could be controlled—which was *everything* in the human. The Nine Lives Effect produced, with minor exceptions, Heaven on Earth—and the Cepee.

The Never-Ending Problems of Never Dying

This chronicle, the first about the Cepee, has focused on how and why the Cepee came to exist. There is another story to be told, another question to answer: How do the Cepees manage themselves and their societies, both of which never die? The questions go on and on: How is the population controlled? How is it decided which Cepee stays young or grows old? When does a Cepee retire? Does he? If so, when does he begin to draw retirement benefits? Does the age-old, yet ageless Cepee lead to decreased or increased health care (preventative maintenance) costs?

The first chapter of the Cepees, of how they came into existence, is nearing its end. The subject of how the Cepee fares in this existence must wait to be told another time.

Conclusion

This narrative has examined a very small sampling of the extraordinary changes the humans made to themselves in the twenty-first and twenty-second centuries, but enough to understand how the human became the Cepee; initially by default, later by design. The humans never came to grips with all the issues surrounding these changes. Nonetheless, gene by gene, protein by protein, bit by bit, and byte by byte, the humans eventually reconstructed much of their phenotype and genotype to become the Cepees.

[1] Aldous Huxley, *Brave New World* (New York: HarperCollins, 1932, 1946), xi.

[2] This quote is in Chapter Four of the online copy of *Brave New World*. The online version did not have an accompanying page number. With the "Find" command available for use with electronic copy, the reference to a page number might become passe.

[3] Emerging DNA evidence is increasingly supporting the theory that the Neanderthals did not become extinct. They were absorbed by the *Homo sapiens* who had migrated from Africa into the Neanderthals' territory in Europe.

[4] Many of these procedures are complex and deal with parts of the body that are not commonly known to a layman. My descriptions of these operations are written in a general way for two reasons. First, to make the explanations comprehensible to someone who is not in the medical profession. Second, I am not an expert in these complicated technologies. I have been careful to construct these explanations to accurately convey the general ideas behind them. I hope I have not trivialized these astonishing feats in what can only be described as works of genius.

[5] "Tools for Life," *Scientific American*, August 2010, 17.

[6] "Synthetic Genome," http://www.astrobio.net/pressrelease/3502/synthetic-genome.

[7] Lawrence M. Krauss, "The Real Promise of Synthetic Biology," *Scientific American*, February 2010, 32.

[8] Ibid.

[9] Robert Lee Hotz, "Printing Evolves: An Inkjet for Living Tissue," *The Wall Street Journal*, Sept 18, 2012, http://online.wsj.com/article/SB10000872396390443816804578002101200151098.html.

[10] Ibid.

[11] Chizuka Henmi et al., "Development of an Effective Three Dimensional Fabrication Technique Using Inkjet Technology for Tissue Samples," AATEX 14, Special Issue, 689-692, August 21-25, 2007, 1.

[12] Hotz, "Printing Evolves: An Inkjet for Living Tissue," September 18, 2012, http://online.wsj.com.

[13] "First Ever: UK Scientists Use 3D Printer to Print Human Stem Cells," http://venturebeat.com/2013/02/06/first-ever-uk-scientists-use-3d-printer-to-print-human-stem-cells/.

[14] Ibid.

[15] Neil Gershenfeld, "How to Make Almost Anything," *Foreign Affairs*, November/December 2012, 51.

[16] My thanks to the NOVA series on PBS for this example.

[17] Clifford J. Rosen, "Restoring Aging Bones," *Scientific American*, March 2003, 71-77.

[18] Pam Belluck, "Device Offers Partial Vision for the Blind," *The New York Times*, February 15, 2013, A1-A3.

[19] Ibid., A3.

[20] According to Ms. Belluck, endnote 18, these two areas are under research.

[21] Brett Barrouquere, "Hand Transplant Recipient Doing Well," AOL Newscast, January 23, 2004.

[22] D. Kacy Cullen and Douglas H. Smith, "Bionic Connections, " *Scientific American*, January 2013, 54.

[23] Ibid.

[24] Ibid., 57.

[25] Ibid., 55. This scenario is what the authors see in the foreseeable future. I use the word *routine* as I have moved their "foreseeable future" past our lifetimes. I'm likely being too conservative.

[26] Coralie Carlson, "Transplant of 8 Organs to Baby Girl Announced," *The Spokesman Review*, March 20, 2004, A9.

[27] "Growing Liver in Lymph Nodes," *Discover*, 03.2012, 10.

[28] Ibid., 11.

[29] Steve Sternberg, "Lab-grown Windpipe Saves Cancer Patient," *USA TODAY*, July 8, 2011, n.p.

[30] Ibid.

[31] Ken Numeoka, Manjong Han, and David M Gardiner, "Regrowing Human Limbs," *Scientific American*, April 2008, 57- 62. This example is the first human self-change operation described in this chapter that has yet to happen (as of the publication date of this book). I have taken the liberty of including it because of the possibility of we humans being able to grow back a lost body part. What seems far-fetched in 2014 will likely be commonplace within a few decades.

[32] William Leventon, "Synthetic Skin," *IEEE Spectrum*, December 2002, 30.

[33] Christine Gorman, "A Transplant First," *Time Magazine*, December 23, 2005, 58. A summary of this article is available at http://content.time.com/time/classroom/glenspring2006/pdfs/CEU_spring_2006.pdf, 28.

[34] "World's First Brain Prosthesis Revealed," *New Scientist*, March 12, 2003, http://www.wireheading.com/misc/brain-prosthesis.html.

[35] Microsoft's Encarta Reference Library.

[36] Michael Shermer, "The Political Brain," *Scientific American*, July 2006, 36.

[37] Giovanna Ponti, Paolo Peretto, and Luca Bonfanti (2008), ed. Thomas A. Reh, "Genesis of Neuronal and Glial Progenitors in the Cerebellar Cortex of Peripuberal and Adult Rabbits," *PLoS ONE* ,http://www.ncbi.nlm.nih.gov/pmc/articles/PMC2396292.

[38] This writer can attest to the validity of these studies—if not in the neuroplasticity of my brain—then in its reaction time. I am certain several years of hitting tennis balls against more skilled players played a role in my improved ability to react to a fast ball coming to me while I was at the net. I began to react, not even knowing what I was doing until I did it. The end result was my having occasional flashes of mediocrity on the tennis courts.

[39] Michael S. Gazzaniga, *The Ethical Brain* (New York: Dana Press, 2005), 101-102.

[40] "Human Cloning and Human Dignity: An Ethical Inquiry," The President's Council on Bioethics, Washington, DC, July 2002, Chapter One, "The Meaning of Cloning: An Overview," www.bioethics.gov.

[41] This point is made several times in the Howard Hughes Medical Institute, Alfred P. Sloan Foundation, Films for the Humanities and Sciences video series on human self-change.

[42] Peter Ward, "What Will Become of the *Homo sapiens*?" *Scientific American*, January 2009, 72.

[43] "DNA," Howard Hughes Medical Institute, Alfred P. Sloan Foundation, Films for the Humanities and Sciences # 32868, Princeton, "Curing Cancer," 2003.

[44] Microsoft's Encarta Reference Library.

[45] Rick Weiss, "Monkeys Control Robotic Arm with Brain Implants," *The Washington Post*, October 15, 2002.

[46] PBS, Channel, KCOT, Spokane, November 26, 2006. The quotes are taken from an interview with MIT engineers, who discussed their robots being able to "feel" and show "emotions." One asked, "What if you could get people to relate to a robot in the same way a parent relates to a child?" The answer should have been, "Who would want to?" Small wonder the Cepees turned off funding these well-meaning innocents' Tinker Toys projects.

[47] "DNA," Howard Hughes Medical Institute, Alfred P. Sloan Foundation, Films for the Humanities and Sciences # 32866, Princeton, "Playing God," 2003.

[48] W. Wayt Gibbs, "Synthetic Life," *Scientific American*, May 2002, 75-81, http://online.sfsu.edu/rone/GEessays/SyntheticLife.htm; "Life 2.0," *The Economist*, September 2, 2006, 67-70.

[49] Ibid., "Life 2.0," 67.

[50] "DNA," Howard Hughes Medical Institute, Alfred P. Sloan Foundation, Films for the Humanities and Sciences # 32869, Princeton, "Pandora's Box," 2003. Dr. Mario Capecchi discusses this idea. He does not bring in the concept of BCM libraries in his discussion, but I see BCM as a necessary tool for programmable chromosomes.

[51] Olivia Judson, "The Selfless Gene," *The Atlantic Monthly*, October 2007, 98. The term *mediating friendly behavior* is taken from this article.

[52] Tali Sharot, "The Optimism Bias," *Time*, June 6, 2011, 41-46. Posted online, May 28, 2013, at http://content.time.com/time/health/article/0,8599,2074067,00.html.

[53] Paul J. Zak, "The Neurobiology of Trust," *Scientific American*, June 2008, 88.

[54] Ibid., 95.

[55] Jeffrey Kluger, "Race and the Brain," *Time*, October 20, 2008, 59.

[56] Ari N. Schulman, "What Mass Killers Want—And How to Stop Them." *The Wall Street Journal*, November 8, 2013, C1-C2. Mr. Schulman reports on a study conducted in Vienna Austria, in which the suicide rate on subways quickly decreased by 75 percent when the story was moved off the front page, and the word "suicide" was not used in the article's heading. The subject of this endnote is mass murder, not suicide. Nonetheless, studies backup this assertion. For an introduction to the subject, see: http://usatoday30.usatoday.com/news/opinion/forum/story/2012-07-20/aurora-colorado-batman-movie-murder/56376566/1.

[57] W. Wayt Gibbs, "Synthetic Life," *Scientific American*, May 2002, 80.

[58] Mohandas Gandhi, *Young India*, March 9, 1922, in Frank, *Quotationary*, 232.

[59] Telomeres are structures on the tips of the cell's chromosomes. They prevent the ends of chromosomes from attaching to the ends of other chromosomes.

[60] David A. Sinclair and Lenny Guarente, "Unlocking the Secrets of Longevity Genes," *Scientific American*, March 2006, 49. The initial research was conducted on rather simple organisms. Later, humans applied their findings to the human genome.

[61] "Forever Young?" *The Economist*, September 5, 2011, 95.

[62] Ibid.

[63] John Cloud, "Why Genes Aren't Destiny," Time, January 18, 2010, 49-53.

[64] Ibid., 50, 51.

[65] Ibid., 51.

[66] It is not known how many epigenetic marks are in the genome. Nor is it known if each cell type has a different epigenetic pattern. Only two cell types have begun to be mapped (an embryonic stem cell and a fibroblast).

[67] Cloud, "Why Genes Aren't Destiny," 51.

[68] Ibid., 53.

[69] E. O. Wilson, *The Social Conquest of Earth* (New York: Liveright, 2012), 193, Kindle edition, loc. 3119.

[70] As noted in endnote 3, emerging DNA evidence is increasingly supporting the theory that the Neanderthals did not become extinct. They were absorbed by the *Homo sapiens* who migrated from Africa into the Neanderthal's territory in Europe. This quote is paraphrased from a NOVA television program aired on PBS, January 14, 2013.

[71] Zak, "The Neurobiology of Trust," 95.

CHAPTER 12

HEAVEN ON EARTH

Not everything that can be counted counts,
and not everything that counts can be counted.
—Albert Einstein

Earth, by the twenty-second century, can be turned,
if we so wish, into a permanent paradise for human beings,
or at least the strong beginnings of one.
—E. O. Wilson[1]

Our behavior is embedded deeply into our souls,
chiseled onto our genome and gray matter with the
imprints of ancient human tribal hierarchies.

The ascension of the Cepee came about in less than two centuries. In this short time span, the conventional human was changed to become a significantly altered individual, one with no pain, ample good looks, few faults, and an eternal warranty on life.

For a while, the humans' early EGO initiatives resulted in people with beautiful faces and trim neck lines. But eventually, plastic surgery declined in popularity. Gene manipulation, biosynthetic skin, and anti-aging therapies made the cutting and stretching of human epidermis unnecessary. The tattoo industry boomed for a few years, but like all fads, receded into obscurity, leaving legacies of shrunken, wrinkled, and faded portraits hanging loosely on the skins of retirement home residents. Genetic and brain engineering led to the demise of the antidepressant and steroid pills industry. A "feel good high" was obtained with gene manipulation and brain enhancements. Consequently, the Cepees had little need for their ancestors' EGO programs.

Likewise for the ILLS enterprise. After decades of frustrating dead ends and dead people, the emerging Cepees finally engineered themselves and germs such that the formerly deadly organisms did little harm to the Cepees. Indeed, many heretofore harmful germs were modified genetically to aid the Cepee. The SANE programs took ILLS to another effective level.

The ASSES initiatives, critical to the well-being of the twenty-first-century humans, relied on the technologies developed by the EGO, ILLS, and SANE programs. Eventually, their cumulative alterations came into play. The many changes applied to the human over almost two centuries unintentionally resulted in the Cepee. Nonetheless, the early Cepees were not so haphazard in their changes. Many were intended to produce more streamlined versions of their lineage.

As a result of earlier conflicts and associated 1984 Orwellian fears, they resolved to find solutions to the Deadly Trinity by 2084. Beyond that date, the humans made further progress in self-changes that led to the Cepees.

Finally, those egregious humans who were a minority in their species, but who did great harm to the members of their race were no longer egregious. These beings and the other members of their species were no longer humans, at least in the strict sense of the word. They were now Cepees. The combined autocatalytic effects of EGO, ILLS, SANE, and ASSES led to an altered linage of the human: a perpetually well-adjusted, healthy, contented assemblage of human parts, greatly enhanced with biosynthetics, genetic tailoring, and organic computers.

Transition Problems and Opportunities

In 2084, the humans held ceremonies to mark the 100th anniversary of the George Orwell's book, *1984*. These ceremonies were held to acknowledge and commemorate their race avoiding the dangerous and dreary 1984 Orwellian world. The events also celebrated the humans' remarkable progress in coming to grips with their self-induced Deadly Trinity. The ceremonies were named *2084 and Beyond.*

As shown in Figure 11-1 (Chapter 11), by 2084, the many changes that had been made to the humans during the twenty-first century reinforced and fed on one another, leading to an exponential explosion of human self-change technologies. The result was an Autocatalytic Cycle (Figure 2-2, Chapter 2) encompassing innumerable discoveries, inventions, and technical breakthroughs.

The Cepee pauses: *I recall a term, plus ultra, that was coined by the French around the time of the ninth century. Several other languages borrowed the term, and it took on several but similar meanings. One was "more beyond." Another was "further beyond." The Human Archives document that the humans in 2084 were aware of how rapidly they were changing themselves and the world around them. I suspect if they had known what lay in the future, their year of celebration would have been named "2084 Plus Ultra."*[2]

Nonetheless, the transition of the human to the Cepee was not an easy passage, because the issues regarding human self-change were controversial. As the humans marched along in their procession to transformation, bitter debates accompanied their ongoing alterations. As noted earlier, segments of the human were a quarrelsome lot and did not take kindly to opposing opinions about self-change and an everlasting life. In keeping with their approaches to contentious issues, some members of the opposition were "eliminated," with the resulting effect of ending the debate regarding the deceased's view on the subject. Notwithstanding these casualties, the momentum resulted in most humans jumping aboard the self-change bandwagon.

A substantial majority of the race embraced the ideas behind self-change. Their views were aptly affirmed by a twenty-first century human, "Man is not going to wait passively for millions of years before evolution offers him a better brain."[3] As well, man and woman were not going to wait for millions of years for better bodies.

Living in the Cepee World

The modern humans debated the pros and cons of living an infinite life. During these debates, they assumed the universe would accommodate their race to an endless stay on earth, and the travails of day-to-day living would be eliminated. They assumed their offspring would eventually experience no pain, aggression, jealousy, or envy; no aging parts that could not be replaced; no angst or anger; no hunger, thirst, cold, poverty, and other vicissitudes of life.

These humans came to realize their future relatives would be admirable, contented creatures, ones who would make good neighbors to equally superior beings. In effect, the many syndromes, principles, laws, and attendant miseries described in this narrative would no longer be part of the life of earth's future beings.

The reaction to this situation depended partially on a person's religious beliefs. If a believer, the human had come to expect death and understood he or she must wait a short time to be redeemed, and therefore, wanted no part of the Cepee scenario.

The nonbeliever took the position that nonexistence followed death. Taking a practical view, the thought was, "Why not stick around on earth and see what happens?" The Cepee life would certainly be more stimulating than a void of nothingness.

Yet another approach to the subject was espoused by those who followed the philosophy of Epicurus, "Death itself is not bad for the dead, because they are dead, and not bad for the living, because no living person can be dead."[4] Surely a testament to practicality and a pragmatic approach to dealing with grieving relatives.

Neitzsche and other existentialists said humans should embrace death with joy by choosing when to die. Of course, this approach did not set well with people who espoused only their god could determine when death took place.

Then there was the skeptic, the latter-day human who was not a pure believer or an atheist, the fence straddler. The being who thought, "Oh God, if there is a God, save my soul, if there is a soul." This person questioned the purpose of living in such a world.

On occasions, this individual favored being a Cepee.[5] Those occasions were instances when he realized his life on earth was nearing the end; when he found himself losing his physical powers and mental prowess; when, during the deadly and chaotic times of the humans' weapons of mass destruction wars, he crossed a conscious Rubicon to the realization the world had become a less pleasant and more dangerous habitat, at least in comparison to the days of his younger years.

On other occasions, the latter-day human preferred a non-Cepee world and wanted this way of life to continue. In doing so, he marveled at the legacy of the human race, of its creativity, of the race's ability to imagine and dream, its empathy, its desire and need to love and be loved, its inclination to touch and be touched, its humor, its sense of irony, its members' day-to-day deference to one another as they tried to pass through life relatively unscathed. He reflected on the joys of birth, of childhood, parenting, even old age. He thought about the passages and transitions associated with closure, of events coming to an end and the joy of reflecting about those endings. On those occasions, he said to himself, "I'll take my chances with a non-Cepee existence."

Yet it was impossible to visualize accurately a Cepee world because of the many changes that would ultimately be made to the mind. If brain functions were changed significantly (which they were), this person could only have guessed how future operations would have been further altered.

Living in a Semi-Cepee World

The latter-day humans found themselves living in a semi-Cepee world, a world they did not yet know would rapidly evolve into an existence beyond any fantastical imaginations they currently harbored about human change. Within a few generations, the older members of the human race would become different from their offspring. Their outward appearances would be the same. After all, it was noted earlier that no one was going to countenance unsightly humans springing forth from the biotech lab, even if their physical changes would have made them more efficient. But their mental dispositions, their behavior toward one another, their approach to life in general, were not the same as their predecessors. The result was a tranquil race consisting of productive, intelligent, and energized members who respected and tolerated one another's peculiarities.

The several generations of the transitional humans and emerging Cepees who shared the planet earth at the same time were increasingly different from one another. How different? That was the thorny question. How different did a human want to be from, for example, his or her grandparents, even the parents? Ultimately, it was the individual who determined the extent of the transformation.

For a while, some governments placed limits on DNA and brain manipulations. Other countries somehow functioned without a functioning government and had no laws restricting the use of genetic tailoring and brain engineering. Whoever dictated the changes, the questions were daunting. What changes would be made in regard to aging? Intelligence? Looks? Disease immunities? To name a few.

Eventually, the human race came to the conclusion it would not deny treatment to innocent sufferers or even miscreants who could find relief by using these technologies. Of course not! How could a person deny the use of such palliatives to a fellow human, when ultimately, this very person might have need of them as well?

There was no stopping it. If the Joneses across the street gave their kids Ritalin to improve their kids' SAT scores, the Smiths had to do the same.[6] If the Smiths patched up little Billy to increase his intelligence, the Joneses had no choice but to take their little Sally to a nearby out-patient clinic for the same operation.

Heaven, as Advertised in the Holy Books

The biggest road block to humans' self-change, to becoming Cepees, were the holy books of several religions. These documents claimed heaven was a place where God, gods, or other spiritual beings dwelled. Heaven (and Paradise for the Muslims) was a place and/or a condition of perfect supernatural happiness for those who had been redeemed after they died.

The holy books never mentioned anything about a human-manufactured heaven. Indeed, humans doing their own thing regarding heaven and an everlasting life was not in keeping with the teachings of the holy books. After all, according to these documents, heaven had already been created and was awaiting those who qualified for entry. A human-made heaven was an invasion onto the turf of the heaven sanctioned in the holy books. Consequently, the holy book interpreters—the priests, friars, imams, and preachers— those occupying positions of power because of their take on this issue, condemned any suggestion that there might be another way to achieve everlasting life.

Heaven was quite important to many humans. Yet one of the holy books, the Bible, contained only thirty-one verses about the subject of heaven. Less than one page from a text of 1,389 pages of this Bible was devoted to heaven. Nonetheless, those who read and followed the passages of this book often conjured up images well beyond what the Bible actually said. For example:[7]

> Since the resurrection of Christ, the souls who are free from sin are admitted immediately after death into the firmament, which is called heaven. Their joy consists in an unclouded vision of God known as the beatific vision. Their bliss is eternal, but at the general resurrection their souls are to be reunited to their perfected or glorified bodies.

But the Bible contained no references to: "unclouded vision of God," "beatific vision," "bliss is eternal," or "reunited to their perfected or glorified bodies." Because heaven was advertised as the final stop, heaven was a significant concept to most humans. One would have thought the Bible would have been more expansive on the subject. It appeared the Bible's approach to enticing a person to read about a subject that was of considerable interest to the reader was to take a minimalist approach in its advertising.

As mentioned in Chapter 11, humans were particularly intrigued and puzzled by one verse about heaven. It was Matthew 24:35: "Heaven and earth shall pass away, but my words shall not pass away." Even heaven may not have been permanent. According to other verses in the Bible, heaven was where a person was supposed to be headed for afterlife. Yet, if heaven passed away and the human was left without the afterlife's residence, what happened next? Was the human to be relegated to the position of a heavenly homeless person?

Nothing was simple in a human's life or in the afterlife. Lucky for many humans, they watched televangelists on Sunday morning. These preachers apparently had possession of a stealth Bible and a direct filament to the firmament, because their shibboleths explained the details of heaven…those not in the Bible.

Regardless of these inconsistencies and unknowns, Chapter 11 revealed that religious Cepees were indeed allowed to practice their religion by returning to aging, death, and these Cepees hoped, an afterlife that was somewhat promised in their holy books.

Natural Laws: How? Why?

After centuries of celestial ignorance, the human race began to understand how the universe worked. Galileo's revolutionary scientific investigations and Newton's machine-like explanations opened vistas to the mysterious galaxies surrounding earth. Others followed these great men. They developed mathematical descriptions of the universe, how it began, and how it continued its existence by executing additional laws discovered by the human race's brilliant Plancks and Einsteins.

These laws defined how phenomena behaved. The propagation of light, radiation, and electromagnetism were well understood. The rules defined physical occurrences, such as how atoms decayed, how energy had mass, and how time changed during high speed travel. They were brilliant constructions, erected with the authority of equations.

But with all these enlightening numerical compositions, the human race was unable to explain *why* these events occurred and continued to occur. The humans were adept at answering *how* but inept at answering why.

Beyond the questions of how the cosmos operated, if the humans tried to answer why it even existed, the natural laws did them little good. Indeed, as recounted in Chapter 5, some questioned whether their universe was ultimately governed by natural laws. The humans' description of the universe bordered on the supernatural. The scientific community could not even come up with answers to gravity. In their latter stay on earth, scientists discovered an antigravity dark energy that appeared to defy known "natural laws."

What were natural laws? They were little more than observations through humans' woeful physical senses, little else than their earth-centric, telescopically limited opinions about a baffling universe. They were little more than perceptions from their impressive but limited brains, scribbled into formulas and their mathematical models of the universe. Rather extraordinary, modeling something that was only partially known.

Natural laws meant the values on each side of the equation were equal. This fact was an important construct, but it revealed little about the most important question, why? In addition, so-called natural laws were not laws at all, just observations or opinions.

To cite an example, Euclid *defined* a straight line as the shortest distance between two points, a natural law of geometry. He did not *prove* a straight line was the shortest distance between two points, he simply declared it to be so. He formed an opinion. In fact, the shortest distance between London and New York was not a straight line, but a bowed line that veered north between the two southern points. Euclid's limited flat world did not translate accurately to a round world. The same idea held true for the largely inexplicable universe.

In the end, the humans' algorithmic explanation of the universe, even of life itself, proved inadequate to their needs. Their closed loop axioms were not up to the task. Their mathematics, "seeking neither utility nor truth, but self-consistency," could not answer the fundamental question of why?[8]

Consequently, many of these beings continued to believe in religion, even after the human had become the Cepee. Their views about heaven and an everlasting life also underwent changes. But they were not radical changes. Because the holy books were vague about the exact nature of heaven, the Cepee's *heaven on earth* was now understood to be the human's *heaven in the firmament*.

The Mind

For centuries the humans argued about the nature of the mind and how it operated within the brain. Its existence was not questioned, but the mechanisms through which the mind functioned led to endless philosophical discourses. During his discussion about the mind, Descartes argued there were no sure signs to distinguish a waking experience from a dream. Therefore, all human experience was an illusion.[9] An illusion? Why not a dream? A critic of Descartes dismissed his ideas by stating his concepts were, "The dogma of the Ghost in the Machine."[10]

Some humans spent their professional careers attempting to understand the relationship of the mind to the brain, to understand how the brain enabled the mind, and to understand the physical underpinnings of the mind: ethics, morality, judgment, empathy, love, hate, and yes, pathological aggression.

Scientists agreed the mind was a part of the human's brain for thought and memory. No one contested that certain areas of the brain were responsible for specific mental processes. This knowledge was used to perform extraordinary enhancements to the central nervous system.

But the vague term *part* could not be defined or explained. Neuroscientists were able to measure the brain activity contributing to a physical action, say, the movement of one's hand. They were able to calculate the time delay between the mental activity and the associated physical action, including the time required for the neural signal to travel from the brain to the hand.

They could account with extraordinary accuracy the chemical and electrical functions involved in these actions. However, they were not able to account for 100 milliseconds of this total process. They plotted brain waves and created models of the brain's electrical and chemical operations, but they could not explain the mysterious 100 milliseconds. They knew something else was going on in the brain, but they never discovered what it was.[11]

Memories Are Made Of?

Equally puzzling was the mind's memory. Neuroscientists could not agree on how memories were coded, stored, and later decoded. They knew some memories were linked to the hippocampus. This discovery was made after surgeons removed the hippocampus from a man's brain and noticed, "he could no longer make new long-lasting memories."[12] Putting one and one together, they deduced the hippocampus had something to do with memory.

One school of scientists believed relatively few neurons (a thousand or so) held a recollection. Another school stated "bits and pieces" of a memory were distributed across millions, perhaps billions of neurons.[13]

Socrates declared that memory was the mother of the Muses and left the matter alone. Of course, Socrates was a philosopher, and uttering vague platitudes was a trademark of his profession. The neuroscientists of the twenty-first century were not satisfied with inexact proverbs, even if spoken by Socrates.

They came up with what they claimed was a specific answer to the question of what is memory? They explained that memory happened through concept cells. The "elegant coding scheme" of concept cells allowed the mind to store "many instances of one thing as a unique concept—a sparse and invariant representation."[14]

This "exact" explanation could not define what the elegant coding scheme was. Furthermore, what exactly was a sparse and invariant representation? Perhaps it was Socrates' Muses fiddling around with the hippocampus.

No one could explain how concept cells behaved or how the coding scheme worked. Thus, the memory of the mind was as elusive as the dark energy of the universe or the molasses-like invisible bath of the Higgs boson.

The Self

The self was as enigmatic as the mind and memory. The humans believed the self was part of the mind, but how? Why? They were able to correlate brain activity in the prefrontal cortex of a human on the occasions when a human was thinking about oneself.[15] They also established that questions posed to a human about oneself fired more synapses in the brain than did questions about someone else. This should not be surprising. After all, ego centrism was a hallmark of humans' behavior.

The humans also concluded brain damage could put a damper on one's self-image. They made this astonishing discovery when, in the nineteenth century, and as a result of a railroad construction explosion, Phineas Gage had a tamping iron travel through his skull. Understandably, Mr. Gage's behavior changed after this experience. Friends said he had difficulty thinking about things. They said he was, "no longer Gage." Imagine that! An iron missile had rifled through his entire head. Small wonder he was no longer himself.[16]

The Soul

If the mind and its memory were beyond the understanding of the humans, the soul was even more mysterious. The soul was viewed by the humans as the source of all bodily activities and mental functions.[17] Almost all human cultures believed a soul existed as an entity distinct from the body.

Some ancient philosophers, such as Epicurus, believed the soul was composed of fine particles that were spread throughout the body. They also believed the dissolution of the body in death led to the dissolution of the soul, which could not exist apart from the body. Therefore, no afterlife was possible. Because death meant total extinction, it had no meaning, either to the living or to the dead. As Epicurus declared, "When we are, death is not; and when death is, we are not."[18]

The scientists failed to reveal the soul or how the brain enabled it. They claimed the soul could not be discovered because it was a concocted idea of the religious mystics. The religious mountebanks argued the soul was beyond the scope of the scientists' measuring devices and their soulless minds.

Free Will

Like the mind and the soul, free will was an abstraction and elusive to quantitative analysis by the humans' scientists. The philosophers who believed in free will described it as a complex set of moral and ethical blueprints imprinted on unknown regions of the brain. An assemblage of mental principles, it allowed an individual to choose a course of action without regard to antecedent events. That is, an action that was a cause and not an effect.[19]

As an off shoot to this debate, some religious leaders preached determinism. If a human professed acceptance of and belief in the tenets inscribed in the appropriate holy book, this person was preprogrammed for the Pearly Gates. Other religions did not go this far. They pontificated that a mixture of free will and determinism was the best way to behave, "Give in sinner. Submit yourself to the Almighty, and you will be saved! But you still have to get up in the morning and go to work."

If free will existed, the uncertainty principle was in question, which displeased the scientists. As observed in chapters 5 and 6, the uncertainty principle stated it was impossible to specify the position and momentum of a particle (such as an electron) with precision. The mere observation of the electron would change the behavior of the electron. In other words, one could say that an electron had free will. Being a shy sort of particle, it reacted to observers by altering its behavior.

How did the scientists address this problem? With quantum mechanics in which they created probability calculations to account for the free will of the electron and other members of the universe. As an example, some scientists concluded: There is a probability that the constants of the immediate universe surrounding earth are not the constants that govern the more-distant universe. Therefore, there is also a probability that what scientists have been espousing as universal natural laws are not universal at all.[20] Small wonder that many scientists, including Einstein, embraced mysticism.

Reality and Illusion

Some philosophers informed a less informed human populace that everything was an illusion, including the philosophers and their philosophies. They argued that the entire cosmos was a construct of humans' minds, that there was no reality outside human thoughts.[21] George Berkeley, the eighteenth-century Irish philosopher, espoused this idea. This concept intrigued many people. It was an easy out.

René Descartes' utterance of, "I think, therefore I am" allowed many humans to forego both scientific rigor and religious rigidity. They declared, "I think, therefore the universe is."

Seemingly silly, but the notion was not all that frivolous. After all, what humans could observe in their physical world was far removed from the tiny universe of micro particles and the immense universe of macro objects.

Unsolvable Micro-Secrets and Unobservable Macro-Mysteries

The humans were never able to solve the mysteries of the micro mechanisms in matter or the macro operations of the universe. They discovered tiny particles, such as the boson. They discovered massive galaxies.

They knew all matter, including humans, was made up of protons, neutrons, and electrons. But these objects accounted for about 5 percent of the entire universe. The remainder of the universe consisted of dark energy and dark matter. Their very existence and the existence of the universe were, "only because of subtle connections between the very small and the very large."[22]

These beings could not explain with certainty the very phenomena they thought they may have discovered. As stated in Chapter 5, they had a hunch they knew about dark matter, anti-gravity, parallel universes, and infinite universes, but they were not certain. After all, they knew the universe could very well extend beyond the boundary they could observe. They studied galaxies whose light had traveled more than 13 billion years to reach earth. But beyond those distant systems, beyond the effects of the Big Bang, what was there? No one, including the Cepee, ever knew.

They even began to accept that their treasured constants were not constant. They came to know more about how, but the why remained elusive.

They also came to understand the anatomy of the brain, but they comprehended little beyond the physiology of synapse firings and other corporeal activities. They were able to trace activities in the brain correlating to different emotions and physical movements, but they could not explain how the brain performed them. The mind and its memory? It existed, but no one knew how. The soul, the self, and free will? Even more enigmatic.

How to account for the seemingly free will and independent intelligence of a modest human cell? As told in Chapter 11, cells had their own sense of sovereignty, "They knew what to do. It was as if cells possessed an invisible and undetectable intelligence of their own, that their simple structure contained a cerebral astuteness of their making and under their control."

The Cepees marvel at the acumen of these microorganisms. They have no frontal lobe or cortex, nothing that would have ordinarily bequeathed to them a discernible locus of insight. But they indeed have insight. Why? Usually, to facilitate the life of the human and later the Cepee. How? The interactions of chemicals and electricity. No. *How?* Beyond corporeal observations, the humans did not know, nor do the Cepees.

An Unsolvable Legacy

For the better part of the twentieth and first part of the twenty-first centuries, researchers believed the humans descended from a common ancestor of the chimpanzee. The fossils that were discovered up to around 2011 pointed to this single lineage. From that time, additional fossil discoveries pointed to two startling revelations: First, the last "common ancestor of humans and chimpanzees [was] not particularly chimplike." Second, humans did not evolve from one lineage, but multiple lineages.[23]

The evolutionary trail of some of these lineages went far beyond the trail of the 3.2 million-year-old Lucy (*Australopithecus afarensis*). A small creature named Ardi (of the *Ardipithecus ramidus* species) lived 4.4 million years ago. Ardi was thought to have been one of the humans' ancestors. Ardi was a member of a species that had a closer relationship to humans than to chimps, one that did not have much in common with chimps.[24]

Fossils were also found that offered strong evidence of primates, quite possibly ancient lineages of the human, assuming upright postures eight million years ago, well before the chimps appeared on earth.

Because of the inability to glean DNA from these specimens, because fossils could not be found that would yield an uninterrupted evolutionary tree, because different lineages were known to develop the same trait independently (*homopasy*), because these like traits may have come about in species separated by millions of years, scientists knew there was a limit in tracing relationships over this wide expanse of time.[25]

In the final analysis, knowing exactly who the humans' ancestors were was not as important as what the humans had come to be. The wiser humans, those less anal about their primate pedigree, found consolation by assuming a more accepting posture, "He who knows says, 'We do not know.' "[26]

The Cepee pauses a moment to reflect on these discoveries: *Perhaps these findings led to a bit more tolerance between the pro-chimp and anti-chimp camps on humans' ancestry.*

Religion Is Not Subject to Objectivity

Nor could these beings prove or disprove religion. The religious folks began to distrust the scientists because they kept altering their supposedly immutable natural laws. Eventually the unified field theory and dark matter/energy concepts were successfully postulated. But the question remained: So what?

The arguments about the existence or absence of a God or gods never ceased. The believers said yes. The atheists said no. The fence straddlers said maybe. But even some atheists did not discount the grand possibility of a supernatural force behind the universe. Notwithstanding this prospect, they rejected the "parochial" view of the believers of an earth-centric God whose Jesus was to descend to the planet to lay waste to evildoers.[27] They believed this opinion was a very limited view that had been imposed on the human race by ancient theologians who were circumscribed by their ignorance.

The Imprints of Ancient Human Tribal Hierarchies— and Their Dislodging

After centuries of intra-species killing, the humans came to understand their genetic and cerebral makeup was a more serious problem than their intramural wars over wealth, politics, sciences, philosophies, and religions. Indeed, they realized these battles came about *because* of the specific compositions of their brains and genes.

They came to understand their age-old behavior was embedded deeply into their souls, chiseled onto their genome and gray matter with the imprints of ancient Human Tribal Hierarchies.

The changes to save themselves from themselves were not easy to make. Some humans thought it an impossible task. Nonetheless, they altered the deadly course on which they were headed. In so doing, their greatest accomplishment was dislodging the Deadly Trinity from their makeup.

In the early part of the human's twenty-first century, the known part of the human genome and its associated behavioral underpinnings was quite small. At that time, the ability to alter the genome (and thus, the human) lay at the visible tip of the genetic iceberg. The part of this iceberg that was not visible, and unknown at that time, ultimately determined how the humans evolved. The changes they decided to make to their DNA and brain ultimately dictated their temperament, character, personality, disposition, humor, and individuality—even their morals and ethics.

Eventually, the latter-day humans began to address the profound issues of what they wanted to become, what they wanted to be like, how they wanted to look, and how they wanted to behave. After their genome was mapped and gene therapy became commonplace, as organ replacements became a routine matter, as synthetic skin, bones, and cartilages became a reality, as brain engineering became an accepted way to enhance the species, the humans embarked on a remarkable and astonishing journey to make their lives more pleasant and less antagonistic.

Beyond 2084

For the universe, change is the bedrock of its existence. On earth, time passes as change continues to play a role in the Cepees' life. They realize time is their never-ending partner. How do they deal with this everlasting cohort? Just as their ancestors did, with their natural zeal and curiosity, they use never-ending discoveries to take up much of their time. Habits, even in these advanced times, die hard.

With their flair for excelling in arts, sciences, and sports—it might appear the Cepees are contented beings. After all, their day-to-day life now takes place without war, revenge, and aggression.

Given this idyllic world, how do these earth-bound beings living beyond 2084 occupy their time? As told earlier, those who choose to keep their telomeres intact have a lot of time on their hands.

Even with their great minds and insatiable curiosities, the Cepees are not content with living in a sterile, secure world, one with no challenges. While they have become inoculated against and isolated from the past vicissitudes and transgressions of their forebears, they are still subject to boredom.

True to their nature, they have made changes to their behavior. They have turned their attention and creativity away from their minds and bodies. They have turned outward. They have begun to explore the universe in earnest. Not with limited telescopes and suppositional equations, but with physical journeys to distant bodies. First, they built and launched manned exploratory spaceships. Then, like their ancestors who centuries ago, set out on quests to discover and populate their world, the earth, the Cepees have set out on quests to discover and populate what they now believe to be their new world: the universe.

But this odyssey is not being undertaken just to quell curiosity and meet a challenge. The infinite Cepees have had to deal with the reality that their stay on earth is not infinite. Eventually, millions of years away, the core of the earth will cool, and transform earth's atmosphere to one that will not support photosynthesis. Besides, the sun itself has a limited life, even if measured in billions of years.

But what are a few billion years when viewed in the context of an infinite number of years? Thus, the story of the Cepee, and thus the story of the human, has only just begun.

How far have they reached into their new world? How have they gone about doing it? This chapter, like their stay on earth, is for another time.

More Human Than Cepee?

The latter-day human and the emerging Cepee traveled a long way on the Promethean path of altering nature and nurture. They remade themselves to fit their habitat needs, fulfill their desires, and of utmost importance, to save their societies. But in the end, the Cepees kept intact the mind, soul, and free will of the humans, because they never learned what these things were anyway. Neither brain scans nor genome mappings revealed the specific locations of morals, ethics, responsibilities, and a myriad of other characteristics loosely associated with the mind, the soul, and free will.

One point was uncontested. With few exceptions, the aggregate of human behavior, including the elusive mind, soul, and free will, existed for one reason: betterment of the race. Granted, mutant anomalies on the genome and the Law of the Instrument created serious obstacles to the safety and advancement of the *Homo sapiens* during their latter stay on earth. But in relation to the age of the human species and the everlasting life of the Cepees, the era of wide-spread use of weapons of mass destruction was little more than a short blip on a screen. In the long run, a small bit of noise in the human/Cepee spectrum of existence.

Nonetheless, given that the race was in great danger in the twenty-first century, it is fair to conclude the rapid evolution of the human to the Cepee was really nothing more than the manifestation of evolutionary principles: changes (mutations) and natural selection to improve and perpetuate the species. With one exception: The Cepees took control of many of the mutations by doing their own selections.

These changes led to—not a new species, but one that was dramatically altered. But then, the humans had been retooling their bodies and brains for centuries. The twenty-first and twenty-second centuries witnessed their speeding up the process.

In remaking themselves, it could be argued that humans bent nature to their will. But did they? After all, they never solved the mystery of free will, or for that matter, the nature of the universe itself. In addition, an increasingly accelerating universe of bodies moving away from earth meant the traces of the Big Bang would disappear. The red shift would be too elongated to be detected. These extraordinary beings might find themselves back in pre-Galileo days before their ancestors could look beyond the Milky Way.

But they did not confine themselves to an isolated earth, suspended in a cosmos filled with arcane dark energy, dark matter, and the elusive boson. What their ancestors did on earth, the Cepees are doing in the universe. Once again, they have embarked on journeys into what is largely unknown, a place of uncertainty and danger.

Regardless of the stunning discoveries they made with their telescopes, of brilliant inferences they made from red-shifted light waves, of findings they honed with experiments, they are awed by what they can now experience personally. They are as transfixed by the beauty and expanse of the universe as were their forebears who traveled across vast deserts, colossal forests, and seemingly never-ending prairies. For human and Cepee alike, awe is relative to past experience.

Beholding the galaxies they explore, they come to appreciate an idea of their distant cousin (Oscar Wilde) who offered that the visible is more mysterious than the invisible.

Notwithstanding their universal odyssey and their finding answers to many questions about themselves and the universe in which they live, many other questions remain unanswered. Did the humans remake themselves through their own volition, or were the changes guided by someone or something else? Was the Cepee race preordained? Was Darwinism a factor? Was God involved?

No one, be it the human or the Cepee, ever discovered the answers to these questions. The imponderables of the universe, the enigmas of the mind, the puzzles of science and religion remained as elusive to the Cepee as they had been to the human. And the Cepee knows this situation is the ultimate beauty of existence.[28]

> The most beautiful and most profound emotion we can experience is the sensation of the mystical. It is the sower of all true science. He to whom this emotion is a stranger, who can no longer wonder and stand rapt in awe, is as good as dead. To know that what is impenetrable to us really exists, manifesting itself as the highest wisdom and the most radiant beauty which our dull faculties can

comprehend only in their most primitive forms—this knowledge, this feeling is at the center of true religiousness.

The Cepee closes the Human Archives. Once again, he reflects on what he has learned: *At times, it seems my ancestors learned so much, yet knew so little. But they knew enough to alter the dangerous course they were on. Because of what they learned, because of what they came to understand, I came to be. I carry their gift, their legacy.*

---

[1] E. O. Wilson, *The Social Conquest of Earth* (New York: Liveright, 2012), 297, Kindle edition. loc. 4777.

[2] Earl Rosenthal, *The Palace of Charles V in Granada* (Princeton, NJ: Princeton University Press, *1985*), n.p.

[3] Michael S. Gazzaniga, *The Ethical Brain* (New York: Dana Press, 2005), 71. (Quote from Corneliu E. Giurgea, 1970).

[4] David Papineau, ed., *Western Philosophy* (New York: Oxford University Press, 2004), 71.

[5] As stated at the beginning of this book, I use male gender because males have been on the center stage of human human aggression, one of the subjects of this narrative.

[6] Gazzaniga, *The Ethical Brain*, 72.

[7] Microsoft's Encarta Reference Library.

[8] L. W. H. Hull, *History and Philosophy of Science*, sourced from Uyless Black's notebook without further attributions. I make an exception in this note to reference conventions and standards of endnotes. I came across this thought during a 1962 lecture at the University of New Mexico. The course was "The History of Science." The lecturer furnished Hull's quote and source. I was intrigued by the idea behind this quote. I remain intrigued.

[9] Papineau, *Western Philosophy*, 49. Decartes discussed this idea in his *Meditations*.

[10] Microsoft's Encarta Reference Library.

[11] Gazzaniga, *The Ethical Brain*, 92-93.

[12] Rodrigo Quian Quiroga, Itzhak Fried, and Christof Koch, "Brain Cells for Grandmother," *Scientific American*, February 2013, 35.

[13] Ibid., 34.

[14] Ibid., 35

[15] Carl Zimmer, "The Neurobiology of the Self," *Scientific American*, November 2005, 93-101.

[16] This case study on self and (more generally) on being out of sorts when one's head becomes a target for an iron projectile is cited in many journals and articles. My quote here is also from Gazzaniga, 96,98.

[17] Microsoft's Encarta Reference Library.

[18] Ibid.

[19] Ibid.

[20] See Chapter 6 for the details and references about this subject.

[21] Alan Lightman, "Our Place in the Universe?" *Harper's*, December 2012, 34.

[22] Michael S. Turner, "The Universe," *Scientific American*, September 2009, 43.

[23] Katherine Harmon, "Shattered Ancestry," *Scientific American*, February 2013, 42-49.

[24] Ibid.

[25] Ibid.

[26] Leonard Roy Frank, *Quotationary*, 430.

[27] Richard Dawkins and Frances Collins, "God vs. Science," debate between Dawkins and Collins, *Time*, November 13, 2006. This idea, spoken by Mr. Dawkins, is taken from p. 55 of this debate.

[28] Lincoln Barnett, *The Universe and Dr. Einstein* (New York: Bantam, 1980), 108. This quote is from Albert Einstein.

EPILOGUE

Less than a century for humans to make significant progress eliminating pathological aggression from our makeup? Less than two centuries to become a significantly altered race? If these times seem too short for you, extend them. The timeline does not matter. Whether we like it or not, we are on the road leading to a spectacularly altered human being. Most likely it will not be a new species, but by the next century, a decidedly different person will emerge from what we are today. The startling progress made in genetics, brain engineering, and body and organ replacements might make the timelines pointing toward 2084 and 2150 seem modest.

Are humans evil? The Prologue of this book claims we are capable of evil acts. The Prologue also claims we are capable of acts of selflessness and compassion. Altruism is part of our makeup and has species-enhancing attributes. Altruism, even friendliness, often translates into cooperation, which is important to any species competing for survival.

Will humans accept the self-change scenarios described in this book? Over 40 percent of adult citizens in America believe humans appeared on earth in their present form within the last 10,000 years.[1] If they accept this idea, which is based principally on religious beliefs, will they accept the idea of a perpetual existence on earth in lieu of a heaven or other after-life paradises?

Will there be terrorists' nuclear and biochemical attacks that serve to break the camel's back against human self-change? If this scenario seems too far-fetched to you, discount it, but I am convinced we humans will make changes to our DNA and brains in attempts to quell Homo sapiens' genetic and cerebral underpinnings of pathological aggression. I used the fictional wars in the Middle East and the fictional assault on Washington, D.C. as a tool to make my case about our fixation on violent intra-species aggression and our penchant for revenge.

A so-called camel's back may not be needed. We have already begun the journey to re-make ourselves. The extraordinary human self-change wonders described in Chapter 11 represent a stunning (yet conservative) view of what lies ahead for our species.

Will the changes lead to a radically altered species? Will they lead to a new species? Will meaningless aggression be culled from our behavior? Will the genetic and epigenetic discoveries we are making about ourselves lead to schools that no longer have security guards posted at their doors? Will our race succeed in creating leaders who are dedicated to feeding their helpless underlings instead of feeding their own egos? Will our race evolve to one where contentious opinions about religions do not cause beheadings? Or will our race find itself unable to cope with the problems it alone has created? Will our race eventually self-destruct?

It is clear that science and religion need to work more closely together and become more accepting of each other's views. It is also evident that religions should practice what they preach, and religious factions should seek ways to avoid killing one another. We intelligent humans carry out amazingly unintelligent actions against ourselves. In the long-run, these actions are little more than self-defeating rationalizations for our own shortcomings.

Many new medical inventions and discoveries have paved the way for humans to change and create a much better world in which to live. Let us hope that instead of ensnaring ourselves in self-destructive cycles of aggression and revenge, we can move forward, leaving the Deadly Trinity in the dust.

It is painfully clear we humans must work more closely together to find ways to preserve and foster ourselves and our cultures. We should pursue these efforts…yes, aggressively. As I state in the final chapter, I believe we can remake ourselves, yet preserve those traits that make us human. We need not fret about the mysterious nature of free will, the soul, the mind, and the miracle of memory. We need only to respect these wonderfully puzzling aspects of human nature. We do not need to change them, but perhaps tweak them a bit.

This epilogue has posed several questions that our race must answer. Who knows the answers to these questions? Of course, that would be the Cepee, but we can also add our opinions to the Cepee's wise observations. As events transpire, I will be posting my ideas from my email account. I would like to know your views as well. You can reach me at UBlack7510@aol.com.

———————————

[1] Jahnabi Barooah, "46% Americans Believe In Creationism According To Latest Gallup Poll," June 6, 2012, http://huffingtonpost.com/2012/06/05/americans-believe-in-creationism_n_1571127.html.

The Rules of Life

The Aggression Tools Cycle
The successful use of a weapon leads to the invention of a more powerful weapon.

The Aggression Cycle
The successful execution of an aggressive, violent act leading to more aggressive and violent acts.

The Autocatalytic Process
A positive feedback cycle wherein a process reinforces another process, which in turn, reinforces the first process, on and on.

The Creeping Momentum Principle
A gradual expansion of what begins as a modest endeavor, therefore escaping notice and concern, until the effect of the endeavor renders it too big to be ignored and sometimes too pervasive for its momentum to be reversed.

The Deadly Trinity Truism
A collective term describing the interplay of The Law of the Instrument, The Aggression Cycle, and The Revenge Cycle.

The Disproportionate Impulse Effect
An effect in which the primitive part of the brain drives a human to commit an act before the more recent gray matter takes control. Often, the impulsive act causes damage to the person or others. The typical response to this effect is "I lost my head."

The Disproportionate Ratio Effect
A ratio defined as n:m, where the value of n is very small and the value of m is very large.

The Drugstore Terrorist Syndrome
A phrase to describe the ongoing bandwagon of killers and terror-

ists, based on a modern incident when bottles of Tylenol were laced with poison.

The Equal Extermination Opportunity (EEO) Factor

An equal opportunity for anyone to be assassinated by a terrorist, regardless of one's beliefs, skin color, or cultural preference.

The Excessive-Plastic-Surgery-Surprise Effect

The sensation of glancing at one's face in the mirror for the first time after plastic surgery and encountering a stranger.

The Exponential Consequences Curve

The consequences of an action in which the consequences are far greater (non-linear) than any one predicted (doomsayers aside).

The Fear of Farming Syndrome:

An acute bias against tilling the soil in a mine-littered field. Medical studies have confirmed this disposition is not an illness but a syndrome. It is prevalent in the minds of many people who live in third-world countries. It is absent in the minds of citizens who reside in the countries that manufacture land mines—and coincidentally have no land mines in their soil.

The Feel Good Law

A phrase to describe a human who will disregard almost any taboo, law, ruling, or prohibition in order to feel good. And in accordance with The Immediacy Syndrome, to feel good as quickly as possible.

The Geographically Undesirable Law

A potential attacker will not go to the trouble of assaulting a potential victim if the victim is located in an inconvenient place in relation to the potential attacker.

The Graveyard Shift Law

Not to be confused with a work schedule. Rather, the shifting of priorities to implement a long-known solution to a long-known problem, but only after the problem has resulted in unnecessary damage, perhaps loss of life.

The Hearse Carriage Effect
As more killers jump on the bandwagon to copy other killers' actions, more corpses are piled into hearses for delivery to the local cemetery. These bandwagon killings are often accentuated by the Autocatalytic Effect.

The Homogenization Factor
A term to describe a homogeneous world in which people eat the same foods, wear the same kinds of clothes, read the same books and magazines, listen to the same music and radio shows, watch the same movies and TV programs.

The Ignorant Therefore Doctrinaire Syndrome
A common human behavioral trait in which a human who is devoid of any knowledge on a subject holds an unyielding—and often belligerent—opinion on the subject

The Immediacy Syndrome
The desire for an immediate fulfillment of a wish, a trait common to the humans' prehistory forebears based on necessity, and all too common in modern humans, based on desire.

The Innumeracy Syndrome
Those who lack a basic knowledge of mathematics, are unable to use figures in calculations, and do not consider 0 to be a number.

The Lag Effect Law
A time lapse (called the lag window) between the occurrence of an action and when the consequences of the action are revealed

The Law of the Instrument
Exemplified by a child with a hammer who looks for something to pound.

The Monks Do Not Dissolve Monasteries Rule
A rule in which the name of the rule defines the rule itself. Therefore, here is an example. Monks do not dissolve their own monasteries. To do so, would put them out of work. In fact, monks attempt to build additional monasteries in order to enhance their jobs and add another layer of hierarchy to their organizational

structure. Also see bureaucrats, the military, Congress, banks, business, et al.

The Preventative Attack Cycle
Attacking someone before being (possibly) attacked by this someone.

The Pride Anomaly
A person who is proud of an act or situation to which this person has made no contribution. This anomaly disappears when a person changes, "I am proud of your success." to "I am proud for your success."

The Revenge Cycle
The desire of a person to attack anyone who has previously attacked that person. The cycle is then reversed, with the attacker becoming the attacked.

The Threshold Lowering Syndrome
An act by a human, who by committing the act, makes it easier for this person or another person to repeat the act. This term is derived from the psychologist, B. F. Skinner and The Skinner Effect: A behavior or state of affairs which tend to reinforce and perpetuate the same behavior or state of affairs.

The Unintended Consequences Law
An action that yields results different from those expected. The consequences of the action may be far greater (non-linear) than any one predicted, as in The Exponential Result of Unintended Consequences Phenomenon.

The Unlike-Dislike Axiom
Anything that is dissimilar to a human's expectations or customs is suspect and disliked.

Key Acronyms in *2084 and Beyond*

ASSES: **A**lterations to **S**ave **S**ociety from our **E**gregious **S**elves

EGO: **E**nhancements to **G**lorify **O**urselves

ILLS: **I**ncurable **L**atent **L**abile **S**icknesses

SANE: **S**upplying **a** **N**ew **E**go

INTERVIEW WITH A QURAN
SCHOLAR AND CONTRARY VIEWS

The following dialogue took place with this writer and Sohaib Nazeer Sultan through the Internet (September 15, 2004). Sultan is the Muslim Life Coordinator and Chaplin at Princeton University. He is a graduate of the Hartford Theological Seminary, earning a master's degree in Islamic Studies & Christian-Muslim Relations. He is the author of *The Koran for Dummies*, part of the well-known series published by Wiley Publishing Inc. He is also the author of *The Qur'an and Sayings of Prophet Muhammad: Selection Annotated and Explained* (Skylight Paths Publishing).

I have made a few edits to this text for purposes of readability. I have been careful to keep the context of the questions and answers intact.

Following this interview are excerpts from two commentators who have a different opinion than Mr. Sultan on the issue of Islamic extremism.

Uyless Black: It is my understanding the Koran does not sanction the killing of civilians, non-combatants, women, and children. Is there a passage in the Koran that so states?

Sohaib Nazeer Sultan: In general, the Quran provides some basic outlines and broad moral teachings, which are then often fleshed out by Prophetic sayings and deeds. In chapter 2 of the Quran when the first passage comes about the permissibility of war within the context of self-defense, the verse says, "But do not transgress the sacred bounds, for God loves not the transgressors." This verse clearly indicates that even just war has certain legal bounds that cannot be crossed. From Prophet Muhammad's sayings, we learn that one of these bounds is not to kill women, children, and non-combatants.

Also, in chapter 22 of the Quran the very reason given for the permissibility of war is in defense of those innocent people who are killed and driven out of their homes. As such, by logical conclusion Islamic ethics of war cannot possibly permit the violation of basic human rights.

Also, capital punishment is prescribed for those who commit murder in the Quran, so this shows you how severe of a crime it is to take the life of innocents. This is also backed up by a verse in Chapter 5 that says, like the Torah, "killing one innocent life is like killing all of humanity, and saving one life is like saving all of humanity."

Lastly, in chapter 25 of the Quran, it says that among the worst of sins is the taking of an innocent life without any just cause. From these verses and other supporting Prophetic sayings, the scholars have concluded that taking innocent life even in just war is outside the ethical bounds of warfare in Islam.

Black: The Koran, chapter 47, verse 4, "When ye meet the Unbelievers in battle, smite at their necks; At length, when ye have thoroughly subdued them, bind a bond firmly on them: thereafter is the time for either generosity or ransom: Until the war lays down its burdens." I take this passage to mean the victor has a choice about how to handle captives?

Sultan: Yes, you are correct in your analysis. I must also point out that the Quran always encourages the way of mercy rather than revenge. For example, in the verse that prescribes capital punishment for a murderer, the Quran gives the option to [a] victim's family to take some other compensation instead of capital punishment for the murderer and encourages this mercy as the higher path.

Also, from the Prophetic practice we learn that prisoners of war can be released with non-monetary compensation. For example, in one instance the Prophet asked the prisoners of war to teach his companions how to read and write as [a] way of getting their release.

Also, in chapter 9 of the Quran, it says that if a Pagan comes to you (writer: "you" means the Muslims) seeking protection, then give him protection and take him to a secure location. So Muslims are not allowed to kill a prisoner of war for no just reason; it is only when this person is clearly a threat to the security of the Muslim community or has committed some egregious war crimes.

Black: It appears the Koran places limits on this matter. I quote chapter 7, verse 48, "...pain of the sentence be less than the pain inflicted by the murderer upon his victim." I take this passage to mean the Koran places an emphasis on mercy?

Sultan: Yes.

Black: A fatwa is issued by a respected Islamic authority, a trained scholar, about an interpretation of Islamic law. Bin Laden is hardly an Islamic scholar; he is a road engineer by training. Yet, he issued his own fatwa. Is this permitted?

Sultan: Osama bin Laden and his types have no authority to issue fatwas or religious opinions, simply because they have not been trained to do so. It is like practicing medicine without a license.

Black: I have also read that Muhammad directed Muslims not to kill any soldier who had turned his back to battle. It appears his remonstrance describes a soldier who is in retreat as well as a deserter. However, I cannot find a passage in the Koran that so states? Do you know of one?

Sultan: Once again, this is a teaching you won't find specifically in the Quran but generally referred to when it says 'not to transgress the sacred bounds...' This teaching of not killing one from the back is found in the Prophetic example in which Prophet Muhammad clearly forbade it, and also there is an instance in which the Prophet reprimanded one of his companions for killing a retreating soldier during one of the battles.

Comments from Ayaan Hirsi Ali

Hirsi Ali is a known critic of Islam, and has this to say about Islamic faith and violence:

> I think fortunately the majority of Muslims today will not commit acts of terrorism. But to argue that there is nothing in Islam that leads to violence—that would be a weak argument to a false argument, because if you define *Islam* as "submission to the will of Allah," then you find out what that submission means...you find out that...the sixth obligation is to convert others to Islam, first by peaceable means, then by violent means.

> So when Islam is violent—you can't argue...that it's not a violent religion. Then you will say, "What about Judaism? What about Christianity?" Now, adherents of these religions over the centuries have been pacified to understand and accept the separation of the divine and the worldly...Nowhere in the Muslim world has that profound pacification of Islam...taken place. And I think that is the difference.

Comments from Charles Krauthammer

Charles Krauthammer is a columnist, known for his conservative views, and has this to say about Islamic faith and violence:

> Hamas is fighting not to create a 23rd Arab state but, as its charter explains, to recover "an Islamic Waqf." Meaning? Territory claimed under the Islamic precept that "any land the Muslims have conquered by force...during the time of [Islamic] conquests" more than a millennium ago belongs to Muslims forever because "the Muslims consecrated these lands to Muslim generations until the Day of Judgment."

> This declaration includes a substantial part of Europe, including Spain, which was conquered by the Muslims in the eighth century and taken by the Christians in the fifteenth century.

I thank these three learned scholars and journalists for their contributions to this discussion. Permit this writer to offer a few thoughts as well.

These debates are important and must be amplified to the general public. But in consonance with the theme of this book, they represent external wrappings around what actually matters: Ancient DNA gene strands and brain components dictate our behavior. Our fixation on external factors camouflages our primeval disposition. We disguise our real reasons for our aggression, because we have not had the courage to face the fact that they are not based on some noble ideology.

We have come to disguise our true nature, that of survival, in the cloth of various wardrobes such as patriotism, religion, language, and nationality.

For the victims of the World Trade Center assaults, the London subway explosions, the Madrid train attacks, the Boston Marathon, ad nausem, we can refute or support the claims of experts such as Sultan, Hirsi Ali, and Krauthammer. But the fact remains the bombing victims remain dead.

Religious idealism, religious dogma, take your pick. Political idealism, political chauvinism, take your pick. They all come face to face with the reality of human nature, which transcends these human veneers, to shake hands with the Deadly Trinity.

---

[1] "Ideas and Consequences," Aspen Institute's Aspen Ideas Festival of 2007. *The Atlantic Monthly*, October 2007, 54.

[2] Charles Krauthammer, "Actually, The Middle East Is Our Crisis Too," Time, August 7, 2006, 31.

ACKNOWLEDGMENTS

Several authors and their works are cited on numerous occasions in this book. They are Jared Diamond (*Guns, Germs, and Steel, Collapse,* and *The World Until Yesterday*), Konrad Lorenz (*On Aggression*), Philip M. Tierno Jr. (*The Secret Life of Germs*), Richard Wrangham and Dale Peterson (*Demonic Males*), Eric Schlosser (*Fast Food Nation*), Michael Scheuer (*Imperial Hubris*), Mahmood Mamdani (*Good Muslim, Bad Muslim*), and Edward O. Wilson (*The Future of Life* and *The Social Conquest of Earth*). William Langewiesche, a remarkably capable journalist and fine writer, is also cited several times in this book.

I make reference to the DNA series of videos produced by the Films for the Humanities and Sciences about work being done by the Howard Hughes Medical Institute, Alfred P. Sloan Foundation—a wonderfully rendered explanation of research on our genes. I cite *The 9/11 Commission Report* a number of times as well.

George Orwell deserves special mention, as I base part of my book title (*2084 and Beyond*) on his *1984* classic. I have taken a different slant from that of Mr. Orwell about the long-term state of the human race, but I mirror his theme on the subject of perpetual war.

* * *

This book pays a special acknowledgment to five men: Abraham Maslow, Konrad Lorenz, Jared Diamond, E. O. Wilson, and George Orwell. I studied Abraham Maslow during my early days in the U.S. Navy. His hierarchy of needs concept stuck with me and led me to create the Human Tribal Hierarchy. I modified Maslow's hierarchy with my own views about human behavior and listed the "rungs" of his original hierarchy in Chapter 2. I learned about Lorenz and Diamond later. Lorenz's concepts are fundamental to my Threshold

Lowering Syndrome, as well as the aggression and revenge cycles. Diamond's ideas are found in many parts of this book. My "geographical roll of the dice" catch-phrase is based on the research of Diamond, as is the Autocatalytic Process. E. O. Wilson's research on tribal hierarchies and human aggression substantiated my views on these subjects. As I mentioned, part of the book's title is based on George Orwell's book.

The great achievements of several of the authors mentioned above came from their research in the field and their conducting a rigorous, disciplined analysis of their investigations. My writing the essays and reports that led to this book came from my long-held interests in human nature, which led to my undergraduate work in psychology; as well as my life experiences, while reading and learning from those mentioned here, as well as others. Over the past fifty years or so, I have come to a number of conclusions about how we humans deal with one another, many of which are reflected in this book. As examples: the concept of tribes for each human endeavor (religious, political, military, etc.), the principle of tribal hierarchies, the dual and often contradictory aspects of human behavior, the propensity toward violent, pointless aggression and revenge, and the predisposition to kill our own species without regard to our own survival.

I am gratified that most of my views, ones of observation and experience, have been corroborated by the rigor of academic analysis and peer review by others.

* * *

The essays that led to *2084 and Beyond* are titled *The Deadly Trinity*. I made the title change after friends, colleagues, and reviewers conveyed to me that they viewed the word "trinity" to be about the religious trinity. It is not, as I used the term as "a group of three." However, I understood their point. Also, as mentioned in the readers' comments section, as I was working on this book, I realized the time lines for events unfolding were not detailed enough. Consequently, using 1984 as a benchmark, I expanded the narrative to include other important dates, one being 2084. Because this date is an important focal point in the book, I decided to use it as part of the book's title.

* * *

My team (separate contractors, but still my "team") continues to come through on my behalf. Holly Waters, Beth Waters, Alvart Badalian, Sylvia Gann Mahoney, Dawn Hall, Susan Britt, and Jerry McClain often corrected my wayward prose and visual creations, and also offered sound advice on other parts of this book and other works. Bill Ellefloot has been a great supporter in working with me on mailing lists, booth displays, and brochures, as well as offering personal encouragement of my work. They never fail to improve my original composition.

Readers' Comments

I have discontinued the practice of placing readers' comments on the back cover of my books. They extol the virtues of the book and the wisdom and wit of the author. I know of no book that has a reader's negative comments on its back cover. Of course not, why would an author include such a note? It would be self-defeating. Besides, these comments stoke the writer's ego (I am not immune to praise), but they do not give the reader much meaningful information about the book. My approach is to place the comments, warts and all, in a section at the back of the book, as you see here.

During the time I was writing the material that lead to this book, I sent it to a list of readers whom I had asked to read several of my essays about the subject. After I placed some of these essays online, I received more comments in the form of e-mails or comments on my blog, as well as a few telephone conversations. Some came from readers I did not know. I also received comments from a selected list of readers for my more recent essays that became part of this book. I have included some of these comments below. They do not constitute all the responses, but they do represent typical examples of the feedback I received.

These comments do not have names attached. In some instances, I do not know who the sender is, as my material was later sent to unknown readers who responded with an e-mail address, or from a less-identifiable blog response.

If I do have names, for privacy purposes, I have deleted the name of the sender. If you would like to know the sender, and if I have his/her identification (I have domain names for most of these e-mails), I will contact the sender and ask for his/her permission. In this way, you can also verify the accuracy (pro and con) of this correspondence.

Unless a person included something personal, I have altered no words (or grammar) in this material. I have used **** in place of profanity or other words a reader might find offensive. On a few occasions, I must substitute a person's name with a noun or pronoun, in which case I place brackets around my change. Any notes I add are also surrounded by brackets.

I have made the text the same font size and type and changed minor formats. In some cases, an e-mail was several pages. I took the liberty of cutting some of the paragraphs. Both ego inflator and ego deflator passages were deleted. Some readers sent me more than one communiqué. As space permitted, I included them in this section.

I look forward to your thoughts about my book and the ideas from my readers.

++++

One hundred fifty years to become a different race is farfetched. Your emerging race could not pass genes and interbreed with current humans, and that's what you suggest. I doubt that will happen in just a few generations. [I was lax using the words "new or different race" in three phrases in these essays. I have corrected this oversight in this book, and clarified the relationships of the devolving human with the human's evolving successor.]

++++

When I first looked at the manuscript, I said, "Futuristic! This isn't the kind of book I usually read." Could I ever become used to all of these acronyms for things I have never heard of. I had to tell you that because after reading Part One, I am so surprised to find your book intriguing.

++++

I truly hope you publish this manuscript. [He was reading parts of the essays.] I think it is everything a satire should be. [The final manuscript took out many passages dealing with satire. I thought my writing was attempting to do too many things.] You engage the reader immediately in the Prologue and make him/her (me) want to find out more about why the world as we know it came to an end.

[The Prologue in the book was reformatted to help clarify points. But with the exception of the Christian cross and the Klu Klux Klan cross sentences, it remains almost the same as it was in the original essays that led to *2084*.] You have used your sense of humor to lighten the mood throughout what I've read of the manuscript. [Although I did eliminate much satire, I hope I have retained enough to provide a change of pace to what are admittedly less than joyful themes.]

++++

I never cease to be amazed at your talents. ...You should submit to *Atlantic Monthly*! [I made some inquiries to *Atlantic Monthly* and received polite rebuffs. In spite of their rejection of my work and my resulting ego deflation, I continue to subscribe to this fine magazine.]

++++

I am working my way through *Heaven on Earth* [the initial working title]. Very clever and well written, but somehow it troubles me a bit. Will try to figure out why and let you know.

++++

I am getting a little deeper into your essays. My first impression is astonishment. You put a hell of a lot of work into this thing! It really is quite impressive. I also like how you are using the literary device of lectures, as well as the third person perspective for analysis. I am really enjoying the read. It also has a little Douglas Adams - Restaurant at the end of the Universe feel to it. [I have deleted these lectures. The length was becoming to resemble a Thomas Wolfe manuscript in its size. I made the decision to break the material into three books. The other two, *The Cepee Dialogues* and *Coming to You Live from the Dead*, are finished, and awaiting my decision about their future.]

++++

I laughed out loud when I read the "side effects" [of this essay.] We're all instructed to read the fine print regarding side effects for a medication.

++++

[This correspondence came to me from a literary agent working out of London.]

Thank you for taking the time to send your mss. to me for consideration. It's obvious that you're a good writer, but as a work of fiction, I think there are a number of problems with your mss. It seems that you're trying to write fictional stories in the same style that you've written the 30+ non-fiction books that you've already published, which makes sense - you've found a writing formula that works, so why not stick with it? Still, I don't think it works when you try to cross over into fiction. For example, you coin numerous terms, e.g. Save Society from our Egregious Selves (ASSES), Incurable Latent Labile Sicknesses (ILLS), and changed entity, programmed for extended eons (CEPEEs) to name but a few. Whilst this works for books about emerging technologies or academic publications, i.e. coining new terms as a way of making a name for yourself, it doesn't work for fiction because it actually distracts readers from the story. With fiction, it's more a unique turn of phrase than a series of acronyms which people remember.

[I am not alone in wanting to make a name for myself. But I was confused why the agent would come to the conclusion that my coining terms was my way of making a name for myself. I thought about Aldous Huxley's *Brave New World* and his coining terms which I assume this agent thought were acceptable, such as Fordism, free martins, Arch-Community-Songster, etc. I also considered George Orwell's *Nineteen Eighty-Four*, and his terms of ingsoc, doublethink, Newspeak, memory hole, and others.]

[Modesty aside, I think my EGO, ILLS, SANE, and ASSES acronyms stand at least as well as the terms invented by these writers. Acronyms whose letters from an *existing* word that is *integral* to and *reinforcing* of the words in the phrase itself are not all that easy to create. It's not difficult to create, say, PETA, NATO, or radar—all shortened forms of more than one word. But none of these sets of letters were words found in the dictionary *before* they were invented as pronounceable acronyms.]

[My four "coins" disliked by this agent form words that are closely associated with and reinforcing of the meaning of longer sequence of words. *Ego*, *ills*, *sane*, and *asses* are in the dictionary. In this book, they also form acronyms whose dictionary definitions reinforce the meaning of the words in the four phrases. Try it, and get back to me.]

And lastly, when I pitch a book to the author, it needs to be clear what genre it falls in and what its target market is likely to be. Neither of these were clear to me when reading your book. These would need to be more clearly defined by your narrative.

[Given the extensive research (and endnotes), this agent should have known,—even with the Cepees' presence—that this material was (is) a nonfiction work.]

++++

I was overwhelmed by your insights and philosophical musing on the past, present, and the possibilities of what the future holds for the planet earth and its current inhabitants. Your writing not only connected with me, I think you defined the phrase "Preaching to the Choir." Each chapter read as if it were my own personal hymnal.

As I was reading, I would ponder your thoughts, be totally amused by your humor, and want to mark it so I could return to it later. However, I did not want to put marks on or highlight the manuscript, so I put a sticky note on the page I wanted to save for future reference. When I finished the book, I realized there was a yellow sticky note about every 5th page. (I have a lot of rereading to do and reference points for friends.)

I have really wrestled on how to convey my thoughts upon receiving your work and your invitation to read it without sounding unduly maudlin. But I shall try. I thought the book was excellent but, as I stated above, it fit my thinking, personality and view of how I perceive life to be.

++++

I finished your manuscript. It is truly a great creation. I will be delighted to write a review for use by your agent. I hope your agent reads it and understands it.

++++

I love the mainframe term, and then read your definition of same. ...I am more amazed than ever with your mind flow, your ability to convey your story and your vocabulary!!!!!!!! [sic], [I promised to retain all readers' verse as written. I was tempted to delete these exclamation points, but chose a sic instead.] Thank you for sharing your wisdom and your human-ness. Yes, the book was "heavy" in weight, and I considered that to return to the near beginning and read it in its entirety, I could lay it on a table. How novel! [In its original form, it was a bit heavy.]

...The whole steroid thing, to mention just one topic. I liked that I laughed out loud a few times in what I read of yours yesterday.

++++

I would have liked to know a little bit about the world the Cepee's [the successors to the humans] were now caretakers of...did they resolve the problems relating to global warming, pollution, etc...were some Cepee's related to physical work-type functions while others did Sage-type duties...in other words, how did they resolve class issues, or did they not have any of those...it doesn't appear that sex was a part of their existence (what a shame!!) so why would looks really matter, or self-image for that matter...in a constructed and controlled world would it not be possible to determine exactly how many Cepee's of various functions were necessary to adequately perform their mission and limit production to that number, thereby eliminating the need for a Sage as a Cepee never dies or needs replacement?...would it be possible to have a "lemon" that just couldn't be fixed. [In the final manuscript, the subject of sex was addressed.]

One final thought...the driving impetus to the creation of the Cepee race was simultaneous nuclear terrorist attacks [I added biochemical attacks after this reader had read a draft.]...it occurred to me that the ability to create this kind of change rests on the survival of the technological infrastructure necessary to accomplish it...it is quite possible that any attack, terrorist or otherwise, of this magnitude could actually doom civilization by collapsing the components of global economic and technological cooperation that is a prerequisite to effect this change and result in the next dark ages, somewhat akin to the fall of Rome...in that case we would just have to see if the survivors would reject technology as they reorganized their world...and in that respect, the terrorists would "win."

++++

This really is an intriguing and largely successful effort to synthesize a staggering amount of information developed in the scientific context in a broader environment. As you will see later, I don't find some of it developed enough, but it is an excellent effort.

One of your strengths as a writer is your ability to do dialogue, even if upon occasion I think you stretch a little to be humorous. Can easily see why you want the humor, as heavy as the general topic is, but I think humor is the hardest thing to write, and one has to be careful not to get over the top. [As mentioned, most of the humor (as well as dialogue) was moved to two other books]

I think one thing that will give potential publishers cause for some concern is the complexity of it all, not only the topics, but also the intricate construction. Can see why you want to use the Cepee dialogues and the Saturday Night Live About the Dead shows to get in material, and humor, that would be tedious in the regular narrative, but they can be a little distracting. For the moment, I would leave them as is (except maybe to see if there is a better title for Saturday Night.....) and see what a publisher says; I may be wrong. [I took his advice and moved this material to the other books. I also changed the "Saturday Night" title to "Coming to You Live, from the Dead."]

++++

Probably because you wrote different chapters at different times, I think the timing gets garbled in places. You seem to say things happened in the earlier part of the 21st century at one point, and at the end of that century in another. You might want to put together a timeline for your own purposes to keep straight, and if it is helpful, include it as a text illustration. [I took this reader's advice and created the timeline.]

++++

Is there really a "Howard Hughes Medical Institute" [There is, and doing good things.] or is this a convention to get stuff in that you need?

++++

As your afterword suggests, there is nothing totally new under the sun. While there is some passing resemblance to *Brave New World* and *1984*, there is even more similarity to some of my uncle's stuff [name withheld], Bradbury, Asimov, maybe Ursula Le Guin. What they tend to do is "parallel universe" constructs, that allow them to manipulate variables to see what difference it makes. One example is my uncle's (name withheld), which is a 1980 collection of a lot of earlier stuff. I am not suggesting that you try to incorporate this stuff, but rather that you might want to indicate that you know it exists, in your Afterword.

++++

I really enjoy the Dialogues. [The dialogues are now in the book, *The Cepee Dialogues*. As mentioned, I have not decided what to do with this piece of writing.]

++++

I scanned [your material] *today*. It fits together so well and has so much depth to it. A person could read it a dozen times and still find missed gems.

I am a true believer that you have a one-of-kind book that will have an impact on the philosophical thought of humans; however, it will take time for a publisher to comprehend that he/she has a unique book that will someday be viewed as a pristine review of the past and a preview of future options for humans to survive. Your book is written in a style lightened with parody, satire, and irony.

++++

Hmm. It's very eclectic.

++++

My reaction to the concept of the Cepee as the successors to the human race is that it is a less likely scenario than simple, sudden extinction or devolution based on our propensity to overuse and abuse our resources as well as each other. I don't believe nature is sentient, but I do believe God created a system that self-corrects.

If we survive the next 25-50 years pretty much intact, I would assume we had solved the major terrorist problems and perhaps could look forward to an age of enlightenment where humans are generally allowed the freedoms we enjoy in the west (and take for granted) and have found a way to meet basic needs for most populations while suppressing the dictatorial tendencies inherent in too many of our species.

I think the power of the species to corrupt and misuse all gifts would not allow the Cepee to evolve in a positive manner. It's difficult for me to think of a single invention, discovery, or development that we haven't found a way to abuse. If we were to develop a prototype Cepee, the military and the porn industry would immediately create super warriors and whores to destroy our enemies as we **** our own brains out. Pretty negative...sorry.

I do look forward to your version of the future. It sounds more positive even if it doesn't include any of my genetic material.

++++

[A reader responds again.]

Well, I was able to spend about an hour or so on the Cepees last evening and to my surprise I found that we are on the same page in many respects.

After our discussion of Konrad Lorenz's *On Aggression* I came away believing you thought it was possible to overcome our evolutionary roots and temper our aggressive impulses as a result of reason and civilization. Now I'm not so sure.

I believe the only way to rise above a successful survival strategy (aggression) is to wait for evolution to catch up with the environmental changes that make it less desirable (if that ever happens). Anything else is just putting lipstick on a pig. We cover it over with social graces, laws, and moral imperatives but in reality our reptilian brain isn't having any of it.

I think I understand your position on religion and agree with it. Christians, Jews, and Muslims, to name just a few, all espouse a peace-loving philosophy that has led to more deaths than anything else mankind has ever created (to date).

++++

I have read quite a bit of your tome! What a lot of work and what a lot of creativity. I find it very humorous, in your particular brand of humor. Do you have a publisher? I think your book would create quite a stir in the literary world. Also, you should send a copy to George Lucas--a movie done well (is that an oxymoron?) would be a blockbuster!

++++

[After the London subway bombings]:

Your manuscript needs to be published as its predictions are unfolding much like you have indicated they would. The way you have adumbrated the results, it is so logical that your predictions have to occur. Would people change if he/she knew for sure that destruction was coming?

BIBLIOGRAPHY

Ade, P.A.R., N. Aghanim, C. Armitage-Caplan et al. (Planck Collaboration). "Planck 2013 Results 1. Overview of Products and Scientific Results-Table 9." March 22, 2013. "Planck 2013 Results Papers." and "First Planck Results: the Universe Is Still Weird and Interesting." March 31, 2013. *Astronomy and Astrophysics* (submitted). arXiv:1303.5062. Bibcode:2013arXiv1303...5062P.

Allen, Scott. "Widespread Abnormalities Stump Scientists. Pesticides, Parasites among Explanations." *The Boston Globe*, July 28, 1997, B01.

"Al Qaeda May Have 'Briefcase' Nukes." *The Spokesman Review*, March 22, 2004, A1.

The al Qaeda Training Manual. http://www.usdoj.gov/ag/manualpart1_1.pdf.

Anderson, Fred, and Andrew Cayton. *The Dominion of War.* New York: Viking, 2005.

"Ann Sexton." *Time*, September 24, 2007, 17. http://www.poemhunter.com/best-poems/anne-sexton/as-it-was-written/.

Arendt, Hannah. Cecil Rhodes' Quote. *The Origins of Totalitarianism*, in Frank. *Quotationary*. 392.

Argano, Tim, and Michael R. Gordon. "Sectarian Strife Again Imperils Future of Iraq." *The New York Times*, March 20, 2013, A10.

Aristotle. *Nicomachean Ethics.* 10.1. Translated by J. A. K. Thomson. 1953, in Frank. *Quotationary*. 604.

Arnsten, Amy, Carolyn M. Mazure, and Rajita Sinha. "This Is Your Brain in Meltdown." *Scientific American*, April 2012.

"Autocatalytic." *Dictionary.* Bing.com.

Bacevich, Andrew J. *The New American Militarism.* New York: Oxford University Press, 2005.

——. *Washington Rules.* New York: Metropolitan Books, 2010.

Baker, Aryn. "The Jihadi Next Door." *Time*, March 31, 2008, 81.

"Balance of Power Changed between Shia and Sunnis." http://www.bbc.co.uk/news/science-environment-20447422. Assessment by Roy Sutton, a specialist on the Middle East.

Barnett, Lincoln. *The Universe and Dr. Einstein*. New York: Bantam, 1980.

Barooah, Jahnabi. "46% Americans Believe In Creationism According To Latest Gallup Poll." June 6, 2012. http://huffingtonpost.com/2012/06/05/americans-believe-in-creationism_n_1571127.html.

Barrouquere, Brett. "Hand Transplant Recipient Doing Well." *AOL Newscast*, January 23, 2004.

Barrow, John D., and John K. Webb. "Inconstant Constants." *Scientific American*, June 2005, 57-63.

Bates, Claire. "15 Million People Worldwide Had Plastic Surgery in 2011... But Why Are South Koreans so Much More Likely To Go under the Knife?" http://www.dailymail.co.uk/health/article-2271134/15million-people-plastic-surgery-world-just-year--SOUTH-KOREA-leading-way.html.

Bautman, Elif. "The Sanctuary." *The New Yorker*, December 19 & 26, 2011, 81.

Begun, David R. "Planet of the Apes." *Scientific American*, August 2003, 80.

Bekenstein, Jacob D. "Information in the Holographic Universe." *Scientific American*, August 2003, 59.

Belluck, Pam. "Device Offers Partial Vision for the Blind." *The New York Times*, February 15, 2013, A1-A3.

Benn, Aluf. "Israel's Warlords." *Foreign Affairs*, March/April 2013, 164-169.

Biema, David Van. "Undercover: Christianity in Muslim Lands." *Time*, June 30, 2003, 39.

"Biosphere." http://web.geology.ufl.edu/Biosphere.html.

Bird, Adrian. "Perceptions of Epigenetics." *Nature* 447 (7143): 396–8. doi:10.1038/nature05913. PMID 17522671.

Blackshear, James. "Boots on the Ground." *New Mexico Historical Review* 87 (Summer 2012): 329-358.

Black, Uyless. *Coming to You Live from the Dead*. Santa Fe: Privately published, 2009.

——. *The Mediterranean*. Privately published, 2006.

Bobrow, M. 1995. "Redrafted Chinese Law Remains Eugenic." *J. Med. Genet.* 32 (June): 409. doi:10.1136/jmg.32.6.409. PMC 1050477. PMID 7666390.

Brennan, W. "Aggression and Violence: Examining the Theories." *Nursing Standard* 12 no. 25 (1988): 26-37.

"British Mandate for Palestine." http://www.mideastweb.org/Middle-East-Encyclopedia/british_mandate_palestine.htm.

Brown, David. "Joys of Revenge Documented." *The Washington Post*, August 30, 2004, A13.

Brunner, H. G., M. Nelen, X. O. Breakefield, H. H. Ropers, and B. A. van Oost. October 1993. "Abnormal Behavior Associated with a Point Mutation in the Structural Gene for Monoamine Oxidase A." *Science* 262 (5133): 578–80. doi:10.1126/science.8211186. PMID 8211186.

Burnett, John. 2005. "The Navajo Nation's Own 'Trail of Tears." *NPR All Things Considered*. (June 14). http://www.npr.org/2005/06/15/4703136/the-navajo-nation-s-own-trail-of-tears.

Carlson, Coralie. "Transplant of 8 Organs to Baby Girl Announced." *The Spokesman Review*, March 20, 2004, A9.

Carter, Jimmy. *Our Endangered Values*. New York: Simon and Schuster, 2005.

Clarke, Richard A. "Ten Years Later." *The Atlantic Monthly*, January/February 2005, 61-77.

Cloud, John. "Why Genes Aren't Destiny." *Time*, January 18, 2010, 49-53. http://www1.cbsd.org/sites/teachers/hs/chchoe/Honors%20Reading%20Articles/I_Genetics_WHY%20GENES%20AREN'T%20DESTINY.pdf.

Coll, Steve. *Private Empire: ExxonMobil and American Power*. New York: Penguin Press, 2012.

"Corn Products and Byproducts." http://www.csmonitor.com/2002/1031/p17s01-lihc.html.

Crumpton, Henry A. *The Art of Intelligence*. New York: Penguin Press, 2012.

Csordas, Thomas J. 1999. "Ritual Healing and the Politics of Identity in Contemporary Navajo Society." *American Ethnologist* (Blackwell Publishing on behalf of the American Anthropological Association) 26 (February): 3–23. http://www.jstor.org/stable/10.2307/647496.

Cullen, Dave. "What a Killer Thinks." *Newsweek*, August 6, 2012, 31-34.

Cullen, D. Kacy, and Douglas H. Smith. "Bionic Connections." *Scientific American*, January 2013, 54.

Cullison, Alan. "Inside Al-Qaeda's Hard Drive." *The Atlantic Monthly*, September 2004, 60.

The Dalai Lama. *The Universe in a Single Atom*. New York: Random House, 2005.

Dawkins, Richard, and Francis Collins. "God vs. Science." Debate between Dawkins and Collins. *Time*, November 13, 2006.

"Definition of Anthropogenic Forcing." http://www.chemistry- dictionary. com/ definition/anthropogenic+forcing.php.

Deloria, Vine, Jr. *Red Earth, White Lies*. Golden, CO: Fulcrum, 1997.

Diamond, Jared. *Guns, Germs, and Steel*. New York: Norton, 1999.

——. *Collapse: How Societies Choose to Fail or Succeed*. New York: Viking Press, 2005.

——. *The World Until Yesterday*. New York: Penguin, 2012.

"DNA." Howard Hughes Medical Institute. Alfred P. Sloan Foundation. Films for the Humanities and Sciences # 32866, Princeton. "Playing God." 2003.

"DNA." Howard Hughes Medical Institute. Alfred P. Sloan Foundation. Films for the Humanities and Sciences # 32868. Princeton. "Curing Cancer." 2003.

"DNA." Howard Hughes Medical Institute. Alfred P. Sloan Foundation. Films for the Humanities and Sciences # 32869. Princeton. "Pandora's Box." 2003.

"Drying Up." *The Economist*, May 21, 2005, 46.

"Early Craftsmanship: Implements in Stone and Bone." http:// www.becominghuman.org/. Also, https://www.facebook.com/ BecomingHuman.org.

"Economic Cooperation and Development Review," Organization of the Islamic Conference 3, no.2, September 2010. http://www.sesric.org/ files/article/422.pdf.

"The Effects of Nuclear War." Washington, DC: Office of Technology Assessment, Congress of the United States, 1979. http://www.pbs.org/ wgbh/amex/bomb/sfeature/1mtblast.html.

Eisenhower, Dwight D. "Quotes." http://www.eisenhower.archives.gov/ all_about_ike/quotes.html.

Englert, Francois, and Robert Brout. 1964. "Broken Symmetry and the Mass of Gauge Vector Mesons." *Physical Review Letters* 13 (9): 321–23. Bibcode 1964PhRvL..13..321E. doi:10.1103/PhysRevLett.13.321.

"Estimated Causalities." http://csis.org/files/media/csis/pubs/090316_ israelistrikeiran.pdf. Also, http://www.globalsecurity.org/wmd/world/ iran/karaj.htm.

"Eugenics." *Novaya Gazeta*. December 12, 2005.

Falconer, Bruce. "Murder by the State." *The Atlantic Monthly*, November 2003, 56-57.

Falkenrath, Richard A. Harvard University: John F. Kennedy School of Government. Microsoft's Encarta Reference Library.

Federation of American Scientists. "Status of World Nuclear Forces." http://www.fas.org/programs/ssp/nukes/nuclearweapons/nukestatus. html.

Filkins, Dexter. *The Forever War*. New York: Alfred A. Knopf, 2008.

"First Ever: UK Scientists Use 3D Printer to Print Human Stem Cells." http://venturebeat.com/2013/02/06/first-ever-uk-scientists-use-3d-printer-to-print-human-stem-cells/.

"Forever Young?" *The Economist*, September 5, 2011, 95.

"Forgiveness in Islam." Summary of a Friday Khutbah. April 14, 2000. http://www.islamawareness.net/Salvation/forgiveness.html.

Foss, Brad. "All Fired Up." *The Spokesman Review*, Spokane, WA, January 25, 2004, D1.

Frame, T. *Losing My Religion*. UNSW Press, 2009, 137-141. http://books. google.nl/books?id=1mb-h1lom9IC&pg=PA137.

Frank, Leonard Roy. *Quotationary*. New York: Random House, 2001.

Franklin, Benjamin. *Poor Richard's Almanac*. April 1756.

Freeman, Chas W., Jr. "National Security in the Age of Terrorism." Remarks by Ambassador Freeman to the Congressional Research Service Seminar for New Members, January 6, 2006.

Friend, Tom. "Elusive Gene Therapy Forges On." *USA Today*, February 24, 2003.

Fukuyama, Francis. *America at the Crossroads: Democracy, Power, and the Neoconservative Legacy*. New Haven, CT: Yale University Press, 2006.

Gamow, George. "Crunch, Bang." *Scientific American*, March 1954. Excerpted from March 2004 section, "50, 100 & 150 Years Ago." 15.

Gandhi, Mohandas. *Young India*. March 9, 1922.

Gazzaniga, Michael S. *The Ethical Brain*. New York: Dana Press, 2005.

"Genocide Statistics." https://www.google.com/#q=definition+genocide.

"George Packer Quotes." http://www.goodreads.com/quotes/376986-ideology-knows-the-answer-before-the-question-has-been-asked.

"George W. Bush Quotes." http://www.brainyquote.com/quotes/authors/g/george_w_bush_4.html#T7lsbVgSYkrFX3UM.99.

Gershenfeld, Neil. "How to Make Almost Anything." *Foreign Affairs*, November/December 2012, 51.

"Getting Worse." *The Economist*, July 14, 2012.

Gibbs, W. Wayt. "Synthetic Life." *Scientific American*, May 2002, 75-81. http://online.sfsu.edu/rone/GEessays/SyntheticLife.htm.

 "Glaciers." http://www.greenpacks.org/2009/04/17/worlds-7-largest-glaciers-by-continent/.

Gladwell, Malcolm. *Blink*. New York: Little Brown, 2005.

Goodwin, Doris Kearns. *Team of Rivals*. New York: Simon and Schuster, 2005.

Gorman, Christine. "A Transplant First." *Time Magazine*, December 23, 2005, 58. http://content.time.com/time/classroom/glenspring2006/pdfs/CEU_spring_2006.pdf, 28.

Greene, Brian. "Fabric of the Cosmos." PBS, July 25, 2112. http://www.thedailybeast.com/newsweek/2012/05/20/brian-greene-welcome-to-the-multiverse.html.

——. "The Mystery of the Multiverse." *Newsweek*, May 28, 2012, 23.

Grossman, Lev. "Drone Home." *Time*, February 11, 2013, 33.

"Growing Liver in Lymph Nodes." *Discover*, 03.2012, 10.

Guralnik, Gerald, C. R. Hagen, and T. W. B. Kibble. 1964. "Global Conservation Laws and Massless Particles." *Physical Review Letters* 13 (20): 585–587. Bibcode 1964PhRvL.13.585G. doi:10.1103/PhysRevLett.13.585.

——. "Science's Great Leap Forward." *The Economist*, July 7, 2012, 13.

Harmon, Katherine. "Shattered Ancestry." *Scientific American*, February 2013, 42-49.

Harris, Sam. "The Case against Faith." *Newsweek*, November 12, 2006, 42-43.

Hebebrand, J., and B. Klug. 1995. "Specification of the Phenotype Required for Men with Monoamine Oxidase Type A Deficiency." *Hum. Genet.* 96 (September): 372–6. doi:10.1007/BF00210430. PMID 7649563.

Henig, Robin Marantz. "The Quest to Forget." *The New York Times Magazine*, April 4, 2004, 32-37.

Henmi, Chizuka, Makoto Nakamura, Yuichi Nishiyama, Kumiko Yamaguchi, Shuichi Mochizuki, Koki Takiura, and Hidemoto Nakagawa. "Development of an Effective Three Dimensional Fabrication Technique Using Inkjet Technology for Tissue Samples." AATEX 14, Special Issue, 689-692, August 21-25, 2007, 1.

Higgs, Peter. 1964. "Broken Symmetries and the Masses of Gauge Bosons." *Physical Review Letters* 13 (16): 508–509. Bibcode 1964PhRvL..13..508H. doi:10.1103/PhysRevLett.13.508. http://prl.aps.org/abstract/PRL/v13/i16/p508_1.

Hinshaw, Gary F. 2008. "WMAP Cosmological Parameters Model: lcdm+sz+lens Data: wmap5." (April 30).

Hotz, Robert Lee. "Printing Evolves: An Inkjet for Living Tissue." *The Wall Street Journal*, Sept 18, 2012. http://online.wsj.com/article/SB10 000872396390443816804578002101200151098.html.

"Human Cloning and Human Dignity: An Ethical Inquiry." The President's Council on Bioethics. Washington, DC, July 2002. www.bioethics.gov.

Human's Self-indulgent Ways." Announcement. Bush Administration, February 14, 2002.

Hunter, Philip. "What Genes Remember." *Prospect Magazine*, no. 146 (May 2008); Web.archive.org. 2008-05-01. http://web.archive.org/web/20080501094940/. http://www.prospect-magazine.co.uk/article_details.php?id=10140.

Huxley, Aldous. *Brave New World*. New York: HarperCollins, 1932, 1946.

Huxley, Julian. "Transhumanism." *New Bottles for New Wine*. 1957, in Frank. *Quotationary*. 253.

"Ideas and Consequences." Aspen Institute's Aspen Ideas Festival of 2007. *The Atlantic Monthly*, October 2007, 54.

"Impact of global warming." http://www.youtube.com/embed/hC3VTgIPoGU?rel=0.

"Iran: Foreign Policy Challenges and Choices." November 2006. http://www.david-kilgour.com/2008/pdf/iran/Iran%20Report.pdf.

Isaacson, Walter. *Einstein*. Audioworks. Simon & Schuster, 2007, disc 13, track 6.

"Islam." *Encyclopædia Britannica Online*, 2010. http://www.britannica.com/EBchecked/topic/295507/Islam.

"Israeli Military Decorations by Campaign." http://www.google.com/#psj=1&q=Israeli+Military+Decorations+by+Campaign.

"Issues related to mitigation in the long-term context." http://www.ipcc.ch/publications_and_data/ar4/wg3/en/ch3.html, in IPCC AR4 WG3 2007.

Ivanchik, A. V., A. Y. Potekhin, and D. A. Varshalovich. 1999. "The Fine-Structure Constant: A New Observational Limit on Its Cosmological Variation and Some Theoretical Consequences."

Astronomy and Astrophysics 343: 459. arXiv:astro-ph/9810166. Bibcode 1999A&A...343..439I.

"Jesus." http://www.gospel-mysteries.net/teachings-jesus.html.

Jones, Seth G. "The Mirage of the Arab Spring." *Foreign Affairs*, January/February 2013, 62.

Judson, Olivia. "The Selfless Gene." *The Atlantic Monthly*, October 2007, 98.

Junger, Sebastan. *War.* New York: Hachette, 2010.

Karmen, Andrew. A rebuttal to Daniel Patrick Moynihan's "Defining Deviancy Down." www.albany.edu/scj/jcjpc/vol2is5/deviancy.html.

"Keeping Back the Sea." *Fortune*, December 3, 2012, 20.

Kennedy, John F. "Man on the Moon." A Special Presidential Address to Congress on the importance of Space. May 25, 1961. http://www.homeofheroes.com/presidents/speeches/kennedy_space.html.

Khatchadourian, Raffi. "Azzam the American." *The New Yorker*, January 22, 2007, 63.

Kluger, Jeffery. "Race and the Brain." *Time*, October 20, 2008, 59.

Knickerbocker, Brad. "Classic Guerilla War Takes Shape in Iraq." *The Christian Science Monitor*. Excerpted from *The New Mexican*, September 20, 2004, A-5.

Knickmeyer, Ellen, and Alex Delmar-Morgan. "Gulf States Balk at Regional Union." *The Wall Street Journal*, May 14, 2012, A10.

Kolbert, Elizabeth. "Mr. Green." *The New Yorker*, January 22, 2007, 35.

Komatsu, E., J. Dunkley, M. R. Nolta, C. L. Bennett, B. Gold, G. Hinshaw, N. Jarosik, et al. 2009. "Five-Year Wilkinson Microwave Anisotropy Probe Observations: Cosmological Interpretation." *Astrophysical Journal Supplement* 180 (2): 330. Bibcode 2009ApJS..180..330K. doi:10.1088/0067-0049/180/2/330.

Kossuth, Louis. *Speech.* Lexington, MA. May 1982, in Frank. *Quotationary.* 712.

Krauss, Lawrence M. "The Real Promise of Synthetic Biology." *Scientific American*, February 2010, 32.

Krauthammer, Charles. "Actually, the Middle East Is Our Crisis Too." *Time*, August 7, 2006, 31.

Kringelbach, Morten L., and Kent C. Berridge. "The Joyful Mind." *Scientific American*, August 2012, 42.

Kuhn, George W.S. "Nuclear Weapons." *World Book Online Reference Center*. March 23, 2004. http://www.aolsvc.worldbook.aol.com/wb/Article?id=ar396520.

Kummer, Corby. "Back to Grass." *The Atlantic Monthly*, May 2003, 138.

Kyle, Chris. *The American Sniper*. New York: Harper, 2012.

"Lab Report." *Time*, October 4, 2010, n.p.

Lacey, Robert. *Inside the Kingdom*. New York: Penguin, 2009.

——. *The Kingdom: Arabia & the House of Sa'ud*. New York: Avon, 1981.

Landau, Elizabeth. "Scientists More Certain That Particle Is Higgs Boson." CNN, March 13, 2013.

Langewiesche, William. "How to Get a Nuclear Bomb." *The Atlantic Monthly*, December 2006, 80-98.

——. Interview by Elizabeth Dougherty. http://www.theatlantic.com/magazine/archive/2005/11/the-world-in-which-we-live/304361/.

——."The Point of No Return." *The Atlantic Monthly*, January/February, 2006.

——. "The Wrath of Khan." *The Atlantic Monthly*, November 2005, 63.

Leonard, Mark. "Why Convergence Breeds Conflict." *Foreign Affairs*, September/October 2013, 125-135.

Leventon, William. "Synthetic Skin." *IEEE Spectrum*, December 2002, 30.

"Life 2.0." *The Economist*, September 2, 2006, 67-70.

Lightman, Alan. "Our Place in the Universe?" *Harper's*, December 2012, 34.

Lineweaver, Charles H., and Tamara M. Davis. "Misconceptions about the Big Bang." *Scientific American*, March 2005, 38-39. http://space.mit.edu/~kcooksey/teaching/AY5/MisconceptionsabouttheBigBang_ScientificAmerican.pdf.

Liu, Jian-Miin. "Formula for Red-Shift of Light Signals Coming from Distant Galaxies." Department of Physics, Nanjing University, Nanjing, The People's Republic of China. Document1http://arxiv.org/ftp/physics/papers/0505/0505036.pdf.

Loeb, Abraham. "The Dark Ages of the Universe." *Scientific American*, November 2006. Online;"The Dark Ages of the Universe."

Lorenz, Konrad. *On Aggression*. San Diego, CA: Harcourt Brace, 1963.

"Los Angeles' Water Sources." *Life & Times*, January 26, 2007. PBS/KCET, 8 p.m.

Lyons, James. "Civilian Casualties vs. Rules." *The Washington Times*, September 3, 2006, B1.

The Making of the Modern Near East 1792-1923. Harlow, England: Longman, n.d.

Mao X. January 1997. "Chinese Eugenic Legislation." *Lancet* 349 (9045): 139. doi:10.1016/S0140-6736(05)60930-0. PMID 8996454. http://linkinghub.elsevier.com/retrieve/pii/S0140-6736(05)60930-0.

"Mapping the Global Muslim Population: A Report on the Size and Distribution of the World's Muslim Population." *Pew Research Center*, October 7, 2009. http://pewforum.org/Muslim/Mapping-the-Global-Muslim-Population%286%29.aspx.

"Marc Rich." *The Economist*, July 6, 2013, 86.

McCullough, David. *Truman*. New York: Simon & Schuster, 1992.

McHenry, H. M. 2009. "Human Evolution." In Michael Ruse and Joseph Travis. *Evolution: The First Four Billion Years*. Cambridge, MA: Belknap Press of Harvard University Press, 2009, 265.

McKenna, Maryn. "The Enemy Within." *Scientific American*, April 2011, 48.

Meacham, Jon. *Franklin and Winston*. New York: Random House, 2003.

Merali, Zeeya. "Gravity off the Grid." *Discover*, 03.2112, 49.

Montefiore, Simon Sebag. *Jerusalem, the Biography*. New York: Alfred A. Knopf, 2011.

Mooney, Chris. *The New ExxonMobil: Has the Tiger Changed Its Stripes?* June 13, 2012. http://www.desmogblog.com/new-exxonmobil-has-tiger-changed-its-stripes.

"More Jewish Than Thou." *The Economist*, July 28, 2012, 9.

Moynihan, Daniel Patrick. "Defining Deviancy Down." *American Scholar*, 1993. www2.sunysuffolk.edu/formans/DefiningDeviancy.htm.

Natural Resources Defense Council. *USA Today*, February 26, 2004, 12A.

"NPT." http://www.un.org/disarmament/WMD/Nuclear/NPT.shtml.

Numeoka, Ken, Manjong Han, and David M Gardiner. "Regrowing Human Limbs." *Scientific American*, April 2008, 57- 62.

Obama, Barack. President. March 21, 2013. Aired on major television stations.

"On the Trail of the Black Market Bombs." http://news.bbc.co.uk/2/hi/3481499.stm.

Orr, H. Allen. "Testing Natural Selection." *Scientific American*, Dec. 18, 2008, 51.

Papineau, David, ed. *Western Philosophy*. New York: Oxford University Press, 2004.

Patterson, Richard North. *Exile*. New York: St. Martin's Press, 2007.

Peers, John, Gordon Bennett, and George Booth. "Sam's Dispair." *1,001 Logical Laws*. New York: Fawcett Columbine Book - Ballantine Books, 1980.

Pillar, Paul R. *Intelligence and U.S. Foreign Policy*. New York: Columbia University Press, 2011.

Polk, William R. *Understanding Iraq*. New York: HarperCollins, 2005.

"Pollution." www.usgs.gov/themes/FS-189-97/.

Ponti, Giovanna, Paolo Peretto, and Luca Bonfanti. 2008. Edited by Thomas A. Reh. "Genesis of Neuronal and Glial Progenitors in the Cerebellar Cortex of Peripuberal and Adult Rabbits." *PLoS ONE* 3 (6): e2366. doi:10.1371/journal.pone.0002366. PMC 2396292. PMID 18523645.

Quiroga, Rodrigo Quian, Itzhak Fried, and Christof Koch. "Brain Cells for Grandmother." *Scientific American*, February 2013, 34-35.

Rando, O. J., and K. J. Verstrepen. February 2007. "Timescales of Genetic and Epigenetic Inheritance." *Cell* 128 (4): 655–68. doi:10.1016/j.cell.2007.01.023. PMID 17320504.

Ratliff, Evan. "Taming the Wild." *National Geographic*, March 2011, 41.

Reik, W. May 2007. "Stability and Flexibility of Epigenetic Gene Regulation in Mammalian Development." *Nature* 447 (7143): 425–32. doi:10.1038/nature05918. PMID 17522676.

"Religions." CIA. *The World Factbook*, 2010. https://www.cia.gov/library/publications/the-world-factbook/fields/2122.html.

Remini, Robert. "The Reform Begins." *Bill Nye the Science Guy*. http://www.billnye.com/.

Remnick, David. "Danger Levels." *The New Yorker*, July 31, 2006, 22. http://www.newyorker.com/archive/2006/07/31/060731ta_talk_remnick.

Reston, James, Jr. "Seeking Meaning from a Grand Imam." *The Washington Post*, March 31, 2002, B4.

"The Road to Renewal." *The Economist*, January 16, 2013, 54.

Rosen, Clifford J. "Restoring Aging Bones." *Scientific American*, March 2003, 71-77.

Rosenthal, Earl. *The Palace of Charles V in Granada*. Princeton, NJ: Princeton University Press, 1985.

Rousseau, Jean-Jacques. *Discourse Upon the Origin and Foundation of Inequality Among Mankind*. New York: Perennial Library, 1994.

Roy, Olivier. *The Politics of Chaos in the Middle East*. New York: Columbia University Press, 2008.

Rucker, Phillip. "We Scared Every Night." *The Washington Post*, July 24, 2006, B2.

"Saudi Police 'Stopped' Fire Rescue." *BBC*, March 15, 2002.

[Scheuer, Michael]. *Imperial Hubris*. Washington, DC: Bassey's, 2004.

Schlosser, Eric. *Fast Food Nation*. New York: HarperCollins, 2002.

Schulman, Ari N. "What Mass Killers Want—And How to Stop Them." *The Wall Street Journal*, November 8, 2013, C1-C2.

Schweitzer, Albert. *The Psychiatric Study of Jesus*. Boston: Beacon Press, 1948.

"Science's Great Leap Forward." *The Economist*, July 7, 2012, 13.

Scott, A. L., M. Bortolato, K. Chen, and J.C. Shih. May 2008. "Novel Monoamine Oxidase A Knock Out Mice with Human-Like Spontaneous Mutation." *NeuroReport* 19 (7): 739–43. doi:10.1097/WNR.0b013e3282fd6e88. PMID 18418249.

Seabrook, John. "Suffering Souls." *The New Yorker*, November 10, 2008, 72.

Shaivit, Ari. *A Promised Land*. New York: Random House, 2013.

Shakespeare, William. Hamlet. 1.5.27, 1600, in Frank. *Quotationary*. 2001.

——. *Troilus and Cressida*. 2.3, 164, in Frank. *Quotationary*. 713. Frank. *Quotationary*. 654.

Shane, Scott. "The Moral Case for Drones." *The New York Times*, July 15, 2012, 4.

Sharot, Tali. "The Optimism Bias." *Time*, June 6, 2011, 41-46. http://content.time.com/time/health/article/0,8599,2074067,00.html.

Shaw, George Bernard. *Preface to Plays, Pleasant and Unpleasant*. Vol. 2, 1898. 1898, in Frank. *Quotationary*. 713.

Shermer, Michael. "The Political Brain." *Scientific American*, July 2006, 36.

Shidduchim. Program Dor Yeshorim. Accessed Nov. 11, 2011. http://www.shidduchim.info/medical.html.

Silverman, Paul H. "Letters to the Editor." *The Atlantic Monthly*, June 2004, 14.

Sinclair, David A., and Lenny Guarente. "Unlocking the Secrets of Longevity Genes." *Scientific American*, March 2006, 49.

"The Sociology and Psychology of Terrorism: Who becomes a Terrorist and Why?" Library of Congress. A report prepared under an interagency agreement by the Federal Research Division, September 1999.

"Something in the Air?" *The Economist*, January 19, 2013, 47.

Spotts, Peter N. "Spooky Action at a Distance." *The Christian Science Monitor*, October 4, 2001. Web; "Spooky Action at a Distance."

Stern, Jessica. *The Ultimate Terrorists*. Cambridge, MA: Harvard University Press, 1999.

Sternberg, Steve. "Lab-Grown Windpipe Saves Cancer Patient." *USA TODAY*, July 8, 2011, n.p.

Stringer, C.B. 1994. "Evolution of Early Humans." In Steve Jones, Robert Martin, and David Pilbeam. *The Cambridge Encyclopedia of Human Evolution*. Cambridge, MA: Cambridge University Press, 1994.

"Studies on a Possible Israeli Strike on Iran's Nuclear Development Facilities." http://csis.org/files/media/csis/pubs/090316_israelistrikeiran.pdf.

"Sunnite." *Encyclopædia Britannica Online*. 2010. http://www.britannica.com/EBchecked/topic/574006/Sunnite.

"Sunni vs. Shia." and "Sunni and Shia Wars." "Religions." *CIA. The World Factbook*. 2010, in "Islam." https://www.cia.gov/library/publications/the-world-factbook/fields/2122.html.

"Synthetic Genome." http://www.astrobio.net/pressrelease/3502/synthetic-genome.

Syrus, Publius. *Moral Sayings*. 987. Translated by Darius Lyman Jr. 1862.

Tagliaferro, John Samut. *Malta, Its Archaeology and History*. Luqa, Malta: Miller House, n.d.

"Tattoos—From Taboo to Mainstream." *National Geographic News*, October 11, 2002.

"Team Jesus Christ." *The Washington Post*, June 4, 2005, A16.

Tegmark, Max. "Parallel Universes." *Scientific American*, May 2003, 41.

Tierno, Philip M. Jr., *The Secret Life of Germs*. New York: Atria Books, 2001.

"Tools for Life." *Scientific American*, August 2010, 17.

"Treaty for the Non-Proliferation of Nuclear Weapons (NPT)." http://www.un.org/disarmament/WMD/Nuclear/NPT.shtml.

"Tribe." *The Random House College Dictionary*. New York: Random House, 1984.

Turner, Michael S. "The Universe." *Scientific American*, September 2009, 38, 43.

Tyler, Patrick. *Fortress Israel*. New York: Farrar, Straus, and Giroux, 2012.

United States Congress. *The Effects of Nuclear War*. Office of Technology Assessment. PDF files at Princeton, 1979.

Vedantam, Shankar. "FDA wants Anti-Depressants to List Warnings." *The Spokesman Review*, March 23, 2004, A1.

Vick, Karl. "The Ultra-Holy City." *Time*, August 13, 2012, 48.

Vishnivetskaya, Galina B., Julia Skrinskaya, Idabelle Seif, and Nina K Opova. 2007. "Effect of MAO A Deficiency on Different Kinds of Aggression and Social Investigation in Mice." *Aggressive Behavior* 33 (January 1): 1–6. doi:10.1002/ab.20161. PMID 17441000.

Wain, John. "A Song about Major Eatherly." *Weep Before Gods*. 1961. 1961, in Frank. *Quotationary*. 425.

Walker, Williston, Richard A. Norris, David W. Lotz, and Robert T. Handy. *A History of the Christian Church*. 4th ed. New York: Charles Scribner's Sons, 1985.

Ward, Peter. "What Will Become of the *Homo sapiens*?" *Scientific American*, January 2009, 70-72.

Webster, Paul. *The Guardian*, July/August 2003.

Weise, Elizabeth. "Report: Rodents May Offer Insight to Monogamy." *USA Today*, June 16, 2004, 2A.

Weiss, Rick. "Monkeys Control Robotic Arm with Brain Implants." *The Washington Post*, October 15, 2002.

"What's the Point?" *The Economist*, January 12, 2013, 42.

"When Corn was King." http://www.csmonitor.com/2002/1031/p17s01-lihc.html.

Wilson, E. O. *The Future of Life*. New York: Alfred A. Knopf, 2002.

——. *The Social Conquest of Earth*. New York: Liveright, 2012. Kindle edition.

——. "What's Your Tribe?" *Newsweek*, April 9, 2012, 44.

Wong, Kate. "First of Our Kind." *Scientific American*, April 2012, 31-39.

——."The Human Pedigree." *Scientific American*, January 2009, 60.

——. "Lucy's Baby." *Scientific American*, December 2006, 78-85.

"World's First Brain Prosthesis Revealed." *New Scientist*, March 12, 2003. http://www.wireheading.com/misc/brain-prosthesis.html.

Wrangham, Richard, and Dale Peterson. *Demonic Males*. New York: Houghton Mifflin, 1996. http://www.sfgate.com/news/article/Al-Qaeda-bluffing-about-having-suitcase-nukes-2776832.php

Xinhua News Agency. "China's 1st Notables' Sperm Bank Opens." June 24, 1999.

Yapp, Malcolm E. *The Making of the Modern Near East 1792-1923*. Harlow, England: Longman, 1987.

"The Year of the Drone: An Analysis of U.S. Drone Strikes in Pakistan, 2004–2012." New America Foundation. http://counterterrorism. newamerica.net/drones.

Yokovlev, Alexander N., Anthony Austin, and Paul Hollander. *A Century of Violence in Soviet Russia*. New Haven, CT: Yale University Press, 2002.

Zak, Paul J. "The Neurobiology of Trust." *Scientific American*, June 2008, 88- 95.

——. "The Trust Molecule." *The Wall Street Journal*, April 28, 2012, C2.

Zimmer, Carl. "The Neurobiology of the Self." *Scientific American*, November 2005, 93-101.

INDEX

Other Works by Uyless Black
Essays available at Blog.UylessBlack.com

Lea County Museum Press:
The Light Side of Little Texas, 2011

Note: Winner of 2012 Centennial award from The Historical Society of New Mexico for the "Best Book Depicting Domestic Life" in New Mexico.

Finalist for 2012 award from The New Mexico Book Co-op for "Non-fiction, other."

IEI Press:
A Swimmer's Odyssey: From the Plains to the Pacific, 2011
The Nearly Perfect Storm: An American Financial and Social Failure, 2012
2084 and Beyond, 2015

The following books (some of the first books on Internet protocols and architecture) offer historical perspectives on early data communications networks. Note the copyright dates.

SAMS:
Teach Yourself Networking in 24 Hours, 2009

IEEE Computer Society:
Physical Layer Interfaces and Protocols, 1988
X.25 and Packet Switching Networks, 1991

Prentice Hall/Pearson Publishing:
Data Communications, Networks, and Distributed Processing, 1983
Computer Networks: Protocols, Standards, and Interfaces, 1987
Data Networks: Concepts, Theory, and Practice, 1989
The OSI Model, 1991
Data Link Protocols, 1993
Asynchronous Transfer Mode (ATM) Networks, Volume I, 1995
Wireless and Mobile Networks, 1996
Emerging Communications Technologies, 1997

SONET and T1, 1997
ISDN and SS7, 1997
The Intelligent Network, 1998
Asynchronous Transfer Mode (ATM) Networks, Volume II, 1998
Asynchronous Transfer Mode (ATM) Networks, Volume III, 1998
Residential Broadband, 1998
Second Generation Mobile and Wireless Networks, 1999
Advanced Intelligent Technologies, 1999
The Point-to-Point Protocol (PPP), 2000
IP Routing Protocols, 2000
Internet Security Protocols, 2000
Quality of Service in Wide Area Networks, 2000
Internet Architecture, 2000
MPLS and Label Switching Networks, 2001
Internet Telephony, 2001
Voice over IP (VOIP), 2002
Networking 101, 2002
Optical Networks, 2002

McGraw-Hill:
TCP/IP and Related Protocols, 1992
Network Management Standards, 1992
The V-Series Recommendations, 1995
The X-Series Recommendations, 1995
Frame Relay Networks, 1998

Foreign Editions of Books:

Japanese: *Network Management Standards; Internet Security Protocols; Data Communications and Distributed Networks; IP Routing Protocols; TCP/IP; Multi-protocol Label Switching (MPLS)*

Korean: *Voice over IP (VOIP); Communications Networks: Protocols, Standards, and Interfaces*

Russian: *Communications Networks: Protocols, Standards, and Interfaces; Internet Security Protocols*

French: *Teach Yourself Networking in 24 Hours*

Chinese: *Advanced Features of the Internet; Voice over IP (VOIP)*

Spanish: *Data Communications and Distributed Networks; Communication Networks: Protocols, Standards, and Interfaces; TCP/IP; Advanced Features of the Internet*

United Kingdom: *Data Communications and Distributed Networks; Data Networks: Concepts, Theory, and Practice; Computer Networks: Protocols, Standards, and Interfaces.*

Magazine Articles:

Structured Programming:

InfoSystems magazine (circa 1975): "Gestalt Psychology Applied to Software Design" (An article explaining the brain's partitioning mental tasks to facilitate solving problems, based on Gestalt theory. A concept fundamental to a programming idea called structured programming, a revolutionary idea at that time.)

Metadata defined before it was named:

Data Communications magazine, November, 1980, McGraw Hill, Inc: "An Automatic Pilot for the Growing Distributed Network" (To my knowledge, the first known explanation of *metadata*.)

Subjects under research, with plans to publish:

Fractured: How the Cold War and Class Wars have Divided America
My Capital, My America (working title)
The Light Side of Little Texas, Volume II

Short Stories:

Available upon request.

Essays available at Blog.UylessBlack.com:

America's Capital: Memories of author's experiences in Washington, DC.

America's Cities: Journeys and encounters in USA's towns and cities.

America's Finances: A series on issues such as Medicare, Social Security, and debt.

Computers and Networks: Essays on Internet "net neutrality" and software complexity.

Creatures and Computers: Drawing analogies to wildlife and Internet life.

Customs and Cultures: A look at America and Americana.

Eating and Drinking: Surveys of food fairs, cafes, and restaurants.

Food Effects and Drug Defects: Reports on toxic foods and drugs' side effects.

Foreign Affairs: America's relations with other countries.

Foreign Places: Taking roads, ships, and trains through parts of the world.

Immigration and Emigration: America's immigration practices and related problems.

Politics in America: With several reports on National Press Club speakers.

Presidential Places: Presidential homes, museums, and grave sites.

Privacy: NSA activities, right to Internet privacy in relation to other rights of privacy.

Sports and Games: Essays on competition and the beauty of sport.

Traveling America: Taking roads through America and America's cultures.

War Zones: Essays on cold, warm, and hot wars.

Listings of some newspaper articles. Uyless Black has published numerous articles on various topics with the local newspaper, *The Coeur d' Alene Press*. **Here are some samplings:**

- "When Political Correctness and Freedom of Speech collide," December 13, 2017.
- "The FCC Rulings on Net Neutrality," December 2-3, 2017.
- "What Walls Should America be Building?" November 1, 2017.
- "A Deeper Issue in Immigration Debate: Separation of Church and State," November 27, 2015.
- "Beware the Freedom to Kill the Freedom of Religion," November 28, 2015.
- "Muslims in America, a Personal Look," December 28, 2015.
- Ten articles about "The Internet and Society," January 4, 2016– January 15, 2016.